METAROMANTICISM

METAROMANTICISM

AESTHETICS,

LITERATURE,

THEORY

PAUL HAMILTON

The University of Chicago Press
Chicago & London

PAUL HAMILTON is professor of English in the School of English and Drama at Queen Mary and Westfield College, the University of London. He is the author of *Coleridge's Poetics* (1983), *Wordsworth* (1986), *Historicism* (1996), and *Percy Bysshe Shelley* (2000) and the editor of *Selections from the Journals of Dorothy Wordsworth* (1992).

The University of Chicago Press, Chicago 60637
The University of Chicago Press, Ltd., London
© 2003 by The University of Chicago
All rights reserved. Published 2003
Printed in the United States of America
12 11 10 09 08 07 06 05 04 03   1 2 3 4 5

ISBN: 0-226-31479-0 (cloth)
ISBN: 0-226-31480-4 (paper)

Library of Congress Cataloging-in-Publication Data

Hamilton, Paul, D. Phil.
Metaromanticism : aesthetics, literature, theory / Paul Hamilton.
         p.   cm.
Includes bibliographical references and index.
ISBN 0-226-31479-0 (cloth : alk. paper)—
ISBN 0-226-31480-4 (pbk. : alk. paper)
1. Romanticism—Europe.   2. Romanticism—Great
Britain.   3. European, literature—19th century—History
and criticism.   4. European literature—18th
century—History and criticism.   5. English literature—19th
century—History and criticism.   6. European
literature—18th century—History and criticism.   I. Title.

PN751 .H25 2003
809'.9145'094—dc21   2002155087

CONTENTS

5

ACKNOWLEDGMENTS

This book represents a decade and more of thinking and puzzling over romantic theory and writing. I am very grateful to those who provided the initial hospitable occasions for the papers and discussions which turned into the chapters below. In particular, I would like to thank James Chandler, Warren Chernaik, Stephen Clarke, the late Stephen Copley, Thomas Docherty, Richard Gravill, Mary Jacobus, Anne Janowitz, Vivien Jones, Ed Larrissy, Marjorie Levinson, Reeve Parker, Tilottama Rajan, Robert Rehder, and John Whale. I owe crucial debts of conversation and controversy, some momentary and inspirational, some perennial and of long example, to these people and to many others, including Isobel Armstrong, Andrew Benjamin, Richard Bourke, Kath Burlinson, Andrew Bowie, Marilyn Butler, Tony Crowley, Greg Dart, Seamus Deane, Peter Dews, Terry Eagleton, Ken Hirschkop, Cora Kaplan, Timothy Morton, David Norbrook, Jacqueline Rose, Michael Rossington, and Robert J. C. Young. An especial thank-you goes to James Chandler and Jon Klancher for the needful, detailed criticism I could build on, and, at Chicago, to Alan Thomas for his faith in the project and to Randy Petilos for his typographical optimism. Closer to home, at home, in fact, Roxana and Leon have pointed the way forward, and the conclusion this book reaches is for them.

Portions of this book have appeared, in earlier form, in the following publications. Chapter 3 appeared as "Coleridge and Godwin in the 1790s" in *The Coleridge Connection,* ed. Richard Gravill and Molly Lefebure (London: Macmillan, 1993), 41–60; reprinted by permission of Palgrave Macmillan. Chapter 4 appeared as "Keats and Critique" in *Rethinking Historicism,* ed. Marjorie Levinson, Marilyn Butler, Jerome McGann, and Paul Hamilton (Oxford: Basil Blackwell, 1989), 108–43; reprinted by permission of Basil Blackwell. Chapter 5 appeared as "*Waverley:* Scott's Romantic

Narrative and Revolutionary Historiography" in *Studies in Romanticism* 33 (winter 1994): 611–34; reprinted by permission of the Trustees of Boston University. Chapter 6 appeared as "A French Connection: From Empiricism to Materialism in Writings by the Shelleys" in *Colloquium Helveticum* 25 (1997): 179–92; reprinted by permission of Peter Lang AG. Chapter 8 appeared as "Andrew Marvell and Romantic Patriotism" in *Marvell and Liberty,* ed. Warren Chernaik and Martin Dzelzainis (London: Macmillan, 1999), 75–94; reprinted by permission of Palgrave Macmillan. Chapter 9 appeared as "The Romanticism of Contemporary Ideology" in *Intersections: Nineteenth-Century Philosophy and Contemporary Theory,* ed. Tilottama Rajan and David L. Clark (Albany: SUNY Press, 1995), 302–21; reprinted by permission of the State University of New York Press. (c) 1995 State University of New York. All rights reserved. Chapter 10 appeared as "The New Romanticism" in *Textual Practice* 11, no. 1 (spring 1997): 109–31; reprinted by permission of Taylor and Francis, http://www.tandf.co.uk. Chapter 11 appeared as "From Sublimity to Indeterminacy: New World Order or Aftermath of Romantic Ideology" in *Romanticism and Postmodernism,* ed. Edward Larrissy (Cambridge: Cambridge University Press, 1999), 13–29; reprinted by permission of Cambridge University Press.

INTRODUCTION

Metaromanticism

Metaromantic Moments

"Metaromanticism" is a necessary word for describing the subject matter of this book: the specific ways in which major writers in the romantic period generalize their practices. It is also a misleading word. In my use of it, "meta" does not indicate a defining distance from the activity of romantic writing. Metaromanticism does not, as might have been expected, belong to a language outside romanticism, but is a characteristic product of romantic discourse. Metaphysics, were it possible, would tell us of the nature of reality from a position outside reality, immune to its vagaries. Similarly, a metalanguage, were it possible, would define language without being itself subject to linguistic fallibility. But metaromanticism embraces the implication in its subject these other pretenders to external objectivity want to shake off. Like the metacritiques of Kant by Herder and Hamann, metaromanticism exploits this discursive sufficiency to trump critique. Or, looking ahead, metaromanticism is "perspectival," its content relative to each romantic example in which it occurs. It is not, however, at ease with this proto-Nietzschean dispensation from objectivism: it is fundamentally discontented with the immanence to which its own critique is restricted.

Another way of saying this would be to claim that romantic period writing is often simultaneously a position paper on its own kind of significance. Students of this literature are now expected to be familiar with a critique of its ideology of internalization, a critique whose philosophically definitive moments start with Heine and Marx and continue through Nietzsche, Irving Babbitt, Carl Schmitt, and Georg Lukács to the near-contemporary polarities of deconstruction, cultural studies, feminism, and new historicism—none of whom would necessarily accept this compartmentalization. Marx attacked the immanence of romantic self-critique in his early polemic *The German Ideology*. Self-critique of this kind, he argued, only perpetuated the self it criticized, adding to its substance, extending rather than contesting its narrative. Characteristic of romantic discourse, self-critique is just the fashion in which it struggles with itself, is about itself, beside itself even. Critique is another way in which it becomes what it is, not a way in which it posits an alternative to its own *Weltanschauung*. It produces, in Friedrich Schlegel's terms this time, rather than Nietzsche's, "the poetry of poetry." It takes itself as its subject, but then struggles with itself, as if against an unwelcome limitation. It wrestles with its angel. It is literature typical of what Kant and Schlegel after him called a "critical" age. But, again, this criticism always finally seems self-serving, a discontent with poetic solutions whose unhappiness still produces the poetry of poetry, not something else.

This book tries to identify moments when romantic period writing encounters this defining limitation. Critique of its habits of recuperation has been taken to great lengths over the last two decades. Growing more audible in the course of the prosecution, though, has been the voicing by writers of the time of their own discontent with the prison of self-consciousness in which they find themselves. It has not escaped many of them that each act of removal from the position criticized sets it up once more. Writers working outside the dominant mode of imaginative expression, or knowingly disadvantaged by it, can, for example, see its typically masculine contours and expose their entrapment by that configuration. The vast upsurge of scholarship of women's poetry in the romantic period has made us aware as never before of this fascinating heterology and its writerly tactics. Nevertheless, the "economy" of the indictment of mainstream romanticism—boosting our critical "capital," giving us something to say—has gradually become more apparent.[1] For heterodox as much as orthodox writers look for ways to redeploy an aesthetic grasp of the self whose utopian potential is too powerful to be justifiably abandoned. The texts examined in this book are linked by this function, a philosophical function of the ability of texts, often nonphilosophical, to interpret each other. This "new" romanticism, as it is called here, charts no certain line of flight from romantic subjectivity; but it is studied in its expression of the major convulsions that subjectivity enjoys in order more quickly to close on the problem such paroxysms (fail to) represent. It therefore asks for a treatment different from the kind of archival decentering of canonical romantic thought prevailing now in romantic studies. But my reworking of the immanence of romantic self-critique bids to recover at its center a neglected philosophical archive of a kind.

To anticipate, it may help to offer a preliminary formulation of my general argument in the terms David Simpson uses when he appears to tie English romantic writing into an ineluctable, commonsense, national literary tradition, constitutionally skeptical of the adequacy of any critical reflection of its own complexity. In contrast, I am endeavoring to uncover not variations on this "radical *literature*" but indeed a "*radical* literature," one whose immanent unease rhetorically encourages translation into more effective means of discursive transmission, and, in so setting aside its traditional privileges, becomes a document of radicalism. This literary development parallels the evolution of a post-Kantian philosophy now, in its most recent, Habermasian incarnation, influentially interpreted as itself forgoing mastery to occupy the more ancillary role of facilitating better communication between different discourses. The collaboration between English literature and German philosophy in the romantic period, intuitively helpful in the past but hard to prove, can thus take on a new dimension. Framed in this way, the literary/philosophical dynamic of metaromanticism possesses implications for both how we read the literature of a historical period and for how we do philosophy. Philosophy, unlike the "theory wars" to which Simpson's admirable work relates romanticism, connects romantic writing to a discursive critique of its own sufficiency, the radical project they historically share.[2]

Romantic self-consciousness, pushed to its limits, seeks to shatter the reflection or image of plenitude it has created. In the language of John Keats's *Hyperion*, it is exposed "to the most hateful seeing of itself." As in Keats's cyclic poem, this self-disgust is perhaps a more telling critique than the new order with which it supposedly replaces but in fact blindly reconstitutes the aesthetic hierarchy which has been the problem all along. Certainly self-disgust can appear to be the epitome of romanticism. It ostensibly fits a stereotype of the romantic endeavor *par excellence*. It expresses its unrealistic resistance to inescapable boundaries, its irrational discontent with constitutional limitations, its desire, in short, for death rather than life. Like Chateaubriand's René, the romantic feels the death-wish perversely as *la puissance de créer des mondes*. Yet Schlegel can call this self-transcending drive both "progressive" and "universal." Percy Shelley's poem *The Triumph of Life* ghosts most of this book's effort to expose an inherent romantic struggle *against* being required to think authenticity as self-disgust. It attempts to preserve Schlegel's sense of progressiveness amidst the damaging estrangement from the material self—"all that is mortal of great Plato there"—wrought by idealism of all kinds. English romantics as different as William Wordsworth, John Keats, Percy and Mary Shelley explore and examine, rather than morbidly indulge, the obligation to cast self-redefinition as a fatal expansion. The second generation of English romantic writers, though, confronts that self's political existence; they redefine the citizenship consequent upon new imaginative affiliation here and now rather than in the kingdom of God to which Wordsworth's *Excursion* tries finally to convert the nascent British empire. Like Giacomo Leopardi, but less explicitly, they examine pessimism for its power to enjoin a new solidarity *(social catena),* an association redescribing personal extinction as a transforming natural sympathy or political future.

In this posthumous ambition, I argue (in chapter 2), they are anticipated by Rousseau. They become his children, his afterlife, primarily through their resistance to that institution of art which appears to be their necessary environment. As ever with Rousseau, this is a complicated and suspect procedure, caught in the abject yet liberating transformation by which his metaphorical progeny, his appreciative readers, are meant to replace his natural children, children abandoned to likely death in an orphanage so as to be excused from experiencing his bad offices as a father. Perversely again, this suffering would have been measured by his failure to educate them to be sympathetic readers of his work, his failure to make them aesthetic children. The loss incurred by a characteristically aesthetic trajectory away from its original expression into another kind of discourse capable of mobilizing its radical potential more effectively is thus early seen by Rousseau and borne witness to in an astonishingly self-lacerating romantic manner.

I use Friedrich Schiller's Kantian aesthetics, though (in chapter 1), to demonstrate the elaborate finesses by which the enhancement of our powers to conceive of fulfillment is gained in an aesthetic realm necessarily de-clutched from social process and political instantiation. We easily forget how dazzling must have seemed the versatility of a romantic aesthetic capable of uniting these opposites of transfiguring vision and of resignation to living in terms of the actualities that gave that transfiguration its difference. This dialectic and the "criticism of life" it inaugurates are here called to account by the metaromantic *reductio* or espousal of its aims so vociferously partisan that its cover is blown. Through critical performance, the romantic artist can exceed an aesthetic to which, propositionally, he or she seems committed. In so overstepping the mark, though, the romantic writer anticipates and makes intelligible an ensuing tradition of artistic self-criticism that is not simply self-serving. The aesthetic reveals the arts by which power and vested interests had used it to disguise their purposes. In this metaromantic moment, stepping aside from the ideological plot in which it had seemed imprisoned, the aesthetic inaugurates a critical reception capable of reformulating its ends. At full strength, metaromantic writing is Rousseauian, indifferent as to whether or not its future retains an originally aesthetic function. Otherwise, its criticism remains immanent, and from within a Schillerian orthodoxy it exposes the trick by which the aesthetic is indemnified against dissent because critical departures from it simultaneously double as the metaphorical distance or troping of an original—as further aesthetic production. My two opening chapters on Schiller and Rousseau set out the framework for these metaromantic debates.

Immanence, in particular, has its discontents. Keats's unexceptionable lodging of his better speculations in the realms of art sets up what is perhaps best described (in chapter 4) as a "run" on art. The more convincing its promises, the more we desire to call in the tabs, to redeem these extraordinary poetic riches which turn out, however, like the currency of the time, to have just moved off a tangible standard of specie and to exist only as paper, as credit, as their own power of circulation, the stories we tell to each other for comfort, "Here, where men sit and hear each other groan." Of course, one can rejoice in the aesthetic recompense on offer, one can profit from its irresistibility, the sureness of its temporary assuagements in contrast to the uncertain promises of schemes of political amelioration such as William Godwin's. This aesthetics of distraction, I argue in chapter 3, had no more knowing and bewitching performer than Coleridge, although his strategies of reticence, his "mystery" poems, converge upon that discursively constructive reserve with which Godwin's 1790s novels characteristically empower a political reader.

I believe that to appreciate the sensuousness of Keats's "critique" one has to be versed in the more skeletal articulation of it in theory of the time and its uses of immanent critique. That theory is almost entirely German. One does not, perhaps, need to go as far as Mme de Stael and proclaim northern Germany (that anachronistic construct) *la patrie de la pensée* in order to acknowledge many reasons for pursuing a knowledge of Kant and the post-Kantians. The vigorous anti-German reaction after the high romantic period in England confirms its unspoken influence at the time.[3] Where the period's literature and philosophy are concerned, though, the advantages of translating between one and another for the better articulation of both have never been obvious to critics of romantic writing in

English. Irresolvable questions of influence are embodied unforgettably in the disastrous figure of Coleridge, that desperate housing-problem for both English criticism and the continental tradition of philosophy he plagiarized. Carlyle, who painted the remembered portrait of Coleridgean decline, fostered the attitude which has bedeviled the acquirement of an easy fluency in both literary and philosophical discourses, the virtue which this book bets on as an unambiguously worthwhile aspiration. In his essay on Novalis he pronounced, incredibly, that there was no need "to enter into the intricacies of German philosophy." Actually, the trick is to get the balance right: to deal with the philosophy in enough detail to make its inclusion sensible in relation to its own highly sophisticated, defining traditions, and to read the literature closely enough to see the power of its particularity to skew any too easily preconceived philosophical gloss, and thus to bring out philosophy's flexibility and creativity in response to its own. Large mythological parallels between philosophical structure and epic plot, as recorded, for example, in *Natural Supernaturalism* by M. H. Abrams, are obviously exciting and suggestive, but detailed moments of logical maneuver and revision of philosophical tradition can be just as scintillating.[4] That, at least, is the thinking behind the marshaling of much of the philosophy here, but the reader's patience with the theory is humbly solicited at those moments when the philosophical exposition fails to communicate enthusiasms as infectious as literary ones. Let me, however, sketch the groundwork for their integration.

The Philosophy of Metaromanticism

Popularly Kant was and still is thought to exert the major influence of German idealist philosophy on British romanticism. "The mind alone is formative," summarized Hazlitt, and the level of generality he employs here is representative of the manner in which Kant was domesticated. Skill in rendering Kant fit for home consumption was, René Wellek lamented, the salient characteristic of his reception in English.[5] The romanticism which followed Kant exerted a more complex and less familiar influence. To appreciate its possible extent requires more detailed consideration of its own philosophical evolution. As critics like Thomas McFarland have stressed, Kant's dualism of phenomenal and noumenal worlds happily consorts with Christian faith in a way that the monism of the post-Kantians did not.[6] This dualism, though, is difficult to justify. Its inherent instability led Kant's romantic successors from revisions of Kant's system into their own distinctive attempts to overcome the entire subject/object way of thinking it epitomized.

Traditional criticisms of Kant from Fichte onward, therefore, concentrate first on his unstable dualism. They point out the derivativeness of descriptions of things-in-themselves, noumena, from the phenomenal categories to which they are supposedly anterior. Noumena should, for example, stand outside the causal relations by which we are logically obliged to order experience. But if noumena don't cause phenomena, if things don't cause their appearances, then how do they play any part in our knowledge at all? Maybe we experience their authority in moral and aesthetic experience? But, again, the cognitive question of what is added to experience by saying this remains unanswered. Hegel argued that, at best, we can say that our notions of things-in-themselves are at least parasitical on the phenomenal knowledge of a particular period by always being *its* outside boundary, *its* inverse world. Our ideas of what we don't know vary with what we do know and so are relative to perceived scientific progress. If, however, we freed our understanding of noumena from this historicism, our position would be antinomian: the reality existing outside scientific knowledge, beyond our ken, might for all we know be completely at odds with the system of laws by which we currently find our experience to be regulated. "Messianic," was Walter Benjamin's calculatedly anachronistic ("wizened") term for this discontinuity impossible to realize.[7]

Kant's transcendental dialectic supplements his analytic in order to suggest why he thought antinomianism impossible. We are obliged by ideas of reason to judge that nature, of its own accord, combines itself in such a way as if to make our coherent experience of it possible. We cannot, of course, *know* this, but our judgment that we are justified in so speculating is founded on aesthetic experience and on teleological assumptions we cannot sensibly give up. The grounding of our knowledge cannot be given in knowledge. Neither subject nor object can be so encompassed. We must assume that, were a suitable vantage point accessible, from it we would see that subject and object, mind and nature, do in fact relate so as to produce knowledge of the one by the other. These assumptions are founded on the exercise of our power of judgment *(Urteilskraft)*, aesthetic and teleological. The problem, though, remains that the structure Kant describes for the reflective judgments of teleology and aesthetics shadows the subject/object model he had prescribed for science. Judgment needs to observe this parallel in order to maintain its credentials as rational process, while strategically falling short of cognitive achievement.[8]

This is a fairly desperate recourse, though. As it is, we cannot check that a representation corresponds to the world *tout court,* because we have no access to the world independently of another representation of it. As Hume saw, consistency with other representations—a coherence theory of truth—is more defensible than a correspondence theory of truth, which in any case assumes without explaining the coherent phenomenal packaging of reality necessary for correspondence to have been possible in the first place. But if we reflect on the sense of orientation we get from the consistency of our representations, or what Kant called the "finality" of our judgments, we are no closer epistemologically than before to something outside representation. In fact, the inside/outside distinction, like that of subject/object, seems to be the problem not the solution here. This persistent nit-picking is necessary if we are to understand the enormous status that post-Kantian romantics felt compelled to attribute to ways of understanding the world other than those gained through our representations of it and reflections upon those representations. Even Hegel's historicism, after all, only opens up another can of epistemological worms if, as Lovejoy argued, we take a romantic view that history is not simply linear and progressive but charged with a diversity of new possibilities at each moment. "Man," ventured Friedrich Schlegel, "is nature creatively looking back at itself," a productivity which defeats the standardization to which reflective judgment aspires. Hegel's account is standardizing: it allows all oppositions to circulate within an absolute subject, individually incomplete but, in completion, absolutely individual.[9]

If we look at the problem again, this time from the subject's end of the knowledge relation, we find that the self, too, always escapes its own forms of knowledge. It has to, otherwise it would cease to be the subject having the knowledge and would have become another item on its own scientific inventory. Its distinctive subjectivity would have vanished. From Descartes to Sartre, some philosophers have been content to consider the subject sufficiently defined by its power to separate itself from things known. It is a *pour soi*, and that's all that can be said. *Ego sum, ego existo.* The romantic reaction to Kant, though, argued that we must come by our apprehension of subjectivity in a manner outside the subject/object paradigm of knowledge altogether. What might this other way of grasping ourselves (and natural possibilities beyond scientific jurisdiction) be? Fichte argued for a basic *act* subtending knowledge in which the ego spontaneously posited its opposite and so intuited both itself and the world in this mutual productivity. The intuition comes from the fact that in each act of knowledge an absolute ego gets defined in opposition to the not-self it has posited. Fichte can forget about noumena; they drop out of consideration in this monistic theory, one in which nature is simply the resistance we produce in order to make it possible for us to act, in order to give us something to act against—a *Bestimmung*, determination, or vocation. The object is internal to the subject's self-constitution. Thus, Fichte's theory of knowledge is a general theory, but its evidence is always particular: the world is the resistance intuited in the accomplishment of specific acts of knowledge. His absolute ego can only be got at individually. Correspondingly, each individual act should be understood as one performance among the many open to an unconstrained subject. That is why Friedrich Schlegel famously held Fichte's *Wissenschaftslehre*, along with Goethe's *Meister* and the French Revolution, to be one of the main tendencies of the age. All three proffer their individual actions with an ironic reserve, signaling awareness of an untapped potential. It is in making something of this reserve, instead of meticulously preserving the epistemic suspense it incurs, that Schlegel frees creativity from strict loyalty to an original aesthetic moment and urges its historical proliferation.[10]

This, though, is to anticipate. Reserve is an important concept in the studies that follow. But to continue the philosophical tale, Fichte's creative intuition, though, can appear yet again to resurrect the subject/object paradigm to which it was supposed to provide an alternative. Certainly, Fichte's vocabulary of this practical awareness of the self can still unhelpfully point to that self-defining activity as if to an object.[11] A more convincing escape is offered by the Jena group's aesthetics.[12] The poeticization of philosophy and the theorization of poetry practiced by Friedrich Schlegel, Novalis, and Schleiermacher, often aphoristically, can appear exaggerated or overingenious. Equally, these investigations can rehearse and help explain much later philosophical positions trying to solve the same problem. Art is something increased rather than judged by reflection. Critical reflection upon art does not say what art is but generates more of what art is. Art is not known as an object by a subject, the interpretations it releases are not different from its being. Its power to provoke a series of different interpretations throughout history, at different times, characterizes its nature. Conversely, we can say that critical activity, the attempt to know what the work of art means, does not belong to a different order of existence from the work of art itself. Romanticism is also metaromanticism. As did Heidegger and Gadamer, we have to devise a critical language of indwelling categories assisting mutual disclosure adequate to the common being of critique and object of critique, a being more primordial than can be identified as an object by a subject.[13]

Can the aesthetic offer a model of apprehension different from that of scientific practice? As Schlegel puts it in *Ideen*, "Whatever can be done while poetry and philosophy are separated has been done and accomplished. So the time has come to unite the two."[14] The new aesthetic must preserve the alternative which Kant wanted aesthetics to offer to determinate judgments, but without surreptitiously relying on Kant's reflective model deriving from the scientific paradigm of a subject reflecting on its object. This kind of reflection is an activity, as it was for Fichte, but an activity belonging indifferently to both sides of the relation, one in which their common being, the being of art and its critical understanding, are identically perpetuated. Schelling called this point of indifference (meaning not "apathy" but belonging neither to subject nor object) the Absolute and regarded it as the moment explaining all knowledge, uniquely grasped for us in art because productivity has replaced reflection as a mode of understanding. Art, as Schelling describes it in his 1801–4 lectures on the philosophy of art, almost a coda to the Jena philosophical collaboration, is "knowledge which has completely become activity. That is, the indifference of both."[15] This situating of oneself ontologically in life-process as a creative form of orientation, a grounding knowledge, is precisely what is forbidden those characters over whom life triumphs in Shelley's *The Triumph of Life*. We do not here need to go into the wider implications of the romantic aesthetic for philosophy in general, but we should dwell further on the historical character thus evoked for art.

Metaromantic Historicism

Walter Benjamin's early dissertation on the idea of art criticism in Schlegel evinces sympathy for the romantic aesthetic which helps explain Benjamin's later ideas about the radical possibilities for critical transformation open to the work of art. In an age of mechanical reproduction, though, the aesthetic itself appears subject to destruction. For Novalis, "The true reader must be the extended author." For Friedrich Schlegel, more equivocally, the true critic had to be "an author to the second power."[16] Is the romantic aesthetic open enough to reproductive possibility to be able to part company with its particular authorial occasion and survive only in the self-criticism it has given rise to? Can that original specificity be historicized as mere "aura," and can the ensuing democratization of the image, the making of it readily available in forms owing nothing to its occasion and everything to its critical currency, be accomplished without incurring a critical loss as well, a "messianic" interruption?[17] It is a sense of irreparable individual loss that provokes

Rousseau's entrusting of his reveries to the miscellaneous activation of future readers. Adorno, although sympathetic to any noninstrumental apprehension of nature, balks at the "regression" he believes consequent on this critical *laissez faire.* He privileges the elite individual artistic performance, and dreads its demotion as he does effacement of the pastness of the aesthetic critically perpetrated by the "culture industry."[18] Again, fortunately, we don't need to decide between Adorno and Benjamin here. But we should note that these later tensions have their originals in the romantic mobilizing of the aesthetic, the work of art's incorporation of its own critical reflection.

Kant's aesthetic shadowing of the subject/object relation means that his aesthetic can suspend this relation but not abandon it. Aesthetic experience must articulate itself through its characteristic power to hold the two terms of subject and object apart in a non-identifying act that, for Kant, becomes the "chief portion," to quote Frances Ferguson, of aesthetic interest.[19] Ferguson distinguishes the "reciprocal quotation" of the opposites, art and nature, in her reading of Kantian aesthetics, from Adorno's famous insistence on "non-identity" as the privilege of art. Like all Kantian theories, however, hers exists on the assumption that aesthetic objects "are autonomous . . . because they cannot be exclusively assigned to either subjectivity or objectivity."[20] Schlegelian theory, leading not to Adorno but to Benjamin, Gadamer, and beyond, tries to replace this aesthetic hesitancy, or "solitude" as Ferguson calls it, with something more than art's abstemious quotation of the thing with which it cannot be identified. For Schlegel, the non-identity of subject and object enjoys a critical extension as ontologically indifferent as Schelling's Absolute to the jurisdiction of either subject or object. In the space of non-identity cleared by fiction, Schlegel's art is already and "characteristically" fashioning critical alternatives to and historical departures from its original generic performance—that is what is creative about it, its inherent plurality. Benjamin only emphasizes the application of Schlegel's concept of the *Mischgedicht,* or generically conflicted work of art, to the institution of the aesthetic as a whole.[21]

Paradoxically, art's growing power to comment on and offer models for understanding the age can therefore raise discontent that it is to art that this critical function has been historically allocated, a self-impugning discontent which arises from the creative projection of romanticism into metaromanticism. Metaromanticism is skeptical of the aesthetic's critical empowerment. My sixth chapter, on Scott's *Waverley,* looks at an example of this, reading a representation of romanticism into its hero, Edward

Waverley. His name, to become the running title of the great edition of all Scott's novels, echoes a common English assimilation of the romantic irony theorized by Schlegel's Jena group. Wavering typifies the German philosophical attitude as characterized a bit later, for instance, by Franklin Blake in Wilkie Collins's *The Moonstone*. "Have you ever been in Germany?" Blake asks Gabriel Betteridge, and then proposes an explanation which, "taking its rise in a Subjective-Objective point of view," claims that "one interpretation is just as likely to be right as the other." But, as well, *Waverley* represents the Jacobites as romantic, living a life of irony, perpetually disempowered and yet signifying by default the revolution of Scott's own time, the French Revolution, and its power to disorient historiography. The appositeness of aesthetic categories to describe the Revolution does not save Scott's writing of its history but invalidates it. The Revolution was an unassimilable event from which his historiography had to recover, and Scott's widely accepted aesthetic displacement of French onto Jacobite Revolution became a self-confessed alternative to historical explanation. While critics have been sensitive to his transformation of genre, there has been less attention paid to ways in which his aesthetic successes critique their own maladjusted historical empowerment, the incongruousness of their political inflation, in a manner once more evidencing the metaromantic activity at work.

Like Scott's conservatism, Jane Austen's is worried by the degree to which its proper instantiation relies on the exercise of aesthetic responsibilities. In *Waverley*, the fantasy, dream, and immature indecision aesthetically enjoyed by Edward Waverley was known for what it was by the novel's more capable art. The embarrassment, nonetheless, of its aesthetic profit from this dangerous investment was also there for all to see. My chapter on Austen's attack on what Carl Schmitt called "political romanticism" (chapter 7) pursues her comparable use of the character of the flirt to figure an art which, as in politics, must then disown itself to carry conviction. But its fictional function preserves party-principle when the Conservative establishment isn't itself up to the task. Conservatives resist theorizing this political reserve and making it answerable to principles, as I discuss in the contrast between Coleridge and Godwin in chapter 3. Yet their reticence allows all sorts of competitors to lay claim to the political space outside positive institutions and class divisions, the natural or patriotic interest which Conservatives assume is theirs. This is a contested space (as expounded at more length in chapter 10), one to be occupied by purposeful conversation, binding together in society like-minded interlocutors. To have conceded so much, though, is to have identified a responsible use of aesthetic activity that is no longer necessarily Conservative. Either we are returned to the indecisiveness Schmitt deplored, or else the "conversibility" allowing different classes to enjoy each other's society suggests multivalent possibilities whose outcomes could be decisively *multi*cultural. Austen's strength is to acknowledge this indeterminacy in the process of arguing for its Conservative resolution.

I take up these implications in the last three chapters. When viewed as holding a place for a more adequate political dispensation still to be empirically established, the sublimatory or compensatory function of the aesthetic is replaced by the notion of it as the currently hypothetical state in which the better life is logically obliged to exist, for the moment. It shares this logical constraint with the aspirational character of all language toward full communication. It keeps a place open for voicing that priority. It doesn't pretend it has achieved it already, nor that it will always be valuable not to have achieved it so as to be able romantically to imagine it. This "new romanticism" (chapter 10) is both more modest than and breaks the mold of Schiller's aesthetic. The use of Habermas here is intended to do justice to the critical force of meta- or "new" romanticism, as I define it, without letting it collapse back into itself in another recuperation—as more romanticism or aestheticism, like the "German ideology." On the way to these chapters' discussions, though, I look at the varieties of patriotism (in chapter 8) which romantic period writers used to articulate their aesthetic. Again, the romantic contribution is characterized as their ability to think different possibilities within an occasionalism which is not the willful indecisiveness taken to task by Carl Schmitt but a Machiavellian openness to unprescribed possibilities, one appreciative of the *virtù* they occasion.[22]

But precisely what might be "natural" to us, our human *patria*, can itself be straightforwardly contested. The materialism of Mary and Percy Shelley provides one such confrontation, not often appreciated as such partly because its formative traditions (canvassed in chapter 6) are Lucretian and French, neither of which have much currency after Erasmus Darwin in English writing of their period. The *philosophes* are effaced from English philosophical genealogies by all sorts of philosophers— commonsense, dissenting radicals, romantics like Coleridge and Hazlitt—because of their unacceptable materialism and its atheistic subversiveness. But the philosophes had in their turn suppressed the scandalous materialism of La Mettrie, partly because of its evident compatibility with La Mettrie's lack of subversiveness. Mary Shelley, more obviously than her partner, recycles La Mettrie's shocking degree of acceptance of a completely physical definition of our lives. In her work, the contrasting horror and uncanny surrounding this materialism satirize those obliged so to demonize it; and her feminism arises from recognizing women's frequent role as the bearer of male abjection of this horror. The body, then, carries a philosophy which has been disallowed as a theory, its physical origins made to disqualify it as an intellectual position. Galvanized, this materialist philosophy moves in monstrous guise, from the figure of the creature in *Frankenstein*, through Heine's class-inflected reworking of it, to the story Engels tells of the bourgeois abandonment of the universals of philosophy for those of the market, and the consequent settling of philosophy's mantle on the proletariat—that unthinkable, *lumpen* fate: "The German working class is the inheritor of German classical philosophy."[23] This is the new *patrie de la pensée*, one which would be for most of his polite readers, as Engels knew, interchangeable with the idea of the "end" of philosophy.

In his 1835 *Zur Geschichte der Religion und Philosophie in Deutschland* (On the History of Religion and Philosophy in Germany), an ironic reply to Mme de Stael, Heine had declared it the immediate task of modern institutions to facilitate the rehabilitation of matter. Germany's pantheism was, in fact, an open secret. Political parallels invited by the philosophical progress of this desired reconciliation, though, were inauspicious. They seemed to end in Schelling's reactionary "restoration" of nature after Kant's terroristic *Convenzion* and Fichte's Napoleonic *Kaiserreich*. The young Marx favored Feuerbach's brand of materialism and also attacked Schelling's. Heine had found more frightening than the call of the disenfranchised for a voice, a new philosophy's demand for a body.[24] For Engels too, writing in 1888, it is the discrediting of the sublimatory purpose of German idealism that has made theory's materialization happen in unlikely creatures frightening to a bourgeois sensibility: "to the same degree that speculation abandoned the philosopher's study in order to set up its temple in the Stock Exchange, educated Germany lost the great aptitude for theory which had been the glory of Germany in the days of its deepest political humiliation. . . . Only among the German working class does the German aptitude for theory remain unimpaired."[25] Of course Engels means that if theory worthy of the name has to be generated anew from a material source, then the proletariat will be the group with something new to contribute: first of all because they have been silenced up until now, and secondly because, according to Marxist "science," all authentic material change derives from the proletariat's progress in particular. Without taking this metaphysic literally, we can find in its outcome an understanding of why romantic ideology tried to keep alternatives to itself unthinkable. In chapter 9 I examine this self-confirming habit as spectacularly dramatized by Stendhal and Sade. This knowing refusal of any critical position outside a self-confirming belief-system is what I call the "ideology of immanent critique." In this character, though, romantic ideology played into the hands of its enemy. For when that enemy predominated, it could argue consistently with the romantic opponent it had defeated that what mattered was no longer philosophical. For Georg Lukács, this was the founding act of irrationalism, inaugurating the "destruction *(Zerstörung)* of reason." Schelling's identification of aesthetic and intellectual intuition represents primarily his privileging of good taste, his "tendencies to aristocratism" in epistemology, not an incipient materialism. Schelling's method prescribes all the future materialisms Lukács holds to be false alternatives to scientific Marxism. Schelling's method "defines the problematic/sets the terms of inquiry *(Problemstellung)* for Schopenhauer as later for Nietzsche, for Dilthey's 'descriptive psychology,' for 'intuition of the essence' *(Wesenschau)* in phenomenology, for ontology in existentialism."[26]

Metaromantic Afterlives

Nevertheless, interpretations continued.[27] Materialism needed a philosophical rationale as much as romantic philosophy needed an afterlife. If the Hegelian tradition had indeed been "annihilated," then "the new content which had been won . . . had to be saved."[28] The aesthetic was deployed in new ways. Means for resisting idealism and subjectivization were devised which were still philosophical. Only recently has it appeared valuable to return to romantic period writers' and philosophers' resistance to the immanent self-critique to which they were confined and to look for a "contemporaneity" in their treatments. As a "post-Marxist" perspective emerges, or a Marxism more historicized than Lukács's classical reconstruction, there seems more point in returning to romantic thought to search out materialist possibilities different from the inversion of idealist philosophy which romanticism invited and Marxism originally proclaimed. Hence chapter 10, "The New Romanticism," looks at near-contemporary reworkings of the romantic concern for particularity or a material individualism which would call the shots where philosophical pretensions to competence are concerned. The aporia we saw arrived at by idealist deployment of the subject/object epistemological paradigm was in practice got round at the time by discursive versatility. The failure to achieve a position of critical authority outside forms of self-knowledge and object-knowledge, a transcendental position, is thematized by writing of the time. The examples I cite complicate, I hope, Habermas's attempts to update these alternatives as forms of discursive reserve, stand-ins for their eventual articulation in that ideal situation when we will be able to tell all. In the meantime, our idealizations show a highly practical respect for cultural difference which makes communication historically possible. Habermas, therefore, doesn't want "ideal" to mean here what it does for an idealist philosopher, but he can often appear, not unhelpfully, to be systematizing a pragmatics of romantic discourse.

This verdict returns us, in chapter 11, to Schiller's chiasmic structure. The postmodern eschewal of romantic creativity has itself to invent an original, ungrounded identity in order to be sure its own indeterminacy doesn't collapse into the original ungrounded identity of romantic sublimity. The particular facts, events, or individuals it treats with exemplary singularity materially resist prescribed definitions. But in this tactic it develops metaromantic writing's own creative resistance to that aesthetic naturalization of the particularity it couldn't get hold of in any other way. This opposition can explode from within romantic sublimity by dwelling on a moment of its sequence, a savoring of particularity prior to aesthetic legitimation, in the manner of Dorothy Wordsworth's *Journals.* From an ancillary position within romanticism, her success strikingly suggests romanticism's instability and increases its usefulness as a precursor of postmodern materialism and views of human creativity released from aesthetic institutions, or, in her case, an ascendant brother. This is to take a cynical view of her situation as a writer, one encouraged by the explicit cynicism of Friedrich Schlegel—unlikely commentator on Dorothy Wordsworth, but an expander of the definition of poetry well beyond strictly aesthetic control and a writer much influenced by female readers and collaborators.

The reserve required by the logic of communication is therefore fostered by both these authors in their different ways. Dorothy Wordsworth's cultured hesitation before the particularities of her life reserves judgment on which form their authentic presentation should take. Schlegel's cynical detachment leaves his individuality comparably unconfined. By disowning any unique expression, he makes all self-expression over to public ownership. Schlegel socializes Kant's notion of genius. Originality involves a reflection upon its own artifice, immediately placing itself on a level with its imitation by others. This reversing of Kant's emphasis means that we can make any original display, if it is a valid one, into our own accomplishment. All things are potentially ours, though not ours uniquely, and the true original is the one who gives most away for public consumption. It is best, therefore, not to own anything, but to treat everything as if you did own it, as if it were yet another fragment of your identity. Like Rousseau, Schlegel casts his vote, as it were, in a republic, entrusting his self-definition to its commonwealth rather than insisting on his rights to a private existential property as unlikely to be conclusive and as likely to be fragmentary as Kantian self-coincidence or apperception. But of course it has been his emphasis on his *own* exclusiveness, his cynical refusal to identify with any given character, which has allowed him to contribute to this commonalty. This is the "logical sociability" which he defines as being philosophical wit in the *Lyceum Fragment* 56. He rejoices in the mixed and contradictory results of this poetic franchise. I consider the possible contribution of this republicanism to ideas of multiculturalism in the final chapter.

There I develop in a Schlegelian direction aspects of Habermas's Kantian theory of how the freedoms of private perception might model the emancipatory dynamic of a public sphere. As in chapter 10, I stress the difference between Habermas's notion of a *Platzhalter* and aesthetic prefigurations of an eventual plenitude. Not consolation for fulfillment indefinitely postponed but current skills in negotiating cultural difference are the benefits of such "stand-ins" for ultimate rationalization. That is what they keep room for. In this evaluation, Habermas could have been following Walter Benjamin's reading of Schlegel (as well as Novalis and Hölderlin). On this interpretation, Schlegel turns the indeterminateness of Kantian and Schillerian aesthetics into an open-endedness, not to linear progress *(Fortgang)* but to the possible connections or affinities *(Zusammenhange)* Schlegel's own mixed-genre approach to writing actually performs.

The most cited situating of the thought of the Jena romantics in current debates is probably *The Literary Absolute* by Philippe Lacoue-Labarthe and Jean-Luc Nancy. The authors show the "absolute" of literature to equivocate between the expansion I have been describing and a theoretical self-sufficiency that perfectly justified the literary turn philosophy was taking in France in 1978, on the heels of Derrida and Deleuze.[29] Either, like "the poetry of poetry," the ontological increase criticism gives to the artwork it criticizes folds back into that artwork—then criticism aestheticizes itself out of its obligations to any further discursive sphere in which it might belong and we are enmired in the dilemma to which metaromanticism, it is proposed here, is a solution; or else, peculiarly attuned by its object to productivity, criticism perpetuates the liberality of artistic conception elsewhere and gains its entitlement to aesthetic "civil rights" by virtue of its generous, creative behavior in another sphere. This latter interpretation, advanced by this book and following the language of no. 117 of *Kritische Fragmente,* equates the ontological momentum of criticism's "presentation of a necessary impression in the state of becoming" with that "open tone" within the expanding franchise of "civil rights within the realm of art."[30] As Benjamin put it (and Lacoue-Labarthe and Nancy occasionally reiterate) "the idea of poetry is prose."[31] Criticism, divinatory in Schleiermacher's sense, descries the revelatory legacies of an originally aesthetic experience ready to precipitate itself creatively in other discursive spheres.

Habermas criticizes Adorno in *The Theory of Communicative Action* for collapsing into aesthetics "the placeholder" of an undistorted apprehension—"the surrender of all cognitive competence to art." He himself continues to rephrase that same placeholding function to make respectable his own retrieval of a future for philosophy. He commends the "interdisciplinary materialism" of critical theory's original project over its subsequent critique of instrumental reason.[32] Perhaps it is not too Quixotic to see Schlegel's cynicism concerning the defining singularity of Cartesian self-consciousness as comparable to Habermas's own abandonment of an exhausted "paradigm of the philosophy of consciousness" for that of the logic of communication? That move exhibits its results in a philosophical ability to interpret different disciplines to each other. Philosophy cultivates a sense of connectedness which renews the Schlegelian step aside from a unique philosophical project into the world of the *Mischgedicht,* or what Habermas calls those "hybrid discourses" he believes may well mark "the beginning of new research traditions."[33]

In the essay from which Paul de Man's reading of the rhetoric of romanticism effectively starts, "The Rhetoric of Temporality," de Man too writes that we should revise traditional explanations of romanticism centered on the dialectical relationship between subject and object. We should no longer subscribe to that same philosophy of consciousness rendered tautologous by the intentional structure of its own images. Schlegel is also crucial to de Man, and my reading of him can be further clarified by its difference from de Man's deconstruction of him. De Man, unlike his then equally influential colleagues Geoffrey Hartman and Harold Bloom, shifts on to other ground the romantic problematic of squaring a homeless subject with a natural object. Hartman and Bloom had provided a genealogy of existentialism, one of Lukács's discredited irrationalisms, in the process of reading major romantic poets such as Wordsworth and Shelley. With more respect for Lukács, de Man argues instead that the relationship crucial to romantic construction is not between subject and object but one within temporality, between genres. Romanticism typically stages the conflict between an "authentically temporal" self acknowledged in allegory and its own symbolic defenses against such shocking recognition of mortality. I argue that the truth which intermittently surfaces within romantic theory and writing is that we are natural products, and that the mind which supposedly returns upon its origins to master them as objects external to it, objects of scientific knowledge, deceives itself as to this authoritative difference and is better employed in finding ways of explaining its common ground in nature and expressing this natural orientation. Viewed as one such tactic, symbolic genres do not propose an "illusory" union between consciousness and the alien constrictions of mortality; they get behind scientific differentiations of ourselves from nature in order to figure the infinitude such loss of individuation entails.[34] The crisis in romantic temporality is then no longer de Man's one of a repressed *memento mori*, but, as I argue in my first chapter on Schiller, the temporizing by which the aesthetic symbol is defined to imply that the realization of its imagined, better life is always still to come.

By making its predating of the satisfactions the aesthetic promises identical with its constitutive figurality, Schiller postpones aesthetic satisfactions forever. It is a category mistake to expect such fulfillment ever to occur. The disabling paradox here, which I examine in this book, lies in the fact that the symbolic figural aesthetic nonetheless has its *raison d'être* as an expression of the larger noumenal reality to which we belong. The category shift in fact denotes the alternative access to reality the aesthetic sets up. The entire Kantian narrative assumed here has the aesthetic join up our consciousness of the world with the world itself, but unconditionally, without making one an object of the other, although this paradigm of acquaintance disablingly haunts Kant's formulation. Romanticism calls Kant's bluff and makes the distinction between literal and figural no longer sustainable. We have to use symbols to get on terms with the literal reality to which we belong. The aesthetic enacts this knowledge but is unjustifiably instituted, by its shadow-play of science in Kant's *Critique of Judgment,* so as to make its experiences neither knowledge nor action.[35] As in Schiller, so in de Man's later essay on Shelley, figuration made literal is disfiguration, a malformation charged with a horror and disgust taken to discredit its access to an encompassing material reality.

Here lies the inconsistency against which the metaromanticism of Kant's successors is mobilized and against which the metaromantic writing of the romantic period grates.

Let me rephrase where I think my thesis differs from de Man's. Schlegelian irony need not, as de Man seems to think, in its "infinite agility" perpetuate Schiller's postponement of and deluded longing for satisfaction. It may indeed, as Walter Benjamin argued, concretize infinite satisfactions at every stage of its process. Its "permanent parabasis" *(Parekbasis)*, in the Schlegelian phrase on which de Man alights, steps aside from the individual cognitive project in which it is situated.[36] De Man, though, overemphasizes the authorial intervention signaled by parabasis at the expense of the communal, Choral voice which Schlegel knew was always allotted parabasis in Greek drama. Parabasis takes a Choral view of everything topically adjacent to a moment in the unfolding dramatic progress to which it is otherwise the purpose of the play to harness our attention. Irony is therefore not a history of inauthentic foreclosures of an infinite linear progress, but a branching out into lateral connections, a sideways rolling expansion socializing the infinity present at each moment. To see " 'a World in a Grain of Sand' " we do not measure anything. Blake's symbolic logic is performative, enjoining a collaborative readership, not charting a territory. De Man's late (1983) writings on the sublime do move on from his earlier figurative/constative problematic to an appreciation of this performativity, but in order to imagine performativity culminating in an ultimate "prosaic materiality of the letter." De Man's materialism here also solicits a collaborative vision, one pursuing the non-identitarianism of Kantian aesthetics to the pure unintelligibility alone adequate to the noumenal, intelligible world aesthetics is supposed to get on terms with. We are asked to picture language somehow converging more closely on what it is in itself by shedding the signifying character constituting for us just what it is to be a language. De Man's "materialism" is thus one exquisite poetic fashioning among other possibilities. It renders, perhaps, Rilke's displacement onto the animals of the knowledge, inaccessible to us, that we are not reliably at home in the interpreted world *(und die findige Tiere merken es schon, / dass wir nicht sehr verlässlich zu Haus sind / in der gedeuteten Welt)*. But another poetic effort might conjure up another poetic possibility, inventing Schlegelian departures along the way. In a chiasmic formula, de Man transvalues Kant's aesthetics into materialism, but a materialism whose conceptually intransigent particularity requires a distinctively imaginative effort to isolate. His materialism needs to remain conspicuously aesthetic, raised

anew in each of its instances, never determinate, in order not to per-
petrate the phenomenalist reification he is using it to expose. One is
struck by de Man's deconstructive need to believe that the aesthetic, if
not a Kantian self-defeat, habitually mystifies and can never instantiate a
reality absolutely indifferent to our contradictory modes of being in it.
For him it never records a history we cannot disown.[37]

For de Man, Schiller's deferral of fulfillment keeps at bay for ideological reasons the dead typographical landscape actually accessed by the
fullest exertion of our aesthetic powers. Like Schlegel, Walter Benjamin
steps aside from this aesthetic one-way street and looks for the prosaic
proliferation of aesthetic education in adjacent discourses critical of its
original aura or formulation. Benjamin's suspicion of unidirectional progressiveness starts early. In his first work on Schlegel the necessarily empty
(leere) understanding of deferred fulfillment is satisfied, as a mathematical
function is satisfied, by mediations of infinite possibility founded on the
liveliness or living reality of connectedness *(vermittelte Unmittelbarkeit . . .
auf der die Lebendigkeit des Zusammenhanges beruht).*[38] Initially, this lateral
rather than onward movement, diversifying rather than advancing, is exemplified for Benjamin in Schlegel's idea that criticism intensifies rather
than judges its object, squaring its possibilities "to the second power,"
satisfying another aspect of its being rather than mastering it from a different order of knowledge.[39] Thus understood, art is constitutionally variegated, and, departing from Benjamin now, my last chapter shows that
Schlegel's early political theory proposed a republicanism consistent with
the *Mischgedicht* or inherently mixed form into which he had directed
the "universal, progressive" impetus characteristic of romantic *Poesie*. Its
theoretical future lies in the direction of a Bakhtinian poetics whose poetics is a *culture* crisscrossed by different stylistic aptitudes.[40] A lateral
or comparative inclusiveness allows literature to free improvements or
striving toward the better life from the model of linear progressiveness.
Thus emancipated, literature puts multicultural politics into practice in
its own sphere, rather than prefiguring that desirable outcome through
a compensatory aesthetic of consolation.

In this metaromantic character, romanticism can, I hope, convince
us of a critical function, refusing the indecisive relativism its detractors
accuse it of indulging and inaugurating a new progressiveness, multifar-
ious rather than linear, maintaining difference through sympathy and
tempering idealization of the other with the demand that, in fairness, he
or she make comparable efforts to imagine a workable commonalty. The
aesthetic's cynicism about its own self-sufficiency fragments into a local

politics, a grassroots democracy: the manner in which different generic views of the world—epic, heroic, tragic, comic, or whatever—cast their votes within a common aesthetic structure shows a heterological politics in action. From this perspective, metaromanticism gives us a salutary political vision extending beyond the confessional state, beyond the commercial consensus of liberal democracy that succeeded it, and beyond the communitarian alternatives to that supposedly final settlement. This vision reaches toward a society possessing the arts of accommodating the mixed allegiances that have to remain in dialogue for the frail postcolonial civilization in which we live to survive.

AESTHETICS

Schiller's Temporizing

Herr Settembrini spoke more than once, with great enthusiasm, of the revolutionary principle, and about rebellion and reform—which is no very peaceful principle, I should think—and of the mighty efforts still to be made before it triumphs everywhere, and the great universal world republic can come into being. Those were his words, though of course it sounded much more plastic and literary as he said it.

—Thomas Mann, *The Magic Mountain*

Figuration and Temporality

Friedrich Schiller is the prime expresser of a romantic ideology common to English practitioners and German theorists of the romantic period. Secreted in his logical virtuosity lies an ingenious justification for ruling out of court any alternatives to the aesthetic as location and description of the transforming power of art. Schiller's aesthetic prohibits that knowing "metaromanticism" or "new" romanticism with which this book tries to surround it.

As a key to this chapter and what follows, I should reiterate the way in which Habermas is at the heart of my attempt to think through an alternative to the romanticism implied by Schiller's aesthetics, a new romanticism. The contrast I develop comes from the fact that throughout his work Habermas does *not* idealize full communication out of existence. For him idealizing is part of the machinery communication needs to function, something we actually experience *in* communicating. It is enacted in the counterfactual dimension allowing sympathetic communication between opposing cultures, disciplines, and standpoints. And the reserve in which our own ideals repose evolves "stand-ins" and "interpreters" as a pragmatic way round that opposite idealizing-as-postponement I explain in this chapter. Schiller's temporizing follows from the heritage of Kantian and post-Kantian philosophy which linked idealizing to deferral in the description of any ameliorative discourse, such as poetry. I try to make Habermas's reflex but reforming recourse to that philosophical tradition also power my own readings of the new romanticism.

The aesthetic theory Schiller worked on over a ten-year period is frequently neglected, yet it marks a crucial passage between the thought of Kant and Hegel. The intellectual framework of the major philosophical texts, *On Grace and Dignity* (1793), *On the Aesthetic Education of Man, in a Series of Letters* (1795), *Naive and Sentimental Poetry* (1795), and *On the Sublime* (1801) is Kantian. But Schiller treats problems in Kantian aesthetics and modifies hierarchies within Kantian speculation in order to elicit their meatier implications for a definition of culture, and he offers culture the role of preserving a civil society lying behind the state apparatuses or executive institutions of the State. If one wants to write about the culture and politics implied by the discourse of romantic philosophical aesthetics, Schiller is very important. He repeatedly describes the State as intended for human cultivation, and the chiasmic turn of his thought repeatedly leads his reader to expect the corollary: the achievement of our proper end would be the creation of a State capable of the satisfactions we have so far had to make do with in the form of aesthetic experience. Art ought to render itself otiose. For Herbert Marcuse, this dissolution of art in material life is only consistent with the purpose of Schiller's aesthetic education to integrate our "higher" rational powers with a common sensuous base. "Advanced capitalism has revealed real possibilities of liberation which surpass all traditional concepts. These possibilities have raised again the idea of the *end of art*. The radical possibilities of freedom (concretized in the emancipatory potential of technical progress) seem to make the traditional function of art obsolete, or at least to abolish it as a special branch of the division of labor, through the reduction of the separation between mental and manual labor. The images *(Schein)* of the Beautiful and of fulfilment would vanish when they are no longer denied by the society. In a free society the images become aspects of the real."[1] As Habermas points out, Marcuse can challenge Schiller to redeem art's promises only because he shares Schiller's view of art as ideal. Were one to forsake this view and understand art to be capable of reintegration with other forms of creativity and labor, then art would no longer be under threat. Nor would we be barred from enjoying its former idealisms, provided we historicized that enjoyment. This would be Walter Benjamin's view, both more radical and more conservative than Marcuse's at the same time.[2]

But Schiller's way of avoiding an "end of art" scenario is by insisting on a necessary passage through art to politics, which he believed incumbent on any emancipatory idea. Ideas achieve full expression in aesthetic experience, but consequent upon that fullness is the demand for their practical realization in life. Marcuse challenges Schillerian aesthetics to keep its promise: to efface itself in the real benefits it is its purpose to inspire. As we shall see, the lengths to which Schiller goes to preserve the aesthetic function belie this radicalism. His aesthetic does indeed seem bent on rendering itself redundant by commanding us to create the better world in which its ideals will no longer be ideal but real, a way of life.[3] Whenever such desuetude threatens, however, Schiller removes his aesthetic from the chronology where it had shone as the temporary prefiguration of an eventual fulfillment. He temporizes. He plays around with time in order to keep the aesthetic figurative of and autonomous from the life whose completion it was meant to urge. And another way of saying this is that Schiller's aesthetic defers the better life so that, perversely, we can still enjoy the benefits of having to imagine it.[4]

Schiller describes the aesthetic state as one which is free from all determination: it is universal because it is an experience of that sense of plenitude we possess before we enter into any scientific or practical determination of our nature. As soon as we do that, we necessarily narrow ourselves down, temporarily, to one or other of the functions, sensuous or rational, which we moderns typically employ in isolation from each other to get things done or find things out. To experience the common ground of our otherwise divided natures, though, is to experience something indeterminate, something whose antithetical difference from "mere indetermination (without limits because it is without reality)" is its potential for any future determination (145). Crucial, then, for distinguishing Schiller's educative aesthetic from a state of "mere indetermination" is a question of temporality. At stake is whether one sees the aesthetic state as prior to a determinate one, and the condition of its possibility, or sees it as subsequent to determination, and thus only recognizable as the "mere" abeyance of that determining function. The latter would exhibit the indecisiveness or "occasionalism," rather than historicity, for which critics of romanticism from Hegel to Carl Schmitt have reproached it.

An ironic attitude is forced on the aesthetic understanding of the provisional nature of all understanding and expression. The reserve with which any definition is offered in the light of its aesthetic foretaste can work in either of two ways. Either it can remain progressive, hanging on to its claim to prefigure, charting each moment of incompletion as a stage on the road to something better, each fragment as pointing toward the fulfilling whole; or else this metonymic logic is replaced by that of catachresis, in which the shortfall of any attempt to express something already savored in its aesthetic possibility generates the attitude of the dilettante. This *flâneur* regards reality as a mere trifling with his own far richer stores of sensibility, something not to be taken seriously except as figurative stimulus to a sense of the infinite. Like Kierkegaard's aesthetic seducer, he can claim, "I myself am a myth about myself."[5] Progressiveness too is a false limitation placed on the universality he apprehends aesthetically, and the fragmentariness of nonaesthetic understanding reveals only its mistakenness (catachresis), not its historical part in a better future (metonymy). Friedrich Schlegel, master of irony, predominantly adopts the first, progressive meaning of aesthetic reserve; but the second kind, growing out of "sheer indetermination" or a superiority to any specific condition in which we find ourselves, although memorably dallied with by Schlegel too, inadvertently comes from Schiller.[6]

The young Friedrich Schlegel's republican idiom, this book's trajectory aims to show, by contrast with Schiller, accesses a present experience of the Ideal. What attracted Walter Benjamin to Schlegel (and led, later, to Habermas's departure from romantic pragmatics) was his alternative to an eternally postponed fulfillment, necessarily deferred to ensure the prefigurative substance distinguishing the aesthetic. Schlegel's own philosophy reached out sideways, laterally and synchronically, into all the reaches of contemporary possibility, holding contradictory genres in aesthetic solution (tragic, comic, epic, lyric, etc.) and accommodating opposing class interests within a politically mixed constitution. In the British tradition, such a political settlement has an obvious radical pedigree, although not radical enough for Tom Paine, as we shall see. It perpetuates the Machiavellian moment favoring productive class conflict and debate, through Harington's separation of powers in *Oceana*, figured in the republican Marvell's representative poetic dialogism, and recovered in the fruitful self-divisions of the metaromanticism studied here.[7] In Europe, Schlegel's republicanism clearly opposed absolutism, while its tolerance of contradiction opened up a multicultural rather than leveling franchise, one in which the women active in the Jena group of romantics (principally Caroline Schlegel and Dorothea Veit) would have their say. Schiller, conversely, tries to overcome both the division of labor and its Jacobin leveling by constructing an aesthetic recourse to which all citizens may repair, but without prejudice to the hierarchies causing their need to re-create themselves.

Schiller's argument is mentalistic. The narrowing specialisms his aesthetic redresses are imbalances in a desirable psychic equilibrium made up of Kantian faculties. But the faculties themselves unavoidably sound politically self-selecting, without any need of allegorizing: sense obviously enjoys a wider dispensation than reason, and their interaction precipitates a raising of one and democratizing of the other. Schlegel's aesthetic does not prescribe ideal political remedies. His republicanism and his notions of aesthetic order, in *Poesie* or *Roman,* set standards for each other. His republic's independent citizenry model the aesthetic association of the contested forms within the *Mischgedicht,* whose inventive combinations return the compliment. In Habermas's terms, they can "stand in" for or "interpret" each other. Neither legislates a priori the conditions of the other.

Schiller, however, never satisfactorily establishes the priority necessary to secure for the aesthetic state an existence more positive than the absence of any determinate state. His aesthetic is always secondary, in the way that the figurative is always preceded by the literal. Yet Schiller persistently claims that the aesthetic possesses a retrospective authority. Were it not for the potential of which the aesthetic state is the repository, no future determinations would be possible, and no past ones could have been various or different. The aesthetic is "the ground of possibility of them all" (151). Its literal outcomes turn out to have been tropes after all: metonymically they stood in for much wider possibilities. But we can't get at the aesthetic itself except through this having of an aesthetic, playful attitude to what is not aesthetic. Aesthetically, we judge the determinations of our character to symbolize much larger and more integrated capabilities. Schiller contrives to make us think that to grasp the aesthetic literally would be a contradiction in terms.

The aesthetic thus becomes suspended in that future-perfect state, that "will have been," utilized by postmodern theories of judgment such as Lyotard's. It is identifiable as a present experience, but only with reference to its future determinations, which will turn out to be metonymic postponements. It is inherently proleptic. These future destinations are expressible only in a future-perfect tense which, in an apotheosis of liberalism, is to escape the prescriptions of rules and their source in the supposed tyranny of the enlightenment's emancipatory narratives of the coming of reason. I will examine this view in more detail in the last chapter. In the meantime, it is worth noting that it is rather more committed to idealist precursors than is usually admitted. It repeats, for example, the dilemma besetting Kant's depiction of the object of "inner sense": the self which, can only be intuited as our temporal difference from it. In Kant's account (added to the second edition of the first *Critique*), we cannot experience the self, we can only experience self-consciousness or the mind "as it is affected by itself, and therefore as it appears to itself, not as it is" (B:68–69). The hypothesis of an up-to-date self, not thus clouded by a time lag, becomes purely formal: a condition of the possibility of knowledge, a transcendental presupposition, it is not part of the "empirical data" available to inner sense (A:107). The transcendental self is always ahead of or gone by the time of its latest appearance because it is the elusive thing of which the appearance is mere appearance. As soon as we grasp its appearance, we know the thing itself has escaped us. The best we can do is to take the appearance figuratively rather than literally in acknowledgement that its referent has departed. Schiller's aesthetic state is similarly constrained to give only the "appearance" of appearing, despite his attempts to escape the Kantian dilemma in which, "unfortunately" *(leider)*, as he describes it in the first of the letters in *On the Aesthetic Education of Man*, "intellect must first destroy the object of Inner Sense if it would make it its own."[8]

All the language of Schiller's aesthetic is therefore borrowed. The aesthetic can guarantee its own autonomy only through such derivativeness. Any characterization of itself—as "state," "experience," "freedom," "education"—must refer back to determinate conditions; but since it is the essence of Schiller's aesthetic to have preceded these conditions, as their potential, its use of these terms must be *already* aesthetic. In other words, when one says that the aesthetic is condemned to use borrowed terms, it is just its typically figurative use of them that is supposed to make sense of the idea of the aesthetic as originary. The disabling time lag that derivation might have otherwise signified is recuperated as the figurative detachment from determination intended to render the aesthetic universal plausible. Thus, the notion of the aesthetic as the ground of possibility becomes a hypothesis which can be indicated only in a language of temporal displacement. Its derivative expressions are not literally belated but figuratively point up the borrowed time on which the aesthetic survives.

Schiller's aesthetic, the fullest documentation of our humanity, is in fact nothing other than the power of figuration which such dislocation enjoins. Under the aesthetic dispensation, nature becomes semblance or illusion *(Schein)*—the "appearance" of appearing—because of our simultaneous apprehension of its possibilities over and above the determinate shapes of our experience of it. The corollary of this is that nature, when experienced aesthetically, becomes utopian. Nature defined as the better place it might be matches Kant's involuntary definition of the self through its figurative departures from self-reference. Nevertheless, Schiller's entire effort in his aesthetic writings remains that of appropriating for his utopian aesthetic the universal validity Kant assigns to his noumenal extremes of reason and nature, a transcendental self and the thing-in-itself. It would be another move altogether, a Hegelian one, to resign oneself entirely to the phenomenology of the self and abandon all hope of coincidence with its ulterior essence. It is Schiller, though, who has made acceptable the idea of an aesthetic composed entirely of metonymies of itself.

Schiller is no more prepared to shelve his aesthetic's Kantian, universal ideal than he is to ditch that of a "naive" poetry that *would* be literally aesthetic. Yet our difficulty with the notion of the *literally* aesthetic, its paradoxical appearance to us, shows the degree to which we have naturalized Schiller's effective collapse of the aesthetic into its aestheticizations, our fullest humanity into figurations of it. Either this is fraudulent prevarication, or else (as Theodor Adorno might argue) it ensures the non-identity of art with existing consumables which are bound to be ideologically contaminated and themselves false substitutes for fulfillment. Redemption of aesthetic promise must remain a "standpoint," a "demand thus placed on thought," a Kantian imperative.[9]

Without such a transcendental signified of the "naive," the economy of Schiller's aesthetic would be very insecure, living off future investments, "futures" in market parlance, which it must never redeem if its function is to remain perpetually metaphorical, always in the likeness of a future return. In his own time, Schiller shapes, without subscribing to, the phenomenological poetics behind the redemptive sagas of succeeding romantic philosophies from Schelling's *System of Transcendental Idealism* to Nietzsche's Dionysian vision in *The Birth of Tragedy*. These more obviously archetypal romantic narratives demonstrate that "nature which has become alienated, hostile or subjugated, celebrates once more her reconciliation with her lost son, man"[10] According to the Schelling of 1800, aesthetic experience as an intermediate grasp *(Auffassung)* of a final poetic pattern once again fully exists only in the future tense. These are the exigencies that Schiller anticipates in trying to make the aesthetic state available but also indeterminate.

Aesthetics and Politics

Schiller's difficulties and saving ingenuities are especially apparent in the political application he claims for his aesthetics in the early 1790s. In the second of the letters in *On the Aesthetic Education of Man*, he dismisses the charge against him of "culpable indifference" (9) toward French

Revolutionary politics purporting to debate the "very fate of mankind." His justification is once more the temporal prioritizing of the aesthetic. To "put Beauty before Freedom . . . because it is only through Beauty that man makes his way to Freedom" demands an activity in which "retracing" *(ruckwarts zu tun)* and "transforming" *(unzuscheffen)* (11), anteriority and figuration, as I have been suggesting, go hand in hand. Schiller's *Mensch* awakens to consciousness that he or she exists in a state of "compulsion" *(Notstaat)* and retrieves as "a fiction" a state in which they could live according to laws given to them by their own reason. But this fictionalizing rather than historicizing of Rousseau's state of nature appears to reach a historical terminus in the sixth letter's comparison of modern alienation with the "polypoid nature *(Polypennatur)* of the Greek States" (35).

Here a specific political construction fleshes out Schiller's aesthetic state, an organization "in which every individual enjoyed an independent existence but could, when the need arose, grow into the whole organism." In contrast to Greek democracy, subsequent political developments resist organic fulfillment and are better portrayed as a sort of mechanism or clockwork. Schiller, though, has now to project *back* an ideal status onto the Greek model in which the individual can figure the whole organism through political action. Not to do this is to risk two things. In contemporary political thought, such immediate empowerment of the citizen would recall the contemporary Jacobinism Schiller abhorred. Secondly, even when Jacobinical dispensing with political representation is safely consigned to the Greeks, not to make it *ideal* would be to render aesthetic education determinate: what happened at a certain place at a certain time. Schiller again uses historical difference to generate figuration by arguing that had the Greeks "wished to proceed to a higher state of development" they would, "like us," have sacrificed the holistic economy for which they are valued for modern specialism and its clockwork activity (41). Ingeniously, our affinities with them both guarantee the validity of their example and ensure the already aesthetic status of their priority. We can, in Schiller's scheme, trace our political lineage only as a falling-off from Greek organicism when we see the Greeks similarly able to catch the value of their political system only in ideal retrospect. In other respects, Greek democracy remains primitive and undeveloped in comparison to the progress offered by specialization.[11]

Schiller's political history (his Hellenism) and his epistemology (his Kantianism) reflect each other. In each, the aesthetic is shown to be a figurative construction of an otherwise irretrievably dislocated essence. Kant's noumenal world appears to collapse into rhetorical performance.

The figurative status of its display follows from the impossibility of the plenitude which it successfully stages. Franco Moretti, following Carl Schmitt, puts this paradox well: "The best thing we have had is an experience which, not having taken place, can be reexperienced in a totally unconstrained and subjective way. The Romantic charm of indecision has found its most adequate *temporal* expression" (my emphasis).[12] These formulations furnish those chiasmuses which, Schiller's English editors Wilkinson and Willoughby show, are intrinsic to the design in *On the Aesthetic Education of Man*. An impossible plenitude is experienced in an aesthetic legitimated by the impossibility of getting to that plenitude in any other way. Through chiasmus, Schiller devises "a linguistic analogue of the dynamics of the psyche," rhetorically doubling the content of his strictly philosophical analysis (xcvii, lxviii). This rhetorical "birth in language" of Schiller's argument, as the editors call it, is not its supplementary analogue, but represents the way in which characterizations of the aesthetic state are already always aesthetic. Any metaromantic knowingness, implying that the aesthetic formulation is one among a number of linguistic alternatives, is locked out by the chiasmus. Unlike Derrida's dangerous supplement, Schiller's prior rhetoric does not deconstruct but reinforces the hierarchies he desires. Philosophical definition of the aesthetic state must already be metonymic of its object, according to Schiller's argument, which is exactly to guarantee the priority of the aesthetic to everything else. In other words, the relation between Kant's two worlds, phenomenal and noumenal, determinate and indeterminate, is still the thing; but the dramatic failure to establish this distinction where the aesthetic is concerned is Schiller's successful play, an aesthetic excuse for otherwise reprehensible philosophical indecision.

Schiller's aesthetic, then, instructs us in desire for the imaginary: not desire for any specific state of affairs or political achievement, for as the Greek example confirmed, these could only embody aesthetic values retrospectively, at a figurative distance from themselves. For this reason, the aesthetic can, in Schiller's view, help in effecting running repairs to "the living clockwork of the State," which must never be allowed fully to run down (13). Why can the aesthetic be trusted not to rebuild the State on an entirely different model? Because it hasn't any models of its own, and its uniqueness can only be limned in the metonymic status it can confer on any existing definitions. Furthermore, to talk of the State's "clockwork" is to identify the State's machinery with temporality itself, for to what else will the State keep time? So any attempt to revolutionize the State must be unrealistic, mere temporizing, playing with time. The only direction in which it can be turned round is the one along which it is revolving anyway.

Like Gramsci's notion of "civil society," the aesthetic backs up the State with a skeletal structure which will hold firm when the executive totters. Only when the aesthetic can be relied upon in this way is "it safe to undertake the transformation of a State" (17): a moment when, presumably, the Terror following the French Revolution could have been forestalled. The crucial difference from Gramsci, of course, is the ruling out of any struggle for hegemony while determining the nature of this residual "support" *(Stütze)* and thus *what* it supports. The universals of Schiller's aesthetic state still draw on the supernumerary authority of the atemporal Kantian universals which underwrite its figural, aesthetic specificity. It is still "a pledge in the sensible world of a morality as yet unseen" (14). The phrase *sinnlichen Pfand* suggests not a detachable object to be given in trust, but an integrated experience, always sensuously invested, never redeemable or cashable on its own—like the "already aesthetic" or the inescapable figuration. The Gramscian pattern, though, is reinforced by Schiller's essay *On the Sublime*. The disjunction between reason and sensuous understanding essential to the Kantian sublime might have seemed so far to have been exactly what Schiller's aesthetic is trying to overcome. According to my argument, we have seen that in Schiller's utopian aesthetic we experience the self as temporal displacement rather than some original or noumenon free of figuration. But the noumenal original must remain in play as the thing figured to prevent Schiller's aesthetics from collapsing prematurely into Hegelian phenomenology.

Sublime Politics: Schiller and Wordsworth

Hence Schiller claims still to need the sublime, both to reiterate his idea of our noumenal vocation and yet to maintain the politically stabilizing function of the aesthetic form in which it is expressed. In *On the Sublime* (1793?, published 1801),[13] he argues that the sublime gives us reason to remain in "equanimity": beneficent, biddable, and altruistic, even when deprived of the sensuous, material side of life spiritualized in the beautiful unity of character experienced in the aesthetic state (201). Clearly it won't do to tell the cultured but suddenly impoverished bourgeoisie that material loss only reenacts the aesthetic of its refined sensuousness. It is still likely to rebel; and, given Schiller's "pledge" to make out of the aesthetic a present experience of the noumenal satisfactions Kant had infinitely postponed, the bourgeoisie would be justified. Instead, Schiller has to embark on a revisionary critique of his own aesthetic (suggesting a later rather than earlier date for *On the Sublime*). The aesthetic problem addressed in *On the Aesthetic Education of Man* was that of raising the sensuous to harmonize with the rational, and so to supplement the arid one-sidedness of Kantian formalism. Now, however, the Kantian dichotomy is reinstated: "refined sensuousness" is described as a "net" restraining us from a sublime apprehension of our unlimited "absolute moral capacity" (201–2). This *"pure daimon"* (210) takes on responsibility for furthering an aesthetic education which might else have sanctioned an image of ourselves lacking proper "dignity": "the sublime must complement the beautiful in order to make *aesthetic education* into a complete whole and to enlarge the perceptive capacity of the human heart to the full extent of our vocation *(Bestimmung)*; beyond the world of sense in any case" (210). In this way, Schiller tries to reincorporate the sublime in the pedagogic unity to which it had earlier proved an exception, identifiable precisely when that unity failed.

Schiller recalls the Kantian sublime, a further reserve of equanimity, to stand behind the aesthetic state as a safeguard against even its collapse, an ultimate bulwark of civil society. Disintegration of the aesthetic state, the failure to refine sensuousness into symbols of perfection, would not now utterly efface its stabilizing function, but would force it to recover an earlier Kantian configuration, effacing instead Schiller's protodemocratic initiative on behalf of sensuousness upon which Marcuse had seized. Hence Theodor Adorno's caustic remarks on Schiller's idea of sublimity, in the section "The Sublime and Play" in his *Aesthetic Theory*: "Deeply etched into the sublime are characteristics like domination, power and greatness, and yet nature protests against domination. This is alluded to in Schiller's dictum that man is fully human only when he plays. In other words, when man has consummated his hegemony he rises above its spell. The more impervious empirical reality is to this kind of transcendence, the more art accentuates the moment of sublimity. With the eclipse of formal beauty it seemed as though the sublime was the only idea of traditional aesthetics to survive and to live on in modern art."[14] Lyotard's recourse to the sublime toward the end of *The Postmodern Condition* neglects Adorno's point here that a resolutely indeterminate aesthetic can evince *contempt* for nature in its determined forms. Adorno attacks Schiller for legitimating the destruction of any nature incommensurate with human dignity, a privileging of the subject he especially links to Schiller's *On Grace and Dignity* (1793). There, after all, Schiller begins the section on dignity with the assertion that "just as grace is the expression of the beautiful soul, so dignity is the expression of a sublime mind/principle/sentiment" *(Gesinnung)*.[15]

Schiller's aesthetic educates us in the art of being educated. Tractability is the quality which will ensure our loyalty to a shared ideal, another irredeemable *Pfand* or "security." Cultivation is its own reward; the ability to find a tangible experience in the figures which substitute for an inconceivable millennium and sustain us in its absence. This, at any rate, is the conservative interpretation of Schiller's ostensible radicalism, or his bold claim that "if man is to solve the problem of politics in practice he will have to approach it through the problem of the aesthetic."[16] The conservative interpretation reveals Schiller's underlying constitutionalism and the crucial role the aesthetic plays in its articulation. It is a useful interpretation for showing the complex manner in which the importance of art was defended by exposing how much else hung on its reflexivity. The autonomy that might have been thought to devalue art in comparison to the scientific and the practical now has the role of entertaining and containing revolutionary ideas, extracting them from any possible train of events, ostensibly in the interests of their fuller development. In the words of Settembrini that head this chapter, their violent conclusiveness is self-defeatingly prolonged in the "plastic and literary" terms which make them so attractive.

The aesthetic which Schiller worked out in the 1790s rationalizes major canonical English poetic practice and its developments from Wordsworth to Keats. I offer here an uncontentious (I hope) sketch of the plotting of Wordsworth's long poem, *The Prelude*, to show Schiller's usefulness in exposing its logic of entrapment. From the poem's 1799 two-part version onward, the difference between now and then, the narrator's present consciousness and his putative childhood, is meant to have been educative: as a result of nature's early ministrations, he possesses criteria for the proper evaluation of the here and now, the "this" in which he finds himself. Maturity and poetic creativity are to merge in the narrator's power to put aside childish things and, still in a Pauline spirit, find an adult expression for "That spirit of religious love in which / I walked with nature" (2:406–7). The value of the naive is to be recovered through a conscious displacement which measures the naive's pedagogic success— the finding of a poetic subject by a poet able now to treat it worthily.

In fact this is not quite what happens, and the truth takes Wordsworth's project nearer to Schiller's theory and its instabilities. The difference between then and now (childhood poetic election and present artistic capability) should be overcome by the figurative nature of the narrator's recall. Instead, the new subject does not emerge, as the 1805 *Prelude*'s passage between the "glad preamble" of 1799 and the reprise of the 1798 start of the two-part *Prelude* demonstrates. The narrator is obliged to renew his attempts to establish an educative logic of difference between his present and his childhood consciousness. The aesthetic substance precipitated by the displaced narrator should turn him into a poet once and for all. But Wordsworth's poem has a critical dimension which remains unsatisfied by such straightforward recuperation. His two consciousnesses of past and present, in David Bromwich's haunting reading, turn memory into sympathy, or a feeling more properly "shared by discrete persons." The resulting "memory-fragment" can even make poetry out of an alienation the poetry has almost always been interpreted as having had as its mission to overcome.[17]

The narrator fails to fail in a poetically productive way to coincide with his former self, and this double failure generates the poem's distinctive art. He fails, that is, to close on a naive wholeness, but then he fails again, this time unable to find sufficient aesthetic recompense in the figurative portentousness which that primal unity consequently bestows. In the larger story the poem tells, it leads him into "visionary dreariness" or its political counterpart in Revolutionary sympathy. Yet in this impairment the restoration of imagination can still be found. Eventually, the narrator thinks he can't write the poem, even a poem substituting for the naive but unspeakable fullness of those "years that bring the philosophic mind," following the plot of the "Immortality Ode." But the double failure is doubly aesthetic. A second aesthetic emerges, licensing as poetry even this vexing frustration.

In the first of *The Prelude*'s aesthetics, the spots of time, "fructifying" (1799) or "renovating" (1805), are the formative childhood experiences which, necessarily troped already as growth-points, speak the power that tropes them. Their priority or inaccessibility becomes irrelevant as Wordsworth temporizes, finding the act of remembering them now to tell him more of what they really were and signified. Notoriously, however, large stretches of *The Prelude* are bereft of this transaction. Also, it remains conspicuously obscure why some "spots of time" should provide the stimulus to troping rather than others. "It was in truth / An ordinary sight." But if the narrator isn't just going to tell lies about it, the linguistic challenge comes from a truth his figurations cannot enhance. They must, therefore, critically figure their own deficiencies. This local texture memorializes the alienation whose affective power Bromwich uncovers. The poetry must lie there, in the evocation of the words the narrator hasn't got. How else do you figure with any particular felicity a universal scene for which any words will do equally well? The sublime has to intervene quickly. A calculated reticence concerning why some moments rather than others are preeminent can generate romantic mysteriousness, certainly. These moments can also register uneasiness with an aesthetic which seems able to profit from the metonymic status of anything, whatever its meaning, without concern for its "dignity." Love of nature leads to love of mankind, but it is the abstract nature of these allegiances which propels the narrator into his dangerously undiscriminating historical sympathies. A further monitor is needed to police the insufficiencies of the aesthetic life, or to dragoon its indiscriminate occasions into line with an idea of what is genuinely dignified. Having to do this, having to overcome an equally constitutional alienation, is also what the poem is about. When we finally hear that readers of the poem will find it "Instruct them how the mind of Man becomes / A thousand times more beautiful than the earth," we know that Schiller's second, sublime aesthetic of dignity is firmly in place. Its aesthetic duplication registers an ultimate stabilizer moving into action when too democratic an aesthetic receptivity threatens.[18]

In Wordsworth's version of the Schillerian aesthetic, what might have been expected to have observed a law of diminishing returns instigates a kind of galloping inflation. The example of Wordsworth's *Prelude* shows that within the economy of Schiller's aesthetics, the character of the naive state is reconstructed retrospectively out of its power aesthetically to valorize subsequent ideals because they have to trope it. The insufficiency of even this relation only adds further to the poem's wealth of figurative displacement, its dignity growing with its impoverishment. A bourgeois cultural generosity prepared to underwrite even these losses promises to outdo the aristocratic patronage of the arts which, historically, it might be thought to succeed. It also locates "humanity" or the "self," which this poetry claims to document so fully, in a position of invisible obviousness. An inaccessible transcendental reality is both necessary as the source of the figuration at work and yet is only grasped as a function of it. Like Poe's purloined letter, the object desired is right under the reader's nose, provided he or she accepts its presence as the sign of its concealment or absence. For Wordsworth's narrator, the syntax suggests, the "self-presence" of his childhood days as much as the intervening "vacancy" makes for his divided apprehension of himself as "Two consciousnesses." The incorrigibility of autobiographical logic—my former existence is also characterized by my failure to grasp it now—depends, as Paul de Man puts it, on a

"substitutive exchange that constitutes the subject."[19] Its "specular structure" is ghostly only to those with unrealistic (i.e., realist) expectations of
the substantiality of the self.

That this endless specular inflation need not necessarily be the fate of
art is suggested by the Rousseauian resistance to aesthetic exclusiveness
that I examine in the next chapter. The afterlife which Rousseau solicits
for his formative experiences, in discourse and reverie, implies the surrender of aesthetic privilege and of the exclusive authority of Rousseau's
own, autobiographical situation. These are bequeathed to the power of
later readers to historicize them creatively, critically reworking them in
good faith for an authentic present. Rousseau, notoriously, is prepared to
forgo all dignity in the process. But in so doing, as we shall see, he sets up
a pattern for romanticism's critical reflection upon itself, one escaping
sublime recuperation and facilitating metaromanticism proper.

Rousseau's strategy should here remind us of Schlegel, or the use to
which Walter Benjamin put Schlegel's aesthetic of fragmentation in contrast to the aura of completeness with which Schiller invests the aesthetic.
For Benjamin, the aesthetic particular, the symbol, takes its place among
the other particulars whose endlessly illuminating differentiation it encourages. The privilege of the aesthetic is not that of being autonomous
but that of precipitating a tradition of commentary or reformulation in
other critical discourses that contributes further to what it is. Schiller's
symbol, though, is a *nonpareil*, possessing autonomous self-sufficiency. If
his aesthetic state became in reality what it is *in potentia*, we wouldn't necessarily find out anything more about it ontologically. The risk, though,
in Benjamin's aesthetic dissemination is, as pointed out above, that the
originating aesthetic occasion typically loses all definition and disappears
in its characteristically critical prolongation. Rousseau's reveries, we shall
see, similarly hazard all for a future existence and premise their own per-
petuation on a willingness already to surrender property rights to and
ownership of a unique experience. Wordsworth's "spots of time" surely
dally with this poverty? The "ordinary sight" gets the poet universal recognition by beggaring distinction, disseminating its restorative affect beyond his own power to articulate. *The Prelude*'s conclusion that "what we
have loved, others will love," equivocates on the discursive and critical
freedoms conferred when the poet passes on the baton. Behind the apparent transparency of Rousseauian reverie to all sorts of re-creation, a
very specific egotistical sublime sets about consolidating a definite aesthetic.

Toward the end of *On Naive and Sentimental Poetry*, in a recapitulation of contemporary class politics, Schiller argues that this indeterminate creature—"the beautiful unity of human nature that is destroyed for the moment by any particular task" (174)—can be preserved *(aufbewahren)* solely by those belonging neither to "the labouring" nor to "the contemplative portions," but to "such a class" *(Klasse)* which actively occupies the middle ground, in hegemonic dress, "borne by the current of events without becoming its victim" (174–75). Nietzsche, too, in *The Birth of Tragedy,* sees that to criticize aesthetic self-possession of Schiller's kind requires one to attack the individualism characteristic of a particular social class. The *principium individuationis* of Apollonian "illusion" (Schiller's *Schein*) which is surrendered in Dionysian abandon, is connected in Nietzsche's prefatory "Attempt at a Self-Criticism" (1886) with the dwindling of the German victory in the Franco-Prussian War from a Dionysian manifestation of the "German spirit" into a bourgeois *Reich.* Schiller's relation of naive to sentimental repeats the chiasmic logic of *On the Aesthetic Education of Man,* and the unity of human nature created by this figurative shuttling serves the class most likely to profit from its specular inflation. In other words, the legitimacy of this class grows in proportion to the unrestrained expansion of the human universals it patronizes.

Schiller had already told this story the other way round when he described the successful rebellion of a commercial class against an absolute monarchy in his *History of the United Netherlands Secession from the Spanish Government* of 1788, just before the ten years or so he devoted to aesthetics. Wieland's preface of 1791 to Schiller's *History of the Thirty Years' War in Germany* stressed the education in national unity it provided for a country whose "contradictory system" had divided it into small states: in the absence of a political universal, it was the writers who had become "the men of Germany."[20] But Schiller's earlier history was much more clearsighted about the social specifics involved in modern nationalism; and the aesthetic subtext of that book is much more visible and partisan than the "edification" his Weimar compatriot Wieland believed was "produced by our national history."

The tale Schiller tells contains anticipations of his aesthetic theory, such as his psychological analysis (Burkean, to his English translator in 1807) of Philip II of Spain, who remains trapped in that divided state of mind Schiller was later to unify through aesthetic education.[21] More than this, Philip is characterized as the old sublime, a "mighty mortal" (7) cutting an anachronistic figure in a modern age whose collective commercial enterprise defeats him. Belgian financial success during the war with Spain happens because a common bourgeois spirit transcends particular allegiances in a manner just like Schiller's aesthetic state. For, almost comically, Philip cannot prevent trade taking place between his own subjects and the Belgians with whom they are at war. In Schiller's narrative, the new measure of capital is not fixed by determinate possessions, kind or specie, as are the treasures looted by the Spanish from South America. The trouble is that the more capital of this kind which Philip spends on his war, the more he makes it possible for his opponents to profit from the resultant inflation throughout the Spanish empire. The drop in Spanish reserves cheapens Spanish money, raises the price of commodities, and makes the trade between Spain and the Netherlands, which can't be stopped, more lucrative to the latter. I don't think the exact truth of Schiller's economic history matters so much as the picture he creates through it of a capitalist class free of national determination.

At one point in all this, Schiller claims that "the history of mankind is as invariable in its principles, as the laws of nature: and as simple in its machinery, as the human soul" (45). This soul, which furnishes the moral of Schiller's story, here works free of the inherited and fixed allegiances to absolute authority or to its rebellious subjects. It flourishes, instead, in the commerce between the two. Its commercial character both survives their outright opposition and has its economic importance significantly inflated in the process. But in contrast to the sublimities of antiquity, the history of this modern ascendancy will, Schiller fears, appear to be constituted by "a total absence of magnanimity and heroic virtue" (6). In 1788, before his revision of Kant, Schiller's positive political sympathies had still to establish the new aesthetic credentials whose ostensible independence from these political sympathies would begin the process of universalizing them, recycling naive, classical virtues in modern sentimental dress.

To stress the political economy of this romantic aesthetic is necessary if one is to have any chance of explaining the self-criticism that followed. Within it, there seem to be two kinds of defense or repression at work. From our account so far, the most obvious one is the institutionalization of the aesthetic as imaginary: not as any particular art but as the containment of such a universally applicable interest within a sphere of disinterest and impracticability, prompted by something like a Socratic fear of the democracy of rhetoric. It could easily be argued, though, that such overt institutionalization of art as autonomous, prompting my slightly vulgar historicist account, in fact contains another fear: the anxiety that a fully realized humanity *is* only a figment of imagination. The conspicuousness of its aestheticization is then what allows us falsely to believe it is artificially sequestered and could after all be realized in different political circumstances. The only way out of this nihilism is the view that we are creatures censored by our own notions of emancipation, notions which leave everything outside that aesthetic idealization looking deceptively random, alien, contingent, or apocalyptic. This is a postmodernist view, but one anticipated by Hegel's critique in his *Aesthetics* of a "romantic" art in which "external experience can no longer express the inner life" because "the inner, so pushed to the extreme, is an expression without any externality at all."[22]

We have seen that, for Schiller, because of its universality, aesthetics can render any particular expression figurative: from an aesthetic point of view, anything can be rendered metonymic simply by virtue of its determinacy. Hegel agrees. Art "in our day" has become "a free instrument" brought to bear "in relation to any material of whatever kind" (1:605). Hegel's agreement, though, is also diagnostic. Schiller's aesthetic has overreached or, better, overstayed its purpose. By making its universality synonymous with the loss of specific content, it shows to Hegel that its time has passed. What the aesthetic presaged for him was not the realization of its ideals but the more complete expression of those ideals in another discourse—"art . . . acquires its real ratification only in philosophy" (1:13).

To resume: just as inflation erodes belief in the value of money, a discourse which claims to double its profits with each failure will eventually lose the confidence of the polis. Schiller's clever chiasmus kept the aesthetic in transcendental credit: Kant's noumena collapse into figurations identified as such only by their failure literally to represent noumena. But that chiasmus appears to wither under the gaze of Hegelian speculation. Nevertheless, Hegel in fact repeats the Schillerian finesse by having aesthetics superseded by another discourse rather than by the better life it prefigured. The aesthetic function is philosophically displaced and reconfigured as Hegel "ratifies" rather than discredits its mechanisms. To its opponents, this circularity finally characterizes Hegel's philosophy as a whole.[23] Hegel, then, repeats the act of containment to which other writing of the period can still be consciously resistant. His critique reproduces its object. He thus declares his membership of what Marx was to diagnose as the German Ideology and shows its romantic character. More than that, he helps us understand its persistence.

Hegel's attack on the imperialism of romantic inwardness nevertheless inaugurates a variegated tradition extending to Heidegger, Adorno, and beyond, powered by the sense that the subjective has got quite out of hand and that objects now reproach us with the authority to prescribe the sort of creatures we ought to be if we are to be fit to live in a world shared by them. This is not the experience of the inanimate becoming uncannily animate, although romanticism is a source of that too. Rather, as a consequence of having reached that pitch of internalization attributed by Hegel to romanticism, we long to ascribe to the inanimate an organizing principle in virtue of its inanimateness. Much of this book examines the degree to which this drive for materialism was already troubling romanticism's subjective excess and so does not indicate our unquestioned advantage over romanticism. In any case, the radicalism of the materialist move looks compromised to the extent that it furnishes a tradition which is professionally and institutionally productive. Like the process by which Schiller's Kantian sublime was seen to be standing guard behind his aesthetic state, philosophical failure or self-abnegation still drops into another philosopher's lap with predictable regularity. Hence we have the paradoxically traditional "end of philosophy" style of thinking started by Hegel. Failures to be definitively radical set up a philosophical and literary typology, their sense of their own ending once more betraying the temporizing habit that lets them get written again and again. Either we can do something else entirely, as Marx advocated, and that is an option, or else we are back with Schiller's chiasmus, sharing the problems of those writers of the romantic period who, as we shall see in the succeeding chapters, wrote under and against its spell.

TWO

Rousseau's Children

Historical Confessions

Many have written about who might have been Jean-Jacques Rousseau's children or heirs, fewer about the process of becoming one, a process Rousseau was tormented by as if in penance for the fate he dealt out to his real offspring. To remain a child of Rousseau was an impossible business.

> We chose a discreet and safe midwife, Mlle Gouin by name, who lived at the Pointe Sainte-Eustache, to undertake the depositing of the baby; and when her time was come, Thérèse was taken by her mother to be delivered at Mlle Gouin's. I went to see her there several times, and took her a set of initials [un chiffre—monogram, or might just have been a number] which I had written on two cards, one of which was put in the child's swaddling clothes. It was then deposited by the midwife at the office of the Foundling Hospital [*Enfants-Trouvés*], in the usual manner. In the following year, the same inconvenience was removed by the same expedient, except for the *chiffre* which was overlooked. No more serious reflection on my part, and no greater willingness on the mother's; she obeyed with a sigh. In due course it will be seen what vicissitudes this fatal conduct occasioned in my way of thinking [*mon façon de penser*] as well as in my fate. (*Confessions*, 322; 1:344–45)[1]

Three more children went the same way: "I thought I was acting as a citizen and a father, and looked upon myself as a member of Plato's republic," confessed Rousseau (333; 1:357). A famously devastating paragraph in *Émile*, however, states bluntly that such dereliction of parental duty can never be excused (49; 4:262–63). In 1761, when he thought he was dying, Rousseau had the Duchesse de Luxembourg try to trace his children's whereabouts, without any success. According to biographer Lester

Crocker, the mortality rate at the *Enfants-Trouvés* was withering: "No less than two thirds died in their first year; fourteen out of a hundred survived to the age of seven. Of the five out of a hundred who reached maturity, almost all became beggars or vagabonds."[2]

How might guilt at his "fatal conduct" have permeated, and, through the vivid figures of children, perhaps clarified Rousseau's *façon de penser*? More generally, I want to ask what this chilling tale has to tell us about the historicizing of one's moment—the regulation of the past and the control of the future—Rousseauian themes which target critical understanding of any time and at any time. Rousseau, popular father of romanticism and of revolution, complicates the problem of his own transmission, characteristically enjoying a critical distance at the very moment that he propagates his views or anything else. His first and greatest follower, Kant, famously sundered what is right from what is good, or what it is our duty to do from the pursuit of happiness. From Schiller to Hegel, philosophers struggle to reunite these divided obligations: content has to be restored to Kant's otherwise strictly formal moral reasoning. When, however, moral content derives from *Sittlichkeit* or institutional determination of what are to count as duties, these prescriptions still must justify themselves rationally. Sometimes the standards reason sets seem impossibly high, as unlikely as becoming the child of Rousseau's state of nature. We have seen Schiller overcome the problem through an aesthetic redoubling which sweeps up the aesthetic's failure to represent anything into the defining example of its figurative character. The return to Rousseau, then, in this second framing chapter, is salutary when it restores a critical awkwardness to romantic self-reflection that makes it institutionally recalcitrant and therefore genuinely metaromantic in my sense. Because the institution and its critical reflection are interdependent, this interpretative activity will be a self-damaging one. Who better, then, to test its historicizing power than Jean-Jacques?

For Irving Babbitt, writing in 1919, a preoccupation with Rousseau was easy to explain: "It is [Rousseau's] somewhat formidable privilege to represent more fully than any other person a great international movement." That movement Babbitt called "Romanticism." Nowadays, romantic scholars are less confident of romanticism's unity; we are also, alas, less knowledgeable about the international context which Babbitt easily marshaled for his discussion. Babbitt's academicism was admired by T. S. Eliot but attacked as "obtuse" by F. R. Leavis.[3] It is certainly hard not to feel that Babbitt's older, more leisured proficiency in European letters ought to have stoked a skepticism concerning the definition of romanticism: an impressively learned awareness of the variety of writing in different cultures of the romantic period ought to have displaced the critical category supposedly subsuming and authoritatively naming that variety. Proleptically, Lovejoy should have triumphed over Wellek in the contest of discriminating romanticisms. Our contemporary scholarship has tended to acknowledge that the literature of a historical period will always outrun our means of knowing it, although we may know those means or critical specifics better as a result. Romantic period writing is writing which historically relativizes the once-dominant critical idea of "romanticism" applied to it. This revisionism explicitly confesses its own periodicity, and so suggests, perhaps, that there is no reason why its own critical understanding will not be reified in turn by later dissent from its defining, pragmatic emphasis. But Rousseau is perhaps before us here as well in his skepticism of contemporary cultural institutions and his belief in the need to historicize their founding *raison d'être*? Babbitt, though, could only see such skepticism as confusion.

Babbitt attacked in Rousseau an "incomplete positivism" which, had it been complete, would have highlighted that quantum-leap of faith argued by Lessing to be required to save us from pantheistic naturalism. Positivism, in this context, means the behaviorist reduction of otherworldly values to forms of human experience—psychological, animal, emotional. In *Rousseau and Romanticism*, however, Babbitt's target is not behaviorism but Rousseauian affect. If it is thought that we can, without offense to them, dissolve religious and ethical certainties in emotional correlatives, sufficiently preserving their credibility by translating them into felt life, then, according to Babbitt, we lose all discrimination. To save standards under threat simply by sympathizing with them, however resourceful the literary expression of that sympathy might be, is not to preserve them at all. (One can see immediately why Leavis would regard Babbitt as an enemy in his battle to establish the centrality of literary experience.) Their value rather lies in their recalcitrance, their eternal otherworldliness which becomes visible only through *exclusion* from a thoroughly positivistic, skeptical vision. If we waver in the thoroughgoingness of our modern skepticism, thinks Babbitt, then we accommodate a debased morality and a pseudoreligion. They enjoy a merely eleemosynary existence; they become the pathetic beneficiaries of our philosophical generosity and large-mindedness. Romantic tolerance, from the religion of the Savoyard vicar to the ironic reserve of Schlegelian philosophy, is sheer confusion: a kind of intellectual synesthesia matching the aesthetic version Babbitt had attacked in his reworking of Lessing's thought in *The*

New Laokoon. Romanticism of this kind is indeed what T. E. Hulme called "spilt religion," a mental set happy to use sympathy as a proof for anything it can't believe in.

His attack shows that Babbitt rules out of court the idea that the sympathetic incorporations of conduct and religion in positivism which he anathematizes might be suspect for the opposite reason. We apparently cannot ask the question: Why might sympathy not be the *euphemism* we use to make tolerable the successful reduction of these distinctively human vocations to material nature? Rousseau did confront this option, but for Babbitt a proper, "critical" humanism accepts that the materialistic description of what human beings are capable of makes clearly visible the external, immaterial support they need to realize their potential dignity. Babbitt's Rousseau is like Jean Starobinski's comparably epochal figure to the extent that Starobinski's Rousseau is defined by a desire for transparency in political and cultural life which obstructs his sense of "otherness." He sheds his awareness of those boundaries and limitations to the sympathetic self, constraints which encourage discipline and normality. Rousseau generates an inferior humanism which Babbitt wants to replace, and an inferior phenomenology which Starobinski wants to redeem with more existentialist sophistication.

Starobinski argues that for Rousseau to treat people exclusively as equals, even within his own social class, is to dismiss all other differences possibly important to their self-definition. To treat them as the same on political principle is to be egotistical and totalitarian at the same time. The madness of this equivalence in Rousseau's thought is meant to be evident in the confiding quality of his autobiography which has fascinated, shocked, and alienated readers from Edmund Burke to Thomas McFarland.[4] McFarland, in his recent book on romanticism as Rousseau's "heritage," argues that the "shabby genius," Rousseau, "perverted a central function of the Catholic Church" in his *Confessions,* much as the *Encyclopaedistes* demystified esoteric techniques of knowledge for public consumption.[5] This sounds quite admirable to me, but McFarland's real worry concerns the democratically abject self whose literary achievement in expressing itself he nevertheless feels forced to admit. He shows little sense of Rousseau's challenge to our perception of other far more reticent literary selves whose calculated reserve his all-embracing ideas of equality in nature ask us to revise. The provocation of *Confessions* is partly to get us to concede that we are much more like him in essentials than we can decently admit. Consequently, accusations of totalitarianism where, say, sexuality is concerned, usually look like desperate attempts by the

reader to salvage decorum. Also, that distinctive collocation of the normal and the aberrant, that persistent historicizing of his own theories,
his logic of the supplement—these signal that Rousseau was unusually
alert to the extent to which we live lives in which what we can legislate
for and what we cannot are problematically continuous. Our self-esteem
(amour propre), often disreputably quirky, can be as much an avenue to
our knowledge of other people's defining needs as nonidiosyncratic intu-
itions. We obviously could not run a society on the basis of these peculiar
sympathies, but they are relevant, if difficult to discipline.

For Rousseau, this difficulty is historically inevitable. Given his belief
in the progressive corruption of his society, all attempts to enforce sociability will actually disguise private interests unconnected with the general
good. Attempts, that is, to assert norms all must observe will, in the absence of a social contract properly grounded in the general will, conspire
to serve private interests and create inequalities. Conversely, these efforts will evince a general blindness to private interests which are indeed
part of our common nature. Rousseau's skepticism has two main consequences. The first, bad consequence is that his social theory borders
on conspiracy theory and so raises the question of his paranoia. Stanley Cavell, though, has a point when he calls this an "original madness,"
historically expressive.[6] The second, better consequence of Rousseau's
skepticism of altruism is to make him a past master at detecting his own
and others' tactics for disguising from themselves the content of their actions. Or when his unmasking fails to convince, he has still made available
the evidence for what he admits is an open contest in the interpretation
of Jean-Jacques. When critics of Rousseau differ, it is usually over which of
these two alternatives is at work in his text—paranoia or self-analysis. But
the possibility of both happening at the same time is surely a dilemma we
negotiate from day to day?

How far can we take this last defense? Need Rousseau's sense of the
otherness of other people be disadvantaged because it is presented as
coming from his confessions of his own uniqueness? The *Confessions*,
after all, offer a contested portrait in explicit competition with others.
Rousseau fights his enemies not by proclaiming his own purity but by
being a more convincing interpreter of his own *amour propre*, and thus by
being true to his own theory of the distortions visited on our natural state
by historical circumstance. The reader's further worry that the writer is
en abyme, swallowed by his own theory, will be consciously exploited by
Rousseau later in his *Rêveries*. In *Confessions*, though, he famously wanted
to tell unsavory truths about himself because the stories others were

telling were even worse—or so he thought. Does paranoia efface otherness, or does it unbearably sharpen the sense of others? Paranoiacs are deluded about being persecuted but not deluded, presumably, about the otherness required for them to be making a mistake? If they were complete fantasists, they couldn't sensibly be said to believe that other people were getting at them. These considerations arise, though, from acknowledging fully the variety with which Rousseau writes about the need to establish a base for self-understanding outside the tradition of the arts and sciences he has inherited. The more we are invited to invade the personal Rousseau, to risk the idiosyncratic, the more he tries to persuade us that we are being led into an area where discussions of a general nature can take place without the usual preconceptions. Consistently, in *The Social Contract*, he endorses a species of secret ballot in which the general will is expressed by private individuals without consultation. Indeed, legitimate common views are those established *without* reference to any group interests. To see the consistency of this theme, modulating throughout his work, is to concede persistent problems in disciplining *his* meanings *now*. It also begins to let us ask how a major precursor of various cultural practices called romanticism could also, in advance, be their critic and disowner. In other words, if Jean-Jacques Rousseau was the father of romanticism, how does he let us identify his typically abandoned, anonymous foundling?

We can get closer to Rousseau's personal historicism by moving from a Kantian reading of what he might mean by a "state of nature," a reading associated with Ernst Cassirer, to a more Hegelian, phenomenological interpretation reaching out to Starobinski and beyond.[7] Either Rousseau's state of nature is to be interpreted as achieving full definition only in Kant's idea of freedom, or else it sets in motion a thinking much more like Hegelian dialectic. Through Kantian spectacles, the state of nature as it appears in Rousseau's *Discourses* exists only as a regulative idea. What does commend it is that its inhabitants live in accordance with needs determined for them by the kind of beings they are. The state of nature is stable and static because it is universal. This universality accounts for the much longer periods of so-called prehistory—aeons of lower, middle, and upper Paleolithic lifestyles—compared with the frenetic "progress" since then. This factual basis underpins Rousseau's "hypothetical and conditional reasonings" (50) in the *Discourse on Inequality*, but the speculation he is really interested in indulging, on the Kantian interpretation, is to conjure up a state in which the individual acts spontaneously in accord with his nature because, in an unbreakable tautology, human nature is just that pattern of behavior in accordance with which everyone *can* act freely. The revival of a virtuous republican tradition to which Rousseau wanted his native Geneva to belong is obvious. Rename human nature "reason," and the Kantian content also becomes clear. The general will spontaneously identifies individual and general interests to create what Rousseau calls the "social contract." Kant's moral theory can never let us know that we are acting morally in any instance, only that *if* we do, we act from reason alone (lots of room for conspiracy theory here). In the same way, Rousseau's social contract remains a hypothetical possibility, in the past or in the future, although an eternally present categorical imperative for political rectitude. Where Hegel himself mentions Rousseau, he tends to identify him with this Kantian idealism. But elements in Rousseau's writings could also have informed a Hegelian critique of the Kantian separation of morality from definition by actual ethical practices and existing political institutions.

On the Hegelian reading of Rousseau, then, the state of nature shows humans to be self-alienating creatures. They are universally driven away from unreflective contentment by a typical passion for perfectibility. They are, in Rousseau's famous distinction, impelled as much by *amour propre* as by *amour de soi*. Kant had his own uses for *amour propre* or human competitiveness, the crooked timber which tempered and proved our rational vocation. But insofar as Rousseau historicizes, the state of nature fits better with a Hegelian account of history as a series of generalizations by which humans typically politicize themselves—that, thinks Hegel, with Aristotle, is *the* human activity. Successively, though, they find each politicization inadequate, a false universal, requiring a still wider accommodation of what it is to be human. *Amour de soi*, in other words, repeatedly turns out to be *amour propre* in disguise. *Amour propre* must nonetheless retain credit for our progress as the consistently imperfect, idiosyncratic, personal form in which we seek perfection. Again we encounter Rousseau's difficulty in conferring intellectual respectability on, or disciplining, his systematically unreliable historicism.

Hegel's phenomenology, however, makes Rousseau's paradoxes into the motor of history. In the *Discourse on the Origin of Inequality*, these paradoxes look like cul-de-sacs: a Kantian impasse between morality and politics, the noumenal and the phenomenal. People bind themselves together in defense against common enemies; but in so doing they create inequalities that cause the ruin of their republic and the rise of a "hideous" despotism (67–68; 3:190–91). They are "oppressed from within as a consequence of the very precautions . . . taken against what menaced . . . from without." (67; 3:190) But other passages suggest that

Rousseau was a historicist who abandons transhistorical standards. Universals are the universals of a particular time: "the human race of one age is not the human race of another age . . . savage man and civilised man differ so greatly in the depths of their hearts and in their inclinations, that what constitutes the supreme happiness of the one would reduce the other to despair" (69; 3:192). Denunciations of modern citizenry fill the rest of the *Discourse*, apparently consigning us to a tragic fate; the contemporary citizen is a contemptible spectacle and leaves Rousseau, as in Percy Shelley's version of him in *The Triumph of Life*, questioning "why God made irreconcilable / Good and the means of good." When Percy Shelley's Rousseau says, "I was overcome / By my own heart alone," he could be criticizing the intransigence of an *amour de soi* which will not compromise so as pragmatically to power its way to happiness through its historically idiosyncratic, temporary form of life, *amour propre*. Rousseau has, in other words, conceded enough to historical relativism here for Hegel's purposes. As a result, one *can* ask the question of Rousseau's *Discourses*, Is it in fact a failure of *historicizing* that they diagnose? The source of value, the state of nature, can appear inaccessible, and our ideal dependence on it for values we in reality legislate against can look self-defeating. But we are not, as Nietzsche thought, condemned by Rousseau to live thus belatedly, full of *ressentiment* against our anachronistic situation.[8] We ought to be able to recover our natural state in contemporary form and to understand that the original state of nature was itself time-bound and consequently limited. In *Émile* we are told it would be "absurd" to "confound what is natural in the savage state with what is natural in the civil state" (406; 4:764). The same flexibility informs Rousseau's sensitivity to national differences, appreciated by the Corsican and Polish patriots who solicited his comments on their respective constitutions and governments.

Retrospective and Retroactive Writing

Preeminent among the implications of a Hegelian reading of Rousseau are the implications for writing. We are left with a challenge to imagine new forms with which to gain access to and transmit anterior value. To construct an explanatory state constructed retrospectively and retroactively is the Rousseauian pattern of romantic hermeneutics. Latterly, the retroactive rather than retrospective version has predominated, one in which the source we discover discomposes the procedure which uncovered it. Obvious examples of this might be the way the "Unconscious" problematizes Freud reread by Lacan and others, the linguistic turn

forced on Heidegger by the disclosure of "Being," or how a polymor-
phous and polyphemous nature which our technologies, argues Adorno,
don't control is stimulated to unpredictable riposte. We might characterize these retroactive effects overall as ecological: the investigation of
nature eventually shows up the interests lying behind apparent scientific
objectivity and discloses a larger category to which our understanding
belongs and on which, therefore, it cannot objectively pronounce. The
writing of those interests will be correspondingly original, paradoxical,
or just incomprehensible. Above all, they will not repeat, albeit at a
higher level as does Hegel's philosophical displacement of aesthetics,
the understanding they criticize. Retrospective rather than retroactive
constructions of romantic hermeneutics, though, confidently simulate
lost knowledge rather than historicize knowledge itself as just one among
other possible contemporary ways of being in the world. Rousseau's ha-
tred of thinking may appear to approach the latter, retroactive relaxation
of the scientific paradigm. His *Rêveries*, though, where he comes closest
to retroactive writing, are always dynamically retrospective supplements
to and then improvements on original experiences. They approximate,
in Starobinski's words, "a *memorised immediacy* richer and warmer than
the immediacy of actual sensation" (237).

Do Rousseau's writings lend themselves unambiguously, though, to
romantic transformation? It looks at first as though it is the romantic
recuperation of literal failure as symbolic expression which provides
the most economical model for explaining Rousseau's historicism. Far
from advocating a return to the state of nature, Rousseau dismisses such
anachronistic identifications in favor of new ways of communicating the
obligations of natural law in contemporary society, maintaining that in
the unreflective state of nature that absence of "communication" was
the "essential vice" modernity could remedy. In a chapter in the Geneva
manuscript of *The Social Contract*, Rousseau claims that in a state of nature
"all our happiness would have consisted in not being conscious of our
wretchedness" (171; 3:283)—so no innocence except that lost in its experienced recognition, no naïveté unless sentimentalized, no Dionysian
nature without an Apollonian gloss, and so on. Nevertheless, Rousseau's
romantic precursiveness here obscures how suspicious he remained of all
current versions of a virtuous dependence on nature. At the start of *Julie*,
a natural passion is generated whose affront to virtue is still measured in
virtue, or the passion's superior power to tailor itself to the conventions
which couldn't stop it arising. The rest of the novel, though, undoes this
compromise in its journey toward Julie's death. Whatever he might have

thought of later, romantic discourse, he refuses to align his own rhetorical endeavor with any cultural establishment, or, more significantly, with the attempt to create one. It is this aesthetic entropy at the heart of his project which both problematizes fascinatingly his usefulness for the romantics and anticipates critiques of the aesthetic resumed in their own metaromantic practice.

Rousseau's historicism is most visible stylistically in his tendency to write retroactively rather than retrospectively. There is more of a letting-go, one commending a surrender of subjectivity to its environment, distinguishing Rousseauian reverie from Wordsworthian elegy.[9] But doesn't such materialism, when the Rousseauian subject apparently accepts the formative character of its circumstances, flatter to deceive? Isn't it part of a bourgeois will to naturalize its own experience in order to displace prevailing aristocratic assumptions of hereditary representativeness? That aristocratic confidence in its own human paradigm is to be forced to cede to a new classicism in which the proportions of human nature are rediscovered. This symmetry belongs to all; it is not nurtured unequally in an exemplary few. But of course the difficulty of achieving and maintaining the insight creates its own elite. Still, this elite must be defined by its attempt to dissolve its own specialness in the universal franchise it has uniquely imagined. I say "attempt," but the anxious apprehension of this paradox in writing from Rousseau to Shelley is far more ambivalent. Marx faces up to the idea that his own revolutionary class disintegrates in the success of creating a classless society. In *The Communist Manifesto*, he mocks the limited content of bourgeois emancipations that nevertheless still try to hang on to the distinctiveness of bourgeois culture. Cultural studies these days can too insouciantly take as read Marx's view that cultural privilege is of an age and not for all time. Rousseau, though, more than most, seeks out ways of writing which prefigure and acknowledge the need to make livable this paradoxical dissolution of authority. His apparently pathological isolation at the end of his life is scripted as a reverie in which he surrenders to his own nature, his antisocial sensibility, as if it were authentically natural because of its compulsiveness. When, at the end, he seems determined by his own peculiarities, he welcomes and repeatedly describes as exemplary programming the unfortunate circumstances which have imposed upon him. In the eighth *Promenade*, for instance, he can translate being "completely disorientated . . . overwhelmed . . . in the horrible darkness in which they did not cease to keep me immersed" into the understanding that since "all I had yet to do on earth was to regard myself on it as a purely passive being, I ought not to

use up in futilely resisting my fate, the strength I had left to endure it"
(112, 115; 1:1076, 1079).

In these surrenders and sequestrations, Rousseau seems as effectively
opposed as ever he was to the establishment of the arts and sciences he
shot to fame by attacking. Yet he is as nervous of the increased chances of
being misinterpreted and misconstrued which such extraterritorial freedom from convention carries with it, a fear he transfers to women and
children throughout his writings. He frequently uses women and children to figure for him the natural distortions of an original, rather than
to endorse the conventionally romantic view of them as natural originals
subsequently distorted by social artifice. They thus repeat the paradoxical plot of the *Discourse on the Origin of Inequality*. The formal structure of
these contradictions is striking enough for critics like Paul de Man to read
Rousseau's entire *oeuvre* as a treatise on metaphor, which tells us everything and nothing, because one wouldn't expect it not to be that as well.
Rousseau's choice of generational and gendered metaphors to figure
metaphor is not explained by their metaphoricity. Women and children
encode for him the best and worst of civil society. Back in 1751, Rousseau
had written with spectacular self-righteousness to Mme Franceuil: "You
know my situation: I earn my living from one day to the next with difficulty; so how could I feed a family as well? . . . Do you say one should
not have children if one cannot feed them? I beg your pardon, Madame:
nature wishes us to have children because the earth produces enough to
feed everybody; it is the style of life of the rich; it is your style of life which
robs my children of bread."[10] His *amour propre*, outraged by hers, assumes
the dimensions of *amour de soi*. His children traduce him because their
natural claims on him muffle the social inequalities actually dictating his
treatment of them. Rousseau's indignation, interactively metaphorical,
laments the usurpation of the natural right to breed by a universal economic constraint which, historically, has taken the place of the state of
nature. But, as we have seen, there is no state of nature which is not historically relative: artificially induced scarcity characterizes the only one
available to him at this time. Thus Rousseau, in complying with economic
and social necessity, wriggles off his own hook to escape the charge that
he is an unnatural father.

Children arguably represent for Rousseau the truth that we reproduce ourselves in all sorts of ways, not just biologically. Reproduction appears to him central to being human, and so his treatment and characterization of children expose his unease at this defeat to self-sufficiency. His
peculiar disowning of his own and his conciliation of other children—

prominent in the *Rêveries*—are as paradoxical as his valuations of women and civil society. At their worst, children are distortions, the burlesques of oneself which, Rousseau despairs, any form of self-expression becomes at the hands of a competitive society. Yet, at their best, children may also act as redeemers, in spite of historical degeneration, of one's true nature— ideal readers. People who make themselves your children through sympathetic, positive efforts of identification rehabilitate the role of children, as Rousseau's *Rêveries* are meant to ensure. Curiously, artificial children or ideal readers can restore the natural self-sufficiency of their author which natural children threatened, and for which they had to be abandoned.

In the *Dialogues, or Rousseau, Judge of Jean-Jacques* (1772–76), immediately preceding the *Rêveries*, the competitiveness of *Confessions* intensifies as the dilemma to which *Rêveries* would offer a solution becomes more extreme. In *Dialogues* Rousseau explicitly raises the question of which form of writing would be adequate to the communication of the truth about himself. He settles on a dialogue between "Rousseau" and "the Frenchman" on the subject of someone else called "Jean-Jacques." His need for dialogical inventiveness arose from the deafening silence of public neglect in which he had to work. He had no public image against which to set a different portrait of himself justified by inner familiarity. He had to invent the public as well. In this utter solitude, though, Rousseau was advantaged rather than disadvantaged in his attempts to be objective both about himself and about the distorted picture of himself which must, he believes, be current in the society which so militantly ignores him. As if by magic, a familiar pattern of explanation reasserts itself. Rousseau is called upon to excoriate civil society in contrast to the natural man it cannot assimilate. The fiction that he belongs to neither category is then guyed by the concession that the "Jean-Jacques" whom "Rousseau" defends is, of course, actually writing the defense "in the form of a Dialogue," a dialogue which, Rousseau tells "the Frenchman," is "rather like one that may result from our conversations" (136; 1:836). The objectivity with which judgment was pronounced on "Jean-Jacques" was only a pretense, even one made in bad faith, argues Starobinski. Yet this complication is still true to Rousseau's consistent relativism or belief that our best selves are philosophical hypotheses, natural principles awaiting realization in contemporary idioms, never adjudged once and for all. Nevertheless, it is true that Rousseau was always haunted by the fantasy of a complete self-coincidence, a once and for all. Such ideal materialism or complete merging with one's historically natural self would enable one to dispense with further speculation or philosophical reflection because

you know you've got it right, that your mode of living, since natural, is automatically virtuous. Derrida famously seized on the contradiction here
in privileging self-presence over its representation while in fact just inaugurating another mode of representation—not another obstruction, as
Starobinski would have argued, for there is no alternative to representation, and so, as Rousseau appeared to appreciate, no sense in seeing it
as an impediment. Every Rousseauian aspiration to an unmediated natural encounter with himself simultaneously debates the kind of writing
required to achieve it.[11] This reflex, or automatic self-criticism invoking
alternative forms of writing, again looks less like Schillerian redoubling
or Hegelian displacement and more like metaromanticism.

In *Confessions*, therefore, ensconced in Mme d'Epiney's "Hermitage,"
Rousseau ponders "an external regulation *(régime extérieur)* which, varied according to circumstances, could put or keep the mind in the state
most conducive to virtue" (381; 1:409). He began sketching his conclusion under the title of *La morale sensitive ou le matérialisme du sage.* However, the handing over of philosophical authority to environmental influences which might beneficially "act on our machine" *(agit sur notre
machine)*—terminology recalling that other bugbear of the philosophes,
La Mettrie—was an abdication not fully embraced by Rousseau until the
Rêveries. Before them, in *Émile*, the *Dialogues,* and elsewhere, the tutelary
figure of the philosopher *supposé savoir* still presides. In *Rêveries*, though,
he courted philosophical abjection to found a form of writing which
might implicate its future readers, its progeny, in the natural process of its
own production. While this reenactment "varied," no doubt, "according
to circumstances," its historicism could at least be imagined to be secure
from the authoritative intervention of any critical establishment.

The Vanity of Reverie

"Vanity" was what came to mind when Burke wished to use Rousseau to
discredit the leaders of the French Revolution in 1791. He recalled the
visit to Britain by "the great professor and founder of the *philosophy of
vanity*" twenty-five years before.[12] The supremely confident claim on his
readers' attention which opened the *Confessions* and popularly justified
Burke's prejudice was, however, replaced at the end of Rousseau's life by
a kind of writing suggesting that the process of self-analysis had scarcely
begun. Explicitly postconfessional, Rousseau's *Rêveries*, published before
but written eleven years after his posthumously published *Confessions*, immediately puts in question the confessional subject and all it might be
truthfully said to own. The *moi seul,* myself alone, provocatively trumpet-

ing the arrival of a completely different kind of book, has now with cruel irony come to describe estrangement and exile, not self-sufficiency. The unique has given way to the solitary individual. Only in "solitude and meditation" is Rousseau "fully myself and for myself" (12; 1:1002). Not in corrective opposition to society but in isolation from it can he hope to recapture his natural goodness. While Montaigne wrote in seclusion for others, Rousseau will write only for himself. He accepts the solipsism this implies and the consequence that its reveries, as he calls this self-recording, puts his writing *en abyme*. He will "let my ideas follow their bent without resistance or constraint." At any point in the *Rêveries* where a judgment is ventured, Rousseau must reflexively concede that he is expressing a random association of ideas. In trusting to the wisdom of life as "a purely passive being," he believes he will be "what nature willed" (115,12; 1:1079,1002). His reader, though, must have faith that this coincidence is confirmed rather than undermined by Rousseau's professedly undisciplined method: "I no longer have any other rule in conduct than in everything to follow my propensity without restraint" (89; 1:1060). Rousseau's utter self-abandonment, the logic of that curious phrase implies, must reveal a world of subjectivity over which he has no control. Readers must renew their trust in Rousseau through something akin to the Wittgensteinian idea that ultimately solipsism and realism coincide. The ultimate in self-abandon dissolves subjectivity in circumstances; and the realist will hardly dispute the egotistical capitulation that has played into his hands. The self that has thus given everything up to him can now retain its freedom unchallenged because it no longer represents any claim the realist has to acknowledge. Its sacrificial generosity, though, remains *the* defining experience for the solipsist.

Reverie is Rousseau's final mode of self-education in the ways of necessity. The freedom he inculcated in Émile he now tries to rediscover for himself—"I have never believed that man's freedom consisted in doing what he wants, but rather in never doing what he does not want to do" (83; 1:1059). In other words, he must happily "do what nature wanted," making its will his own. The trouble is that he keeps telling us that he has been driven to this exigency by the cruelty of others. How far can he go in persuading readers that what he might be forced into doing is what he really wants? How virtuous can you make necessity? One answer might be: about as much as you can persuade your readers that a highly personal reverie still shows the objective conditions that produced it.

How does Rousseau cope with such rhetorical problems? The diary of reverie, he tells us in the first *Promenade*, is *informe*, "formless"; it admits no principle of order distinct from the reverie's own haphazard succession of memories (6; 1:1000). He describes reverie as its own reenjoyment. When we remember a reverie, we fall back into it again (13; 1:1003). Reverie swallows its own future; it is just the arbitrary recall of circumstantial pleasures like its own. Rousseau can thus further claim that to *read* a reverie is the same as to *have* it. The rereading of Rousseau's *Rêveries* by a future audience cannot, therefore, interfere with the reverie's logic of rebirth, its doubling of Rousseau's existence, because there is no distance between experience and its representation in this form of writing to allow its adequacy to be critically judged.[13] The pleasure of writing or reading reverie is all. But so to safeguard reverie from the critics is also to drain it of content. Unlike the Rousseau of the *Confessions* and *Dialogues*, the Rousseau of the *Rêveries* has abandoned ambitions of communicating or transmitting meaning to future, juster generations (7; 1:1001). Or so he says. Yet this extinction of egoism is also, as we have seen, a calculated merging with the natural state and its commanding authenticity. We are returned to the question of how such abjection can produce authority.

Rousseau's overall claim in the *Rêveries* to be surrendering himself to sensations means that his answer to this question finally does not belong to him. This is part of his strange solution. In the fourth *Promenade*, truth is defined as something which can be owed. Lying is equated with stealing. But, according to Rousseau, one can only owe what is useful and good. You are not depriving someone if you lie to them about what it would be immaterial to know. Where no useful goods are being concealed from those to whom they are owed, strictly speaking, no lie is told. The most precious goods are those which apply generally and impartially, rather than particularly, and the finest general truth is impartiality itself, or justice. Now the Rousseau of the *Rêveries* tells us he doesn't want to owe anyone anything. And if he holds no goods, then no lies can be told about him, nothing can be taken from him, he can no longer be injured. "In making me insensitive to adversity," he writes, "they have done me more good than if they had spared me its blows" (117; 1:1081). Abjectly reversing sublime recuperation, Rousseau finds a good in the deprivation of good things—the pleasures of his *Rêveries*. Are they fictions or fables possessing the moral or allegorical purpose he attributed to history in *Émile*? He seems to be claiming more than that. He seems to want the character he gave himself in the *Rêveries* to embody a good, but a good that doesn't belong to him.

Forced to rely on nature alone for solace, companionship, comfort of all kinds, the Rousseau of the *Rêveries* is best positioned to form a just estimation of the human condition. We cannot steal from him what is a common dispensation. We cannot, that is, lie about him without appearing, ridiculously, to malign ourselves. But this egregious defense mechanism or burglar alarm of Rousseau's *Rêveries* requires, as we have seen, extraordinary sacrifices. Reverie is not just self-perpetuating; the self it perpetuates is generalized and so impoverished of personality as to include the humanity of all future readers. Since Rousseau cannot possess his own goods, he must figure them in a language forever severing the ties of ownership. His descriptions of the experience of reverie do this. In reverie one is most oneself by losing oneself. In merging with the whole of nature, "this beautiful system," one loses touch with particularities, including the stabilities necessary to personal existence (92, 95; 1:1063, 1065–66). In "seeking refuge in our common mother *(chez la mère commune)* [from] the attacks of her children" (95; 1:1066), the reclusive Rousseau identifies with a "continual flux" (68; 1:1046).

Any attempt to represent flux will be undermined by its fluidity and overspill. The satisfying passivity of reverie participates in, rather than represents, this mobility. Recent literary theorists have emphasized the allegory of reading thus provided. The reader analogously submits to the temporality of the reading at once constitutive and misleading; essential—you have, after all, to read the book—and yet at odds with the influxes of prolepses and analepses constituting plot, register, character, and just about every trope imaginable. One can also legitimately stress the convergence of Rousseau's effort to will the abnegation of reverie with his natural descriptions aspiring, so he tells us, to a disinterestedness he attributes to the *échantillons* or samples of botanical classification. In reverie, Rousseau submits to being determined by, rather than directing, a flow of ideas. Yet this alarmingly parallels the indigence he attributes to an old age in which "fallen into mental languor and heaviness, I have forgotten even the reasonings on which I grounded my belief and my maxims, but . . . never forget the conclusions I drew from them with the approval of my conscience and my reason" (39; 1:1022). The same paradoxes besetting reverie reappear here, but in time rather than space, in the isolation of age rather than in environmental solitude. In old age, Rousseau unreflectively lives according to his earlier better nature; but this truthful point of orientation is presented as less important than the virtues produced by submission to it—"patience, sweetness, resignation, integrity and impartial justice" (40; 1:1023). It is as if Rousseau moves beyond truthful confession into a kind of afterlife of what he thought. Again he anticipates readers who may no longer agree with him but who devise various languages—aesthetic, historical, pedagogical—in which

they can still value his representations. In these languages they can produce his heritage; they can, if you like, be his children, following the
re-creative model of reverie.

In the *Rêveries*, Rousseau is touchingly nervous that the physical effects of aging will make him frightening to children. In another act of
severance, he frequently refrained from their company, which he most
desired. "Children do not like old age; the sight of a decaying nature is
hideous to their eyes. Their repugnance, which I perceive, grieves me;
and I prefer to abstain from embracing them than to make them uneasy
or disgusted" (125; 1:1088). Yet, notoriously, he had abandoned his own.
What can we learn from the pathological or overdetermined connection
Rousseau's writings evidence between the transmission of meaning and
the treatment of children? The two kinds of afterlife raise anxieties for
him he cannot separate.

Rousseau is most obviously fascinated by what we can legitimately
make of our past. He recurrently examines the means available for making history work for us. The *Discourses* and *The Social Contract* critique
the tradition of arguing from origins in theories of language, culture,
and politics. *Émile* pursues the logic of education, formulating the rules
with which to govern a developmental past. However, as is just as well-
known, many of these stories turn out to be exemplary narratives pitted
against actual histories of decline and degeneration. Much of his writing,
therefore, also seeks to anticipate posterity's expected distortion of his
own thought: its making ugly of his work to future generations. Typical
of this prophetic knowingness is a scene in the ninth *Promenade* which
has Rousseau in rapturous conversation with an affectionate child while
already being spoken against nearby by an evil-looking spy in conversation with the child's father. The father is a hooper of barrels, a means of
preservation, and in his quickly learned hostility to Rousseau is suddenly
caricatured Rousseau's despair that his reputation will survive in barrels
or anything else.

And he was right; but he made sure he was right by his obsession with
the problem of self-interpretation, a preoccupation which itself brackets
his writing on the subject. Again, his relationship with children figures
his anxiety of reception. In *Rêveries* he implies that he wants to protect
children from an alienating image of him as the senile rather than the
welcome produce of nature. Comparably, his treatment of his own children perversely shows that he wants to protect them from the real father
they would have had in him, one who would have educated them so badly
that they would never have been able to understand his writings anyway.

Once more we find him wriggling off the hook on which he has caught himself. Posterity loses out either way: Rousseau's future interpreters are bound to argue falsely from past origins. Reverie is Rousseau's ideal way of temporarily escaping from the uncontrollable flux of nature and of freeing himself from ownership of as inconstant a self. His lie to Mme Vacassin's daughter in the fourth *Promenade*, when he told her he had no children, was simply embarrassing and mortifying (53–54; 1:1034–35). Reverie, though, imagines a dissolution of the self, an experience of the afterlife which therefore leaves nothing to posterity, which trammels up the consequence in the act, which concerns "goods we carry away with ourselves and with which we can personally endow ourselves, not fearing that even in death they would lose their worth for us" (40; 1:1023). What Stanley Cavell wrote of the rhetorical gamble of the *Confessions* to simulate posthumous knowledge of its subject is still truer of the *Rêveries*: "People who know themselves to be masters of this species of communication, and no other, are likely to welcome the hereafter."[14]

The *Rêveries* raise the question of what we are by making us ask the *Second Discourse*'s key question: What is properly ours as distinct from what is our property? Pressing on this question is the one which asks, Aren't we what we produce? And, if that is true, how are generation and the vagaries attending investment in the future to be controlled so that they do not compromise self-sufficiency or identification with our best selves? If we call the threat of self-alienating productions children, Rousseau's answers become clearer. Anxieties on this score can be overcome in two ways. Rousseau may, as we have seen, disown children except insofar as *they* reproduce *him*, showing themselves to be his heirs by recovering his original meanings in the idiom of their own times. As a form of writing, the *Rêveries* try to ensure this. Or else Rousseau may refuse to take responsibility for his children—women will do that part of his living for him. *Émile* is quite unequivocal on this: "It is up to the sex that nature has charged with the bearing of children to be responsible for them to the other sex" (361; 4:697). Presumably Rousseau is consistent when he disposes of his own children, despite Thérèse's protests, with other women? However, his exquisite bad faith, from whose consequences, he confesses, he suffers for the rest of his life, comes from his own feminization: the inextricability of his own career from forms of self-production he had relegated to women. He makes ridiculous his unequal treatment of women by subverting in his own work the taxonomy or natural order of things with which he justified their inferiority.

This can be briefly reemphasized by looking at some of the ways in which Rousseau's description of women in book 5 of *Émile* plays fast and loose with the distinction between natural and civil society. Of course he *needs* women for this license: they exemplify the historical compromises required to make the state of nature more than an elusive Kantian idea and to give it a social existence. But in *Émile*, his compromises are so outrageous that it is no wonder that they discredit the natural subordination supposedly, Rousseau's argument goes, exonerating him from sexism. The "machine," we are told, is the same in the case of both sexes, but "woman is made specially to please men" (357–58; 4:692–93). This vocation derives neither from reason nor virtue, twin arbiters of Rousseau's discussions elsewhere of what is natural, but from taste (361; 4:697). Through "taste," nature in the shape of woman is made to depend on standards of judgment, propriety, and artifice. Woman "in her conduct . . . is enslaved by public opinion" (377; 4:721), but then even Rousseau worries, "To what will we then reduce women if we give them as their law only public prejudices?" (382; 4:730). The "rule" of "inner sentiment" is hastily reinstated. But the switching from natural to conventional perspectives has become so ventriloquistic that when we are told of them that "even when they are lying they are not false," then women escape the tasteful world of legitimate fictions, the arts of decent coquetry, and become the epitome of Rousseau's own logic (which, of course, they are).

There are many conclusions one could draw from this, the most obvious, perhaps, being Rousseau's corroboration of Luce Irigaray's analysis in *Speculum*. The conclusion I want to emphasize, though, is that it is too easy to assimilate Rousseau's extraterritorial writing to an emergent *aesthetic* self-consciousness which came to be known as romanticism. The idea that Rousseau's rebarbative sentiment of himself, resistant to all other constructions, must find its resting place in art forgets all too quickly his suspicion of the arts. It ignores, too, his suspicion of women, whom he strategically corrals within the aesthetic realm of taste in *Émile*, while guiltily and surreptitiously working their reproductive possibilities into the texture of his own historicist thought. Institutionally mediate, part of civil society, the arts must participate in the distortions which Rousseau consistently attacked. Also, to see him as fostering a new idea of art as inhabiting just that human space which lies beyond social jurisdiction is to replace the historicizing effect he thought necessary to political and social theory with a notion of the aesthetic as the place where, *faute de mieux*, you experience ideals impossible to implement. The embarrassment you ought to feel at this impotence is compensated for by artistic success or its high cultural capital.[15] This Schillerian logic bolsters some of the readings of Rousseau occasioned by his bicentennial. Marian Hobson, comparing Rousseau to Kant, wrote that "For Rousseau, and Kant saw this clearly, it wasn't a question of a return to nature but of a re-creation of nature on the level of art."[16] In the same book of "reappraisals," Samuel Taylor takes this higher resolution to displace an outmoded classicism with a new romantic aesthetic: "the growing apprehension of an incoherent self, with its deviant or perverse elements, and its refusal to be defined within the *bienséances* and *vraisemblance* of the classical code, is the first conscious assertion in art of the *whole* of man's personality."[17] But this is still a Schillerian essentializing of the aesthetic self-encounter which Rousseau would surely have historicized. Like Marx, he would be suspicious of a great to-do about an aesthetic education that sends back into the world a self with better integrated drives but fundamentally unchanged constituents.[18] Why a political imagination, or a hypothetical accommodation of human wholeness, has to be aesthetic is not explained *unless* it is assumed that the aesthetic is the *only* possible location of so wide a definition *and* that there is no shame attached to the collapse of other discursive ideals into art. Again it is not at all clear that Rousseau would have welcomed this exoneration. The worst parts of *Émile* come near the end when he does appear to be savoring the pleasures of an overly fantasized rebirth of his ideals in beautiful souls; but this is far from the bleaknesses and astringencies of the *Dialogues* or the *Rêveries*.

Wise Children?

As Hegel perceived, the problem with Rousseau's general will issuing from collectively purified sentiments is its negative stance toward all institutions. Hegel thought that the political effect of this purism was death or the Reign of Terror. From the point of view of writing, Rousseau's opposition to all institutions and establishments again brings death into the equation, as seen in the *Rêveries*. But this time death comes in the form of an afterlife in which the filial reader must re-create in order to actualize the repetitive, self-perpetuating meaning of reverie. Is it perhaps in the character of one of those wise children that romantic writing confounds from the start its own aesthetic institutionalization?

Rousseau's confessional style exhibits a subject whose transparency to itself is exemplary of the answerability he ascribed to every citizen of his ideal political society. Unimpeded by unnatural artifice, the "people" would spontaneously express what they recognizably possessed in common, and in this expression of the general will political legitimacy would be reconstituted. The obviously revolutionary impact of this bypassing of hierarchical considerations is founded on the authentic self-coincidence which *Confessions, Dialogues,* and *Rêveries* are to convince us is possible. In Rousseau's own time, his argument goes, the appearance of this authentic self must be paradoxical, distorted by its resistance to the artifice blinding his contemporary readers. Existing, as it has to, in such entire opposition to prevailing norms, an egregious egotism is what is needed to set general standards. Or, rephrasing the same paradox, it takes an unnatural father to give up his own children for a posterity in which truly natural paternity can be restored. But what happens to Rousseau's historical gambit? Do immediately succeeding readerships confirm the extenuating circumstances pleaded here?

The shortest political translation of Rousseau's oppositional stance is Jacobinism, the Jacobinism of Robespierre, the "incorruptible," and of the "Mountain" who sat in the seats rising to his left in the *Assemblie National.* Rousseau's paradoxes are mocked by Burke and Wordsworth because they know them as the later contradictions of the Jacobin concept of the self. And the best reply to that mockery is still the remorseless insistence on a return to authenticity in spite of all arts and sciences, typified by Robespierre's famous riposte to Louvet and the other Girondins accusing him of despotism: "Citizens, do you want a revolution without a revolution?" Our postmodernity has accustomed us to the idea of "revolution without a model," indeed, to the idea that only the unpredictable future-perfect, will-have-been revolutionary formulation can avoid limiting revolution to some enlightened prescription.[19] Rousseauian paradox then functioned, it appears, analogously to indeterminacy now, retroactively guaranteeing the disconcertment Burke should only have expected to be produced by "the most astonishing [revolution] that has hitherto happened in the world."[20] Gregory Dart highlights Robespierre's rhetorical question in his recent study of the relation of Jacobinism to Rousseau, deriving its revolutionary self-righteousness from the politics of confession made visible by bringing together Rousseau's political discourses and his autobiographical writings. Dart concedes that it would be arrant culturalism to believe that the actual details of political history could be translated without loss into the politics of reading. Where Rousseau's autobiographical writings are concerned, though, it is his imagined readership that sheds light on the authentic political society he was equally obliged to imagine. The exigencies for the authorial and readerly imagination are the same. So were the difficulties for those who, like Hazlitt, thought they could adopt, rather than refute or historicize, Rousseau's paradoxical style.[21] Hegel's reading of the political outcome of the French Revolution depicted revolutionary action so indiscriminately oppositional that it became indistinguishable from sheer Terror. But comparable repudiation of the aesthetic (rather than its displacement or *Aufhebung*) shows its translation into other discursive configurations. In making sense of this historicizing by the aesthetic of itself, we must redescribe it so as to take account of its creative capability retroactively to surrender its authority to the critical reception of future readers. As with Marx's revolutionary vanguard class, it takes the privilege it is abolishing to achieve the abolition.

The aesthetic immolation is, as I hope I conceded conspicuously enough above, much more easily defended than the Terror, but the critical pattern just described still parallels Rousseau's radicalism. I hope I am supported here by Celeste Langan's clever reading of Rousseau's attempt "to deinstitutionalize citizenship," producing a "citizen subject," defined by a mobile freedom to which reverie is the adequate literary form: a vagrancy whose accidental disfigurations are matched by the reverie's surrender of literary autonomy, of its figures.[22] Such collapse of aesthetic privilege into a wider field of linguistic opportunity provides an immensely influential and genuinely critical alternative to the sublime recuperation, engineered by Kant and then repoliticized by Schiller, of the essentially revolutionary movement in Rousseau's thought. Metaromanticism recovers, often performatively in metaromantic practice, this alternative to an internal self-criticism, eschewing an in-house audit ultimately self-serving in its sublime aesthetic success.

The romantic poetic, to the degree that it attaches to sublimity, has been notoriously difficult to summarize. Symptomatically, manifestos of the time perform much better in this regard than later, purportedly more objective *reductios*, from the dispute between Lovejoy and Wellek onward. A "disabling surplus," as Celeste Langan puts it, perplexes romanticism and leaves critical attempts to define it looking like mistaken efforts to halt something that is processual in nature. Langan follows the idiom of the *Rêveries* to suggest that this characteristically romantic becoming does not lead necessarily to a magisterial Hegelian reprise or retrospect, but rather perpetuates a kind of vagrancy, one formed out of an endless negotiation between the opposite terms romantic poetry makes analogically equivalent. To adapt Nietzsche's diagnosis of Schiller's doubling, romanticism becomes what it already is. Refining on the "literary absolute"

attributed to romanticism by Nancy and Lacoue-Labarthe, Langan epitomizes sublime logic as "the juxtaposition of surplus and distress, or excess
of representation as a symptom of failed presentation."[23] Kant tried to
reshape this contradiction by assigning the surplus and the distress to
different mental faculties: what defeats the imagination consoles the reason. However, the negotiation between the two, whose representation is
required to do justice to the sublime dynamic, leaves the subject wavering
between capacities, homeless at home, nomadic, Carl Schmitt's pathetic
creature of the moment. And I have argued that it is Rousseau and not
Kant who confronts this indigence, making a virtue of the promenade
and a paradigm of the reverie, decisively postponing for future readers
to adjudicate their destination and their definition.

For Langan, the aesthetic accommodation of this lost subject points
beyond romanticism to liberalism, and its uncanny reversals of freedom
and necessity, as the infinite circulation of capital finds its equivalent in
the brutal determinism of market forces. For Kant and Schiller, though,
permission to enjoy aesthetic oscillation between our different faculties
was only given when such negotiations helped build a common culture,
what Kant called "common sense." Rousseau, though, already suggests
the limitations of such aesthetic institutions, and, as we have seen, describes in reverie a form of writing inciting its own re-creation in different
forms, in an afterlife with its own standards of authenticity and naturalness. In Schiller's doubling, the Kantian aesthetic became domesticated,
its sublimity housed in its own constructions. Rousseau, by contrast, exposes aesthetics to the depredations of other discourses. The vagrants of
Wordsworth's *Prelude* protect themselves against any extrapoetic gloss by
the very fervor of their consciousness of sociopolitical circumstance, by
what Langan so felicitously calls the "formal mitigation of their impas-
sioned utterance."[24] Conversely, reverie, in its self-abnegation, seems to
will the new contexts into which its later reading will fall. Its historicism is
metaromantic *par excellence*, twisting round its own authority to ask from
the start where else in the future that authority might better be allocated.
That parabasis, theorized in Schlegelian irony rather than Kantian sublimity, is developed variously in the examples of metaromantic practice
which now follow.

LITERATURE

THREE

Politics in Reserve:
Coleridge and Godwin

Imagining History: *Caleb Williams*

The "connection" which existed between William Godwin (1756–1836) and Coleridge is arguably the main subject of their writings in the 1790s. Both men were deeply interested in the contemporary "Associations" open to them to form with like-minded people. Because of the Pitt administration's suspicions concerning associations, resulting in treason trials, they were also obliged to defend the relation between such fellowships and society at large. In his *Enquiry Concerning Political Justice* (1793), Godwin famously devised a theory entailing the dissolution of government, or any other form of social jurisdiction over private judgment, in the interests of furthering a human perfectibility which could only be realized by the anarchism of true political justice. Coleridge started producing *The Watchman* in 1796 in order to finance a domestic pantisocratic association planned for the banks of the Susquehanna. Hypothetical communities like these turn out to be modeled on the audiences envisaged by Godwin's and Coleridge's writings. This follows from the stress each writer laid upon the circulation of information as indispensable to, even constitutive of, the desired social reality. Coleridge's introductory essay to *The Watchman* contains a history of the "struggle" for freedom of information leading up to contemporary resistance to government censorship.

As the prospectus to *The Watchman* makes unambiguously clear, this fight is identical with a political struggle: A PEOPLE ARE FREE IN PROPORTION AS THEY FORM THEIR OWN OPINIONS.[1] My essay presents some of the arguments for attributing to Godwin's and Coleridge's radical writings this politically constitutive moment and examines the writings' differing awareness of their own potential. I pay much more attention to Godwin, who positively exploits the moment, then watches it passing, registering and helplessly conniving at its idealist reinterpretation by the ideological interests it opposed. The politically Dissenting community converged upon from different directions by Godwin and Coleridge is, on close examination, curiously composed. Godwin, true-born Dissenter, follows the secular tendency of part of his culture to write for circles characterized by a free-thinking no longer obviously connected to a religious genealogy. Advancement toward the abstract community of Reason in *Enquiry Concerning Political Justice* is, in fact, the new self-image desired by a particular class. Godwin's theory, however, claims for this progressive movement a universal validity, paradoxically specifying the social identity of free-thinking Dissenters through their own skepticism regarding any socially defining institutions. Coleridge, coming from another direction, wishes to limit radicalism of the community of pure Dissent in which he finds himself by restoring its religious origins and recovering, through Priestley and Unitarianism, "an *older* radicalism."[2] To use the language of class as I do here is no doubt anachronistic: we are dealing only with class-perceptions and not class-consciousness. Coleridge, though, clearly saw a class-interest at work when, in "A Moral and Political Lecture" of early 1795, he accuses the "third class among the Friends of Freedom" of leveling ranks above them without raising those below; they disqualify schemes for the latter as "visionary," a genre in which Coleridge himself was to become expert. Coleridge, therefore, sees the class-content in the circulation of information when, in *Conciones ad Populum,* he describes it foundering on the distinctions "between the Parlour and the Kitchen, the Tap and the Coffee-Room"[3] and not just on inequalities of understanding.

Yet this class-pressure behind the ideal community of *Enquiry Concerning Political Justice* gives the book its bite. Intellectually constituted, its ideal nevertheless sets in motion a kind of Foucauldian calculus, a discourse constitutive of reality. For example, if it is typical of this class to create opinion, there are no obvious limits set to the public who may eventually profess to *own* this opinion.[4] Property, the qualification necessary to belong to the class of those who, on any mildly radical definition of liberty in the Whig tradition, claimed the franchise, has suddenly become a universal possibility through this commodifying of the intellect. Doubts as to whether or not it would sell in the taproom only point up the liberal openness of its market. In the first of his "Lectures on Revealed Religion," Coleridge asserts: "Property is Power and equal Property equal Power—a Poor Man is necessarily a slave. Poverty is the death of public Freedom."

And in the prospectus to *The Watchman,* he claims that "In the strictest sense of the word KNOWLEDGE IS POWER.[5] Join these together and you have the disruptive concept of intellectual property and, by Whiggish implication, a class entitled to electoral freedoms. Perhaps this sounds farfetched: it is easier to read philosophical radicalism of this sort as backing the attempts of Tom Paine and others to discredit altogether the idea of property as electoral qualification. My point is that if such attempts are, as a result, branded utopian or unthinkable, then it can nevertheless be shown that the structure of their argument at its most philosophical is still amenable to a property-based interpretation of the political liberty it recommends.

Godwin was accused, as much as Coleridge, Wordsworth, and Southey, of political apostasy of a kind to throw doubt on the validity of his early radicalism. There is the spectacular contrast between the author of a book on political theory so subversive that Pitt's cabinet considered prosecution in 1793, and the man appointed to a minor government post forty years later, glad to take up the free accommodation that went with it in the Palace of Westminster. In between had come the eclipse, famously chronicled by Hazlitt, of a once-brilliant public figure, "thought of now like any eminent writer of a hundred-and-fifty years ago."[6] But Godwin's contradictions are often located more glaringly within the 1790s, in the sharp relief of episodes like the marriage in 1797 to Mary Wollstonecraft of the arch-opponent, four years earlier, of the institution of marriage: a utilitarianism which could get round this could only appear unprincipled.

Equally decisive are the revisions of the second and third editions of *Enquiry Concerning Political Justice* (1796, 1798), the populism and the rewritten ending of *Caleb Williams* (1794), the disclaimers of *The Enquirer* (1797), and the championing of domestic affections in *St. Leon* (1799). This latter novel opposes the hero's personal ties and homely virtues to his pursuit of absolute good in the shape of an extravagantly Gothic alchemical project. Godwin thus appears to disown as rationalist excesses key aspects of *Enquiry Concerning Political Justice,* an interpretation licensed by his own preface to *St. Leon:* "some readers of my graver productions will perhaps, in perusing these little volumes, accuse me of inconsistency; the affections and charities of private life being everywhere in this publication a topic of the warmest eulogium, while in the Enquiry Concerning Political Justice they seemed to be treated with no great degree of indulgence and favor. In answer to this objection, all I can think it necessary to say on the present occasion is, that, for more than four years, I have been anxious for opportunity and leisure to modify some of the earlier chapters of that work in conformity to the sentiments inculcated in this" (ix–x).[7]

Already, it can be argued, Godwin has begun to "reinterpret his own career retrospectively in the aesthetic and private terminology of Romanticism."[8] His revisionism has to stop short at the 1793 edition of *Enquiry Concerning Political Justice,* but that is only because he accepts that its radical critique of the separation of public and private life is irrecuperable. He does not develop the theory of perfectibility which powered that critique, but instead reads Hume's *Treatise* in 1795, reinstates "feeling" as the prime mover of human action, and reserves the purely rational act as at best an ideal or limiting case.[9] This conservatism culminates in *Thoughts on Man* (1831), where the cutting edge of the original rationalist drive for a perfect truth is trimmed to fit the immutable diversity of human individuals. Here, Helvétius stands in less embarrassingly for Godwin's *Enquiry Concerning Political Justice,* providing the example of a meliorist system neglectful of individual difference. Repeating Thelwall's and Coleridge's criticism of his own *Enquiry Concerning Political Justice,* Godwin finds Helvétius's hypothesis "unsatisfactory" because "what it sets before us, is too vast and indefinite." Its vagueness merges with what Godwin calls "The Rebelliousness of Man": a constitutional antidomesticity or the "not being at home" which makes us childishly resent, in hopelessly acquisitive fantasies, the privacy of our bodies and the public constraints of our communities.[10]

This stern demotion of Godwin's earlier ambitions for political theory looks unequivocal. However, greater consistency for Godwin's work can be preserved if we take on board the sociological dimensions to Enlightenment theory urged by recent cultural historians. As Roy Porter has argued, the Enlightenment seemed to happen everywhere except in England, yet the Enlightenments of other countries frequently acknowledge English sources for radical ideas never dreamed of in the philosophy of the Augustans. The invisibility of an Augustan Enlightenment is created by the illusion that the influential liberal theorists, from Locke to the Scottish Enlightenment, have no real part to play in the literary culture of eighteenth-century England. Hence that culture is assumed to be divorced from any grand emancipatory narrative. The corrective to this view is to realize the extent to which, in Porter's words, the ideas central to this culture were "a trade, produced for a wide popular readership."[11]

It was Jürgen Habermas, a thinker persistently fascinated by "communicative action" and the political import of the "ideal speech situation," who in 1962 published the first thoroughgoing analysis of the dynamics of the Augustan literary public sphere. In this society of private people, aristocrat and commoner could enjoy a circulation of ideas without implication for their social distinctions. The universality of neoclassical discourse was an abstract, human essence which suspended, without quarreling with, existing hierarchies. In Porter's account, the literary inflection of this commonalty becomes absorbed in a more general "sociability" which furnished the criterion for anyone's seriousness about contributing to the moral order. Porter confidently quotes from an impartial spectator, Prévost—"truly, the coffee houses . . . are the seats of English liberty"— in order to underscore the new political emphasis given to the bourgeois public sphere from Dryden to Johnson.[12]

This is the emphasis whose Dissenting outcome is assimilated to striking effect in Mark Philp's recent work on Godwin. Philp's reading of *Enquiry Concerning Political Justice* is centered on Godwin's claims for the power of discussion, and so is particularly helpful for the study of how Godwin's modes of writing handle distinctions between theory and practice, public and private, fiction and truth, imagination and history. Had he taken his bearings from Habermas, Philp might have argued that the sociability or skeptical community of open debate in the Dissenting circles in which Godwin moved was a recognizable development out of the earlier Augustan public sphere. Dissenting culture possessed features of its own, even when, from the late 1780s, much of it became characterized more by political than by religious nonconformity, its tradition more identifiable through the educational influence of the Dissenting colleges than in worship. This tradition is not isolated from neoclassical culture, but it develops instabilities within the hegemonic paradigm to such a pitch that the circles of Rational Dissent no longer restrain egalitarian or utopian impulses, but provide a concrete experience of just what such emancipation might be like. This claim, without Habermas's Augustan genealogy, supports the most extreme and exciting of Philp's ideas. Godwin's anarchism, his idea that the perfectibility of humanity would gradually do away with the need for government, did not imagine a solipsistic riot of private judgment, nor an ungrounded future state in which reason had acquired unlikely powers over feeling, action, and even biology. Rather, Godwin's anarchism recorded a historical experience of living in a "society" without either state apparatuses or even oppositional political "associations." A noncoercive social group, in which all initiatives were open to debate without (Burkean) prejudice, is projected as a viable general rule. It is after his dismissal in *Enquiry Concerning Political Justice* of "Political Institutions" and "Forms of Government" that Godwin sets such store by "unreserved communication," claiming that "the promoting of the best interests of mankind eminently depend upon the freedom of social communication."[13] By this stage, though, it is already hard to see in what *else* the "social" might consist. Godwin's social milieu does not simply explain how he got his anarchist ideas, but also shows what they were about. As Philp concludes, Godwin's "faith in private judgement and public discussion and his belief that a community of virtuous individuals could survive without state coercion can be seen as empirically grounded . . . a sketch which simply extrapolated from conditions already present in Godwin's circles."[14]

In this case, to imagine a language is very much to imagine a form of life; and such a meeting of idealism and empiricism is the political consequence of a utopian moment which Augustan literary culture had contained and postponed for so long. The political reality attributed to discourse—a real power of discursive construction rather than of ideal, rhetorical sequestration—is what Godwin's writing exploits to the full, and what Coleridge's linguistic practice increasingly opposes throughout the 1790s. The attempt to recover a public sphere, with all its ideological stabilizers back in place, is a prime motivation behind the attempts of Coleridge, Wordsworth, and others to displace their radicalism, and to create through their writing, in the taste by which they were to be enjoyed, ideal readerships such as a "Clerisy" or a "household of man."[15] This restoration of ideality, however, has attracted much more scholarly attention recently, under the name of "romantic ideology," than the radical alternative, so dynamic in Godwin's work, which gives that ideology its defensive purpose.

Philp's thesis softens a number of traditional objections to Godwin. Godwin's elitism has been branded as not politically serious by opponents as diverse as William Pitt and E. P. Thompson. But the exclusiveness of the audience assumed by Godwin's discourse—the "few" addressed by any "literature," according to his *Enquiry Concerning Political Justice*—in fact measures the empirical reality which made it a practical model for his anarchism, and its "literature" an "engine" of reform.[16] Godwin's writings also appear much more consistent when the political substance of his discourse, socially consolidating in all its speech acts of persuasion and rhetoric, is kept uppermost in readers' minds. His *Thoughts on Man,* usually read as capitulatory, has a chapter "On Frankness and Reserve" which, if anything, develops further the power of discursive construction, the empirical underwriting, of the *Enquiry Concerning Political Justice.*

"The very sound of our voice should be full, firm, mellow, and fraught with life and sensibility; of that nature, at the hearing of which every bosom rises, and every eye is lighted up. It is thus that men come to understand and confide in each other. This is the only frame that can perfectly conduce to our moral improvement, the awakening of our faculties, the diffusion of science, and the establishment of the purest notions and principles of civil and political liberty" (313). If one makes the effort to read a cultural materialism into passages like this, rather than finding a dissociated sentimentalism, then the sense of claims such as this slightly earlier one becomes clearer: "An acceptable and welcome member of society therefore will not talk, only when he has something important to communicate. He will also study how he may amuse his friend with agreeable narrations, lively remarks, sallies of wit, or any of those thousand nothings, which set off with a wish to please and a benevolent temper, will often entertain more and win the entire good will of the person to whom they are addressed than the wisest discourse" (309). Godwin is still stressing community as the aesthetic substance prerequisite for moral principle and "good will." An obvious contrast is Coleridge's "Clerisy," which received its fullest expression a year earlier, and whose legislative grasp of noumenal reality informs with absolute necessity the hierarchies constraining sociability. By 1831, though, Godwin is reminiscing. He had experienced the divorce between theory and practice which took place as his kind of Dissent, culturally diffused, reverted to the Whiggery of the 1780s. He bluntly acknowledged the split when he remarked soon after *Thoughts on Man:* "In principle and theory I am avowedly a republican, but in practice a Whig."[17] This separation restores ideality to a sometime way of life. Yet that way of life is recalled in the claims of the conclusion of *Thoughts on Man,* in which the history of his community, "We . . . ourselves," supplies the compass of imagination: "Imagination is indeed a marvellous power; but imagination never equalled history, the achievements which man has actually performed. . . . We are ourselves the models of all the excellence that the human mind can conceive" (470) The relations between fiction and history had been a continuous preoccupation of his from *Sketches of History, in Six Sermons* (1784), to the preface of *Cloudesley* (1830), with its conclusion that "fictitious history, when it is the work of a competent hand, is more to be depended upon, and comprises more of the science of man, than whatever can be exhibited by the historian."[18]

To make history the task of *imagination,* and "the writer of romance . . . the writer of real history" sounds solipsistic, but is in fact the opposite.[19]

The Godwinian context consistently argues that to make *history* the target of imagination is to subscribe to the idea that the romantic individual can be socially constituted in a fulfilling way; that his or her individuality is realized in the communal discourse thus imagined; and that to claim things are this way round is not to diminish or to devalue emotions and feelings romantically thought to have an exclusively individual rather than social origin. The argument of *Caleb Williams* is here resumed, insofar as to imagine a state of affairs more just than "things as they are" is still to take one's cue from the experience of society, rather than unsubstantiated hypothesis, even if that society has never been established in a manner visible to the history of political institutions. The social model offered by the belated rapport between Caleb and Falkland in the published ending, independent of existing legal prescription and definition, is the alternative to Caleb's prison and madness in the unpublished ending. The published choice puts the reconciliation in the novel's and the audience's sphere of public discussion, and that, in Godwin's polemic, is enough. This social emphasis contrasts, for instance, with the internalized, Kantian "law" to which Karl Moor submits at the end of another radical touchstone for liberals in the 1790s, Schiller's *Die Räuber.* In Coleridge's sonnet "To the Author of 'The Robbers,'" sent to Southey in a letter of 1794, he insists already on the ideal status of its appeal, "Lest in some after moment aught more mean / Might stamp me mortal!"

Nevertheless, much of the published ending of *Caleb Williams* appears far from optimistic. Reversing Leslie Stephen's verdict that at the finish "the wickedness of Government . . . has passed out of sight," Kelvin Everest rightly argues that Caleb ends "more desperate than ever," because in vindicating himself he has had "to accept entirely his enemy's premise that truth is commensurate with public credence." The paradox, identified by Thelwall, lies in having a confidence in the integrity of public credence which is more than hypothetical, coexisting with a profound skepticism concerning existing means of communicating the truth.[20] This confidence is specifically at issue in the novel. The novel allegorizes the dilemma of a particular social grouping who should not be precluded by lack of institutional credentials from embodying a political example. "All our happiness and the greater part of our virtues," wrote Coleridge in 1795, "depend on social confidence."[21] "You began in confidence," says Caleb to Falkland, "why did you not continue in confidence?" (321) To see the ending as ruled entirely by Caleb's remorse that his victory surrenders Falkland to the "cruelty" of the law is to repeat that lack of confidence; it is to fail to attribute any weight or material aesthetic substance to the society created by Caleb's oratory, from whose sympathetic perspective the law rightly condemning Falkland can appear unjust. "Everyone that heard me was petrified with astonishment. Every one that heard me was melted with tears. They could not resist the ardour with which I praised the great qualities of Falkland; they manifested their sympathy in the tokens of my penitence" (323–24). This does not merely pity the plumage. A legal antinomy is raised by the audience's recognition of the justness of the penitence of the justified plaintiff. To take this dilemma as signifying either the incorrigibility of society or the effects of an unrealistically generous imagination is to continue to make the separation which the novel questions.

Defending *Caleb* against reviewers' attacks, Godwin insisted that it was not antinomian but practical in its implications for the administration of justice. The gist of his main argument against Lord Chief Justice Eyre in *Cursory Strictures*, published in the same year as *Caleb*, is that Eyre's discretionary charge of "constructive treason" against Thomas Hardy and other members of the London Corresponding Society is imaginary without being historical, having no precedent in legal statute or practice. History, again, backs up his otherwise inconsistent recommendation of discretion over "the vigour of judicial maxims" a year later in the *Considerations . . .* with which he attacks the Two Bills of Pitt and Grenville; although by then he is nervous that activities of the London Corresponding Society as much as of the Government will make incredible his "genuine image of reform" as the approximation of *Gesellschaft* to *Gemeinschaft*.[22]

If we read the two endings of *Caleb* together, as though part of an overarching plot, we see that Caleb has to abandon the support of positive institutional backing in order to enjoy society with Falkland and freedom for himself. If he loses nerve, and thinks that only through established laws will these goods be provided, then he effectively consigns himself to prison and personal incoherence. We have to give the novelist's choice historical credence, and place unusual trust in the fact of publicity, to have an experience comparable to the political faith and daring of Caleb's action. To understand the choice of endings as between pure imaginative possibilities is to miss entirely the way in which Godwin's action informs Caleb's and underlines the novel's resolution of its theme. Godwin's literariness, that is, becomes reflexive; and the critical momentum behind this reflexivity makes it metaromantic. The implied invitation to readers to reflect upon the historical substance of their readership helps explain the enigmatic conjunction of a novel of adventure and historical documentary encapsulated in the title. Readership as society rather than as an imagined alternative to it is the political basis of Godwin's anarchism in 1793–94, recalled by his humanism in 1831. The novel's invitation to consider the possible allegory behind the literary status of its treatment of such matters is precisely its political content. The same is true of *St. Leon,* but the allegory has changed.

Historicizing Imagination: *St. Leon*

While the preface to *St. Leon* encourages the reinterpretation of Godwin's career in terms of a romantic ideology, the novel does much more. As already suggested, the alchemical obsessions of Reginald St. Leon figure an absolute pursuit in disreputable guise. "I am not writing a tragedy, but a history," he claims; but the tragedy dramatized by the novel is just that St. Leon's history can only be expressed as tragedy. The novel's Gothicism records, similarly, its failure as historical record.

St. Leon is pictured as living at a moment when an old chivalric order is giving way before a modern tide of "craft, dissimulation, corruption, and commerce" (26). This unenthusiastic view of what replaced feudalism characterizes St. Leon's aristocratic, Falkland-like prejudice. Equally, St. Leon's chivalry, encapsulated in the fellowship of Henry VIII and Francis I, does carry its own utopian impulse, recapitulating both "the freedom of the old Roman manners" and bursting "the fetters of ages." In the third edition of *Enquiry Concerning Political Justice,* "Greece and Rome present themselves like two favoured spots in the immense desert of intellect," and we are in some ways still "exerting ourselves to arrive at the ground which they formerly occupied."[23] It is, therefore, St. Leon's noble society, about to be superseded, which escapes historical limitation to suggest a contemporary parallel, Godwin's imagined history. But the aptness of that parallel is to show the problems which arise as a community's values cease to be lived and become ideal. St. Leon goes on to embody the contradictions of his class position almost to a fault. He takes up gaming as a show of aristocratic magnificence, a spectacle which his losses reduce to "the magnanimity of the stoic" (30). This frail idealization collapses into the commercial ethos of the bourgeois, as St. Leon realizes that his nobility actually depends on solvency—on his gambling not being aleatory and disinterested. The paradox is repeated when, after terrible vicissitudes, he is restored to wealth by a chance as apparently unearned as any gamble—the gift of the philosopher's stone from a "stranger." All his aristocratic descriptions of this unexampled wealth chime inevitably with the bourgeois ethos of the self-made man: "as if a man could be the author of his own existence" (193). His saintly and extremely high-born wife, Marguerite, has no difficulty in scenting the taint of trade: "An adept and an alchemist is a low character. When I married you I supposed myself united to a nobleman, a knight, and a soldier" (210). However, it is Marguerite who, through her own behavior, begins to educate St. Leon in the contradictions producing his ideals. When he bankrupts himself, her behavior under crisis is also aristocratically exemplary and so especially open to misconstruction as a result. St. Leon cannot describe her unequivocally: "never did human creature demean herself with greater magnanimity" (210). But her mental superiority to material vicissitude loses its value under pressure. "At some times I honoured Marguerite for her equanimity. At others I almost despised her for this integrity of her virtues" (81). Within the oxymoron of demeaning high-mindedness, neither pole is necessarily ascendant. Once St. Leon has sensed its reversibility, his conception of Marguerite is destabilized. The disabling paradox is created by a change in social circumstances which the novel presents as epochal: not simply the individual fortunes of St. Leon, but the disorientation experienced by members of an aristocratic class increasingly forced to live in a mercantile culture whose ethos either replaces chivalric virtue or discredits it through idealization. Anyone naively adhering to the old ethos will appear like St. Leon high-handedly protesting his innocence to an unimpressed Swiss bourgeois magistrate. When the magistrate reasonably asks St. Leon for "the most ample communication" of how he came by his unearned wealth, he receives in reply evidence only that St. Leon is "mighty well spoken" in words that "are big and sounding" (220–21). St. Leon is bombastic, using language too large for its subject, repeating over again the oxymoron of his historical dilemma.

St. Leon clearly fails to justify himself by the standards of communication required in Godwin's *Enquiry Concerning Political Justice*, but one has to make sense of why the novel contrives a situation which renders these standards hopelessly ideal. This is the ingenuity of Godwin's plot and the contribution of the novel's reflexive dimension to the story—quite the opposite effect to the confidence-inspiring self-consciousness of *Caleb Williams*. The tale of the philosopher's stone is what must vindicate St. Leon as an innocent man who has come by his wealth honestly. He has been given this source of wealth on condition that he keep it a secret. His confessions, the narrative, are therefore taken inside the plot. The narrator is systematically unreliable: either he is telling the truth, and in betraying his benefactor's confidence shows himself untrustworthy; or else he is keeping faith with the "stranger," and so is misleading his readers.

The conundrum is deepened by its possible allegorizing of the historical setting of Godwin's novel at the end of the 1790s, after revolutionary excesses have cast Godwin's views on political justice in an impractical, ideal light. The course of the French Revolution has raised a comparable problem for Godwin's own "most ample communication." Either, on Godwin's criteria, the French Revolution was not a "true" revolution, and so his most thoroughgoing expression of human perfectibility does not discuss the most radical event of the decade; or else English reaction provoked by this revolution has historically transformed society in such a way as to dissolve the old factual, empiricist basis of Godwin's anarchism. He is deprived of a radical discourse which is at the same time constitutive of a social group and a standing refutation of charges of utopian idealism. On either interpretation, Godwin is as stymied as St. Leon. The subject of their "literature" is the thing it cannot say. As St. Leon tells his readers: "the pivot upon which the history I am composing turns, is a mystery. If they will not accept of my communication upon my own terms, they must lay aside my book" (215). But to accept the novel on those terms, St. Leon concedes, is to regard it as "Senseless paper!" St. Leon has not only to hide his secret, but "to conceal that I have any to hide" (161). The bluffs are endless, the double-takes undecidable. St. Leon admits that the distinction between confiding the "history and not the science which is its cornerstone" is "vain and frivolous" (161). Like Godwin, he will not differentiate between knowledge and society. But what this science of communication now reveals is its own breakdown: disinformation expresses the reality of social incoherence; historical discourse is thus constrained to tragic irresolution; and the imaginary glosses over an inability to master the facts.

In the "mystery" of St. Leon's life, opposite meanings cannot be kept apart: the unjustifiable private privilege of unearned wealth merges with the trade, the "mystery," of the alchemical "adept." The private cannot be made public, not only in accordance with the Gothic plot, but because of an aristocratic class-pressure which the Gothic "mystery" figures. This, in turn, suggests what we are reduced to, not enriched by, when the discourse of all our emancipatory ideals is no longer in the public sphere. The resultant Gothic growth in feeling and poetic suggestiveness may be considerable and may retrospectively construct the Dissenting discourse of the earlier *Enquiry Concerning Political Justice* (1793 edition) as barren, rationalistic and boring, unequal to the new excitements: we are well on the way to Hazlitt's frequent characterization of Dissent as a *"hortus siccus,"* and Arnold's linking of it with "dogma" as against "literature." But the losses are equally conspicuous. The other gift of the "stranger" to St. Leon was the "elixir of life," bestowing immortality. This alchemical facility is also assimilated to the narrative's duplicity, implying, so St. Leon tells us, a lack of experimental authenticity in any of his sublime effusions on nature and the affections so admired by early readers like Hazlitt and Byron. In fact they are secondhand, just as the novel is brazenly eclectic, their success testifying to another communicative failure, this time indicating the perpetual staleness of a life lived through for the second time.[24] We meet the unavoidable crux of someone forced to use a public language to traduce a private meaning. St. Leon is "obliged to employ the established terms of human description. I cannot interrupt the history of my sensations, by a recital of those pangs by which they have been at every moment interrupted" (356). Except that, in an involuntary, recuperative parody of "Tintern Abbey," and *The Prelude* to come, the expressive failure keeps the secret intact. History, once more, is the loser in what Hazlitt called one of "the most splendid and impressive works of the imagination which has appeared in our times."[25] The novel's power to invite such plaudits is also the ironically inarticulate vindication of St. Leon's claim that "the creature does not exist with whom I have any common language" (356).

The elixir theme's further disruption of narrative authority focuses more sharply the historical contradictions under which the novel was produced. In the revised (1798) *Enquiry Concerning Political Justice,,* Godwin opposed revolutions because their instant egalitarianism had no basis in historical experience: rather than a political freedom constructed out of the discourse of free debate, revolution would be experienced as a massive loss of value. Revolutions "disturb the harmony of intellectual nature. They propose to give us something for which we are not prepared, and which we cannot effectually use. They suspend the wholesome advancement of Science, and confound the process of nature and reason."[26] In addition to his promise to the stranger, St. Leon gives as reasons for not communicating his alchemical secrets comparable threats of the redundancy of value and the deregulation of nature. "The reason why the science may not be developed is obvious. Exhaustless wealth communicated to all men, would be but an exhaustless heap of pebbles and dust; and nature will not admit her everlasting laws to be so abrogated, as they would be by rendering the whole race of sublunary men immortal" (161). The "mystery" of alchemy, then, as of the "revolutions" of *Enquiry Concerning*

Political Justice, is that, like Hume's conservative miracles, it can only be imagined as a new normality, as unmiraculous. Were this "mystery" communal, a trade, then all its advantages would disappear along with the normality of the life over which it had enjoyed its privileges. St. Leon's aristocratic allegiances make it impossible for him to adopt the real indifference required to back a critique of money or of inequality as the natural order. His interests lie in keeping the idea of the alchemical community unintelligible.

In the novel's terms, though, the analogy between its "alchemy" and the *Enquiry Concerning Political Justice*'s "revolutions" is the secret concealing that there is a secret to hide. Following Philp's account, I have argued that historical changes throughout the 1790s deprived Godwin's theory of political justice of its empirical basis. It therefore finds itself on the same footing as the state of revolution which it criticizes. The hidden secret is that Godwin's anarchism, deprived of its experimental vindication, is now helpless to avoid being also construed as idealist scheme and extravagant hypothesis. St. Leon is the figure of the outmoded interest which nevertheless preserves the mystery of its privilege by claiming its historical realization to be an impossible ideal. Even St. Leon's beloved Marguerite must die, rather than be saved by the elixir, to preserve the "mystery." In the character of St. Leon, Godwin watches political justice being absorbed into romantic ideology, unseated from its historical base, and mythologized as an imaginative alternative to social experience. His anarchism cannot resist the slide into identification with revolution because it is now as *déraciné* as St. Leon, its virtues comparable to his chivalry. This revolutionary identification implies, as Robert Kaufman forcefully argues, a non-identity of its aesthetic expression with actual history and politics. It then takes an expansive narrative of the Kantian sublime, a narrative Kaufman himself is prepared to make paradigmatic of modernity, to retrieve value from the growing impracticality of political justice. In contrast with *St. Leon,* though, the endings of *Caleb Williams* suggest instead the necessity of being capable of, precisely, identification. It is the confidence to appropriate justice as a course of action, a confidence equally required of the reader of the published ending, I am arguing, that the novel dramatizes as social possibility. Two years before his death, in the preface to his *Lives of the Necromancers,* Godwin describes perfectly the intellectually disreputable expansiveness of a life of pure imagination, an alternative world in whose anachronistic sorceries, nevertheless, it is "that we contemplate with most admiration the discursive and unbounded nature of [human] faculties."[27]

The plot of *St. Leon* provokes a reflexive style encompassing its mysterious loss of subject. Forbidden to refer, the novel must talk about itself. In contrast to *Caleb Williams*, its reflections on its own fictionality do not inspire a social assurance instituted by the publicity and circulation of ideas, and the metaromantic impulse to see reading as the practical translation of its meanings is thwarted. Rather, its "senseless paper" is designed to short-circuit communication. One of St. Leon's listeners, Monluc, declares to him, "only in a public character am I capable of affording you assistance. . . . [E]nable me to have a reason for acting, that is not merely capable of being felt, but that I may know is in its own nature capable of being stated to another" (227). Like Monluc, we are denied. "Explanation," St. Leon tells us, "is not the business of a man of honour" (226). We are left to savor the mystery so attuned to the literary taste of the time. To *"toss up"* a novel or two like *St. Leon* would be an easy, lucrative matter, Coleridge told Southey. [28]

Godwin's novels of the 1790s allow us to make a more general point. Ronald Paulson has pointed out, in his rich analysis of attempts in different media to represent the French Revolution, the extreme simplicity with which Gothic novels after 1789 allegorize revolutionary events: "Somewhere within all of these novels lurked the allegorical mode with its simple equivalents." [29] In Godwin's versions, I would add, the novels allegorize their own susceptibility to allegory, making its different order of commentary on contemporary events stand either for the political initiative open to a radically confident discourse outside established frameworks or, conversely, for the political unaccountability of a discourse entertaining such alternatives. Susceptibility to allegory shows that fundamental choices can be made, that fictionality as much as fiction is open to historical appropriation of different kinds. Caleb, crouched over Falkland's trunk, is a reader as yet unaware that it is in his power to decide what the social significance of the secret narrative inside will be, over and above what it says. In Tilottama Rajan's brilliant readings of the endings, the "impact on the reader" is all, because the novel looks for future nonnovelistic corroboration to keep its published ending plausible. Godwin "turns the novel back on itself, placing not only Falkland and Caleb but also his own ending on trial." Rajan later describes this movement more pessimistically as Hegelian displacement: "in *Caleb Williams* [Godwin] was able to sublate the failure of political justice into a new utopian ending." She has, though, I think still left it open to the *reader*'s corroborative translation into another discourse to (retroactively) find it metaromantic. [30]

The Politics of Communication

Coleridge, notoriously unsympathetic to allegory, often appears intent on making a decision between such alternatives impossible. In theory and practice, as Mrs. Barbauld found out, Coleridge so convolutes matters at a primary level that the allegorical interpretation is not at all obvious, and certainly does not deal in "simple equivalents." There is, therefore, not the incentive for readers to produce a politics of the text they are reading, the politics thrown up by Godwin's novels' discussion of the thematic significance of their own fictionality. Coleridge's symbolic mode, developed throughout the 1790s, precludes elaborations of this kind from the start, being defined as already consubstantial with its meaning.

Lucyle Werkmeister argued, thirty years ago, that *The Friend*'s essay "On The Communication of Truth" was the closest Coleridge came to providing the "examination" of Godwin's principles repeatedly promised in the 1790s. In that essay, Coleridge emphasized the ideal status of notions of absolute betterment by insisting on the role of genius. When Coleridge writes in this vein, genius significantly lacks the Kantian continuity or Godwinian collaboration with the community it anticipates. Godwin planned "entirely to change the face of education" by abolishing the intellectual privilege of genius or sage: "no such characters are left upon the scene as either preceptor or pupil. The boy, like the man, studies, because he desires it. . . . Every thing bespeaks independence and equality."[31] Coleridge writes instead of "the limited sphere" of the "successive Few" to whom "we owe our ameliorated condition" and from whom come intellectual handouts, apprehended by the great majority of us in their "results," not in their explanatory "Principles."[32]

It is clearly no more the business of Coleridge's "Few" to explain than it was the duty of St. Leon's "man of honour"; and so much of Coleridge's great poetry celebrates the compensatory "mystery" which can be generated as a "result." The slogans of *The Watchman* take on the jejune simplicity of the moral at the end of *Rime of the Ancient Mariner* when contrasted to its "pure imagination." From this perspective, to complain of being limited to the so-called "mystery" poems—*Rime of the Ancient Mariner, Christabel, Kubla Khan*—rather than being granted access to "Principles" makes political nonsense. We are bound to feel more emancipated in a language more adequate to the complex, many-sided reasons for our failure to be just. This equation of poetry with freedom of expression allays doubts that somehow an originally wider political context of debate has been

elided. Elided, rather than discounted, because the reader is still able
to ask the same questions, although the answer assumes the priorities of
a poetic economy. Emancipation of the subject in poetry, in a language
capable of accommodating "the whole soul of man" as Coleridge puts
it in *Biographia Literaria,* is bound to reduce other ostensibly broader discourses to narrow, dismal sciences. But from their perspective, it is poetry
which impoverishes. Coleridge renders this perspective virtually impossible for us to recover with our cultural credentials intact. Coleridge's
development as a poet appears necessarily bound up with a triumphant
progress from Unitarian poems full of political, philosophical, and theological debate to mystery poems whose rhetoric characteristically contrives an adequate reticence on these subjects. The experience of reading
Rime of the Ancient Mariner, Christabel, or *Kubla Khan* raises no nostalgia for
The Watchman's Godwinian moment of a truth that would set us free. Like
St. Leon, Coleridge's cultured readers are persuaded they would lose far
more than they would gain.

Can one bring Coleridge and Godwin closer together? On a Habermasian view of communication we ought to be able to. That is, we ought
to be able to find the utopian impulse in Godwin's communicative logic
which a Coleridgean poetic tried to rule out of court. Equally, we ought
to be able to detect a politics of readership in Coleridgean mystery which
its symbolic mode appears to preclude. But Coleridge's later advocacy of
the Clerisy, the national Church, and his educational commitment to the
dissemination of ideas in quantities appropriately tailored to the needs
of each member of the Clerisy's flock, clearly show that he became, in
fact, as prepared as Godwin to imagine a political reordering of society
through the invention and establishment of a new social class. He wants,
if you like, to give to St. Leon's obsolete aristocracy a vital cultural role
and to fight for the political significance of this cultural innovation to be
acknowledged. In that sense, the reflexivity invited by the mystery poems
metaromantically anticipates or has its consummation within the constructions of another, political discourse. In other words, the readership
imagined by his mystery poems, a readership notionally superior to any
trade in meanings translatable into practicable, utilitarian ends, eventually translates, despite itself, into that substitute for aristocracy Coleridge
was busy imagining from his *Lay Sermons* onward, the period in which the
mystery poems were finally published together. The decline of a landed
class, or one representing a "permanent" interest in the nation, is finally
to be remedied, in *On the Constitution of the Church and State According to
the Idea of Each* (1830), by constructing its philosophical equivalent. This

class is again capable of representing permanence, but is now qualified to do so by its transcendental indifference to individual interests, by its attention to kind rather than degree, on analogy with the way in which the reader of unsolvable mystery poems is thrown back upon reflections on the permanent mental hierarchy habitually engaged by different interpretative possibilities. The politics this Clerisy promulgates, originating in the aesthetic delivery of universal dispositions, may well be full of Schillerian deferrals, but the advocacy of its establishment shows a different, much more practical and determinate politics in action. We may not like the politics, but the longer view shows that they are embedded in the kind of attention the poems draw to the reading of their mysteries. [33]

Godwin's systematic thinking is supplemented by a belief in the power of discussion eventually to perform what his system desires—an understanding no longer bound by existing institutions. In *Enquiry Concerning Political Justice*, Godwin declares himself unable to think of an example of social intercourse which does not leave both participants "better" than before. [34] Is "better" grasped inside or outside ideas of justice current in Godwin's day? Godwin's answer in *Enquiry Concerning Political Justice* is ambivalent in that he suggests that the logical conclusion of following the rational principles partly embodied by existing social institutions is the dissolution of those institutions. The end may be utopian; the means are practical and emphatically begin with things as they are, fostering the rationality immanent in current practices. When Godwin is satirized, as he is by Edward Dubois in *St. Godwin* (1800), for opposing "all political and moral order," his anarchic ideal is strategically detached from its practical implementation by the satirist. [35] While this tactic is unfair, it is nevertheless true to the endpoint desired by Godwin's provisional use of his contemporary discursive framework. Dubois's laughter, though, makes him overlook *St. Leon*'s own satire on the idea of taking up a position, *ab extra*, from which the moral order might be "overcome": an unreal position as illusory, the novel implies, as the advantages of the philosopher's stone or a knowledge of alchemy which can only be envisaged in secret. On the other hand, *St. Leon*'s emphasis on the social affections, in line with changes to the third edition of *Enquiry Concerning Political Justice*, need not contradict the final aim of *Enquiry Concerning Political Justice* to achieve a rational state unimpeded by current institutions, moral, political, legal, and so on. The paradox here is captured in that "unreserved communication" desired by *Enquiry Concerning Political Justice* (288). Godwin there despises an inwardness that, like St. Leon's alchemical lore, does not seek outward expression; but the communication guaranteed by discourse can only be adequate to an unreserved inwardness, a private judgment, if it exceeds or subverts current standards of publicity (315). To champion communication as an overriding aim, therefore, is to breach the jurisdiction of positive institutions. According to the Godwin of *Enquiry Concerning Political Justice*, to generalize one's opinion successfully is to "increase the stock of political knowledge," not, as Everest feared, to assimilate opinion to orthodox concepts. We have seen the published ending of *Caleb Williams* present this enlightened optimism, the long-awaited scene of dialogue between Caleb and Falkland, as constituting not so much an out-of-court settlement as a dispensing with legal arbitration altogether. The sacrifices involved in such absolutism, Falkland's death and Caleb's loss of "character," show Godwin's awareness of the dangers in anticipating the ideal truthfulness to which the logic of communication leads: his discourse is in and about itself, an allegory, I have argued, of its own allegorical possibilities, metaromantic. Equally, the unpublished ending indicates that the suppression of this utopian rational impulse depletes human beings of something fundamental to their ordinary sanity.

For Godwin, as for Wollstonecraft, discursive initiatives create radical possibilities out of the same means by which ordinary communication is assured. The contradiction in theorizing an ideal subject still free to critique its own episteme disappears. Its puzzling metaphysics is replaced by a plausible reserve in communication between individuals, a reserve which both specifies their particular differences and the pragmatics by which they actually communicate. Godwin's theory and novelistic practice repudiate that absolute romantic subjectivity, the role of "St. Godwin" in which he was cast by opponents like Du Bois; he avoids the comedy of *St. Godwin*'s transcendental or arbitrary superiority to things as they are, opting instead for a radicalism expressed through the dynamics of dialogue. The strain put on attempts to honor both the utopianism and the pragmatics of communication produces the split, the two endings of *Caleb Williams* which cannot be entertained at the same time. Whichever ending Godwin had published would have been shadowed, cryptically, by the other possibility his theory of communication held in reserve. Reserve, the distinctive creation of Coleridge's poetic mystery and Godwin's imaginary history, allows for the more explicitly political historical reincarnations of itself which metaromantic writing may not be able to state but which it invites.

—∞—

Keats and Critique

Keats's "Metaphysical Conceit"

The beautiful forms displayed in the organic world all plead eloquently
on the side of the realism of the aesthetic finality of nature in support of
the plausible assumption that beneath the production of the beautiful
there must lie a preconceived idea in the producing cause—that is to
say an *end* acting in the interest of our imagination.

—Kant, *Critique of Judgement*

In this relation [of romantic art] the inner, so pushed to the extreme,
is an expression without any externality at all; it is invisible and is as it
were a perception of itself alone, or a musical sound as such without
objectivity and shape, or a hovering over the waters, or a ringing tone
over a world which in and on its heterogeneous phenomena can only
accept and remirror a reflection of the inwardness of soul.

—Hegel, *Aesthetics*

In a letter of 16 August 1820, Keats wrote to Shelley:

A modern work it is said must have a purpose, which may be the God—
an artist must serve Mammon—he must have "self concentration" selfishness perhaps. You I am sure will forgive me for sincerely remarking
that you might curb your magnanimity and be more of an artist, and
"load every rift" of your subject with ore. The thought of such discipline
must fall like cold chains upon you, who perhaps never sat with your
wings furl'd for six months together, And is this not extraordina[r]y
talk for the writer of Endymion? whose mind was like a pack of scattered
cards—I am pick'd up and sorted to a pip. My Imagination is a Monastry and I am its Monk you must explain my metap^CS [metaphysics] to
yourself.[1]

Keats's readers inherit a critical tradition in which his own language is regarded as being everywhere as loaded and mixed in its blessings as that recommended here to Shelley. His "metap[cs] [metaphysics]," as he told Shelley in the same letter, "you must explain . . . to yourself" (2:323). In an issue of *Studies in Romanticism* providing a forum for the subject of "Keats and Politics," the editor, Susan Wolfson, mentions a "general critical tendency to regard the very conjunction of 'Keats' and 'politics' as something of a metaphysical conceit."[2] Now we have studies such as Nicholas Roe's edited collection *Keats and History* and his own fine monograph *Keats and the Culture of Dissent*.[3] Yet when Keats asks Shelley to curb his presumably political "magnanimity" in the interests of being "more of an artist," he characterizes this aestheticism as devotion to "Mammon" rather than to "God," paradoxically (so it seems) recalling the material interests of politics through his very appeal to artistic idealism. Keats's writings do not explicitly refer *to* but disclose his writerly situation *within* a current metaphysical configuration. His metaphysics have therefore been ignored as much as his politics. But in working them out for ourselves, as he tells Shelley to do, we find that the aura of "metaphysical conceit" that apparently dematerializes Keats's politics is the clue to the nature of those politics.

This is one of the pioneering insights of Marjorie Levinson's book *Keats's Life of Allegory—the Origins of a Style*. At last one can see clearly the conceitfulness with which Keats's poems double and displace their political concerns. Furthermore, we learn to read these concerns not as something under Keats's conscious control, but as part of an exercise in "doing to himself what others do to him." At the same time, Levinson's work discovers in the prescribed perversity that this social effect reveals, the absence of that collective life which would, conventionally, explain the failure of Keats's self-fashioning. Keats suffers the "scandal of a man without a class," the "neither-nor" of someone stationed between the lower and middling orders. In a doubly effacing movement, then, the Keatsian poet is subjected to a social determination which stems from an indeterminate social provenance. Moreover, Levinson shows that the bourgeois culture to which Keats aspires shares his uncertainty of origin and recognizes its prototype in him. *His* visibly disadvantaged perspective on bourgeois aesthetics thus accentuates *its* characteristic nothingness in a subversive parody, betraying its poverty, as Hyperion does the misery of the Titans, "To the most hateful seeing of itself." Levinson's interest in developing a sociology of Keatsian literariness requires a de-emphasis of the familiar semantic questions: "Keats's solutions *do* solve metaphysical and epistemological problems, but it is the others that need explaining."[4]

My own return to "metaphysical and epistemological problems" tries to capitalize on the new visibility which the old problems have gained as a result of Levinson's study. Reimmersion in these problems may weaken the sense of Keatsian parody, but, as Levinson asserts, metaphysical problems *are* solved in Keats's writings; and an analysis like mine, which shows the poverty of these successes, may help us see what happened to the idealist aesthetic when submitted to those pressures which Levinson's cultural materialism has identified. To work within the scheme of romantic idealism in relation to Keats is not, then, to forgo critique. It is, rather, to explore from within a frustrated and inhibited critique which is transformed into effective parody as soon as its strict immanence is abandoned.

The "metaphysical conceit" of Keats's politics is a way to name the manner in which two discourses reciprocally disguise each other. The fact that Keats's metaphysical is political and his political metaphysical makes each invisible and accounts for the proverbial absence of both from his work. The word for this common vanishing-point is the "aesthetic." In the Kantian tradition, the aesthetic is what is left of reality after the critical philosophy has performed its task. A critique which, like Keats's poetry, operates under the sign of the aesthetic might therefore be expected to remain fairly well hidden. The aesthetic is also the area in which politics consolidates itself as culture, in which, again in line with Kantian practice, universals are imaginatively negotiated rather than deduced, and the political character of such transactions is both masked and validated as the exposition of what is metaphysically possible.[5]

My argument is that the interchangeability in Keats's poetry of its ideal status and its political reticence gradually begins to expose the contemporary politicizing of the ideal and the idealizing of the political. Moreover, in speaking that aesthetic function, the poetry breaks the silence on which that function's effectiveness depended, raising considerable problems for the criticism of Keats, both hostile and sympathetic. Hostile critics, in this sense, are neither heterodox nor antithetical but share the aesthetic under critique. Their complicity means that they cannot say what Keats is doing without joining in blowing the whistle on the common aesthetic's political function. Their criticism serves this political interest by becoming theoretically muted; my point is that such reticence still has *its* ideological point and is thus indirectly expressed by the language of social animus which rushes in to fill the theoretical vacuum. The invective covers what Hazlitt, in a passage Keats quoted from his great attack on William Gifford, editor of the *Quarterly,* called "the invisible link, that connects literature with the Police" (2:72). However, paralleling this, sympathetic criticism can point up Keats's political content only by expounding the comprehensiveness of his aesthetic, and so also forgoing differentiation of that content. There is no suggestion of a Hegelian movement into a more historically apt coherence which can escape the inclusiveness of art because it is prepared to abandon art altogether.[6] But Keats's critique is embodied in a writing that reveals that the aesthetic betrays (semiotically and polemically) the political and vice versa, each bringing the other to our notice as its dishonorable disguise.

Jerome McGann has pointed out criticism's neglect of the pun on "leaf" in the first stanza of the "Ode on a Grecian Urn."[7] His reading compels us to see in the Ode a symptomatic paronomasia, the lateral movement of which creates an aesthetic within the aesthetic. This can be fairly obvious, as when the "brede of marble men" implies that in the relief the urn pictures yet another artwork, either statuary or raised figures from another relief. "Overwrought," the brede's key adjective, thus has at least four meanings. It describes the elevation of the "brede" above the surface of the urn, the emotions of the "mad pursuit" of "men and maidens," the transference of figures from one work of art "over" to another, and the overarching umbrage, itself legendary, fringing the urn's narrative. A word branching out in so many directions is itself overwrought, a fact that dramatizes yet again the poem's paronomastic tension. Or, perhaps, the accuracy with which "overwrought" describes itself disables that descriptive function. The word has been overworked beyond what is required, to excess, exhausted beyond usefulness. This result is not, however, the rhetorical effect of an inevitable discrepancy between language's performative and descriptive functions. The reflexive pun thematizes the paradox attributed in Keats's poem to poetic authority. The justness with which the poem refers to itself, and specifically to its radically unauthorized signifying practice, is the means of its special pleading. What is typical of this art is its claims to typicality; all we need know about art is what it says about itself—and it says that too.

Such poetry exposes its limitations by doubling. It critically undermines what its aesthetic ideology obliges it to say, showing even that authority to be one of its inventions as well. Through this oblique critique, this provocative overinventiveness, Keats, I think, lays bare a contradiction in the radical bias of Kantian aesthetics, a bias which Schiller develops. The result is not necessarily the bankruptcy Hegel attributed to romantic aesthetic inflation. Keats's famed sensuousness is fueled by an art which releases in us the desire that it *not* possess that imaginary sphere of undetermined universality which allows it authority to educate our desires, but that it be, rather, a determinate judgment. Keats puts this point with a directness that courts the philosophical scandal involved: "O for a Life of Sensations rather than of Thoughts!" (1:185). Art educates us in wanting to realize the fulfilled humanity we can experience only aesthetically, without being inhibited by the need to observe the autonomy of art, which enabled us to intuit such emancipation in the first place. Keats's poetry makes us want to possess the aesthetic experience it offers on terms which do not allow it to have generated such a desire. Once discovered in Keats's "Monastry," "Mammon" could never have belonged there. This impasse is at the heart of what I am calling Keatsian critique.[8]

Unthinkable Critique

The opening of *Endymion,* John Wilson Croker's test-piece of Keatsian incompetence, is as tricky to read as the openings of Keats's later works. In its obsessive longing for the power to describe the effect of great art, the passage sets the tone for the narrative to come. In this, it continues the preoccupation of the preceding year's sonnets, whose subjects include the experience of seeing the Elgin Marbles and not being up to describing the experience, and the frequent and apparently less problematic evocation of a feeling of inhabiting sensuously the literary space of a great tradition stretching from Chaucer, Dante, and Petrarch, through Spenser and Milton to Chatterton, Wordsworth, Byron, Hunt, and contemporary "Great spirits." As in the conclusion to "The Eve of St. Agnes," temporal distance is used to promote an enabling pathos, whose touch confirms the reader's recognition of an erotic dilemma continuous with present energies. It elaborates the invitation to watch the vanishing point of the drowned Leander when, at the conclusion to the sonnet in his honor: "He's gone! Up bubbles all his amorous breath."

The obsession with matching inspirational influence to felt vocation, and the anxieties arising from possible disparities, tends to disguise the way in which Keats focuses on another subject matter. The advantage to Keats of taking other poems or artistic artifacts as his subject lies in the opportunity to close immediately, from the start, on the nature of aesthetic satisfaction. A deceptively simple point to be taken from these poems and from many of the earlier sonnets of 1816 is that to write of the experience of reading literature is to explore something continuous with other kinds of experience. In this Keats shows, as John Bayley claimed, that "literature can become the most effective vehicle of reality." In classic idealist fashion, to read is to attend to objects with such detachment that we become conscious of their naturalness (what Kant called purposiveness, and Keats "purpose") or sheer appositeness to our experience of them with an intensity that somehow compensates for the otherwise tautological banality of the apprehension. "It implies," in John Bayley's brilliantly succinct words, "a kind of helpless being oneself."[9] Keats, like Hegel, exposes the otiose character of idealist aesthetics, but without advancing from a phenomenological to an evaluative stance. In his early work there is a prophetic concentration on the effects of achieved works of art. The infinite regress of intertextual sources and authenticity (in the visual as well as the verbal arts) does not limit the meaning of Keats's re-creation of the canonical line to a desire to belong to it. The corroborations, correlatives, catalogs, repetitions, and velleities of Keats's sonnets allow him to feel through in a precritical manner what the aesthetic is meant to realize beyond the spectacle of its own construction. In all this there is a latent unease or restlessness with ideas of fulfillment and completion. Even in the most uncritical evocations of an environment of balmy hospitality centrally heated by literary musings, as in "To one who has been long in city pent" or "Oh, how I love, on a fair summer's eve," there is a tentative reach beyond pleasure into discontent. It is this that we sense in the final silence of "an angel's tear," which, like the Satan alluded to in the title, "falls through the clear ether," clouding the otherwise countrified content of the day-tripper in "To one who has been long in city pent." Or one might recall those figures of Puritan resistance, Milton and Sidney, whose "stern forms" sit in silent judgment beside another "delicious tear" with which "Poesy" clouds the eye at the end of "Oh, how I love, on a fair summer's eve." Similarly, the catalogs that conclude other sonnets endeavor rather than succeed in suggesting the conclusiveness of their inventions. Lacking George Herbert's metaphysical "something understood," they have to rely for credibility on their conspicuously imagined choice, an invitation to collude in the enjoyment of a world in which the anecdotal fronts as the essential. This risks tautology and redundancy, most startlingly in the daringly bathetic rounding off of the catalog at the end of "After dark vapours" with "a poet's death."

"The Beauties of . . ." is a predominantly eighteenth-century title which assumes the proportions of a gentlemanly knowledge of literature. Its rationale, however, gets progressively effaced in the romantic period through the commonplace privileging of lyric over narrative, incident over plot, character over argument, and sympathetic imagination over discursive knowledge. One thinks, for example, of Keats's exemplary Kean, with his run of Shakespearean performances in a single season, each one transforming an entire play in the public imagination into *his Othello, Hamlet,* and so on. At the same time, though, the "beauties" rhetoric of Keats's early verse, and especially *Endymion,* characterizes the text as a whole as a succession of achieved moments and quintessential distillations—the "poetical concentrations" Leigh Hunt claimed Byron found unintelligible. "Beauties . . . in almost every page" were, after all, the mainstay of John Scott's rejoinder to the *Quarterly*'s review of *Endymion*.[10] As Keats tells Benjamin Bailey when well into the writing of *Endymion* in October 1817, "I must make 4000 Lines of one bare circumstance and fill them with Poetry" (1:16–70). "Beauties" signals a kind of pure poetry—*Endymion*'s "Poetry"—combating in, for example, "How many bards gild the lapses of time," the association of "gilding" or beautifying with superficiality, and indicating instead Keats's un-Wordsworthian interest in the significance of result rather than process in art. In a letter to Clough of 1852, Arnold senses this Keatsian effect of "beauties" (which he also, ironically, attributes to Shelley) and shrewdly analyzes its components. Arnold wants a modern poetry in which the diction serves the action. In Keats he finds a poet "on a false track" because he sets himself "to reproduce the exuberance of expressing the charm, the richness of images, and the felicity of the Elizabethan poets. Yet critics cannot get to learn this, because the Elizabethan poets are our greatest, and our canons of poetry are founded on their works. They still think the object of poetry is to produce exquisite bits and images."[11] According to Arnold, by the middle of the nineteenth century Keats's success had come to inhibit criticism by forcing it to recognize the particularity of his poetry as the sensuous expression of a pure canonicity. Suddenly, Keats appears as the reactionary quintessence of orthodoxy, opposed by the radical Arnold with his innovatory hopes for a "modern poetry." Such a poetry, with its wider ambitions of becoming "a complete magister vitae as the poetry of the ancients did," will move beyond the metaromantic habit toward an inclusive position of religious authority, oriented toward "the whole." Ironically, in Arnold's story Keatsian "beauties" have lost their pragmatic daring, just as the Elizabethans have been domesticated, and are getting in the way of critical progress. Keats's first critics were silenced theoretically by his style, but exactly because of the experiential consistency with which it made visible cultural prejudice and literary pre-understanding. However, norms which in his poetry become so visible, which have so palpable a design on us, may no longer be able to claim immunity from questioning or, in Hazlitt's terms, maintain the secrecy of their connection with Legitimacy. Keats may be unable to float the idea of a new canon, but he comes much nearer than Arnold does to showing how the canonical might be asked to prove its worth in another court. Terms like "immediacy," "intensity," "proof on the pulses," and "touchstones" all lose their tone of mute abandon when they can be seen to make up the vocabulary of fulfillment, and when their weaknesses can be seen to reflect upon the quality of the experience canonically rendered to us under the imprimatur of fulfillment.

What I hope is more evident now is the paradox by which Keats distanced or disqualified himself from canonical credentials through the very authority of his presentation of these credentials in the form of immediate aesthetic experience. Within one page or so of a letter to Haydon of May 1817, Keats, regarding his own work with some disgust, figures himself as "one that gathers Samphire" while the "Cliff of Poesy Towers above me" (alluding to a famous moment when Shakespearean language substitutes for the impossible scenery and is very much the thing itself) and then dares to conjure Shakespeare as his future presiding genius, thus typically showing himself to have participated in the elevation which puts him down (1:242). When he equivocates comparably in the preface to *Endymion*—"the manner in which this poem has been produced . . . will be quite clear to the reader, who must soon perceive great inexperience, immaturity, and every error denoting a feverish attempt, rather than a deed accomplished"—one of his hostile reviewers, Croker in the *Quarterly,* confesses that "this does not appear to us to be *quite so clear*—we really do not know what he means." John Gibson Lockhart, too, attacks the poem as defying rational commentary. But beneath the sustained gibe of unreadability, the hostile reviews' main trope,[12] lies a serious and understandable bafflement. When Keats's deprecation of his own work suggests it should be read as enjoining or "denoting" a contrary intimacy with and loyalty to the protocols of high art, the politically hostile critic finds his target displaced. To deprecate the work is to take Keats's side, and so *another* reason must be found to account for critical resistance to Keats's presumptuous language of acquaintance.

It is this finesse which generates much of the heat in the early criticism of Keats, denying it the release of direct expression. The shortest way with *Blackwood's* and the *Quarterly* is to say that the overdetermined virulence grows out of this frustration, born in the preface but nourished by the poem. Keats's supposed vulgarity was not a subversive *parody* of high art, precisely because it shared the same founding assumptions of the prevailing idealistic aesthetic. The deflection of criticism of the poem into criticism of the poet's Cockney presumption is what *turns* the poem into a parody; or, it is necessary to see the poem as a parody if the class attack on Keats is to legitimate itself as authentic criticism of his poem. It is this transformation that Levinson so sharply identifies and analyzes. My concern here is with an order of Keatsian critique that required of his critics a foundational shift in order to keep unthinkable the idea that his critique might be nonparodic.[13]

Although Lockhart's own writings of this period, *Peter's Letters to his Kinsfolk,* aspired to Swiftian satire of a sort, he had visited Germany (possibly in the company of the philosopher William Hamilton, later the Sir William Hamilton of Mill's *Examination,* much influenced by Kant) less than a year before his review of *Endymion.*[14] His trip was sponsored by William Blackwood for the purpose of translating Friedrich Schlegel's *Vorlesungen uber die Geschichte der alte und neue Literatur,* the last lecture (lecture 16) of which resumes the German idealist tradition and is full of admiration for Schiller and Fichte. Lockhart's idealist credentials are further supported by his admiration of Wordsworth and Coleridge. In *Peter's Letters,* Lockhart rejects *Blackwood's* caricature of Coleridge's "German" obscurity in *Biographia Literaria,* and he praises that paradigm of romantic irony, "The Idiot Boy."[15] The only way to resist the power of Keats's work to expose the contradictions of the idealist aesthetic (following Kant, the premise that we can grasp fulfillment only as tautology and that any superior ideal has legislative authority only provided it lacks executive authority) was to reveal the political function of those double binds. Of course the function's "cover" lay in the problem of how to reveal a function that did not—could not—operate discursively, but only unconsciously and inarticulately beneath the unquestionable, end-stopped, transcendental valorizations rendered as Keatsian "beauties." This reticence followed from Kant's transcendental principle of judgment, in accordance with which his aesthetic becomes the feeling for how extradiscursive reality is necessarily judged to be contingently organizing itself in discursive support. The implication here that one can therefore dovetail the sublime with the beautiful was seized upon as a prime tactic in counter-Revolutionary aesthetic ideology.[16] However, the resulting, asymptotic congruence between imaginative symbol and conceptual schema sets up the repetitive structure which leaves nothing more to be said. In accordance with the pattern I outlined at the start, to be outside discourse is to be doubly inside it. What Lockhart called the "calm, settled, imperturbable" aspect of *Endymion*'s "drivelling idiocy" froze reviewers in that pose of stymied aggression which they had to transform from theoretical bankruptcy into a new critical paradigm. *Endymion* so consistently enforced the immobility of their traditionally authoritarian stance that they now seem as defenseless to us as Keats must have appeared to them. Their ideological configuration is maintained by a self-censorship which paradoxically inhibits their critical defense. What was required was that their articulate attack on Keats's origins provide grounds for them not to take seriously his qualifications for having produced an immanent critique.

The vituperation Keats suffered had its own logic or pathology, vividly brought to light in Levinson's work. In every diminutive (Jack, Johnny, mankin, etc.) and sexual slur, the reviewers betrayed their insensitivity to an involuntary satire on bourgeois self-sufficiency. Levinson's analysis of that displacement, and of its reconstitution as a legitimate critical focus on the poetry, is an account of what comes of a moment her reading uncovers as having been one of *Zugzwang*, in which any move is the wrong one. In foundational, Kantian terms, Keatsian sensuousness expresses the self-contradictory ideal of living a life constituted by his culture's regulative ideas. This match between felt, Keatsian "excess" and prescriptive, Kantian "impossibility" is the internally disruptive core to Keats's championing of high art. His aspiration to a here-and-now of artistic parity with the canonized poet in fact only exposes his culture's necessarily self-defeating notion of its own goals. To cast this aspiration as vulgar or *arriviste* is a way of isolating it from an endangered idealism. In practice, however, it produces a criticism open to a materialist, sociological analysis which leaves idealism behind. Yet it is the idealist aesthetic that makes sense of Keats's otherwise fatuous "hungering," as Carlyle saw it, "after sweets which he can't get." It is the equation with Kantian aesthetics which most economically explains the words of the *British Critic*'s reviewer of *Endymion*, when he describes how Keats "strikes from unmeaning absurdity into the gross slang of voluptuousness."[17] In the history of attacks on Keats, this repeated juxtaposition of the charges of unintelligibility and sensuous vulgarity now leaves the impression of a tacit pact never to inquire whether either fault might not take its complexion from the other.

Nonsensical Voluptuousness

Croker's difficulties with the opening of *Endymion* arose from his resistance to the poem's invitation that we join in a fiction whereby the flagrantly anecdotal is projected as the essential. We are asked to participate in a parabasis, or stepping aside from the practicable project of amelioration but (no more than in Scott's historiography, as we shall see) without any Schlegelian guarantees of thus closing on an alternative, lateral experience of the better life. Consequently, the full import of an idealist poetry is exposed. "This," runs the fiction, "is what fulfillment is like"—a symbolic adequacy of thought to object, the unproblematic assumption of necessity as one's own freedom, the experience of the random or miscellaneous as a significant catalog, the whole rhetoric of comfort which directs the opening scenes of *Endymion*. Croker, I would suggest, disguises the poverty of this ideal by in effect claiming it has not happened: that it is not there to be observed and so cannot be judged. Keats's poem has, for him, the appearance of having been produced by "an immeasurable game of *bouts-rimés*": this is to say, its equivalences are arbitrary and pat, the random result of auditory associations, risible as a Cockney parody of the heroic couplet and meaningless on the poem's own account. [18] The undoubted difficulties, however, in following the opening of *Endymion* arise from the effort of understanding a further possibility encompassing the qualities which Croker rightly senses, but allotting to them a place within another argument which he would have thought could not be formulated coherently. Since the theme of fulfill-ment is usually thought to exclude critique (critique being properly lim-ited to the policing of the desire whereby fulfillment is to be achieved), the ultimate discontent suggested by a Keatsian critique of fulfillment can only appear to Croker as incompetence, ruled out of court by its suc-cesses. But, as I shall emphasize later, the critique of value is a common feature of contemporary economic discourse. Its bind is inescapable if you want to say something like the following: within romantic aesthetics, fulfillment, which only works as an idea in the normative, prescriptive realm, nonetheless has as its rationale the dissolution of that distinc-tiveness. Fulfillment is when an "ought" becomes an "is," but actually to present it as an "is" may render it so ordinary as to make its previ-ous, legislatory function quite incredible—hence the dissatisfied "Was it for this . . ." which Wordsworth uses all his resources of poetic revision to restore. To preserve that legislative function, the power of aesthetic jurisdiction, it is best to keep fulfillment as the invisible endpoint of desire. It is this contradiction within the realist logic of fulfillment (in Kant's dialectic, "the realism of the aesthetic finality of nature") which is exposed in Croker's and Lockhart's twin accusations of *Endymion*'s unintelligibility and vulgar sensuousness.

The poem's provocative dedication to Chatterton is a guide to the way Keats might have been thinking his way through his own abrasiveness. The dedication invites the reader to remember how Chatterton's youthful fraud is to create a language not natural to him, "the stretched metre of an antique song." This strange and insincere tongue is assimilated to the romantic aesthetic when Chatterton is welcomed, as in Coleridge's "Monody," as "the young-eyed Poesy / All deftly mask'd as hoar Antiquity." In Chatterton's case, the predominant taste *has* found it possible to escape the bind that if he is original, he is not antique; and if he is the genuine thing, he is not original. The parallel escape for Keats, given *Endymion*'s first reviews, would be from the certainty that if he is using a vocabulary of satisfaction, he cannot be critical of it; and if the effect *is* critical, he cannot be in command of his vocabulary.

The doublethink required to escape the Keatsian bind is present at the start of *Endymion,* in its difficult opening transition:

> A thing of beauty is a joy for ever,
> Its loveliness increases; it will never
> Pass into nothingness, but still will keep
> A bower quiet for us, and a sleep
> Full of sweet dreams, and health, and quiet breathing.
> Therefore, on every morrow, are we wreathing
> A flowery band to bind us to the earth,
> Spite of despondence, of the inhuman dearth
> Of noble natures, of the gloomy days,
> Of all the unhealthy and o'erdarken'd ways
> Made for our searching—yes, in spite of all,
> Some shape of beauty moves away the pall
> From our dark spirits.
> (1:1–13)

The pivotal "Therefore on every morrow, are we wreathing" is puzzlingly reflexive. Who is doing the wreathing? Who is the narrator incorporating in the royal "we" wreathing the "thing of beauty"? The poem already appears tied to the task of simulating an image of aesthetic success— a poem about the experience of having read an aesthetically finished poem (good Wordsworthian precedents here). This is the Keatsian logic of catching up on an already poeticized landscape, a wilderness already "dressed" by thought to facilitate the arrival of consciousness.

> And now at once, adventuresome, I send
> My herald thought into a wilderness

> There let its trumpet blow, and quickly dress
> My uncertain path with green, that I may speed
> Easily onward, thorough flowers and weed.
> (1:58–63)

The effect is to continue the earlier sonnets' view of the creation of poetic language as a place of repose—not a characterization of anything but, as in the "Ode to Psyche," the dwelling on apprehension, the treatment of it as a place of arrival, John Jones's "end-stopped feel."[19]

In Kant's aesthetics, this kind of *aisthesis* permits the idea of the world as something that fortuitously coincides with the functioning of our faculties, an experience that dialectically bridges the gap between phenomena and things-in-themselves—"a flowery band to bind us to the earth." *Aisthesis,* or a complete relaxing of the cognitive functions for their sensuous contemplation, pleonastically invokes for Kant, as already suggested, the only legitimate notion of an external world that binds itself together as if to make possible our systematic understanding of it. The rhetorical equivalent of such a guarantee might be parataxis: the random catalog of interchangeable descriptions indifferently standardized. What the paratactic version adds to the idea of getting on equivalent terms with essences is the suggestion that so absolute a guarantee of meaning actually deprives experience of a meaningful (syntactic) order. Nature now falls unnoticeably into place beneath its signs, and the alternative would be equally impossible to demonstrate. Along with this arises the need to repress the suggestion that anyone fobbed off on essentialist terms is being sold short. Cosmology in *Endymion* is inseparable from cosmetics, the "known Unknown" carnally remystified by the poem's romance as "Such darling essence" (2:739–40). The opening passage of *Endymion* continues with a substantial, paratactic passage concluding in the unequivocal ascription of essence to its individual clauses, including the sequence which drove Croker to think of *bouts-rimés:*

> Such the sun, the moon,
> Trees, old and young, sprouting a shady boon
> For simple sheep; and such are daffodils
> With the green world they live in; and clear rills
> That for themselves a cooling covert make
> 'Gainst the hot season; the mid-forest brake,
> And such too is the grandeur of the dooms
> We have imagined for the mighty dead,
> All lovely tales that we have heard or read

> An endless fountain of immortal drink,
> Pouring unto us from the heaven's brink.
>
> Nor do we merely feel these essences
> For one short hour . . .
> (1:13–26)

Pan soon becomes the poem's principle of such a catalog, a physical "leaven" which dodges all conception and so escapes being part of mental "dress," remaining the object of "address" in the shepherds' hymn to him:

> Be still the unimaginable lodge
> For solitary thinkings—such as dodge
> Conception to the very bourne of heaven,
> Then leave the naked brain; be still the leaven,
> That spreading in this dull and clodded earth
> Gives it a touch ethereal, a new birth;
> Be still a symbol of immensity,
> A firmament reflected in a sea,
> An element filling the space between,
> An unknown—but no more!
> (1:293–302)

Pan is the "element filling the space between," the idea of a yeasty consistency behind differences, taken up in the indiscriminate stream of apostrophes to which the bright, essential Cynthia provokes Endymion in book 3 (3:52–102, 163–75), which raises also the idea of a benevolent nature. The paganism which reportedly offended Wordsworth's religious sensibilities seems too a convention under which a realism of fulfillment can be contemplated and its unstable condition examined. Endymion, imagining "happiness" as "A fellowship with essence," is to be "Full alchemized, and free of space" (1:780), a solution that could be entirely ethereal or which might involve his transformation into a material form of infinite extension. The meaning will not settle and remains as oxymoronic as Endymion's dream of an archetypal union with Cynthia—"O unconfined / Restraint! imprisoned liberty!" (1:455–56). To have succeeded in writing a language which raises such equivocations about "that completed form of all completeness . . . that high perfection of all sweetness" (1:606–7) is by implication to have questioned the idea of fulfillment as the adequation of desire and, conversely, of desire as the striving for fulfillment. This conclusion either exposes a use of the aesthetic idea of fulfillment for legislative ends, manipulating people's desires under false pretenses which nevertheless seem inherent in the very logic of desire, and thus safe from criticism, Keats's sense of their falsity expressible only as a kind of nonsense; or else it suggests a willingness to accept the conventionally aberrant and unnatural as imaginative possibilities: following Adorno, we can experience in art the non-identity of things with their labels, an experience that promises the "emancipation" of the aesthetic subject. [20] *Endymion's* hostile critics drew both implications in their charges of nonsensical voluptuousness. Keats's own revision of the "fellowship with essence" passage inspires his most explicit image of a critique of pleasure working through human variables. "My having written that Passage Argument will perhaps be of the greatest Service to me of any thing I ever did—It set before me at once the gradations of Happiness even as a kind of Pleasure Thermometer—and is my first Step towards the chief Attempt in the Drama—the playing of different Natures with Joy and Sorrow."[21]

Kitsch and Capital

So far, the possibilities for Keatsian critique have been largely passive, given shape through the accusations of the first hostile critics of his poems. But the reciprocal, revealing provocation which his writings offer to idealism should now be more visible. *Endymion* is a poem in which Keatsian intensity crowns the narrative far too soon. Endymion finds that he has "raught / The goal of consciousness" early in the second of four books, and the precocious sexual continuation rather than realization of this achievement takes place before the end of book 2. Yet the poem forestalls any straightforward discontent with its apparent structural mismanagement by foregrounding this intensity and overriding other disappointments through its claim to hold in focus a fugitive climax, and so to nudge us beyond the pleasure principle and into a critique of pleasure. The effect is to say: this is the goal of narrative, usually unquestioned, here brought forward for examination. The poem's psychological defense against critical discontent is a phenomenology of the tristitia consequent on pleasure.

Endymion's language of cultural acquaintance, in contrast to the deferential modesty of the published preface, is strikingly ambitious in the possessiveness of its portrayal of "the beautiful mythology of Greece." This presumption takes the form of an intimate inwardness, physical and psychological, by which the empirical reach of Keats's poetic language exceeds its pictorial license, at the same time foregrounding its poeticity.

One thinks of Christopher Ricks's discussion of the "slumbering pout" of *Endymion*'s Adonis or the "limping hare" at the start of "The Eve of St. Agnes." Alternatively, Keats's self-signifying cultivation translates into endless circumscription which never closes on a classical center because such closure is in general epistemologically impossible. Possession is inherently vicarious—Phoebe in place of Cynthia—and poetry is the aesthetic recognition or polemical redemption ("beauty is truth") of that otherwise unhappy fact. Both these versions of Keatsian sensuousness have had their skilful expositors. [22] What they return us to is the notion of a putative endpoint at which we are encouraged to apply what we take to be natural standards of experience to something we cannot have on those terms at all. This is a political as well as an epistemological point, and we have already discussed the politically advantageous self-deception which might be involved. But to expose such a tactic is to impugn the aesthetic collaborator, and in doing so Keatsian critique begins to go on the offensive. On the one hand, *Endymion*'s exaggerations suggest that such satisfaction is an impossible ambition of all art, and one which is, as a rule, decently repressed. On the other, Keats's importunate hyperboles conspicuously disguise the fact that if this view of art had its way, poetry would aspire to the condition of kitsch: an art which meets with no external resistance because it has been purified of all critical difference. This is the moral consequence of the Hegelian reading of the rhetoric of Kantian *aisthesis* quoted at the head of this chapter, a reading to which, Adorno concedes, Kant's formalism makes him vulnerable. The replicatory motives of *aisthesis* are so innocent—so disinterested—that they appear completely complacent in any but the most brazenly self-serving world. For readers who consider themselves cultivated, to meet with the implication that this is what they desire from their reading is highly insulting. It is as if Keats imagines a sudden access of expertise in which the esoteric reflexivity of avant-garde art becomes indistinguishable from the effortless self-evidence of kitsch: caviare for the general at last. [23]

Idealist bourgeois culture legitimates itself by constructing Keats as the *arriviste,* the importunate consumer of what is not for sale. He cannot buy into this culture because it is presented as the system which makes buying possible. This system is analogous to the ubiquitous symbolic order of exchange or credit which, from Simmel through Saussure to Foucault, rationalizes the *paroles* of individual monetary transactions; or to the psychological blueprint which the Kantian tradition deduced and aesthetically savored as the logical prerequisite of every act of determinate judgment or specific cognition. On either of these descriptions, political

interest is disguised as the conditions under which a metaphysic is possible. The specifics of high bourgeois taste pose as an absolute regime—
a universal—and it is the unchallengeable quality of this acculturation
which converges embarrassingly with the self-exonerating logic of kitsch.
One cannot change someone's taste for kitsch by pointing out the easiness or cheapness of the experience on offer, because it is just this facility
of possession which is prized as the distinctive quality of the art.[24] To value
kitsch knowingly, on the other hand, can be to express skepticism about
any alternatives and, also, contempt for the naive belief that more than
an "aura" survives of a sincerely humanist art claiming to escape comparison with kitsch. This is a modernist disingenuousness, reworked in
postmodernism of all kinds from Warhol to Lyotard, which is not at all
Keats's position. The modernist reader of Keats, however, is bound to see
the connection and to find it useful in demonstrating the ways in which
his writing escapes the straightforward recuperations of romantic irony
without simply amounting to the ineptitude and gaucheness attributed
to it by his contemporary critics.

Writing of his suppressed preface to *Endymion,* Keats describes his
"Public" as "a thing I cannot help looking on as an Enemy," and claims
that "if there is any fault in the preface it is not affectation: but an undersong of disrespect to the Public."[25] In this context, the more a poet
risks, not personally but on his own professional behalf, the further he
pushes his readers into a position reflecting the endemic discomfiture of
an audience positioned by an idealist aesthetic. It is hard, after all, to see
how the prefaces, published and unpublished, could be more modest on
their author's part—the true function of a preface according to Keats's
original version. Rather than a labored and straightforward irony, Keats's
persistent wish "to conciliate men who are competent to look, and who
do look with a zealous eye, to the honour of English literature" suggests
that insofar as these critics represent public taste, to allow them to have
their way—genuinely to conciliate them—is insult enough.

The provocation Keats offers to an idealist romantic aesthetic makes
it reveal its ideological basis in the analogy it bears to capital as a whole.
As is the case with Schiller, the universals which are the stuff of aesthetic
legitimacy are symbolic, like Kantian symbols, not just of morality but also
inadvertently of the unquestionable efficacy of the credit on which bourgeois culture subsists. Keats's writing throws in relief the self-defeating
character inflicted on art by this uncritical role. He does not produce
independent critique but uncovers the equivalent of an uncritical moment in the critical philosophy, a disabling contradiction in the mastery

with which art promotes its authoritative humanism. In this way he turns aesthetic success into its opposite and symbolically calls into question the universals of which art is the acceptable expression and legitimating front. The possession of capital is, by analogy, made to seem accidental and disputable rather than the essential, unarguable right of the landed and mercantile classes.

This analogical reading adds to the picture of dominant members of a culture anxiously confronting in Keats's work the precarious importance their culture attributes to art. Art does not serve as something which presents the content of fulfillment, but instead provides the excuse to go on believing in the possibility of utter satisfaction precisely because of the fact that it is never there. To propose, as Keats seems to do, a phenomenology of the ends of art is to reveal precisely that lack by visibly exploiting art as the discourse in which the relation of this discovery leaves us untroubled and reconciled. Art is given credit for what it cannot redeem; and to question this credit—to cause a "run" on art—would be analogous to undermining confidence in the basic fiction by which those in possession of capital possess it by virtue of a universal interest in which all share. The force of Keats's conciliatory critique becomes even more palpable if we consider the contemporary crises of confidence in capital itself, crises whose character offers reinforcement to the aesthetic analogy from the other direction.

This happens especially where controversies over paper money are concerned. In economic debates of the time, value-making was not a Nietzschean overcoming of humanity, but a routine choice between contested options.[26] There is a long tradition in English philosophy and literature of distrust for and ridicule of the gradual ascendancy of paper money over coin, dating from the establishment of the Bank of England in 1694 onward. John Locke had been sure that money was "a Pledge, which Writing cannot supply the place of . . . because a Law cannot give to Bills that intrinsic Value, which the universal Consent of Mankind has annexed to Silver and Gold."[27] The notorious banking adventures of John Law on behalf of the Regent of France between 1716 and 1720 appeared to prove Locke right and gave paper money a bad name and a satirical following, from Daniel Defoe's pamphlet on *The Chimera: or, The French Way of Paying National Debts* . . . (1720) to Thomas Love Peacock's *Paper Money Lyrics*. This last also associated paper money with imaginative activity, moving easily from laughter at the economic theorists of promissory notes to parodies of Southey, Wordsworth, Moore, Coleridge, Scott, and Campbell. Peacock's collection develops the better-known literary skepticism of *The Four Ages of Poetry*. There, the poetic decline is measured in metals—iron, gold, silver, and brass; it would seem reasonable to see no end to Peacock's loss of faith and to construe *Paper Money Lyrics* as imaging the next stage in poetic debasement, "the promiscuous rubbish of the present time to the exclusion of the select treasures of the past."[28] As Peacock's double-edged satire confirms, Law's monetary practices (issuing money to stimulate trade, but causing vast inflation and an unstoppable run on his bank) may have been discredited, but his "superior genius," as Sir James Steuart was to call it, and basic tenets of his theory were not.[29]

The inherent organicism of such theories, according to which the national circulation of money was analogous to the corporeal circulation of the blood, was attractive to would-be philanthropists, motivated primarily by considerations of social rather than fiscal health, as much as to selfish speculators. Both approved of Law's wish that "by this money the people might be employed."[30] George Berkeley, in his *Querist* (1735–37), scandalized by the thought that he might belong to "the only people ["our Irish"] who may be said to starve in the midst of plenty" can find no "vertue in gold or silver, other than as they really set people at work, or create industry."[31] Hume investigated further the benefits of monetary circulation, but his belief that money, "having chiefly a fictitious value, the greater or less plenty of it is of no consequence" is offset by his suspicions "concerning the benefits of *banks* and *paper-credit.*"[32] He might have felt justified in his fears by what happened to the English economy from 1797 to 1819. As Levinson has observed, these years embrace almost the exact duration of Keats's lifetime when, faced with the additional demands of financing the Napoleonic Wars, the government passed a Restriction Act prohibiting the Bank of England from redeeming any of its notes in gold, legislation which held from 1797 until 1819. Even in 1819, only the palliative measure of David Ricardo's Ingot Plan was adopted, and none but relatively large amounts of cash could be redeemed, and then only in bullion, not in coin. Of the 2,028 bars made for this purpose, nicknamed "Ricardoes," only 13 were sold, mainly because the market price fell below the mint price and buyers in the short term lost money. Full convertibility resumed only in 1823. By a striking corroboration, therefore, in Keats's productive years "the realms of gold" would provide the perfect image of the imaginary wealth of literary inheritance, while showing that it would be wiser to stay in credit there, on paper, than to seek a more tangible and realistic standard of value.[33]

Most economic historians seem agreed that it is, after all, very doubtful whether the English economy could have borne the financial burdens imposed by the Napoleonic Wars had it not adopted the device of the Restriction Act and declared Bank of England notes to be legal tender irrespective of the availability of securities. The *Edinburgh Review* opposed Ricardo and the "bullionists" who wanted to limit the domestic money supply and thus facilitate a return to the gold standard. Ricardo took Adam Smith's disapproval of devaluation as precedent, and could have cited Frances Hutcheson in support. [34] In *Queen Mab,* the young Shelley shows himself an out-and-out bullionist. In *The Mask of Anarchy* he continues to attack paper credit as another form of disenfranchisement, straightforwardly opposing its exchange value to workers' labor value.

> Paper coin—that forgery
> Of the title deeds which ye
> Hold to something of the worth
> Of the inheritance of the earth.
> (xlv)

Keats, on the other hand, is a poetic inflationist; one whose work suggests that "the inheritance of the earth" will become more available through the spread of a credit by which, in the inflationary terms of Law, Berkeley, and occasionally Hume, "the people may be employed."[35] Logically, however, Ricardo made it as embarrassing as possible for the antibullionists to defend the expansion of paper credit. In his appendix to *The High Price of Bullion,* he asks his opponent from the *Edinburgh Review:* "is it conceivable that money should be sent abroad for the purpose merely of rendering it dear in this country and cheap in another, and by such means to ensure its return to us?"[36] Clearly it was, and, transposed to the economics of the aesthetic, such pragmatism could be equally sophistical and compromising. Arguably, Keats, in the eyes of *Endymion*'s hostile reviewers, had demonstrated the perversity of Ricardo's logic to the letter. First, he showed that the aesthetic experience of ultimate good depended for its unique value on having been "sent abroad," deferred to some ideal, irredeemably exemplary realm. Secondly, through his "promiscuous" exploration of these aesthetic ends (that is, the hedonistic phenomenology of satisfaction and fulfillment), Keats cheapened them sufficiently to remind readers of their justifiable expectation of enjoying them back in the here and now. Keats's "speculative Mind," as a passage in his letter to George and Georgiana Keats of February–May 1819 shows, carries a Wordsworthian universal, "one human heart," to its shockingly democratic conclusion without fear of debasement "the pity is that we must wonder at it; as we should at finding a pearl in rubbish" (2:80). Not to accept the reality of "speculations," and to lack the courage "to put down his half-seeing," is how Keats's poet "makes a false coinage . . . poetry that has a palpable design upon us—and if we do not agree, seems to put its hand in its breeches pocket." Bad poetry, that is, abandons credit to buy readers off in kind (1:223–24).[37]

In the context of Keats's aesthetic economy, "credit" is less the institutional embodiment of desire through "the perpetual deferral of one's returns" (as David Simpson accurately ascribes it to Wordsworth) than the challenge offered to "value" by a suddenly empowered consumerism.[38] Keats's critical complicity contrasts more sharply yet with Blake's frequent and visionary use of monetary imagery, seen by Kurt Heinzelman to engineer "a momentary triumph over economic discourse."[39] Ricardo's satirical picture, exposing the duplicitous versatility of capital which enabled the economy to survive its greatest crisis, was innocently reflected back to the reviewers less than a decade later by Keats's poetry. Significantly, Croker was later stung to write a pamphlet resuming the history of financial crises from Law onward and claiming the superiority of the Scottish banks over the English banks in maintaining the value of small paper credit.[40] Croker's anxiety sheds further light on the fury aroused by Keats's skewed conformity and harmlessly conciliatory ambitions. The mapping of financial upon aesthetic interests when Ricardo's diagnostic picture is superimposed upon Keats's is unsurprising. As Karl Niebyl has argued, "a theory of money must . . . be an aspect of general economic theory, the latter being itself, or being an aspect of, a dynamic theory of social organization." And Levinson proves that in the "economic allegory" of the Hyperion poems and "Lamia" the "structural contradictoriness of money" reflects "the contradictions in Keats's experience."[41] Theories of money are not static hypotheses but historical explanations whose relativity is visible only in their dependency on other cultural factors. Recent criticism which has usefully explored the common fiduciary and figural logic of financial and aesthetic economies has perhaps insufficiently stressed that it is our inheritance of aspects of a specific, romantic aesthetic and its capitalist affiliations which makes it true that, in Marc Shell's words, "for us the terrible dictum—that nothing will come of nothing—seems to hold true. Except, that is, in the shadowy realms of aesthetics and monetary policy."[42] To understand how Keats's "realms of gold" might, in effect, dispel these shadows is to understand the scandalous fit between his poetry and the contemporary economics of financial survival.

Poetic Redundancy

Keats's immanent critique of the idealist aesthetic is powered by his writing's exposure of the fact that its hedonistic credit is irredeemable and that attempts to redeem aesthetic promise are treated as misunderstandings of the best way to put its fictional wealth to work. The Keatsian example shows that this defense cuts both ways, since the use of art to preserve the idea of transcendental imperatives with categorical claims on our essential nature is now married to a disreputable, inflationary disregard for an economy which thus balances the normative and the natural in opposite columns. Keats's sensuousness and vulgarity dispense with the niceties of idealist bookkeeping and propose phenomenological satisfactions in the speculative field. This is the unacceptable face of an aesthetic which in theory sanctions this proposal, but always under the semblance of economic responsibility. In (Kantian) theory, adventures in the intelligible world can only be recalled in terms which judge without determining a universality bathetically fitting the world of natural appearances; and natural desire is similarly policed by this hypothetical convergence with its regulative ideals. However, to cash the bond by innocently imagining a fulfillment realized threatens the economy's credit by placing under scrutiny the value of its redemption. At best, a cosmetic gloss is spread over its tautologies and parataxes, making them more acceptable but still showing how plenitude can shade into kitsch. To ignore the economy's assumed security of *specie* is, then, to beat it at its own game, enjoying on credit what could never possibly be paid for in kind— kind, that is, as defined according to prescriptions of the natural before the ideal spending-spree began.

Art of this kind is not so much an allegory of reading, as criticism following the work of Paul de Man might see it. By that I mean an allegory reinscribing the disfigurations (exercises in catachresis) by which we supposedly produce the literal. Such art is better cast as an allegory of art. It reinscribes the ideology whereby we agree to accept the impossibility of the literal (the whole, the unconscious, or whatever we choose to call heterogeneity for the moment) provided this loss is told to us in art. We are thus content to get our only glimpse of another possibility in the condescension art shows to us for this purpose. One might see in this model an adaptation of Wordsworth's ingratiating foster mother, "Nature," but shorn of all her metaphysics and knowingly aestheticized— as though tales of that forgotten "imperial palace whence [we] came" could reflect upon her mollifying power to market her compensations with such success as to make indistinguishable from them any wish for something more.

This "reflection" comes nearest to having an independent, critical substance in the staging of the openings of the Hyperion poems, when they are read as a résumé of Keats's immanent critique of the sublime redundancy of Kant's aesthetic, the divine sameness by which it recuperates the aporetic, simultaneously inside and outside its own rhetorical project. *Hyperion* conjures up the availability of a heroic tradition, the enormity of whose immanence has a petrifying effect. The shape of this pressure is initially given through the poem's temporality, or rather its atemporality, in anticipation of that paralyzing *nunc stans* which freezes and monumentalizes the kinetic efforts of its actors and narrators in a series of achieved moments and sculpted poses. The isolation which the opening sentence of *Hyperion* exposes grows more intimate and assured as, again almost in parody of Wordsworth's "Ode," it slips into an inwardness "Far" from the common coordinates of everyday experience— "morn," "noon," "eve." This interiorization does not consequently take on the temporal form of inner sense: there has been no Wordsworthian movement through memory to arrive at this place and so measure its depth. Rather, the vale pictures what it is to obviate all motion, all desire. The landscape apparently described is in fact telescoped into images of its own lack of identifying temporal or spatial perspective. To be "quiet as a stone" is to be so unsurprisingly quiet as to be quiet *simpliciter:* a stone without a dynamic moment or an energizing context because it has absorbed all such as qualities of its own massive equilibrium. The rhetoric of this state is sheer tautology, as in the extended pleonasm with which Thea evokes the Titans' inner life as one of undifferentiated externalization: "O moments big as years! / All as ye pass swell out the monstrous truth, / And press it so upon our weary griefs / That unbelief has not a space to breathe." Truth so protracted can only reiterate its own mass or extension; there is no room for the temporal or spatial progression necessary to Wordsworthian revision. We now realize that what we are "far" from, what we are distanced from, is again distance itself. "Forest on forest hung above his head / Like cloud on cloud" not necessarily because of some fancied visual resemblance between a cumulus of cloud and a formation of trees or hyperbolic foliage vertically stacked, but, more likely, in a proleptic expression of the stillness, "No stir of air," in which clouds could occupy so stationary a pose. In this quality of fixture, it is as if existence has become a predicate, and predicates repeated take on another life. When the "shade" of Saturn's "fallen divinity" deadens the voiceless stream, it deadens it "more," enhancing rather than extinguishing an intrinsic quality; the Naiad's finger was already at her lips for it to be pressed "closer." The undisturbable presence of things is used to impoverish the language which, the poem persuades us, has successfully presented them. The tautologous description that opened the second paragraph—"Along the margin-sand large foot-marks went, / No further than to where his feet had strayed"—is, first, a provocatively unremarkable mapping of the perfect fit of sign and thing, mark and foot. But more than this is the implication of the nugatoriness of epistemological fulfillment and its aesthetic correlatives. Give this language the authority it desires, in which signification is entirely informative and appearance statuesque, and watch it settle into a rhetoric of redundancy. Similarly, an impossibly reflexive ode to the psyche, which already is ("the wreathed trellis of a working brain") the mind it purports to address, tries to euphemize its tautology by becoming an "Ode to Psyche."

The rest of *Hyperion* works on the possibility of something else, something strained for in the early move from pleonasm into the chiasmus describing Thea's expression: "But O! how unlike marble was that face, / How beautiful, if sorrow had not made / Sorrow more beautiful than Beauty's self." Rhetorically flexed in this way, the tautologies of *Hyperion* try to curb their own self-sufficiency and restore a meaningful difference between themselves and their object, impossibly revealing themselves "frail / To that large utterance of the early Gods." Yet the outcome, tragically, falls once more into repetition, and in *The Fall of Hyperion* the further internalization of action within Moneta's brain can only resume the same old Titanic story, the start of *Hyperion*. However, the cul-de-sac is already sketched in the openings of both poems, in the show of a criticism trapped within the ironic elaboration of what it cannot distance, possessing a conscious but unforthcoming insincerity. This dilemma is developed by Saturn's apparent recourse to another, perhaps only closer, language, the "mother tongue" taken up in the opening of *The Fall*. With hindsight, the reader can take Saturn "listening to the Earth, / His ancient mother, for some comfort yet" as listening for a story different from that of the "high tragedy," in which the poet of *The Fall* has to be initiated and which has brought him to this low and deep realization of its archetype. The Hyperion poems can easily appear to blend into the common currency of romantic irony; but, closely read, the poems expose irony's impoverished fulfillment and incorrigible reflexivity. They begin to negotiate the surrender of such self-identity for something less assured, something not inevitably recuperable through the ironies of poetic self-criticism. By the opening of *The Fall,* the "mother tongue" has become the democratic franchise of "every man whose soul is not a clod," in explicit contrast to elitist, a priori prescriptions of who can and cannot be a poet. Fanatic, savage, and poet differ only in powers of articulation, and the resources of articulateness lie in the *mamaloshen.* The only content ascribed to the poet's "dreams" and "visions" comes from the utopian impulse of others, of fanatics who "weave / A paradise for a sect" or the savage who "Guesses at Heaven." Poetry has no content of its own, hence its inability to legislate on its own account and its deference to posterity for its definition. Poetry is nothing but the name given to the effective expression of something better than there is by those who have been educated ("nurtured") in their native language. The narrator's concession at the end of the paragraph—"Whether the dream now purposed to rehearse / Be Poet's or Fanatic's will be known / When this warm scribe my hand is in the grave"—is a paradox which appears covertly to reinforce the nothingness attributed to poetry by the logic of the argument so far. In other words, whatever happens, "the dream now purposed to rehearse" is in language, and any subsequent sobriquet of "poetry" can only appear honorific or supernumerary. Abandoning the whole Hyperion project, Keats writes that it is "English," not an "artful" poetry, which "ought to be kept up."[43]

To read the opening of *The Fall* in this way seems to go against the grain of Keats's poetic ambitions, ambitions caught in that final dedication to posterity, however vulnerable. But again it is worth emphasizing that even this bid for retrospective legislation masks or euphemizes a present lack. The effacement of distance, spatial and temporal, which produces the redundancies of the opening of *Hyperion* is here reproduced within another, more Hegelian conundrum. If the poem will be recognizable as poetry only by a later age, it is not poetry now; yet a concession which can only be formulated in the future is one impossible to write in the poem's present, a concession impossible to have conceded. The narrator is trying to cover up his really disturbing surrender of poetic authority to the "mother tongue" with an artificial crisis. Seeing through this artifice suggests that poetry and articulateness are the same thing after all; "English" is the English of Chatterton (2:167, 212); to question the poetry in one's writing produces a specific kind of poem rather than another form of writing. It is like writing an ode ("Ode on Indolence") in which poetry is one of the options that the poem's "nothingness" circumscribes, as opposed to writing in an explicitly low or rebellious idiom. Keats's isolated attempt in that vein is "the Spirit of Outlawry" of the Robin Hood lyrics, a sally quickly contained again within the literary nostalgia of "Lines on the Mermaid Tavern." The Mermaid Tavern's common table comfortably hosts Robin's prebourgeois idyll of emancipation ("Since men knew not rent nor leases") within an Elizabethan literariness—an imagined unobtrusiveness allowing poetry to startle "not with itself but with its subject," while remaining uneffaced by its success (2:224). There is enough in this and in the opening of *The Fall* to show both that poetry is potentially at hazard and that characteristic of this kind of poetry is perpetually to simulate such crises on its own terms, so that it may have a stake in their plausibility. Keats dramatizes in this way the impossibility of his own parabasis and the gains and losses of a historical appreciation which will be able to see the poetry, but only at the cost of being able to take the aesthetic crisis seriously.

Keats is the poet of dissenting culture described by most recent champions of his political genealogy and subtle readers of his robust application of literary tradition to his cultural station. He shares in the "cult of the south" which Marilyn Butler linked to republican memory. Echoes of neoclassical iconography reminiscent of the French Revolution, emphasized by Roe, indeed evoke a dimension of his odes overlooked by reviews of his purely painterly, canonical sources such as Ian Jack's. Jeffrey Cox is right to stress the radical coterie quality of the Hunt circle, reminiscent of the social support we saw validating Godwin's anarchism in chapter 4 above, coexisting with Hunt's exquisite coziness and Della Cruscan sensibility. But the incomplete yet binding sequences of the Hyperion poems qualify the redemptive quality of their sensuous appropriation of classical orthodoxy and its establishment exclusiveness. To say that "first in beauty shall be first in might" is not to exonerate the aesthetic from hegemonic power politics. Keats's scenario in *Hyperion* reiterates his friend Hazlitt's attack on poetry's political complicity in his lecture on *Coriolanus*. But Keats's attack is more *obviously* a "scenario." He significantly incriminates aesthetic autonomy in the speech of a deposed Titan, someone superseded. Our sympathy for the Titans, though, as beauty and power disappear over their horizon, gives us no grounds for thinking that beauty might be detached from power. On the contrary, the frozenness of the Titans shows the hopelessness of trying to police the aesthetic franchise at all. If Keats's sensuousness points the way forward here, or sideways (off course for an ideal vanishing point and already with that postponed enjoyment), then it does so at the cost of the aesthetic distinction he clearly desired. Hence, *The Fall of Hyperion* makes a drama out of that too.[44]

We cannot take idealism at its own estimation of itself, and so we fail to be limited by and thus true to the constraints of Keats's aesthetic. We see the manner in which his critique and its self-censorship are bound together. We see too what Keats could not when his conspicuously euphemistic and cosmetic style negates his writing's ostensible ideological conformity. By then, however, his aesthetic credit is exhausted. We have to move on to another critical standard. In socially genetic terms, the Hyperion poems situate Keats closest to a class whose radical moment has passed with the French Revolution and whose effaced sign of a former radical interest is the commercial credit it enjoys as a result of the same economic shifts more peacefully achieved in England. As critique, Keats's poetry portrays the ersatz establishment thus created "To the most hateful seeing of itself." But, above all, what is peculiar about such inauthenticity is the inscribed suggestion that there is no alternative; and the tragic strength of the Hyperion poems is their euphemistic betrayal of the historical fact that, within their aesthetic, criticism and creation, disownment and renewal, abandonment and progress have to take place in the same words, through the same effects, powered by the same talents, clenched in the same narratives.

FIVE

Waverley: Scott's Romantic Narrative and Revolutionary Historiography

The Failure of Irony

More than most romantic novels, Scott's inaugural *Waverley* places itself within the contemporary scene of writing, reviewing its own possibilities quite openly—Gothic tale, Germanic romance, sentimental or fashionable upper-class yarn—and self-consciously pondering the problem of recovering a universal subject matter in front of a modern audience sensitive to contemporary generic options. Like Friedrich Schlegel, Scott characterizes his audience as "this critical generation."[1] Like Wordsworth, he wishes to restore an understanding of "the human heart" through a historically colored reading of "the great book of nature, the same through a thousand editions."[2] Cervantes and Calderon, favorites of the romantic ironists, provide him with a background of larger, fashionable models of novelistic understanding. During his Jacobite experiences, Edward Waverley frequently feels that *la vida es sueño,* a dream from which he awakes like Coleridge's Wedding Guest, "A sadder and a wiser man" (170, 296). But if its allusions to contemporary literary expectations suggest Schlegel's ironic reflexivity, does *Waverley* also share Schlegel's agenda for deploying this ironic understanding as the one best suited to representing an age whose most tendentious political event was the French Revolution? In his *Life of Napoleon Buonaparte,* Scott describes the French Revolution as "peremptorily necessary and inevitable" insofar as it recovered rights and liberties alienated during the breakdown of feudalism.[3] Here, Lukács could have found ample justification for reading into Scott's novels "necessary anachronisms" for exhibiting "the prehistory of the present."[4] Despite the Schlegelian ironies, though, Lukács wishes us to transpose from Schlegel to Goethe and Hegel. We must move into the orbit of a typifying model of historicism distanced from the immediate realities of the French Revolution, either as French experience or as English spectacle. To tie Scott's patriotism, for example, more closely to what might be his contemporary class interests is, Lukács famously claims, to pander to "vulgar sociologists"; it is to lose the wider perspective of *The Historical Novel,* in which Scott is the novelist of revolutionary crises in general, and so to lose, also, the novelist of "human capacities" definitively displayed for Lukács in such upheavals (53). In Katie Trumpener's words, "there are high stakes in displacing *Waverley* as a singular yet symptomatic event, to recover alternative forms of historical explanation that emanate from the same historical moment."[5] My treatment of *Waverley* here is still "singular and symptomatic," but in my reading into the novel of historiographical crisis, I hope to show that it registers just those forms of historical explanation it cannot control.

I want, therefore, to examine the self-critical or metaromantic perspective produced within Scott's romantic discourse. Commentary on Scott's *Waverley* has necessarily, given the novel's foregrounding of the generic questions just recounted, had to consider Scott's treatment of romance. Until fairly recently, the general tenor of interpretation has been to suggest that Scott's treatment of romance is ambivalent. While critical of Edward Waverley's romantic, jejune notions, Scott's narrative transforms them into a mature recognition that romance can best express the historical distance of a heritage or cultural ideal still esteemed valuable and potentially regulative.[6] How plausible, though, is this transformation? Could the novel—could, in fact, its aesthetic status rather than a particular genre—entertain the implausibility of fiction as a historiographical resource? We have, as David Kaufmann points out, to avoid dismissing Scott's use of the aesthetic and fantastic "as mere displacements, as diversions from the *real* thing." Otherwise, why bother reading the novels? But what if the real *is* displacement, and *Waverley*'s substitution of Jacobite for Jacobin the thing itself? Then, perhaps, we need a guiding formulation more like Ian Duncan's shrewd conclusion that Scott's "troublesome" achievement is to show that "the powerful pleasures and important truths offered by fiction are precisely those of its inauthenticity."[7]

Lukács appears, then, to return to Scott's concept of "the human heart," announced at the start of *Waverley,* as the ideal text from which the novel will translate. In effect he recovers Coleridge's praise for Scott's depiction of "the two great moving principles of social humanity"; his romantic reader keys into a universal humanism that overcomes any dialectic of historical difference. Lost in this submission to Scott's romantic ideology is any sense of Scott's, or Lukács's, relativism. The local tactics of Lukács's Hegelian period, with its dramatic appropriation of high art to its side of the argument, no doubt explain his comparatively uncritical identifications. Sacrificed, though, is a feeling for the way in which Scott's romantic reach for the universal might be specific to his own historical moment of self-understanding and, less obviously, to the way in which such universalism masks his own local incoherencies in managing the representations of revolution. If we return to Schlegel as the intended ironic reader of Scott's dilemma, we can certainly recuperate Scott's historicism. For the romantic ironist, crises in representation are the means by which what fails to be represented is alternatively evoked. Recently, though, the poststructuralist critiques of this self-righting romantic ideology have aggressively questioned the nature of such alternative figuration: to find, instead of an allegory of revolution, an allegory of reading. In such crises we are made aware not of the difference between writing and something outside writing, but between one form of writing and another; the critical moment simply raises our consciousness of the versatility or generic vocabulary required of the reader. In other words, failure in representation turns out to be a kind of writing and nothing more. The ironists are neither failing more authentically than this nor describing a new mimesis of the recalcitrant event; they are merely switching literary kinds or genres. This deconstructive formulation is an anachronism beyond even Scott's powers. In *Waverley*, however, it is through an incipient critique of romantic irony that the text's historicism produces its own moment.

James Hogg, mascot and butt of Scott and the young *Blackwood's* Tories, claims in his justifiably class-conscious *Familiar Anecdotes of Sir Walter Scott* that Scott "had a settled impression in his mind that a revolution was impending over this country even worse than that we have experienced."[8] This "dread of revolution," if Hogg was right, localizes Scott's Lukácsian interest in discovering an explanatory revolutionary pattern in history. Now this concern looks like his displacement of an analysis he feared to apply to the present. However, the nervousness may not arise from Scott's belief that the Revolutionary analysis *did* presently apply, but from some underlying sense that his compulsion to apply it figured all too accurately a hiatus in his historical understanding. For example, his journal entries for October 1831 record his quite fantastic fears that the Fitz Clarences might be proclaimed heirs by a royalist party opposed to reform, unfolding a plot which "would be Paris all over." This conspiracy would be foiled only if the Duke of Wellington absconded to the Highlands with the young Princess Victoria and raised the loyal standard there. [9] As a Tory argument against reform, this beats most, and defeats ironic redemption in any genre I know. In my reading, the novels do confirm Hogg's private view; they contradict Scott's airy public remarks on contemporary political agitation and reproduce an incoherence which could have provoked the anxious consignment of his Revolutionary analysis to the past.

Waverley enjoys a kind of writing in which the narrative of revolution figures the intrusion of an otherness beyond recuperation: by that I mean a subject matter which remains unassimilable to the aesthetic forms of organization supposed to make sense of it. To the extent to which it might be said to "know" its weaknesses, it can also be said to be metaromantic, or manipulative of them. What I have in mind works mostly in the following way. *Waverley* is ostensibly critical of romanticism, the romanticism of its young hero, Edward Waverley, and of the Jacobite cause constitutionally attractive to someone of this disposition. Yet romanticism turns out to be the very stuff of the Jacobite rebellion, the deep truth for which the narrative must find an image. The narrator disingenuously tells us that "it is not our purpose to intrude upon the province of history" (263), a sleight of hand unmasked when he also tells us, after Waverley's Jacobite adventure, "that the romance of his life was ended, and that its real history had now commenced" (283). The real history of the Jacobites presented here *is* one of misplaced romance: chivalric, visionary, and imaginary—the "great game" (274) of Charles Edward Stuart and the feminine genius of Flora Mac-Ivor. Waverley hovers or "wavers" between alternatives, enjoying a well-endowed "indolence" (in the Baron Bradwardine's Latin gloss on Tory leisure; 57) as richly indeterminate as that of any romantic ironist. The chief of the Mac-Ivors, Fergus, also describes his class as living a life of irony under legislation which allows the Highlander "a sword which he must not draw, a bard to sing of deeds which he dare not imitate,—and a large goat-skin purse without a louis-d'or to put into it" (103). The clans, simmering on the edge of rebellion, frequently demonstrate to Waverley and the reader their own self-government, a legislation unacknowledged by the Hanoverians, but about to be put into visionary practice in 1745 under the romantic Young Pretender, Charles Edward Stuart. It is a romantic discourse which turns the Jacobite entitlement *de jure*, as Waverley's uncle Sir Everard saw it, into one *de facto*, thus pretending to create a political solution in typical romantic fashion by finding a necessity for it in the realm of ideas (25).

The romantic discourse of Scott's novels, then, is perhaps not imaginative simply because the pastness of its subject matter obliges it to be so. Imagination may be more partisan than that. The novels' consciously imaginative reconstructions, even in the most painterly of the set-pieces, are never innocent, always uncanny. Retrospectively they turn out to have been part of a plot. The naive spectator of Fergus Mac-Ivor displaying his troops or of a Highland deer-hunt is always implicated and potentially incriminated by an ulterior purpose. Display turns out to have been military maneuver, the hunt a clandestine mustering of the clan chiefs. Hospitality in a reiver's cave, described with a deceptive drop from the romantic picturesque of Salvator Rosa to a realistic register, later transpires to have been Edward's cunningly wrought undoing by Donald Bean Lean. With Gothic regularity, the ordinary and familiar prove to have contained another meaning. But, more than this, the imaginary character of reconstruction has had a part to play in the novel's historical recall, both interpreting the events so described and historicizing that interpretation. The narrator claims, "I have embodied in imaginary scenes, and ascribed to fictitious characters, a part of the incidents which I then received from those who were actors in them. Indeed, the most romantic parts of this narrative are precisely those which have a foundation in fact" (340). But this attempt to lock romanticism in the archive, and to restrict its sense of history as play or drama to "Sixty Years Since," produces its own uncanny when it resurfaces as Scott's description of revolution in his own time. Scott seems to follow Lord Kames and a host of Scottish Enlightenment theorists when he describes the literary as "that internal sorcery by which past or imaginary events are presented in action, as it were, to the eye of the muser" (17). But the Enlightenment deals in a universal, animal psychology contrasting with Scott's highly topical institutional sensitivity to the adequacy of any mode of representation to epochal change. Scott discovers, I would suggest his formulation here implies, that the literary impugns the object with which it intends to legitimate its imaginative authority. Critical breakdown in the intentional structure of the romantic image is already there to be elicited in *Waverley*.[10]

One of the more persuasive emphases of recent criticism of romanticism has been to improve our understanding of the extent to which its matrix concept, "romance," was especially unstable in Scott's time, peculiarly fraught with a burden of self-criticism arising from its conspicuous literariness. In the reviews, Scott's problematic conjunction of romance and history was frequently discussed, but in terms of his tailoring of their respective proprieties to a new kind of writing: once more, that is, in terms of irony, of recuperation of referential failure within another genre, of the intentional structure of the romantic image. Hazlitt was unusual in anticipating the critical effort perhaps most helpful today. He too steps outside the economy of irony to recover political meanings effaced by irony's exculpation of historical failure: "Through some odd process of *servile* logic, it should seem, that in restoring the claims of the Stuarts by the courtesy of romance, the house of Brunswick are more firmly seated in point of fact, and the Bourbons, by collateral reasoning, become legitimate! In any other point of view, we cannot conceive how Sir Walter imagines 'he has done something to revive the declining spirit of loyalty' by these novels. His loyalty is founded on *would-be* treason: he props the actual throne by the shadow of rebellion."[11] There are no allegories of reading, no saving generic innovations countenanced here. Hazlitt attributes a crudely Legitimist motive to Scott's contrariness. He does not, however, raise the question of whether or not the servility of Scott's logic could indicate a crisis in historiography rather than merely Scott's own tendentious evasion of historiographical responsibility. Yet we can, surely, share Hazlitt's sense of something gone irrecoverably wrong here without having to believe that a shift to Hazlitt's own contradictory stance—Napoleonic radicalism—would restore the authority of historical description. How might *Waverley*'s ostensible critique of romanticism generate a positive representation of history? In *Waverley*, the generous ironies of Wordsworthian idleness or Keatsian indolence register a local class inflection. The "dignified indolence" of Edward's Tory uncle, Sir Everard, goes with his "narrative old age," an undemocratic preservation of the past in a medium "the very reverse of amber, which, itself a valuable substance, usually includes flies, straws and other trifles" (9, 15). Edward's romantic lucubrations clearly share a sublimating mechanism with Sir Everard's selective historical understanding. Both, although suspected as the etherialization of history by imagination, are sure signs of a landed leisure grown precious under the pressure of the times. "A lettered indolence," Flora Mac-Ivor contemptuously calls Waverley's elegant background, temporarily forgetful of the leisured situation forced on her as a woman but necessary for her own cultivation of the culture of the Gael. Flora is impatient with a poetry which does not appear to be practically and politically imperative, simultaneously conjuring rebellion and nationhood. Of course what seems to her a poetry of velleity is—from the novel's perspective "Sixty Years Since"—precisely the reality of her Jacobite allegiance. Eventually she can experience this realism only as tragedy. Contemplating her brother's impending execution, she discovers that a fanciful truth has ceased to represent cultural self-fashioning; it has separated out once more into its originally incompatible categories: "I do not regret his [Fergus Mac-Ivor's] attempt because it was wrong . . . but because it was impossible it could end otherwise than thus" (323). Because, that is, it was an impossible attempt; because while claims *de jure* are frequently adduced post facto, (the rationalization of all faits accomplis), a moral entitlement is not necessarily a legitimate deduction de facto, as the most skeptical Scottish Hanoverian Tory of them all, David Hume, had argued in a publication of 1739, largely ignored at the time.

In *Waverley*, then, literature seems inherently romantic, and is so in the reading-experience of any of the characters. Literature's visionary and imaginary allegiances are what make it expert in delineation of the 1745 rebellion. This happens through a double movement which enhances literature's historical mimesis by restoring it, within the same realist account, to its own status of what can never be. Yet within this ironic delineation of romantic action, critical of Jacobite characters through its realistic application to them, lie the seeds of a further critique. To view irony as a successful alternative to representation, as a kind of "higher" realism, effaces another kind of contemporary history whose literariness records its failure, not its enrichment—a history which inculcates in us the skeptical sense of being determined to view things in such a way that a deceptive fictional coherence occurs. Again, it is helpful to recall Hume's static epistemological skepticism, in contrast to the dynamic skepticism of Schlegelian irony. Consistent with *Waverley*'s Burkean grasp of the history of revolution is its relinquishing of Kant's supposed advance on Humean philosophy: it reverts from the logical necessity of believing in valid representation to Hume's strictly psychological explanation of why we do so.

Philosophically considered, Hume's external world is experienced only as psychological necessity; a compulsion from whose potential uncanny we have to be rescued by the ordinariness of convivial company and billiards. Furthermore, denied the power to represent, Hume's epistemology does not even *figure* an external world but is a figure *of* that figurative alternative to representation. Its success is in giving an image of what it might be like to liken one thing to another from among an actually unconnected stream of impressions. We are thus placed at as uncanny a remove from our figurations as from our representations. In fact, for Hume, the world-building resemblances we are compelled psychologically to imagine between impressions are themselves internal impressions, and so, by a disabling reversal, add to the numbers from which they are meant to abstract.[12]

Waverley's aestheticization of the Jacobite rebellion connects this philosophical defeatism with a Burkean history by defaillance. This history was epitomized for Scott's generation by Burke's valorization—feminized, victimized, Gothic—of the fleeing Marie Antoinette as the bearer of real historical significance, figured as compulsion, rather than active pursuit. The implication is that change or history can sometimes be grasped only in a kind of understanding which abandons claims to mastery, even the mastery residing in an ironic superiority to ironic failure. History, for once, is the story of the defeated, not the victors. Otherness, then, is not the outer edges of what we must know, but the alienation of what we do know without any ironic compensation. The Schlegelian tactic of conceding that our representations are incomplete and fanciful may itself be the fiction by which is masked Hume's and Burke's deeper truth—the utter incommensurability of contemporary events and their history—but a deeper truth growing out of their unwillingness to concede the need to deploy another form of discursive understanding altogether, that critical extension of the original we have seen Schlegel welcome. Radical condemnation of Burkean rhetoric repeated Paine's attack on its "chivalric nonsense." But Burke's heroine remains a target for Hazlitt, perhaps because he realizes that Radicals had to press home their attack to counter the historicist irony otherwise available to Tories: the claim that the capitulation of Burkean history to rhetoric bypasses representational failure to figure successfully the adverse effect of the Revolution in alternative form. But Scott's novel suggests that Burke's pessimism went deeper than this, equating the imaginary mode his history was obliged to use with its own loss of authority. Arguably it is this tougher skepticism which is felt so sharply, for example, by Wordsworth at the end of the 1799 *Prelude* (repeated in book 2 of the 1805 version), when he follows Coleridge's advice to make recuperation of the visionary mode the poem's aim.[13]

The Historiographical Crisis

Writing in this vein is very different, I am arguing, from the optimism of an ironic discourse which, like Friedrich Schlegel's, was complicit with Revolutionary enthusiasm. However, the imbroglio of Revolutionary and romantic ideology can only be teased out strand by strand. Universal progressive poetry was not to be the method of those whose attempts at authoritative Revolutionary narrative were feminized as fanciful surrenders of mastery. Their figurings of determination by an otherness beyond textual recuperation returned the obliquest of ironies to the role of failed representation. A premise of this kind of historical discourse is that not only were genetic explanations or teleologies superficially similar to Scott's, like Hegel's, curtailed from the start; Schlegel's ostensibly more flexible irony was comparably deluded; or, delusion rather than provisionality was its prime significance. Schlegel's encouraging prospect of successive plenitudes made visible through a series of ironic disclaimers, a continually restructured consensus, gives way to Revolutionary divisions.[14] Scott's narrative lacunae never grow (no more than does Keats's sensuousness) into Schlegel's alternative to linear progress: that productive parabasis, that stepping aside from onward narrative into an infinitely ramifying historical complex graspable now. Such modulations record changes in an ideology of progress. For Lukács, Scott was, above all, progressive. The contradictions of his allegiance to progress released him from selfish class-interest and gave his writing truly historical range, allowing it to be necessarily anachronistic in its prophecies of the present without ever becoming a narrowly partisan success story. More specifically, one might say that this is what characterizes Scott's historical narrative as Tory and distinguishes it from a Whig interpretation of history.

My point, contra Lukács, is that Scott's Tory freedom from Enlightenment logic and its romantic teleological successors is won at the cost of any philosophical control at all: his writing is disciplined simply as the description of that breakdown. His otherwise "*servile* logic" discredits rather than connives at its own romance. Schlegel's irony is ultimately ethical and political, its exposure of the limitations of any single viewpoint the simultaneous establishment of a community of viewpoints, its paradoxes evocative of a wider intersubjective experience developing the common sense constructed in Kant's aesthetic judgment. Tory historical narrative of the Revolution abandons this tendentiousness and, like our own contemporary revisionists, refuses to see the Revolution as the logical prosecution of a preexistent bourgeois class interest.[15] The interest and the class may have been there, but the revolution itself was a reactionary thing, *sui generis,* the spectacle of whose own momentum politicized the participants rather than vice versa. As William Doyle puts it baldly: "The principles of 1789 . . . cannot be identified with any one of the prerevolutionary social groups." He draws the only conclusion: " . . . the French Revolution had not been made by revolutionaries. It would be truer to say that the revolutionaries had been created by the Revolution."[16] If this is true, or if a writer thinks so, narrative of a Lukácsian kind has had to give way to another: one which will forgo the bold explanatory schemes it may appear to adopt for the rootless imaginings in which its failed authority lies.

Similarly, the changed emphasis of revisionist historians, attributing original Revolutionary agency to the ill-fated liberal nobility rather than the bourgeoisie, intensifies the picture of a rebellion so self-defeating as to render the notion of "agency" make-believe or imaginary. Revisionist stress on the reactionary and economically disastrous outcome of revolutionary initiatives does the same for historical causality. Simon Schama goes beyond Doyle to give more flamboyant shape to the thesis that the Revolution somehow abstracted itself from historical narrative to cast its own actors and tell its own story. The Revolution thus determined the political composition of its participants rather than vice versa, rather in the way that public spectacle and art of the late eighteenth century could realize its audiences independently of inherited social decorum (Schama, 124–25, 133, 181–82). François Furet had already written that the Revolution "marks the beginning of a theatre in which language freed from all constraints seeks and finds a public characterized by its volatility." Indeed, the possibility that poetic spectacle might be a more appropriate genre for the historian of the French Revolution than sober chronology is a live issue for Carlyle and his reviewer, John Stuart Mill, as early as 1837.[17]

Unlike some other revisionists, and unlike Scott, Schama does not feel his authority as historian to be in conflict with his perception of the power of rhetoric and imagination to generate their own occasions. One can, as does Schama, imply method in the new formations by calling them "the cultural construction of a citizen"; but then his (postmodern?) point is that something "volatile" has taken over which allows "revolutionary utterance," as he calls it, to escape from the determining "discourse" required by grand narratives of historiography, instead producing history by gossip and anecdote. Illuminating arbitrariness is thus the essence of Schama's truthful "chronicle" (xiv–xv). Only if one was, like Scott, committed historiographically to some kind of progressive teleology, genetic or structuralist, would this concession appear embarrassing. Yet the alternative implied by Scott's writing is to take Revolutionary gossip as the norm, consequently to view history as something not in possession of its own explanations, and reflexively to describe this dilemma through the delusions of its actors and audiences to the contrary. As historians, Scott and Schama agree about a number of things, such as the Revolution's reaction against the modern, and the politicization of the financial crisis of the *ancien régime* rather than the crisis itself being of prime significance (Scott, 1:213–14, 105; Schama, 47, 62). They differ where Scott (as I will elaborate in more detail) shows this crisis in historiography to be not redemptively historicist—so that the failure of historical grand narrative ironically becomes historically informative—but the Revolution's rebuff to historical understanding. From this perspective, then, Lukács's patient recorder of gradual change and explicator of the long revolutionary march from feudalism to capitalism is ultimately disabled by a contemporary historical picture. The narrator of *Waverley* insists that the reader is "introduced to the character rather by narrative, than by the duller medium of direct description" (331). But my reading finds Scott's narrative art to be descriptive, its progressiveness frozen in skepticism, and its historicism in the character of its own times. After all, the passage in which this privileging of "narrative" over "description" occurs itself likens narrative to "the progress of a stone rolled down hill by an idle truant boy." In his "Preliminary View of the French Revolution," with which he begins his *Life of Napoleon,* Scott ascribes the same momentum to the Revolution, without the initiating figure of the romantic idler. The *Parlements'* refusal to levy the King's new taxes "was the first direct and immediate movement of that mighty Revolution, which afterwards rushed to its crisis like a rock falling down a mountain" (1:105).[18] Nevertheless, the implied author of the "Preliminary View," the British spectator of the French Revolution and plotter of its narrative, cannot but appear as an idler by comparison with the active participants; and Scott concedes that after Burke's *Reflections* "the progress of the French Revolution seemed in England like a play presented on the stage" (1:280–81). Again, the historical narrative requires a saving "higher" realism, both to compensate for its own concessions to the volatile nature of its subject and to answer Radical criticism, from Paine to Hazlitt, of the histrionics of its Burkean rhetoric. But once more, as we shall see, there is a way of reading *Waverley* which critiques the saving ironies of historicism.

"In the Hands of a Woman"

One can work toward a fuller sense of Scott's Revolutionary "play" through the character of the main heroine of *Waverley,* Flora Mac-Ivor. Initially, Flora seems sidelined by the interest in the clan chief, her brother Fergus. In good Scottish Enlightenment fashion, *Waverley* concentrates primarily on the genealogy and anthropology of feudal patriarchy, but silently maps Tory historiography of the French Revolution onto its novelistic account of the Jacobite rebellion, with all the conundrums for the former genetic historical explanation which this latter displacement entails. For Flora constantly outdoes her brother on his own terms, romanticizing and dematerializing his authority in a movement which first seems to contribute to and then to displace Fergus's framing of the novel's historical interpretation. "Her love of her clan, an attachment which was almost hereditary in her bosom, was, like her loyalty, a more pure passion than that of her brother. He was too much a politician, regarded his patriarchal influence too much as the means of accomplishing his own aggrandisement, that we should term him the model of a Highland chieftain" (101). Throughout the novel, Flora increasingly "models" the Jacobite interest, a role for which in Hanoverian times she is paradoxically fitted by her female lack of hereditary entitlement. She cannot escape the character of "romantic imagination" (101), fascinating to Waverley, a character whose political representativeness is enhanced by the novel the more impossibly she identifies with Jacobite patriarchy.

Her refusal to marry Edward stems from an excessive romanticism. Fergus laughs at the theatricality (109) which Maria Edgeworth thought a fault in Scott's characterization of Flora: "she should be far above all stage effect or novelistic trick."[19] But unrealistic presentation is the clue to her seriousness. Fergus dismisses her coyness with Edward as foolishness "in what regards the business of life" (132); but for Flora "the business" is political, not domestic, and her foolishness is his, distilled to its essence. She is "a triumphant spectator" of early Jacobite successes in a novel where, as already suggested, the spectator is always retrospectively implicated in the action. She finally tries explicitly to assume responsibility as a historical agent on the eve of Fergus's execution. She describes her idealism as gaining a practical application, but then immediately discredits it: "there is a busy devil at my heart, that whispers—but it were madness to listen to it—that the strength of mind in which Flora prided herself has—murdered her brother" (322).

There is certainly a potential irony or higher realism here, in which Flora's paradox figures without representing the political inefficacy of the Jacobites. But justice has also to be done to Flora as the historical agent contemporarily figured as a disempowered woman whose action can only be experienced in the uncanny reversal of her idealism. To appreciate this timeliness more sharply, and with it the significant abdication implied by Scott's use of Flora as a kind of model of revolutions without a model, it is helpful to look further at the figure of the woman in some of the Revolutionary discourses of Scott's time, both pro- and anti-. The common feature is the denial of political efficacy to women in the face of apparently incontrovertible evidence.

The obvious example to pick is the march on Versailles of 6 and 8 October 1789. Most accounts of the October days describe how a large body of Parisian working women marched to the Hotel de Ville and from there to the Palace of Versailles, principally to demand that the King safeguard the supply of bread to Paris. Almost immediately, though, in both favorable and hostile accounts, the agency of the women is discredited. In the pejorative descriptions, a rhetoric in which Scott's "Preliminary View" participates, the women are either depicted as monsters—"half unsexed by the masculine nature of their employments, and entirely so by the ferocity of their manners" (1:185)—through familiar abuse ascribing to them the supposedly male violence of furies, bacchantes, amazons, and so on. Or else they are prostitutes whose loose character not only makes them inherently untrustworthy, but lends credence to the idea that they were the easily bought instruments of others, not autonomous actors but suborned by the Duc d'Orleans. The most blatant detractions from the women's initiative come from accusations that many men disguised as women were the really effective *agents provocateurs* in their ranks. The murder of some of the National Guard at Versailles, before Lafayette came to the rescue, could then be safely ascribed by both conservative and radical writers either to men, or to women whose unnaturalness or hire by men effaced sexual difference.

The polemical cross-dressing of the character of Revolutionary women continues its politically ambiguous story up until about 1795. Feminism at that time, as now, crossed a number of social barriers, but not unproblematically. As Levy, Applethwaite, and Johnson show in their collection and explication of the documentation of women in Revolutionary Paris from 1789–95, feminist interventions ranged from the Enlightened appeals of salon women for legal, educational, and financial reforms to the spontaneous insurrections of the *poissardes* or market-women in response to immediate scarcities.[20] The *Société des Républicaines-Révolutionaires* was a short-lived women's pressure group at the lower end of this social register, but in 1793 it succeeded more than any other formation in aligning radical middle-class feminism with the interests of working women. Once more, the demise of this initiative comes in a discursive impasse in which feminist politics are rendered unthinkable. The *Société* was finally proscribed after a disturbance in which some of its members had tried to persuade the women of the Marché des Innocents to adopt the red pantaloons and bonnets of the Jacobins and Montagnards in their struggle against the Girondins. The report to the

National Convention on this failed recruitment drive records that "a mob of nearly 4000 women gathered. All the women were in agreement that violence and threats would not make them dress in a costume [which] they respected but which they believed was intended for men" (185, 213). The Convention duly banned the *Société* on the grounds that "a woman should not leave her family to meddle in affairs of government." At the Paris Commune, Pierre Chaumette silenced a deputation of protesting *républicaines* by calling the bluff of their cross-dressing: "Since when is it permitted to give up one's sex?" (220).

Clearly, by showing her ability to perform as a political activist, a woman in those accounts loses out both ways—her sex impugns her activism or her activism her sex. Chaumette's play on these uncanny reversals reaches its climax in his casuistical disposal of the predictably embarrassing precedent of Jeanne d'Arc. She was justified, it transpires, only as a corrective to royalist cross-dressing, as confirmation of a proleptic guillotine: "if the fate of France was once in the hands of a woman, that is because there was a king who did not have the head of a man" (220). Within the regime of Revolutionary discourse, whether from counter-Revolutionary, Jacobin, or, eventually, Thermidorean perspectives, female agency is ruled out of court and turned into costume theater through its alleged unnaturalness, vicariousness, or inauthenticity. While this is a recurrent feature of patriarchy, it achieved such unusual intensity and visibility at this moment as to characterize for many the general problematic of Revolutionary action. Ina Ferris pertinently notes the contemporary dismissal of novels as female reading-fodder, and the exception made for *Waverley* as "legitimating novel-reading as a manly practice."[21] Somehow Scott's anonymity seems to have encouraged readers to look for cross-dressing at all stages of the literary process where *Waverley* was concerned, *repeating* the contemporary refusal to give women credence for fiction or anything else as soon as it became serious. But the admission of cross-dressing, or Scott's exception to the feminine rule, lets his novel retain its female mien, and with this comes the failure of its subject to achieve representation, a failure alarmingly converging on a quite unthinkable Rousseauian success.

The Theater of Anachronism

Scott, in his "Preliminary View," described the egalitarianism of the French Revolution as "a gross and ridiculous contradiction of the necessary progress of society . . . a fruitless attempt to wage war with the laws of

Nature." Burke's response, according to Scott, had been one of colorful hyperbole which "ought to have been softened. . . . On the other hand, no political prophet ever viewed futurity with a surer ken" (1;213, 278–79). Burke's histrionics are excused as identifying the Revolution's *lapsus naturae* with its affront to historical logic. Within Scott's own writings, the Revolutionary aberration is corrected not only by the restoration of the Bourbons but by the resumption of a historian's confidence after a definite hiatus. Writing to Henry Francis Scott in January 1831, betraying his private tendency to identify reform with revolution, Scott is more forthcoming about that Revolutionary caesura in historical logic which Burke's imagination rushed to fill.

> About 1792, when I was entering life, the admiration of the godlike system of the French Revolution was so rife, that only a few old-fashioned Jacobites and the like ventured to hint a preference for the land they lived in; or pretended to doubt that the new principles must be infused into our worn-out constitution. Burke appeared, and all the gibberish about the superior legislation of the French dissolved like an enchanted castle when the destined knight blows his horn before it. The talents, the almost prophetic powers of Burke are not needed on this occasion, for men can now argue from the past. We can point to the old British ensign floating from the British citadel; while the tricolor has been to gather up from the mire and blood—the shambles of a thousand defeats—a prosperous standard to rally under. Still, however, this is a moment of dulness and universal apathy, and I fear that unless an Orlando should blow the horn, it might fail to awaken the sleepers.[22]

Here, the initial evocation of the Jacobites as counterrevolutionaries suggests, given *Waverley,* that you counter fantasy with fantasy, the unreal principles of radical projectors with a different kind of unreality. The untenable Jacobite claim, therefore, opposes the Revolution's rationalization of itself, but with a self-confessedly disreputable anachronism. This ambiguity shapes the characterization of Burke's prophecy as a kind of divinatory recourse before reasoning from the past can be rehabilitated. Burke, as "the destined knight," is a character in the romance he is there to demystify. His effort, however successful its outcome, is compromised by the discourse in which it is obliged to identify its subject. That discourse is a dispensable makeshift before the power to argue inductively from the past is regained and the Revolution can be understood as the prehistory of its own disaster, evincing the need for alternative, constitutional reform. The last sentence, though, alluding to the impending

Reform Bill, vindicates Hogg's "anecdotal view" of Sir Walter by having him suggest that another uncharted historical lacuna may be at hand. In his journal, Scott described turning out to vote for Henry Scott in May of that year amid cries by the dissident Border weavers, "the bra lads of Jeddart," of "Burke Sir Walter," a slogan referring by an unintended but rich irony not to the great polemicist but to the fate of William Burke the murderer, Hare's collaborator, recently hanged in Edinburgh. The entry reads like a conflation of Edinburgh under the barbaric Highlanders and Revolutionary Paris agitating for uncountenanceable reforms.[23]

In a letter to Robert Southey of September 1824, Scott had asked his Tory friend: "By the way, did you ever observe how easy it would be for a good historian to run a par[a]lell betwixt the Great Rebellion and the French Revolution, just substituting the spirit of fanaticism for that of soi disant philosophy. But then how the character of the English would rise whether you considered the talents and views of great leaders on either side, or the comparative moderation and humanity with which they waged their warfare. I sometimes think an instructive comparative view might be made out, and it would afford a comfortable augury that the restoration in either case was followed by many amendments in the constitution."[24]

In Scotland, the "Great Rebellion" against Charles I lived on in resistance to the constitutional solution by the ultra-Presbyterian Covenanters. Scott's extended analysis of this, to his mind, unrealistic persistence is to be found in *Old Mortality*. In *Waverley*, though, there is a significant conjuncture in which a group of surviving Cameronian Covenanters serving the Whig cause is detailed to take Edward into custody to Stirling Castle. Mr. Morton, a moderate Presbyterian, recounts the history of Richard Cameron's sect to Edward while they await the Covenanting escort, recalling its "unnatural" support for the Catholic Jacobite opposition to the Union of the English and Scottish Parliaments in 1707 (169). Again, resistance to constitutional change creates analogies between otherwise dissimilar groups who, because they refuse to move with the times, share the same anachronistic, imaginary space. In giving these figures literary houseroom, Scott's fictions again characterize themselves as alternatives to historical explanation, or as places staging the fanciful interregnum between accredited historical discourses.

Chronologically, therefore, the intervening theater is inherently unstable. Edward, perceiving the leader of these belated Cameronians with his captor, Major Melville, "was irresistibly impressed with the idea that he beheld a leader of the Roundheads of yore, in conference with one of Marlborough's captains" (172). Characters are plucked from different periods of history in order to historicize a particular period: the different narratives thus invoked are absorbed in a single descriptive function. As we have seen, this tactic ostensibly belongs to a "higher realism" within history, comparable to that within romantic philosophy when irony is held to compensate for failures in representation. Here, failure of chronology is translated into history by analogy: a failure generating an ironic discourse in which anachronism informs just because of, rather than in spite of, its breaks with history's self-defining sequence. For Scott, this theatrical license reaches its apogee, perhaps, when he stage-manages the Highland pageantry for George IV's visit to Edinburgh in 1822. Historicism competes so successfully with history on this occasion that the Hanoverian King wins applause as the Jacobite Pretender's successor, and the Tory *Edinburgh Observer* can announce that "we are now all Jacobites, thorough-bred Jacobites, in acknowledging George IV."[25] In the novel, however, it is an analogy *Waverley* draws with the new contemporary Revolutionary period which scotches the traditional romantic alibi. This final analogy evolves, as the narrator concedes, from what "may be held a trifling anecdote." As Gifted Gilfillan and his motley, even quaint Cameronian volunteers march into Cairnvreckan to take Edward into custody, the drummer symptomatically falls far short of martial authority in his beating because he has been asked to accompany the 119th Psalm rather than any march known to the British army. The narrative waxes heavily sarcastic at the Covenanters' expense and then, in a final swipe, notes that "the drummer in question was no less than town-drummer of Anderton. I remember his successor in office a member of that enlightened body, the British Convention. Be his memory, therefore, treated with due respect" (171). The sarcasm implies continuity between the narrative and the "respect" Scott himself would have liked to have shown to the Scottish "Friends of the People" who organized the meetings of the "British Convention" in Edinburgh in 1792 and 1793. But Scott's analogy here needs prefacing with more about the knowledge he assumed when presenting his Covenanters.

The Covenanters fuel Scott's historicism with their displaced loyalties, uncanny alliances, and anachronistic potential. When Charles II disingenuously subscribed the two Covenants to secure Scottish support, the Covenanters threw their weight behind the Stuart cause and fought Cromwell at Dunbar in 1650. It was the residue of this interest which joined with the Jacobites against the Act of Union fifty-seven years later. Extremes met in the two groups' opposition to the legacy of the Glorious

Revolution of 1688, which offered religious hegemony to neither. After 1688, the idea of a Whig was detached once and for all from its originals, the radical Covenanters of the Whiggamore raid on Edinburgh of 1648. The ideology of a new moderate Legitimacy deserving of support from Whig and Tory alike was established. The incoherence covered by this consensus, however, is quite considerable. It provides the necessarily unreliable grounds for historians of seventeenth- and eighteenth-century England proposing their own controversial revisionism, a once more self-impugning (Tory) history, weirdly recalling Scott's Burkean moment. For instance, Jonathan Clark argues plausibly that after 1688, far from enforcing Jacobite submission to a new ideology, the successful Whigs accommodate the Jacobite "dynastic idiom" to bolster their monarchical idea. This strategy simultaneously explains the post-1688 consensus, why it lasted, and the ease with which people could change sides. The Whig settlement becomes indistinguishable from its opposite, and thus merits Dr. Johnson's verdict that "Whiggism is a negation of all principle."[26] Clark, however, feels no embarrassment in making this difference without distinction the test of his historical discrimination. He describes how public and cryptic loyalty are expressed in the same words, and in the same homiletic asseverations of monarchic allegiance (*English Society*, 159). But, unlike Scott, he gives no sign of recognizing the threat to a history whose factual basis, the language of established loyalty, has therefore become as uncanny as any post-Freudian view of the normal. This is the Hanoverian Toryism inherited by Scott, which represents an inadmissible division by lying about it: that is, by failing to represent it, employing instead a language whose dreamlike, fantastic working mechanisms have been modeled from Freud to Lyotard as alternatives to representational theories of meaning. Scott clearly has an interest in locating this uncanny entirely in the Jacobite idiom or its extreme Covenanting counterpart. Nevertheless, the inherited contradiction in the original reconciliation of Tory and Whig will out, and surely resurfaces in the nonsense of Scott's Jacobite Hanoverian pageantry of 1822.

In his early novels, though, it is the Covenanting opposition to the Revolution Settlement which Scott presents as a fantastical equivalent to the Jacobites. Either party could, therefore, figure for him the reactionary wrong-headedness of contemporary radicalism. "Education and property," progressive assimilation rather than an alternative "politics" outmoded by definition, were Scott's proclaimed remedies for lower-class discontent.[27] The Covenanting spirit condenses into the democratic radicalism of Scott's own day, again because of rather than in spite of the anachronism involved. [28] Scott, commenting on 1790s radicals and on postwar agitators, possesses the antiquarianism if not the zeal of an Old Mortality retouching the past. The historicism that makes sense of his anachronism is more fully developed in *Old Mortality,* where the Biblical jargon and plebeian crudity of the Covenanters seem intended to cast them already in a primitive light. But it is in *Waverley* that we are first invited to imagine the saving ideological connection between past and present. The imaginary quality of this reenactment not only contrasts Scott's Hanoverian latitude with the dogmatic anachronisms of the Covenanters' Biblical applications to their own actions (259), it also allows his writing to imply room for critical maneuver beyond the historicist solution.

To fill out the modern end of Scott's sarcastic analogy between Covenanters and French-inspired radicals, we must remember that in the early 1790s Scotland was used as a testing ground for how far Government repression against the latter could go. It was, E. P. Thompson claims, the prospect of "an alliance between English and Scottish reformers and the United Irishmen that determined the Government to act." [29] The National Conventions of 1792–93, to which Scott alludes, seemed to offer at least the first half of that possibility, an alliance between Scottish and English radicals. The ferocious Scottish judges, of whom Lord Braxfield (the dedicatee of Scott's thesis for the Faculty of Advocates) became the most famous, went into action, and deportations and executions quickly followed. The potential for a further alliance with the United Irishmen was experienced by Scott in all its implausibility at the playhouse. In the "Preliminary View," the description of the way in which the French Revolution appeared like a play to English spectators continues with a description of the theatergoers themselves, which actually incorporates his own experience. "From this period the progress of the French Revolution seemed in England like a play presented upon the stage, where two contending factions divide the audience, and hiss or applaud as much from party spirit as from real critical judgment, while every instant increases the probability that they will try the question by actual force" (1:280–81). This is what Scott himself did in 1794, conspiring with other hearty young Tory friends to beat up Irish medical students who had been disrupting performances with vociferously antiloyalist sentiments. Scott and other ringleaders of the playhouse riot had to find bail and were bound over to keep the peace. [30] Scott later writes of the Radical War and the Boroughmuir Skirmish of 1820 much in the spirit of his 1790s escapades: "the whole Radical plot went to the devil when it came to gun and sword . . .

the Edinburgh young men showed great spirit. . . . Lockhart is one of the cavalry and a very good trooper. It is high to hear these young fellows talk of the raid of Airdre, the trot of Kilmarnock, and so on, like so many moss-troopers."[31] It is the same unpleasant mixture of high japes for the educated youth playing at militias and hangings for the lower-class radicals.

However, the 1794 brawl grows in seriousness when one discovers that later in the same year it is cited at the trial for high treason of Robert Watt, as "one link of the scheme" for which he is sent to the gallows. To find the life of irony, the theater, realistic in this instance is surely to connive at injustice. The brawl's significance should instead have been to reflect on the admissibility of the evidence on which he was condemned for conspiring to foment "a general rising in Edinburgh." Watt was an unreliable witness, an ex-government spy alleged to have joined the cause he was investigating. The most lurid, unconvincing, but deadly testimony comes from his own confession. The charge that he and others plotted to establish a provisional Republican government in Edinburgh, armed with a few pikes, in concert with London Corresponding Society activists such as Hardy, Thelwall, Holcroft, and others, seems risible.[32] Yet Scott, who stayed in town specifically to witness Watt's execution, ingenuously thought that, on the scaffold, "the pusillanimity of the unfortunate victim was astonishing, considering the boldness of his nefarious plans."[33] The *theatricality* common to Scott's violent overthrow of sedition in an Edinburgh playhouse and the revolting spectacle of an exemplary execution could only be thought of as the *realistic* exercise of justice in a state which was corrupt.

Refusing Ideology

Like other leaders of the Scottish culture of his day, Scott was a trained lawyer, and one might expect there to be a detectable symmetry in the economies of his legal, aesthetic, and historical discourses. Latitude in interpretation of the universal rule of law, such as exonerates exemplary or deterrent exceptions, is as likely to produce opportunism and tyranny as it is to lead to liberal discretion. The power of a judicial institution to survive its failure to implement its own principles does not necessarily redeem its practice, no more than irony necessarily saved epistemological breakdown, nor historicism failures in historical narrative. My insistence on recognizing collapses in the intentionalism of these discourses is finally focused by the pronouncements of two characters within different discourses, legal and novelistic—one a judge, the other a fictional victim of exemplary justice.

Lord Swinton, one of Braxfield's henchmen, remarked during the trial of Thomas Muir, leader of the Scottish Friends of the People, that because sedition included "every sort of crime. . . . If punishment adequate to the crime . . . were to be sought for, it could not be found in our law, now that torture is happily abolished."[34] Swinton's statement, regretfully one imagines, identifies the romantic failsafe in contemporary legal discourse. He acknowledges that there is no longer a motivated relationship of retribution or fit between punishment and crime. This, "happily," is the reason for the law's leniency in only transporting Muir to an early death. Yet it is precisely the new measure of justice, taking over from the old representational theory, which licenses the law's use as a government tool, increasing its scope to the point of oppression. This is the other, darker side of that Burkean view of the law learned by Scott from the lectures of Baron David Hume, in which constitutionalism takes precedence over moral principle, and the law's function as a register of social cohesion identifies its nature more surely than do principles of natural justice. At the end of that road, we find the excesses of Braxfield, discounting Jesus as a justly hanged reformer, and the taking of Joseph Gerrald's able defense as proof positive of his danger to the state and as justification for condemning him to deportation.[35]

Toward the end of *Waverley,* Fergus Mac-Ivor contemplates his fate under a law by which, according to Swinton's judgment, the punishment still fits the crime of high treason. Fergus is quite clear that his execution at Carlyle by hanging, drawing, and quartering will last "a short half hour." He also notes that such torture was not a penalty originally belonging to Scottish law but imposed by England after 1707. Fergus's speech at this moment provides us with a means of seeing through Swinton's sophistry to the way in which, under pressure of coping with the Revolution, the exercise of law, however much it clings to a notion of fitting retribution, collapses into instrumental theatricality of a piece with the aberration it is putting down. " 'This same law of high treason,' he continued, with astonishing firmness and composure, 'is one of the blessings, Edward, with which your free country has accommodated poor old Scotland—her own jurisprudence, as I have heard, was much milder. But I suppose that one day or other—when there are no longer any wild Highlanders to benefit by its tender mercies—they will blot it from their records, as leveling them with a nation of cannibals' " (326).

The legal principle, then, is conveniently effaced, along with the people whom it was its actual purpose as social engineering to devour. Mac-Ivor, though, sees what an ass all this *Realpolitik* makes of the law. He continues, "The mummery, too, of exposing the senseless head—they have not the wit to grace mine with a paper coronet; there would be some satire in that, Edward" (326). A law which refuses to acknowledge its own polemical, ideological design is like a "mummery" which stops short of "satire"; its departure from its own principles is unexonerated by rhetorical compensation in another genre.

Fergus's execution is not witnessed by Edward. The narrative sends Mac-Ivor out of sight under "a deep and dark Gothic arch-way" to his death and remains with Edward. Its silence or blindness here is perhaps its most open admission of the force of its failure to represent the process of revolution. The words with which Mac-Ivor reprieves Edward from the culminating spectacle of his rebellion epitomize literally the instabilities and reversals with which a spectator is undermined: "But what a dying man can suffer firmly, may kill a living friend to look upon" (326).

We have to be careful in deciphering what is rhetorically at stake here. The empowering of spectacle is at the expense of the objectivity of difference. The distance necessary for us to understand power rather than be subject to it is erased. Words which kill have failed to represent. Scott's finally reticent narrative fails to represent this failure of representation which, as theorized by a modern revisionist historian of the Revolution like François Furet, *is* the Revolution in its contemporary characterizations, for and against. Furet argues that in the pre-Thermidor period, especially during Robespierre's ascendancy, "language was substituted for power, for it was the sole guarantee that power would belong only to the people, that is, to nobody." The "basic nature" of revolutionary consciousness was "an imaginary discourse on power" generated when "the field of power, having become vacant, was taken over by the ideology of pure democracy, that is by the idea that the people are power, or that power is the people."[36] Rousseau's unrepresentable general will is imagined in a performative language recognized by devotees and detractors alike. Revolutionary ideology, however, seems unable to break out of its circle and make the further, Rousseauian move, in which the immediacy bypassing representation licenses re-creation of the original in historically different forms. The crisis of representation perceived by Burke to be consequent on the legitimate representatives' loss of power, precipitating his own history's loss of mastery, is related to the Revolution's own discourse about itself. Critique and defense are housed within the same problematic: the more authentic, the more imaginary. This is the confused performance in which *Waverley* finally refuses to participate.

In Furet's scenario, both supporters and antagonists appear locked into the same "revolutionary ideology" which, he argues, also characterizes the work of the first historians of the Revolution: "amazement at the *strangeness* of the phenomenon" (84). Imprisonment by this idea of a radical break with the past, one unintelligible unless as the imagined reincarnation of a temporally discontinuous period (Robespierre's republicanism, Scott's Jacobitism), was of course exactly Marx's target in *The Eighteenth Brumaire of Louis Bonaparte* and elsewhere. He both characterized and attacked the persistent reproduction of the French Revolution as a unique break with the past which set the ground rules for all revolutions to come.[37] Blindness to the historicism and ideological coloring of this interpretation, Marx claims, reduces its later proponents to parody. To see their farcical degeneration also as the apt characterization of their historical moment is to turn historicist recuperation into something indistinguishable from its failure. It lacks the honesty of Rousseau's relinquishment in reverie of his work to future readers. It is like the Hanoverian Jacobites all over again: Scott's pageantry of 1822 for George IV parodies his novel of 1814, in the way that Louis's coup in 1851 parodies, pace Marx, his uncle Napoleon I's coup against the Directory in 1799, almost sixty years since.

Revolutionary ideology parallels romantic ideology in its power to coerce its interpreters into seeing its problematic entirely on its own terms. More precisely, both ideologies share an incorrigible intentionalism which unerringly finds its object. Scott's *Waverley* exposes this common structure and, in his inaugural novel, preserves ideological incoherencies from being utterly obscured by the saving realisms of irony and historicism. Later, his writing could succumb to those recuperations, as in the sentimentalized success of a Jeanie Deans; or in the unconsciously parodic working-up of Jacobite interest again in *Redgauntlet*'s unhistorical figure of a portly revenant, Charles Edward Stuart, in his priest's frock, twenty years on. *Redgauntlet* was published only two years after Scott's "fat friend," George IV, came so implausibly into his Jacobite inheritance in Edinburgh.[38] Darsie Latimer's cross-dressing in the same novel adds to the farcical mockery of the Revolutionary figure of female agency in Charles's disguise. In *Waverley*, though, the imaginary treatment of a historical subject still counts as an insuperable paradox: one in which otherness is evoked, not through successful irony, but through a sense of the novel's having been determined by it in such a way as to misdescribe it.

To summarize, then: Scott on the French Revolution is not Lukács's geneticist. The displaced narrative of *Waverley* shows him to be a historicist. But his historicism expresses the failure of geneticism, not its recuperation in another genre. His ironic use of the imaginary does not save but emphasizes his failure to represent this period in history, finally refusing even the ideological glossing of that failure, offered by both sides, as Revolutionary epistemological break. The quarrel between geneticism and historicism is still alive in the writings of our contemporary historians of the French Revolution, visible in the tripartite debates between revisionists, proponents of the old geneticist view of a bourgeois Revolution, and Marxist reformulations. Furthermore, in his use of the ironic imaginary, Scott demonstrates an internal distance from romantic ideology as much as from Revolutionary ideology. In this he contributes to an antiintentionalist, metaromantic writing which recent critical concentration, however salutary, on exposing the reach of romantic intentionalism has made it increasingly difficult to recognize.[39]

SIX

A French Connection:
The Shelleys' Materialism

Materialism might be called the unacceptable face of empiricism: unacceptable, because it draws the reductive conclusions suggested by the thesis that all our experience originates in the senses. Empiricism might imply atheism, hedonism, and a political equality based on our common physicality, but materialism proclaimed these heresies. As a philosophical doctrine it also appeared to leave little room for concepts apparently central to romantic ideology: imagination, reduced to the play of sensation, must forgo any claims to transcendental importance; organicism in life and art is no different from machinery; perception need no longer strive to find in poetry symbols for a supersensible vocation. Major British romantics, therefore, dutifully took up the task of refuting materialism as a prerequisite for establishing their own credentials. Materialism meshed with anti-Gallic prejudice; the French followers of Locke, philosophes and *idéologues,* while attracting condemnation, rarely provoked the extended discussion accorded native, English, spiritualized versions. In traditions shared by Hartley, Priestley, Darwin, and the usual suspects, materialism could be argued not to deny but to give an alternative account of an animated, active universe ostensibly more congenial to, or building a more helpful launching pad for, the idealist adventures of Wordsworth and Coleridge. Rousseau perhaps straddled both camps. Hazlitt's longer debate with the systems of Helvétius and Condillac was unusual. Materialism, in other words, makes an acceptable intrusion into mainstream late eighteenth-century British philosophical theory in the form of associationism and pantheism; but by then its sting has already been drawn.

An English romantic keen to sting again was Percy Shelley. He is a rare example of a romantic poet who utilized the French materialists, although I believe he is usually thought to have participated in the common abandonment of materialism for a contrary view of the mental formation of experience. "Nothing exists but as it is perceived," said the young Shelley in his "Essay on Life," a statement which could certainly mean with Berkeley that existence is a function of perception. It could also have the implication that anything genuinely existent must be perceivable, through the senses, and so must have a material nature. Already, in Spinozistic vein, Shelley is describing personal differences as "the different modifications of the one mind": articulations of a common substance which itself exists only as it is perceived. He continues to square his empiricism, with its overtones of Berkeleyan or Humean idealism, with the French materialist reduction of thought to the movement of material particles.[1]

Percy Shelley can be read consistently from a materialist point of view, and such a reading interestingly brings Mary Shelley into play not merely as explicatory mechanism, or even collaborator, but as giving the lead in important ways to Percy's thought. Read from this angle, these two authors embarrass a half-hearted empiricism by being unabashedly insistent on the sufficiency of bodily existence. Out-and-out materialism prescinds opposition, each spiritual objection being translated back into a compliment to the body that produced it. You have vigorously to demonize that source in order to make credible the detachment from it of any high-minded effects. The easy urbane materialism of a Hume, a Voltaire, or a Diderot argues against such debasement of the body, but only indirectly, through its discursive suavity and range. Their lack of explicitness, however, elides the initial shock materialism perpetrates on dominant ideologies, and I want to argue that this trauma was perceived to be more important and was countered more straightforwardly at some points in French materialism, in a manner lending definition to the Shelleys' otherwise elusive but persistent materialism.

Empiricism is constitutionally unhappy with its own subject-position. Its stress on the primacy of sensuous input as the source of experience eventually exerts intolerable pressure on the idea of subjectivity, which crumbles into being a sentimental inference drawn from the patterns of data received. Hume retreats gracefully from the problem of locating personal identity elsewhere; Diderot dramatizes the same embarrassment in the figure of Rameau's nephew, a shameless replicator who can apparently transform all interiority into brilliant pantomime, outward display. However disingenuously, both Hume's reticence and Diderot's irony still express the desire to be able to describe the self as other than simply a material effect. One of the eighteenth-century materialists willing to encounter the dissolution of subject into object head-on, the generally unacceptable conclusion to which empiricism seemed to be leading, actually predated the philosophes and scandalized even them. Julien Offroy de La Mettrie, the "center" of French materialism according to Marx, combined an Epicurean delight in nature with a Spinozistic monism to seek explanatory analogies for being human in machinery and vegetable nature.[2] *L'Homme Machine* and *L'Homme Plante* enlist the scientific imagination of the day to invade and explicate subject-areas in ways immediately proclaimed to be reductive and crass by their traditional philosophical and theological guardians. Not that La Mettrie saw his own initiatives as being politically or socially subversive. In fact, the complaint of the philosophes was always that he considered humankind abstracted from the shaping institutions they wished to reform.[3] *L'Homme Machine* opens by specifying La Mettrie's desired audience as an elite capable of shedding prejudice in the pursuit of untrammeled truth.[4] His methodological starting point is his experience as a doctor; and his materialism is frequently backed up by case studies and biological generalizations based on experimental proofs independent of social context. Nevertheless, his scientism seems for almost all his readers to be charged by what it might not necessarily be expected to possess—passion, resistance, eroticism, and wit. He can, that is, be read as dealing with the shock to the readers whom he forces to confront a nature thought obscene when stripped of its ideological overlay. His provocative complacency with physical circumstance aims to overcome their false consciousness, their alienation from and disgust at their material selves, as much as it tries to further the scientific investigation these responses have traditionally impeded.

As a result, symmetries between La Mettrie and the Shelleys' project are easier to detect than affinities with other French Enlightenment materialists. For Diderot and others, La Mettrie had unhelpfully impressed the vested interests of church and state they were out to subvert as being someone highly dangerous or mad, and had, by association, given their materialism a bad name. And yet La Mettrie spoiled the philosophes' attempt to persuade society of the rationality of adopting a new order, because his outrageous scientific frankness appeared quite compatible with his conservatism. He eventually held a sinecure at the Prussian court of Frederick II, where he felt considerably more comfortable than did Voltaire. The aura of sexual license popularly attaching to La Mettrie was less the strategic rubbishing which, for example, Rousseau's *Confessions* attracted to his theories and more connected with his actual intellectual stance.[5] La Mettrie shows that uninhibited investigation of sexuality high-lights the common ground humans share not only with animals but with still more unconscious life processes. Hence, his and Linnaeus's better known sexual classification of plants and, in La Mettrie's case, vegetable classification of man—*l'Homme Plante.* In this "sensitive plant," physical organization displaces psychology, anticipating the practice of Lavater's art of physiognomy or Spurzheim's phrenology, both trashed by a roman-ticism which had located the source of emancipatory knowledge rather in the priority of consciousness to scientific reduction. La Mettrie's prag-matism, though, his insistence on identifying reason in good practice rather than in immaterial isolation supported by an untenable distinc-tion between mind and body, held more political resonance for a later age more alert to the diversity of forms ideology could adopt. Certainly the romantic substitution of aesthetic feeling for bodily aesthesis bol-stered a transcendental psychology which La Mettrie might have happily attacked. He could have reassured us against the need for such romantic sublimations as he did his first readers after dissolving the mind/body distinction: "A true philosopher does not blush, like Pliny, at our miser-able origin" (1:65; 4).

For La Mettrie defines his target as, above all, a priori reasoning. And, confusingly for those of us conditioned by romantic ideology, he found his strongest ally in the imagination. Soul is not a philosopher's assump-tion we have to make concerning what it is to be human. Soul is some-thing we deduce retrospectively from the rational organization of the body to discernible purposes. This immanence of reasoning in the world is the result of imagination. "I always use the word 'imagine' because I believe that everything is imagined and that all the parts of the soul can be reduced to imagination alone. . . . Thanks to the imagination, to its flattering touch, the cold skeleton of reason acquires living, rosy flesh; thanks to it the sciences flourish, the arts are embellished, woods speak, echoes sigh, rocks weep, marble breathes and all inanimate objects come to life" (1:81–82; 14–15). Experience becomes intelligible to La Mettrie as it is perceived to be made up of signs given in imagination. Initially this semiotic move seems to allow nature itself to drop out of the equation. Words, as in Locke, start by taking their meaning from the ideas they sup-posedly represent, but this relation transposes almost immediately into another relation, one holding between words themselves and not *between* words and something else. La Mettrie berates the use of words "to which we can attach no real idea *or distinction*" *(auxquelles on n'a attaché aucune idée, ou distinction réelle)* and describes the brain as touched by words when it "cannot but see their images and *differences*" (*ne peut pas ne pas voir leurs images* et leurs différences) (1:84–85, 80; 14, 17; my emphases). But the collocation of idea or image with distinction and difference removes the representational function of the former: now they exist only as points in a differential system of significance which does not require them to gesture beyond it in order to generate meaning. To avoid a linguistic idealism out of keeping with his materialism elsewhere, though, La Mettrie has to claim that the linguistic structure of our understanding is "marked or engraved on the brain" *(marqués our gravés dans le cerveau)* (1:80; 14). This explains, for La Mettrie, that just as we cannot look without seeing (just as seeing is involuntary), so seeing is impossible without a prior linguistic organization of data simultaneously the production of imagination and the involuntary, physical modification of the brain. Whereas Locke seems to think that we can receive impressions and then, acting on them, produce significance, La Mettrie argues that we could only recognize such elements of knowledge, we could only be impressed by them, if they came to us already organized as forms of signification, each bearing the "traces" of other elements from which they differed in meaningful relations (1:81; 14).[6]

To go on to ask the question of La Mettrie, Which came first— imagination or brain? is to ask a question he thinks is nonsensical. There is one substance, thinks La Mettrie with Spinoza, which can precipitate modes of consciousness without itself being conscious. "Having made eyes . . . without itself being able to see, nature, without itself being able to think, made a machine which can think" *(ayant fait, sans voir, deux yeux qui voient, [la Nature] a fait sans penser, une machine qui pense)* (1:361; 97). This last aphorism comes from a work eventually collected in La Mettrie's philosophical works under the title *Système d'Epicure*. Epicurean philosophy was primarily transmitted through Lucretius's poem *De Rerum Natura*, an intertext for understanding Percy Shelley's earliest and latest long poems, *Queen Mab* (1813) and *The Triumph of Life* (1822). As much as them, the poem most obviously founding Shelley's poetic career, *Alastor: or, The Spirit of Solitude* (1816), shows the futility of trying to recover a sense of self prior to its practical manifestations in reasoning and action. In *L'Homme Machine* La Mettrie insisted that "the excellence of reason does not depend on a grand meaningless word *(immateriality)* but on its force, its extent or its acuteness" *(l'excellence de la Raison ne dépend pas d'un grand mot vuide de sens* [l'immatérialité] *mais de sa force, de son étendue, ou de sa Clair-voyance)* (1:65; 4). To search out a sovereign consciousness anterior to all physical manifestations, and to make this a priori reasoning the object of poetic quest, is bound to be frustrated. All you could arrive at is an awareness of basic physical movements upon which everything subsequent depends. Since there is no subjectivity to be unveiled by the questing poet, his journey back to his own origins concludes in this lack of consciousness, in death. "Everyone leaves life as though he had just been born," says Epicurus. [7] In *Alastor* the Poet's assumption that the "veiled maid" of his vision, self-generated, is someone he must pursue rather than reproduce in actual personal relationship, is his mistake. His movement in quest of her is all that there is to her, to him. The extensiveness of his efforts shows the "generosity" of his error, as the poem's "Preface" has it, but it is the physicality of this spectacularly expressive movement which finally counts. The narrator's infatuation with the Poet repeats the desire for a sovereignty other than that of natural necessity, but the last stages of the Poet's journey have mimed a medically precise return through various anatomical passages toward the womb, a description Shelley could have found in *L'Homme Machine*. Here such travel is totally self-defeating as it closes on the moment of inspiration, the source of self-production, only to show that it is the same as the moment of conception. To approach conception from the reverse direction, leading away from physical diversity of imaginative movement and back to its cause is to retreat from consciousness, not to approach it. Equally, when the Poet of *Alastor* finishes in blindness and decomposition, he has only become integrated with a world he might have affected in other ways. The narrator claims the Poet's future for his "simple strain" (1:706), [8] but this cannibalism only repeats the Poet's delusion that his scrutiny of nature might reveal any other source of conscious movement. Nature does not require help to preserve, or, in La Mettrie's Epicurean idiom: "Everything is replaced, everything disappears and nothing is destroyed" (1:371; 104).

The Poet is obliged to prove this thesis: nothing else could have happened, could it? Had he and the narrator acknowledged that his "mystic" sympathy with nature did not require alchemical or magical alternatives to natural science for its demonstration, they might together have described not an attempt to flee the inevitable but an attempt to face up to it, undiminished. Much of Percy Shelley's own poetry confronts the shock of our subordination to natural process and the self-alienation and despair resulting from such shock. Grasped materialistically, our life can feel like a triumph over other aspirations, paradoxically equally ours. The reduction of our sphere of influence to a single principle of life is like an incestuous imposition. Fastened to the dying animal, we not only imagine other worlds and dispensations in compensation, but conspire in a disgust for this life; scenarios in which the ingenious imaginative organization of experience is detached from a physicality stigmatized rather than celebrated for being mechanical or biological. Percy's political analogy for this impossible discontent is an unwillingness to sacrifice autonomy for the better communal good. The agony of self-dissemination of the bourgeois subject in the interests of humankind can only find an adequate analogue in the thought of death. Shelley could present this exaggeration sympathetically, as in the "Ode to the West Wind," or through the suffering of the poetic madman in "Julian and Maddalo." Or he could exhibit the intolerableness of imagined exemption from proper political obligation in his many figures of tyranny. Or he could, hardest of all, try to evoke an exemplary mobility in reaction to the demands of death and its others, at the ends of *Prometheus Unbound* and *Adonais.*

It is important to detect the political idiom here; otherwise other kinds of acceptance of death-in-life loom, in particular Sade's. When La Mettrie writes his *Anti-Seneca or The Sovereign Good (Anti-Sénèque ou Discours sur le Bonheur)*, he attacks a stoical contempt for mortality and advocates Epicurean acceptance and pleasure. But he is far from recommending an erotics of excess. It is the Stoics who are excessive, who "aspire to be sublime and rise above all events, considering themselves to be truly men only to the extent that they cease to be men" (119). La Mettrie appears able to criticize in advance the inhuman, postmodern destination of the sublime. In *The Triumph of Life*, "Life," the figure in the chariot who leads a procession of almost all the worthies of Western civilization from Plato onward, similarly represents an inhuman compulsion into which people are self-propelled toward their own destruction. Yet this agency is only constructed for life by those who have tried to rule it from above by a priori prescription, thinkers driven into disabling self-abuse by the realization that the object of their science actually dwelt immanently within them, organizing all their supposedly individual responses. As Timothy Morton has shown, Shelley's vegetarianism loses its eccentricity and becomes central to his thought where his materialism is at stake.[9] Meat must be roasted because of its horrific aspect when looked on as food; a taboo as strong as the incest taboo forbids carnivores from thinking of the flesh they eat as the same thing as the body they inhabit. The abjection of the body as food is a striking paradigm of subject-object relations in which the difference between the two also licenses the mastery of one over the other. Such ascendancy requires the casting of the inferior object in a character suppressing the nature it shares with its supposed opposite.

According to Harold Bloom, the "devastation" a long time coming in Shelley's oeuvre is the tragic homelessness of our transcendental vocation experienced as the triumph of life. By contrast, on a materialist reading, this triumph criticizes the artificial alienation felt by those for whom the materialist reductio is traumatic but undeniable, destructive possession but still "life." Rousseau, unlike Dante guided by Virgil, cannot love his dispensation, cannot, that is, see in materialism the image of the body politic, a republic of people in virtuous relationship with each other (for Dante, of course, a theodicy translating Virgilian imperium). Lucretius had described as *foedera naturae* the compacts by which atoms naturally bind themselves together, as if in a republic, to produce such things as "mind."[10] The Rousseau of *The Triumph* instead sees only a vain "deluded crew" (l. 184). He is overcome "by [his] own heart alone" (l. 240), an individualism whose accompanying misery and the affront of mortality could not "temper to its object" (l. 243). I am suggesting that the quickest way with this obscure formulation is to think of the difficulties that most provocatively egotistical of writers, Rousseau, would have had with the idea of himself as an object, as part of a larger physical organization in which he played a democratic part. Rousseau would then stand for a subjectivity typically extinguished by an egalitarian materialism to which it partly subscribed.[11]

I will have more to say on the poem's alternative to Rousseau's agonized materialism later on. His fraught attempt to control a future lived through his readers has already been examined in chapter 2. Percy Shelley's optimistic version of this afterlife is given in *A Defence of Poetry*. But it was in *The Triumph of Life* that he makes a *poetic* subject of the objective process to which we belong and over which Rousseau imagines retaining individual proprietorial rights. Meanwhile, we can get a firmer idea of *The Triumph*'s implications from those novels of Mary Shelley written during or just after her time with Percy which take up this theme. I will try to say least about *Frankenstein*, the obvious novel of *L'Homme Machine*. In the context of this argument, one could stress polemically that *Frankenstein* is not about overstepping boundaries but about accepting them; not about scientific overreaching but about the need to tailor our expectations of human beings to what their physical organization is capable of producing. When the individual beauties of the monster's physical components do not survive his composition, these aesthetic virtues should be relocated without loss in the human expression, need, and appeal which only the society of these parts can produce and which Victor ignores.

The monster exemplifies La Mettrie's materialist language, a physical semiotic in which neither of these categories are intelligibly separable. Victor devalues the effect of organization championed by La Mettrie over any privileged individual organ, material or immaterial.

Mary Shelley's novels ring the changes on this bodily logic with more variety than Percy's poetry could ever manage. *Matilda* is a novel of sensibility. By letting sensibility call the tune, Mary Shelley risks (as her mother did in her novels) writing in a manner in which, because the expression of emotion rules all other considerations, plot seems sacrificed to coincidence, narrative development to the repetition of affective situations, and character to neurosis. Either art of this kind is simplistic in its pursuit of intensity of feeling, or else it is disingenuous, calculated, and strategic. In the latter case, such novels have adopted the later romantic tactic of a higher realism, in which failures at one level of representation are redeemed as successful portrayals at another level of experience. *Matilda,* for example, tells the story of a daughter forced to confront her father's incestuous passion for her.[12] Her shortcomings as a narrator, therefore, and the obsessively foreshortened and predictably catastrophic world the novel builds around her, depict by default the disorientation and loss of any sense of authority nowadays routinely ascribed to the victim of abuse of this kind. The novel, so understood, realistically conveys the horrible traducing and betrayal inflicted by abuse, picturing it as being like living in a bad novel—bad in the sense that all its artificiality and narrative conniving are felt as crude and intolerable impositions. The discrediting of the art of the novel images a loss of faith in authority in general. A "mimetic fallacy" looms, but is itself made part of the novel's thought or plot.

To exonerate *Matilda*'s emotional luxuriance from lack of sophistication with claims for its successful depiction of Matilda's fate is to explain an extreme case of the more general condition under which novels of sensibility labor. Novelistic catastrophe and coincidence provoke extreme emotion when they shockingly corroborate a physically hostile world. Curiously, this world is at its most contrary and opposite to our purposes when it seems to display a design of its own. Its "chain of necessity" (to use Matilda's phrase) is most imposing when least subtle, just as the expression of emotion may be most powerful when an involuntary condition. An abrasive and coercive world repeats itself in the importunities of physiology. Recalcitrant bodies—hysterical, consumptive, overwrought in any number of ways—then presume over other controls, mental or psychological. The resulting emotional disarray is thus truer to our subjection to physical restraint than any response based on Cartesian distinctions between mind and body.

Matilda can be read, through the cult of sensibility, as an extreme version of this recovery of a materialist perspective. Matilda's pathological, self-debilitating but understandable isolation adds to that repeated critique of gratuitous Wordsworthian solitariness discerned by recent commentary in so much of the early writing of the second generation of English romantics. It connects also with Percy Shelley's continuous interest in empiricist and materialist philosophical traditions, in apparent contrast with the idealism usually attributed to mainline romanticism. It is a reading which proves that the reflexive habit of an increasingly ironic literary practice need not just show a romanticism refining itself out of existence but also the search for ways to image the determining power of the material world, along with expressive indications—such as the extreme or limiting case of incest—of the strangeness of doing so in an intellectual climate dominated aesthetically by a cult of imagination and ideologically by religious otherworldliness. Self-consciousness, or "self-anatomy" as Percy Shelley called it, foregrounds the ubiquity of plot and narrative, the prescribed patterns observed by apparent spontaneity, to let a sense of being produced prevail over any pretensions to independent authority.

In keeping with this project, *Matilda* remorselessly engineers its repeated convergences. Matilda's mother dies after the birth of her only child. Her father, half-deranged by the bereavement, abandons home and country for travel overseas. Brought up by an emotionally unresponsive and snobbish aunt, the solitary Matilda makes her father "the idol of my imagination," alleviating her isolation by imagining his return to "claim her" (10, 14). He does so when she is sixteen, comforting her when her aunt dies by comparing her grief to his own now manageable despair. Subsequently, however, he grows forbidding and melancholy, and, after a year, Matilda elicits his confession of an incestuous passion for her. Horrified, she initially spurns him, and he sets off for the coast to drown himself. She follows and arrives too late to save him. Her later verdict—"my folly destroyed the only being I was doomed to love"—shows that guilt at his suicide grows to encompass guilt at his passion for her, surely a classic symptom of the victim of abuse. She unreasonably believes herself to be "polluted by the unnatural love" she had "inspired" (60). She admits that to be in love with her father is, in fact, to be "in love with death," not only in the sense that death would be required to "unite" her with the drowned man, death's insuperable barrier here euphemizing the incest taboo; she has also sacrificed any will for autonomous agency to her emulative desire for him, now grown disastrously mimetic. She is now as uprooted as he was; she now becomes a solitary traveler, her whole life programmed to reenact his inconsolable affections. She meets Woodville, a brilliant young poet who just happens to have recently lost the love of his life. Woodville plays to Matilda the role she played to her father; he elicits her confession of the source of her misery, but only inadvertently to confirm her in her sense that her life is utterly determined by it. Any sympathy from him sharpens her conviction of being "a tragedy; a character that he comes to see act." His attempt to change the script to Spenserian chivalry—"Come, as you have played Despair with me I will play the part of Una with you and bring you hurtless from his dark cavern" (59)—only confirms that a script is inescapable, a further emblem of Matilda's recognition of being marked by another's carcinogenic sign, eating away at her identity (60–61): "perhaps he is already planning a poem in which I am to figure. I am a farce and play to him, but to me this is all dreary reality" (56). The logic here is comparable to that of the debilitating Miltonic and Coleridgean role models testifying to the monster's acculturation in *Frankenstein*.

The autobiographical hits and misses in all this only add to the sense of an imagination working within predetermined bounds. By the time a galloping consumption finally bears Matilda toward an "eternal mental union" with her father, her goal appears already achieved, established (Matilda even repeats Mary Wollstonecraft's deathbed words [57]) on the physical evidence of her life, the enhancement of which by any further "mental" translation looks redundant. In *Matilda*, rather as in Percy Shelley's "Mont Blanc," reflection on nature indicates not an independent, mental, idealist viewpoint, but an effect which nature itself typically produces. Matilda, we are told, is one of nature's "fragile mirrors, that ever doted on thine image." The "of," though, must signal a natural property when we further hear that Matilda's coming dissolution points up nature's power to "create another and another" such mirror, so losing "nought by [her] destruction" (65). In Percy Shelley's later play, *The Cenci*, Count Cenci's incestuous tyranny over his daughter Beatrice similarly transforms her self-reflection from the sign of autonomous agency into further evidence of his own reproductive power, the tragic convergence the play dramatizes.

On a materialist reading, this determinism is morally and politically discredited whenever it is personified. Rather than the tragic condition of life to be ineffectually overcome by poetic myth, it represents a mischievous and destructive attitude toward materialism. Mary Shelley's novels frequently set up singular protagonists whose extraordinariness of situation or character symptomatically disguises an ordinariness from which we have become estranged. She observes the romantic paradigm of the concrete universal, but in order to erode the division symbolically overcome. In her novel *The Last Man*, the lastness of the last man renders in singular fashion a picture of what is true, but taken from an impossible angle. No implied reader can ever hear Verney's words, except as a sibylline prophecy. Yet his isolated mortality is unproblematically true to the unshareable destiny of each one of us. And it seems only human, if culpable, to disguise this incommunicable fate in terms casting it as extraordinary or fictionally distanced from what we know is the scientific norm. Wittgenstein reworks the conundrum in his well-known, Lucretian aphorism about death not being a fact of life; or, putting it another way, death can hardly be a precedent for anything. Blanchot, who also wrote a novella called *The Last Man,* had his Heideggerian version of this paradox, claiming that once dead we lose "the right to death," or the limiting condition arguably making sense of all our actions.[13] Mary Shelley's intervention in what was a voguish topos in the 1820s represents in extended form the difficulty of this commonplace. When the *Literary Gazette*'s reviewer wrote in 1835 that "with that terrible future we have nothing in common," he gets it exactly wrong.[14]

This kind of writing strategy gives Mary Shelley a new take on domesticity, transforming it from the vocational confinement so tricky for subsequent feminist criticism to valorize, into the representative of a fundamental condition men fearfully consign to a feminine or lowly sphere. Her writings, astutely skeptical of this sublimation, have usually been read as a source of horror or of the uncanny. But they might easily be redirected against that exaggerated immaturity which can come to terms with the classical proportions of human life only by casting them in the outlandish forms of fantasy or nightmare. The worst nightmares are those in which you are to die, a dream which, like history, will of course remain undispelled by awakening. The nightmare, from a Lucretian point of view, would be to have become so unreconciled to one's limitations as to find their inevitable measurements nightmarish. Sir Timothy Shelley, one remembers, was for Mary Shelley a Struldbrugg, a figure whose faults were all figured in his pointless survival beyond the material proportions of human life. Materialism is equally about what is material in the sense of relevant or germane. But Mary Shelley also shows this repressing of material limitation projected onto female characters.

In *Valperga: or, The Life and Adventures of Castruccio, Prince of Lucca*, the last novel she wrote in Percy's lifetime, female agency is imaginatively admitted into literary consciousness only as an agonized dependency. The historical truth in this fulfills a male desire to project on women and make theirs the common physical dependency, and the equal circumstances it implies, which male characters wish to repress. The title itself alternates between the Prince of Lucca, his lover the Countess Valperga, and the castle of Valperga which he razes to the ground to enforce her natural subordination while inadvertently symbolizing his own. *Valperga*, emblematic of the "other" Mary Shelley, the one who didn't write just *Frankenstein*, has attracted good feminist readings. These readings are often troubled by worries like Barbara Jane O'Sullivan's, who writes that "Despite her triumph in creating strong female characters, she undercuts her own achievement by her complicity in the repression and discrediting of the voices she herself has created."[15] But Mary Shelley is also using women to show the male characters' need to project away from hegemonic ideas of experience and onto heretics, prophetesses, and power-mad witches what men too easily escape accountability for. The ghastly determinism of the women's lives abjects limitation in general, redoubling its distance from the men. Valperga herself, closer to initiating political action than any of the other women, is nevertheless granted in her death by drowning a dramatic dissolution which is yet again projected onto a feminine process—"the barren bosom of the sea, which, as an evil step-mother, deceives and betrays all committed to her care" (322). This reflex or pathological gendering of determining processes surely knows its own ideological function and epitomizes its own satire of it in Valperga's Christian name of Euthanasia. In contrast to her brave and serene acceptance of all the neurotic luggage heaved her way, the efforts of characters like the usurer Pepe of Cremona to mortgage the future can only appear disgusting, a letting-down of the male conspiracy to hand death and other constraints over to the women and villagers. Pepe reduces his native city of Cremona on paper by lending money to its rich but beleaguered inhabitants on condition they cite their fortunes and properties as collateral. He has impoverished himself to ensure this indebtedness. His credit, though, exists entirely on paper, in the shape of bonds, deeds, and affidavits stored in a chest in an underground cellar. Castruccio's rage at this when taken into Pepe's confidence leads him to call Pepe "not human"; but, revealingly, this judgment on Pepe's attempt to live entirely on the superior level of imagination is elaborated in opposite terms of physical subordination and degeneracy—"in these filthy vaults thou hast swollen, as a vile toad or rank mushroom . . ." (161). Pepe's real crime, the rhetoric seems to be saying, is to discredit the imaginative life by showing it to be complicit in the blind animal drives it is its normal function to discredit. The contradiction can produce only loathing and revulsion. By contrast, Euthanasia's fate keeps everything in place, but ironically, surely?

If Percy Shelley learns from this sophistication, then maybe it enables his materialism to reach its apogee, as do so many things Shelleyan, in his last, uncompleted poem, *The Triumph of Life*. His use of Lucretius here at last allows his narrator, Rousseau, a vision matching Dante's, which a materialist reading can try to make climactic rather than just interrupted. According to book 4 of *De Rerum Natura*, we shed our images like skins: insubstantial, flimsy, but nonetheless atomic particles of the same order as our physical make-up emanate from all objects. These images or films *(imagines, simulacra, effigiae,* translating Epicurus's *eidola* or *tupoi),*[16] penetrating the perceiver usually through the eyes but, if asleep, through pores, render their originals visible. Lucretius's theory is commonly thought to be intended to counter contemporary skepticism or Pyrrhonism. Our senses never lie; what they receive are always "replica," true to life, although we err in our opinions of them. Lucretius gives a literal or materialist theory of metaphor. When we *imagine*, we either apprehend flimsier images, as in the "decaying sense" of Hobbes's account, or else we perceive the exotic results of collisions and amalgams of different images in their varied atomic flights. The vision displacing Dante's toward the end of the poem, then, is the sensuous production of all experience, a material production which gives the lie to skepticism and religious transcendentalism alike. Lucretius's trumping of Dante takes place despite the former's cynical view of "love," with which Shelley could not have agreed, perhaps indicating further the still partially alienated form in which Shelley's Rousseau is obliged to represent materialism.

In *The Critique of Judgement* Kant argued that genius was inimitable: those who claimed to rationalize experiences in excess of our material nature were fanatics. Fanatics need not be revolutionaries, they could just as easily be conservatives.[17] *The Triumph of Life* comparably attacks those who repress for ulterior reasons knowledge of the physical source of our ideas in a common material nature, a shared constitution. Shelley exonerates Dante and Milton from such ideological machinations in *A Defence of Poetry* because they so visibly produce their Lucretian membrane, that mask and mantle in which they approach us across the centuries. A Christianity pretending to a transcendental origin is refuted by the historical imprint of each of its formulators and defenders. In *A Defence of*

Poetry, Lucretius is relegated from the first rank of epic poets—Homer, Dante, and Milton—because he "had limed the wings of his swift spirit in the dregs of the sensible world." But by *The Triumph of Life,* the danger of idealism's consignment of the sensible world to "dregs" is foremost. "The sleepers in the oblivious valley" have (like Beatrice in *Valperga*) been awoken with horror to the physical exigencies of their lives; an enlightenment they should have been prepared for by life, but were shielded from as it shaped human expression to mask rather than replicate its origins:

> And of this stuff the car's creative ray
> Wrought all the busy phantoms that were there
>
> As the sun shapes the cloud—thus, on the way
> Mask after mask fell from the countenance
> And form of all, and long before the day
>
> Was old, the joy which waked like Heaven's glance
> The sleepers in the oblivious valley, died,
> And some grew weary of the ghastly dance
>
> And fell, as I have fallen by the way side. . . .
> (ll. 533–41)

The shedding of masks, then, becomes a depleting and repressive search for truth rather than its Lucretian increase in outgoing self-expression. Understood as a revelatory denuding, it points us in a direction opposite to the positive communication described by the Lucretian projection of simulacra. Life's naturalizing of this swerve away from natural understanding, "As the sun shapes the clouds," fixes us in an unreal, dreamlike state in which all terrors and tyrannies are possible. Poetry, on the other hand, appears in *A Defence of Poetry* to show the wrong-headedness of the pursuit of unadorned, naked truth into phantasmal realms: the removing of veils gives way to the overflowing of a fountain, or is indifferently exchanged for the spreading of a figured curtain. Poetry recovers a universe annihilated by our ideas of it by locating ourselves in its production: it "reproduces the common universe of which we are portions and percipients." Poetry's purging "from our inward sight the film of familiarity" again uncovers ourselves—"the wonder of our being"—but as creatures inseparable from the affective responses with which we clothe the world anew.[18] Poetry does more than implicate subject in object; it displaces them with a nondualist language of creativity. Read with this emphasis, *A Defence of Poetry* collaborates with *The Triumph of Life* by showing that poetry frees us from "Life" when that word signifies the "one sad thought" of those submitting to definitions of it rather than constantly re-creating it from their own historical resources. The poem demonizes, as a Petrarchan triumph, the idea that life is one thing, a single truth to be uncovered by an invariable scientific procedure. Modern relativistic alternatives, accepting the historical variability of truth, have to rescue their own materialism from comparable demonizations as decay, degeneracy, the extinction of higher vision, mechanical subordination, and so on. Shelley's poem's complex survival of its narrator's drive toward a single answer to the question What is life? problematizes the question itself, suggesting that the distance between subject and object which the question assumes is the mistake. This is the error which allows life to be felt as an intolerable imposition from without and our best self to be conceived of as a consciousness anterior to all physical circumstance.

This Lucretian or Epicurean account might seem to bleach the poem of its political coloring. Epicurus's wholesale dismissal of politics and politicians, recorded in epistles and fragments, is deceptive where not understood as itself clearing the way for a political theory properly founded on a just estimate of human possibility. The Epicurean belief that nature is unguided by a teleological principle certainly excludes Platonic and Aristotelian notions that those of us who don't make the grade as philosophers may still be naturally guided toward fulfillment in political life. But there remains an alternative politics to be based on the philosophical acceptance of the absence of such purposiveness, one which was historically productive of its own Epicurean communities.[19] This looks quite close to the communal vision at the end of "The Mask of Anarchy," for example, often thought unrealistic or patronizing. The retrieval of ancient law and the advocacy of passive resistance shaming aggressors into sympathy take a common constitutional stand. The mistake (which Shelley first described in *The Necessity of Atheism*) is to think that mental passiveness leaves the mind supine before an external world rather than empowered to participate in the natural excitation and productivity of that world. An Epicurean or Lucretian reading, though, would again highlight a vision which does not so much refute the anarchic establishment of Shelley's day as seize upon this arbitrariness as its warrant for changing (even abandoning) the rules and locating political authority in that authentic creativity.

The Triumph of Life tempts a similar glossing. Shelley's diagnosis of error then retains political significance. We cannot be expected to subscribe to a political theory if it is completely out of keeping with the truth of what we are. Nonmaterialist theories of how we should live are founded on misconceptions of the animal they try to accommodate. If we let mortality and the primacy of physical organization dictate our common possibilities for happiness, then we might more easily see through the ideologies which either falsely promise something different or else demonize our physicality in order to keep us in fearful thrall to an alternative, unjustifiable authority.

SEVEN

Jane Austen's Conservatism

W
as Jane Austen a Conservative? The answer to this apparently familiar question sheds new light on the political coloring of Austen's values. British Conservatism is a peculiarly British creature, as distinct from conservatism as, say, British republicanism is from American republicanism. Most criticism of Austen balances her reactionary and progressive tendencies (paternalist and feminist, manorial and postcolonial, writing for the gentry, but to secure its reform), but ignores the peculiarly Conservative genealogy that explains their inconsistent society. Conservatism has obsessively retained its character to the present day and so can profitably be examined at close range for historical purposes in its currently available models. That is my contention here, anyhow, along with the view that essential to Conservative polemic is a theoretical reserve whose instabilities are relevant to my study of metaromantic possibility. Austen worries that this reserve can be abused, that reticence about principles can be irresponsible, and she figures her hostility to this unaccountability directly in the flirtation in *Lady Susan* (probably 1793–94) and indirectly in the logic of flirtation periodically mobilizing pejorative characterization in her other novels.

Was "Conservatism" a political concept, current in her own day, describing a self-conscious political grouping? Lord Blake's history of the Conservative party from Peel to Thatcher suggests not. He traces the first use of " 'conservative' in its modern political sense" to an article in the *Quarterly Review* of 1830 once thought to have been written by John Wilson Croker.[1] Furthermore, the merging of Toryism and Conservatism signaled by this usage frequently appears uneasy or incomplete. One recurring strain in Conservative thought regards both its philosophy and its dogmatics as transcending party politics. Bolingbroke and his later admirer Disraeli are perhaps the most articulate protesters that at certain periods in British history the true interests of Conservatism became detached from their supposed representatives. Their reaction was to unearth the true tradition, stemming from Elizabeth I according to Bolingbroke's *The Idea of a Patriot King*, written in the 1730s, and from Bolingbroke himself, the "fiery imagination" of Disraeli's *Vindication of the English Constitution*, published in 1835.[2] Roger Scruton, preaching *The Meaning of Conservatism* at the beginning of the Thatcher era, propounds a Conservatism in league with Hegel—"the theoretical master of the idea of legitimacy"—in its insistence that individuals are socially constructed and possess no original rights and liberties. He has, therefore, to remain magisterially untroubled by those "passing fashions, well-meant, not always misguided" characterizing policies of the Conservative party around 1980. He denies his Conservatism any ideal pattern, identifying such templates with political theories inimical to the practical reason which alone can justify Conservative dogma.[3] Yet the ancestry of the Toryism, often dissident like Scruton's, later to become amalgamated with Conservatism certainly generated ideals—whether the Jacobitism practiced by Bolingbroke and sublimated by Dr. Johnson or the nostalgia for an ancient constitutional patrimony most memorably voiced by Edmund Burke.

I will repeatedly turn to Conservatism's pretensions to elevate itself above party. To mention Burke, though, is to recall a figure who, although identified with rhapsodic idealism by Pitt and others, was nothing if not a rhetorical strategist. This is so much so that Ian Gilmour's apology for Conservatism can plausibly cast him in the role of vindicator of party spirit: "Halifax distrusted parties and 'trimmed' against them; Bolingbroke was excluded from active politics by the ruling clique and sought a non-party kingdom; Hume found in parties intolerance, selfishness and zeal; with Burke, the trumpeter of the Rockingham Whigs, party came into its own."[4] Burke believed party divisions and free government to be inseparable, however mystical or constitutional in the widest of senses he proclaimed to be the interest he represented. He can be seen as a healer of the recurrent rift between a Conservative reaching after something best described as humanist or classical and Tory political practice.

The three historical splits in the Tory party—over the Corn Laws, tariff reform, and now Europe—have always set loyalties to the national interest against loyalties to a wider market. Surprisingly, the broader European dimension in each dispute always carried the commercial, pragmatic attractions, and local chauvinism the Conservative appeal to considerations transcending party. Hence, Burke argued that the French Revolution was a commercial disaster and that it put at risk the European

inheritance of a single culture. The traditional enmity of Protestant England to traces of that Catholic and Latin ancestry must not be allowed to
obscure a hard economic fact: European like-mindedness traditionally
fostered mutual commercial and ideological support among its members
which had then included England. Burke's lament for the passing of that
chivalric culture was far from sentimental; he called it, we remember, "the
cheap defence of nations."[5]

Burke's reassuring example suggests that Jane Austen could have connected an instinctive conservatism, religiose in its convictions, with a particular party at the time (mid- to late 1790s) when she was writing the
first drafts of novels to be published over a decade later. By then, a prime
minister who notoriously never described himself as a Tory, Pitt, could
be contrasted with Lord Liverpool, a figure who arguably held his party
together more effectively than he directed a transitional period in the history of the nation. The intervening ministries of Addington, Pitt again,
Portland, Grenville and Fox, and then Perceval can, with hindsight, be
seen to have stabilized in the fifteen-year reign of Lord Liverpool from
1812–27. He initially presided over a Regency characterized by harsh
Conservative measures rather than anticipations of the inevitable reform
to come—Luddism made a capital offense in 1812, the 1815 Corn Law,
the repeal of Income Tax in 1816 and of Habeas Corpus in 1817, the Act
against Seditious Meetings in the same year.

Norman Gash's biography of Liverpool commends him as a prime
minister who, at a time before party allegiance automatically overrode
all other loyalties, could see to it that parliament was well "managed."[6]
But the virtues of good organization, or the welding together of an original political machine, do not sound Tory only with hindsight. They did,
too, in 1835, when Disraeli sang Bolingbroke's praises as the "organising
genius" resolving "discordant materials" of anti-Whig factions into the
harmony of Tory opposition; the reordering of the public mind which
led, Disraeli thought, to its being ruled by the administrative excellen-
cies of the eventual Tory successor to Walpole, the elder Pitt.[7] Liverpool's
faceless effectiveness in running his administration can therefore be cast
as a Tory virtue. Disraeli, as is well-known, thought Liverpool and his colleagues "mediocrities," but Gash's Tory pattern of justification matches
Disraeli's praise of Bolingbroke to Liverpool's case—the ability to orient
competing individuals with different views toward the national interest.
Of course, the idea that the national interest might entail Liverpool's opposition to Catholic emancipation and a Reform Act just because Liverpool could command his cabinet's consensus hardly follows!

Recently, Austen's novels have been most influentially read as participating in the war of ideas issuing from the Revolution controversy in the 1790s and as complex representations of the Regency Crisis. Common to both interpretations must be her interest in having her characters compensate for an authority either absent or in abeyance, conserving the principle of *ancien régime* or monarchy despite having to be loyal to stand-ins which seem inferior or mistaken. This link between pragmatics and principle, both traditionally Conservative and at work in Liverpool's contemporary management of government, is tested in her novels: for example in Anne Elliot's verdict at the end of *Persuasion* that she had been rightly persuaded to do the wrong thing by a substitute for the right person. Austen writes as if to stretch Burke's identification of party and constitutional interest, or else to refigure a loyalism discreditably close to the fantastic idea that the Prince Regent might be a Patriot King in waiting. Less dramatically, her novels repeatedly contrive the isolation of their heroines from that paradigm of Conservative authority, parental control. From Catherine Morland onward, the circumstance of temporary parting from parents (sometimes doubled as in the cases of Emma Watson at the Edwards' [*The Watsons*] and Clara Brereton at Lady Denham's establishment [*Sanditon*]) shows how primary to Austen's social imagination had become the simulating of authentic standards in the default of their originals.

I want to draw two conclusions from my sketch of Conservatism. One is that the history of Conservatism is littered with attempts of different kinds to make Tory practice representative of a felt but never systematized national identity. This holds true from Bolingbroke to Burke, from the Young England movement to Disraeli's one-nation Toryism through to contemporary varieties of populism or Thatcherite alternatives to "society." The second conclusion is that this intuition of a mandate for political representation, since it cannot be theorized, exists in appeals to common sense, aesthetics, religiosity, or whatever can displace the appearance of prejudice or tolerate contradictions unacceptable to strict political theory. Intrinsic to this finesse is that it be presumed but never admitted; Sidney Smith and Lord Hailsham were agreed on that. A communicative virtue is made out of intellectual inconsistency which is redescribed as a richly realistic appreciation of human vagaries, a *Religio Laici*.

If one introduces Conservatism to discussion of the work of Jane Austen in this way, then maybe the question to ask of her novels is To what extent do they do the work of aesthetic recuperation and to what extent do they mobilize rather than, in Coleridgean fashion, reconcile opposites? In his book *The Binding of Leviathan,* another Conservative apologist and sometime academic, William Waldegrave, argues that Conservatives object to Marxism when it lends intellectual respectability "to the attack by one group in society on all other groups" and when it discredits law and order as ideological expedients in the process.[8] To object that there still might be a case for Conservatives to answer, namely, that they are similarly in the business of universalizing their class interests, is disqualified because of the lack of a Conservative theory that says this is what Conservatives are doing. Take away theory, the argument goes, and you must have what Waldegrave calls "natural community" (123): people living in a manner proper to their kind, perhaps the same as what Mr. Knightley calls "The nature and simplicity of gentlemen and ladies, with their servants and furniture"?[9] Theorize, though, and you create artificial distinctions out of which arise a dictatorial state-apparatus comparable to Hobbes's Leviathan with its inexorable deductions from axiomatic truths or presocial "laws of nature."

Let us take this argument a bit further. Conservatives like Waldegrave argue that it is natural for a certain configuration of classes to pattern forth the State, and proper for us to accept that the State reflects back to us if not our exact station in life then at least the limits of social mobility. Any alternative is hypothetical or theoretical in a pejorative sense that goes against norms natural to community. How has this argument worked in the past? From Sir Robert Filmer, through Burke, to its recycling in Scruton, the conservative imagination has always been paradoxically inhibited by its invention of the natural. Elizabeth Bennett can marry into Pemberley, but for her to desire the franchise, for example, would be a theoretical possibility as inappropriate as wanting, unnaturally, to be able to choose a different role within a family—to want to be a son rather than a daughter, a husband rather than a wife. Radical demands which Conservatives called unnatural before women had the vote they would probably call anachronistic now. Social groupings and cultures can grow within our midst to assert their claims with as natural credentials as their long-time host. But their achievement of Conservative respectability does not alter the fact, which should embarrass Conservatives, that their innovations might once have looked merely theoretically desirable. "What is now proved was once imagined," as Blake might have said. Blake was mad then but is literature now, the Conservative might reply. But before it is proved, Blake's imagined truth inspires the evolving language of universal rights to include unconventional sections of society, a language always anathema to and ridiculed by Conservatives, but necessary to describe the generation or evolution of social states they now call natural. A sometime utopian impulse latterly appears as inevitable and constitutional. A Conservative art which revived this contradiction between "permanent" and "progressive" interests, ordinarily reconciled by romantic Conservatives like Coleridge, might contest Conservatism by enjoying too indiscriminately the license at work when Conservatives invent the natural: when either they marry a kind of transcendental patriotism to pragmatic political decisions, or else disown current policies by claiming that true Conservative values belong to this other realm.

The figure of the flirt in Austen's novels portrays the fictional irresponsibility of those whose Conservatism dallies with actual Toryism and vice versa. Roger Gard writes of Austen's early unpublished novella *Lady Susan* that its "real fault . . . is that we cannot imagine anyone as demonstrably intelligent as Lady Susan really wanting to go in for Dissipation, sexual or otherwise."[10] But is this a fault? And isn't the central point of the character that she can keep other characters guessing as to what she "really" wants? Again, isn't this skill in flirtation represented as being so powerful that it absorbs all its competitors, showing a facility in simulation which accounts for the novel's "single effect," as Gard aptly calls it? Austen's epistolary novel creates a drama in which the reader, lacking authorial guidance, follows the lead of the most intelligent character, the character apparently approximating most closely to omniscience. Disconcertingly, she happens to be the incorrigible flirt, Lady Susan. Not until the "Conclusion" does an implied author intervene, miming embarrassment over the novel's epistolary form—so much money implausibly accruing to the Post Office from all those letters! So Austen's epistolary technique only flirted with realism, it seems? But there is no resolution for the reader here if Lady Susan's teasing art is now simply replicated by her long-awaited judge. Not to be repeated by Austen after this novella is a latitude of treatment, a revealing prominence of flirtatious authority, later to be stylistically curbed and morally regulated. But I should anticipate my argument here and emphasize from the start the multivalency of Jane Austen's flirt. Far from scapegoating the flirt in patriarchal fashion, Jane Austen exploits to the full her power to disturb the settled figures of knowledge and authority, foreshadowing a modernist dilemma fudged by Conservative thinking. Toril Moi provides a *locus classicus* for this positive interpretation when she transvalues Sartre's description of flirtation as, by definition, a woman's bad faith into a female "project." Simultaneously she shows that the *fictional* understanding of flirtation and

seduction, exemplified by Beauvoir's novel *L'invitée*, is "far more complex" than might be given in "documentary" fashion.[11]

In Austen's early novella, the breadth of epistolary interest appears
to displace the conventional profundities meant to anchor the work in
gentrified Conservatism. The experience of writing it while staying in pre-
tentious Bath, after her father's unexpected retirement there, must have
sharpened her sense of a meretricious social variety busily exposing itself.
The two female gold diggers, Lady Susan Vernon and her confidante,
Mrs. Alicia Johnson, sacrifice reason to sensibility and self-knowledge to
convenience. They treat other people as predictable counters in their
selfish speculations and manipulative power games. Austen sometimes
caricatures their presumption with a relish reminiscent of *Love and Freind-
ship* as the two, especially Lady Susan, outmaneuver those who "are not
of a nature to comprehend ours" (92). Again, the joke is that while we, of
course, go along with the prejudice that favors depth over the breadth,
range, and promiscuity of experience of these women, to say so would
be hopelessly dull. "What could I do? Facts are such horrid things!" says
Alicia in camp tones when rumbled. "This eclaircissement is rather pro-
voking," agrees Lady Susan (94). But the novel's joke is also on those who
do not appreciate that to an uncomfortable extent Alicia's and Susan's
virtuosity is its own, their opportunistic miming a comparable exercise of
fictional energies. The novel's moral lesson depends on our skill in reading it, and so on our ability to catch the characters' parody of it, not on
our ability to check the novel's action against some deep truth. Conservative art, from Johnson to Waugh, finds small delight in confirming its
indisputable moral realism. Interest lies not there but in distinguishing its
fluency from the villains' garrulousness, its variations in tone from their
vulgarity, its fancy from their obsessions, its aesthetic from their politics.

From *Rasselas* to *A Handful of Dust*, the fact that we are assumed in-
controvertibly to know what human nature is lets us laugh at those with
pretensions to discover anything about it; yet, surreptitiously, the Conservative novel profits from the fictional significance of the unnecessary
journey to find this out. To put down Lady Susan straightforwardly as
an adventuress would be boring and fictionally self-destructive: the good
characters would write all the letters, expected correctness would always
preempt invention. But Lady Susan is above all "plausible"; she is reputedly "the most accomplished coquette in England." This reputation cuts
two ways (46–47): it makes her professions of feeling untrustworthy, and
her social relationships fundamentally unstable. Yet it is coquetry which
guarantees her continuing acceptability by, in its extreme form, mean-

ing that she can never be still for long enough to have that affair which would ruin her or send her tumbling irretrievably down the social scale. Coquetry is the pale, middle-class shadow of aristocratic license. In her promiscuous misbehavior, Susan Vernon both invites comparison with the defaulting aristocracy Austen's gentry continually surpasses in her novels and shows how far from their freedoms any middle-class hegemony must be content to stay. Indeed, its strength lies in having a very different conception of freedom; its feeling observation of law is frequently contrasted with a lawless indulgence of freedom. Feeling, though, need never issue in action: that's what's wrong with it, but also what may exonerate the devotees of sensibility. Like Susan Vernon, they can be the ultimate artists in keeping up appearances, honoring to a fault what Roger Scruton's Conservative calls "the priority of appearance."[12] Why? Because they never enact heterodox alternatives but only savor feeling in excess of conventional behavior whose rules they, as much as the good characters, are bound to observe out of self-preservation. Or else they exploit inappropriate delights harbored in the safe haven of convention itself, doing right things for the wrong reasons or embodying a will to power they despise others for not using convention to camouflage. Such success may often be achieved by exemplary behavior, when the person predisposed to think ill of the coquette is subdued by her good manners and fair dealing. And only the letters admitting her desire for power over the would-be detractor equip us to distinguish her perfect acting from genuine morality: "There is an exquisite pleasure in subduing an insolent spirit, in making a person predetermined to dislike, acknowledge one's superiority. I have disconcerted him already by my calm reserve; and it shall be my endeavour to humble the pride of these self-important De Courcies still lower, to convince Mrs. Vernon that her sisterly cautions have been bestowed in vain, and to persuade Reginald that she has scandalously belied me. This project will at least serve to amuse me, and prevent my feeling so acutely this dreadful separation from you and all whom I love" (52).

Accomplishment of this kind is nevertheless understood by Susan Vernon's sister-in-law, the Mrs. Vernon, Reginald's sister, obliged to give her house-room and observe the consequences. She calls Lady Susan's behavior "an absolute coquetry, or a desire of universal admiration" (54). But the more accurate this judgment of Mrs. Vernon becomes, the less substance it seems to possess. If one wishes universal admiration, then one has to act the coquette with a disabling number of individual interests, surely? The Conservative persuasion that its class interests identify with cross-party patriotic or human interests must play the field in the same way, perhaps carrying equal lack of conviction to the experienced observer. Austen can only propose universals out loud as a joke, like the one with which *Pride and Prejudice* begins or, less well-known, the claim in *Sanditon* that "Every neighbourhood should have a great lady" (165). Nevertheless, the social proprieties which her plots seek to disrupt and then restore could hardly be more absolute or admit of less debate. Universals are serious things for Austen, although her writing sends up efforts to abstract their essence from individual interests, like Emma Woodhouse's attempt to treat Harriet as pure social possibility. If one objects that, unlike Austen's Conservative, the absolute coquette rather works by insincerely identifying with different interests in succession, once again criteria essential to making this judgment begin to evaporate. Susan Vernon, successfully reducing Reginald De Courcy to her power, "never behaved less like a coquette in my life." Only Mrs. Vernon, she concedes, could "perceive that I am actuated by any design in behaviour so gentle and unpretending" (55). Because she might expect Susan Vernon to exact revenge for Mrs. Vernon's accurate portrayal of her past coquetry, Mrs. Vernon could, conceivably, suspect Susan's lack of coquetry, her unwillingness to flirt with Reginald, her reserve, her lack of familiarity. But this must mean that grounds for imputing coquetry to Susan have nothing to do with the way in which she is acting. Borrowing an example from Derrida, we might put the conundrum this way: to pretend to a Chinese that you can speak Chinese you have to speak Chinese.[13] To toy with a man averse to coquetry, you have to eschew coquetry. Either Susan does not play the coquette to Reginald, or else coquetry loses all definition in order to mean both to flirt and not to flirt.

Susan Vernon is so accomplished a storyteller that she can interpret any evidence in her favor. Her rewriting of apparently damning evidence against her restores her to Reginald's favor in the novel's most memorable volte-face. When Reginald finally denounces her and gives her up, we feel he has relinquished the unequal battle rather than established her guilt. Once more it is worth emphasizing that the coquette exists just in virtue of this lack of answerability to anyone, this lack of individual commitment. A little reserve, in Austen's novels, is a dangerous thing, the grounds, for example, of Knightley's condemnation of the otherwise exemplary Jane Fairfax and the source of her natural (because secret) affinity to Frank Churchill. But while totally disruptive at the personal level, the aporetic logic of coquetry mimes the efforts of a class to make its interests represent the interest of all. Such a universal nature must be the ultimate fiction, the equivalent of making coquetry absolute. Reginald's father, instructed by Mrs. Vernon's unprovable aperçus, opposes his son's "match" to Susan Vernon, "a match which deep art only could render probable, and must in the end make wretched" (58). To which Reginald's reply is that "no character, however upright, can escape the malevolence of slander" (61). Again Austen's text puts us *en abyme*. Uprightness is, if we know enough, what slander, to be slander, must assert. Ironically, nature is best expressed in art through a grace escaping rule. Alexander Pope, a Tory forced like his mentor Bolingbroke into patriotic fantasy, knew this, but for later, more established Tories, the admission was unsettling.

Susan Vernon is a bad mother; but even this piece of demonizing goes wrong. As Reginald notes, "because she has not the blind and weak partiality of most mothers, she is accused of wanting maternal tenderness" (62). We know that she skimps on her daughter Frederica's education, but the correlative of Reginald's defense is Susan's perception that Frederica's artlessness means she could not "bid fairer to be the sport of mankind" (69). Mrs. Vernon holds that Frederica "must not be sacrificed to policy or ambition," but in her solicitude for Frederica she here concedes the political character of Susan's art, perhaps too closely for comfort. Similarly, the rendering of the coquette at work compares too well with Austen's own art: "Oh! How delightful it was, to watch the variations of his countenance while I spoke, to see the struggle between returning tenderness and the remains of displeasure . There is something agreeable in feelings so easily worked on" (85). Were in fact Susan to be a conventionally good mother and to communicate to her daughter, partially, the advantages of her experience, she would furnish her daughter with the interpretative and fictional arts, which politics enacts but disowns, with which to "work on" her circumstances: maybe not quite "the very thing to work on," but just as novelistic. To avoid this visible legacy, the daughter must be detached from the mother as conclusively as possible. Reginald switches, reverses, and then is expected imminently to switch again his affections from mother to daughter, and Susan herself crosses the generations to marry the booby suitor, Sir James Martin, whom she had till then been assiduously foisting on her daughter. Incest, we might remember, was another of Derrida's examples of a concept equivocating between being a natural or a cultural taboo. Even relationships supposedly stabilized between different generations, Austen's novel suggests, can ultimately be remade under the unnerving influence of so adept a shape-shifter as Susan Vernon.

The novel's conclusion, freed, one presumes, of the partiality of the novel's letter writers, wonders whether Lady Susan will enjoy her second marriage. And, at last, the indecidability with which the text has been flirting is openly acknowledged. "Whether Lady Susan was, or was not happy in her second choice—I do not see how it can ever be ascertained—for who would take her assurance of it, on either side of the question? The world must judge from probability. She had nothing against her but her husband, and her conscience" (103). Probability indicates a modest empiricism. Significantly in this respect, Ian Gilmour takes Talmon's "true line of demarcation" in politics to be one between "absolutism and empiricism." [14] Either Lady Susan has foolishly married someone who must make her unhappy, or else an absolute instrumentalism we cannot fathom, in keeping with her virtuosity elsewhere, is at work. At least Susan Vernon has not committed the error she so finely reprobates in her friend Alicia: "My dear Alicia, of what a mistake were you guilty in marrying a man of his age!—just old enough to be formal, ungovernable and to have the gout—too old to be agreeable, and too young to die" (90). The balance of probabilities has finally replaced the idea that, beyond a reasonable doubt, the resources of art cannot replace the satisfactions of what is natural; indeed, they may be indistinguishable.

Jane Austen's own letters show the degree to which she was herself obliged to make up the Establishment which her novels defend and renew. [15] The belief in the moral and intellectual sufficiency of simply relating the details of practical good judgment is Tory, but this assumption is set in the context of a Conservative wit suggesting her grasp of an ideal pattern that is never expected to map onto particular instances. Brothers aside, the letters imply, sailors are no better than they should be and the Admiralty is fickle in its preferment—"Poor Charles & his frigate—But there could be no chance of his having one, while it was thought to be such a certainty." Soldiers are only "sighed for" when they turn out to be good writers, and when marriage to them or to sailors is an opportunity for wives to travel (198, 68). The royal family is, as always, less than ideal; the Prince Regent's being hateful to the "poor" Princess of Wales is her only extenuating circumstance (208). God is hard and eventually unsparing. Jane Austen was aware, according to Cassandra's so convincing letter, when she was about to die and thus experienced the unimaginable pains of separation—"she said she could not tell us what she suffer'd" (344)—the agony whose absence she celebrates whenever possible in her accounts of the deaths of others like her father. She is blessed with children, because she can experience her own writings as children of her own making, the "sucking," "darling" novels she refers to as a mother (201, 182). Cultural superiority compensating for straitened circumstances has to be created and sustained, by establishing Book Societies which are the envy of other neighborhoods, and by generally cultivating a "civility" through one's skills in being "conversible," key words linked in the letters (198–99). "Superiority" in Austen's sense proves both that the genteel poor don't have what they deserve and vindicates a realm of Conservative values transcending party fortunes. Clearly much was to be endured by a mixture of the practicality and ideal inventiveness parodied by Susan Vernon.

Acceptable flirting for the younger Austen is again like making things up, but in a self-conscious and skeptical manner: knowing one's own mind because doubtful of the seriousness of one's partner in crime. Jane Austen describes her own flirtations, especially the one with Tom Lefroy, "for whom I do not care sixpence," as happily taking the risk of making a spectacle of herself: "I can expose myself, however, only once more, because he leaves the country soon after next Friday." Here all is openness, and the immersion in pretense is part of a highly stylized kind of behavior whose conventions are accepted just because they structure and make sense of actions which, if they became the norm, would be indefinable. Flirtation, as Adam Phillips has argued, "is an often unconscious form of skepticism"; and those supposedly capable of explaining skepticism, the philosophers, Phillips continues, "make us doubt that skepticism is erotic."[16] Austen's absolute coquettes, female and male, recover the connection between skepticism and eroticism: they trope an uncertainty in knowledge which she finds unacceptable but whose disreputableness was increasingly embraced by subsequent more radical thinkers. She writes at the start of a tradition in which the consummate pretender—flirt, dilettante, dandy, or *flâneur*—shifts from signifying only an aristocratic trifler to figuring a critical stance which, if it still has no alternative to offer, nevertheless signals a subversive immunity to normally binding social obligations of all kinds.

In the Regency period, the Prince Regent conferred on dandyism associations of an irresponsible, and therefore indeterminate, Whiggery.[17] While the ability to flirt might be part of the dandy's equipment, flirtation focuses the epistemological or communicative problem attaching to an irresponsible radicalism, one not answerable to any programme. The danger, as Austen's treatment of flirtation suggests she sees it, is that mute Conservative assumptions of principle and rectitude occupy the same space or freedom as flirtation when Conservatives rise above party

to an imagined sufficiency in which they are our truly patriotic representatives or, as Disraeli later put it dogmatically, "the Tory, or national party
of England."[18] Radical competitors for this *Lebensraum* must be isolated
from legitimate Conservative ones and then demonized as flirts. But can
they be separated out in this way?

Linda Colley's *Britons* tries to show at length that the nationalism of
British patriots in the eighteenth century grew in proportion to its power
to say what it was not rather than what it was, often through acts of war
and colonialism.[19] This reticence allowed all sorts of competing interests to appropriate nationalism as their form of legitimation. One might
add to Colley's story that in Jane Austen's lifetime successive adminis-
trations sought to safeguard and distinguish the constitutional image of
England from continental models. In the 1790s, overshadowed by the
French Revolution, the threat came from the left; but after the Congress
of Vienna and the Holy Alliance, from the autocratic right. The political shift resulted from England's "being brought into a course," as Liverpool later put it in 1822, "which was quite right at the time" but allowed figures like Wellington to become "rather more continental than
we either are or ought to be permanently."[20] Percy Shelley would not,
of course, have thought of Castlereagh's diplomatic achievement at Vienna as "quite right at the time." But *The Mask of Anarchy*'s nationalistic
appeal to the "Men of England" defines Reform much as Liverpool did
Conservatism: through its opposition to Wellington's "continental direction," epitomized in Shelley's poem by the militia's actions at Peterloo.
Patriotism, evidently, can compass most things, as it imagines communities exceeding any party agenda to which its different acolytes might
subscribe. In *Emma*, the loyal seal of approval on Mr. Knightley's Donwell
Abbey, you will remember, was "English verdure, English culture, English
comfort, seen under a sun bright, without being oppressive" (355). The
sun, of course, does not oppress here because it is not of continental but
of English strength.

An awareness of the history of "flirtation" and its associates in the subsequent history of thought helps us retrospectively to understand better
their apt representation of philosophical uncertainty. My extrapolation
of flirting from its proper meaning of a particular kind of sexual behavior to describe the fictionality of our fantasy that knowledge might ever
be complete is, I have already hinted, characteristically modern, if not
postmodern. In Jane Austen's time, Friedrich Schiller could propose aesthetic experience as the place where we might reencounter a full knowledge of ourselves in contrast to a worldly self-understanding fragmented

by increasing scientific specialism. A century later, Weber and Simmel confront the same problem of the technical refinement of knowledge in an exacerbated form to which the idea of the aesthetic no longer seems an adequate solution. Simmel in particular sees successes in scientific objectification going hand in hand with their advance beyond the reach of the expertise of a single individual, even a single culture.[21] For some centralized purchase on the growth of scientific knowledge to be maintained, a different kind of mastery must be rationalized, one which does not oblige one person to pretend to have specialized in an incredible number of subjects. Accordingly, when Simmel writes an essay on flirtation, the analogies with a timely intellectual attitude toward much more inevitably blossom. Simmel's understanding of flirtation develops the Kantian paradigm of art on which Schiller drew, purposiveness without a purpose, to take it out of aesthetic recession and turn it into an aspect of general discursive competence. He writes: "Here as elsewhere, the relationship between the sexes provides the prototype for countless relationships between the individual and the inter-individual life. . . . Consider, for example, the fact that our intellect can never comprehend all becoming and evolution, real as well as logical, on the basis of a complete unity. . . . Consider the charms of the simultaneous For and Against, the Perhaps, the protracted reservation of the decision which permits a foretaste of the enjoyment of both its aspects together, aspects which in their realisation are mutually exclusive. All this is not only characteristic of the flirtation of a woman with a man. On the contrary, it plays upon thousands of our contents" (149–51).

Simmel, though, is the first to concede, or recall, that the model of flirtation remains a rationalization of failure and frustration, "a tragic moment of life" (152). At best, the pleasure in communication compensates for its lack of a real message to give. At worst, we see at work an endless instrumentalism or manipulation: we may flirt with A in order to flirt with B in a potentially endless chain of partners at no point in which does the "with" connote relationship rather than use, an end rather than a means to something else. In *Mansfield Park*, one of the frightening things about Henry Crawford's comportment of himself in Portsmouth is that one doesn't know who or what his target is. Previously, he might have been flirting with Maria Bertram in order to flirt with her obviously eligible sister, Julia, and then with Fanny in order to flirt at a distance with Maria again; but his elopement with Maria after her marriage to Mr. Rushworth presumably suggests another abeyance of principle which leaves the reader looking for still further motives, further expedients at work. The novel's apparent approximation of Henry's character to animal promiscuity might look prudish, but his simultaneous inscrutability, the difficulty of reading his reserve, also makes him profoundly unsociable. Perhaps that is Austen's point: to exhibit his lack of "conversibility" and "civility."

Nevertheless, Conservative thinking cannot be entirely disentangled from a comparable mysteriousness. Conservatives want both to say that they know what is right, and to deny that they can state systematically what it is they know. Like the unwritten British Constitution, their beliefs are a matter of practical citizenship. Scruton dramatically and disingenuously asserts of Conservatism that "its essence is inarticulate."[22] He means, presumably, as I have been emphasizing, that its exposition must take place in an idiom different from that expected of political theory. For in another sense, the British Constitution has indeed been written—but as partisan history, not a charter of principles; as the vivid histories of Disraeli's *Vindication* and Bagehot's *The English Constitution* (1867) rather than the theories and propositions of John Stuart Mill's *Representative Government* (1861). Politician and journalist carry more weight in Conservative political self-understanding than any philosopher. Defending the Burkean prejudices which replace the conscious exposition of conservatism, Scruton invokes an "instinctive moral sense whereby people come to act with understanding, even if they have no understanding of why they act."[23] Again, though, this simply escapes being questioned by escaping into another genre. Scruton's formulation recalls, for example, the Christian Conservatism of Coleridge's theology in *Aids to Reflection,* where one has to believe before one can understand; a Wittgensteinian language-game which cannot be evaluated from the outside, comparatively. Could Conservatives produce a statement of their principles, could they, that is, abstract their principles from particular implementations, they would be obliged to submit the logic of those principles to canons of fairness and justice. They would have to defend their universal application; they would have to produce a theory, right or wrong. Wittgenstein, confronted with the infinity of constructions one can put on a piece of human behavior, concluded that there must be a way of following a rule which is not just another interpretation of it.[24] Conversely, contra Conservatives, one might argue that there must be legitimate ways of interpreting rules which do not entail that one has to obey them.

Conservative philosophy can look like a philosophy of flirtation. As it is, Conservatives like Scruton flirt with the possibility of a philosophy of Conservatism, keeping it in focus through the predictability and consistency of their actions, while claiming that the essence of this behavior is precisely that it is not generalizable. Let me try to unpack further the analogy between Conservatism and that art of flirtation which shadows the fictional license through which Austen maintains her superior sense of value. Simmel argued that flirtation equivocates between price— flaunting the tag on an attainable sexual commodity—and an intangible value eluding and so transcending individual satisfactions.[25] One person flirts with a view to real relationship, encouraged by the other whose flirtation means nothing of the kind and whose pleasure, one might say, lies in the principle of the activity. Conservative claims to value similarly describe its elevation of interest above party to embody patriotism or nationalism while simultaneously insisting on the priority of local political calculations over abstract principle. Conservatism can then ridicule the attempts of its opponents to make prior universal principles, such as theories of human rights, inform political decisions. Values and prices, like Wittgenstein's duck-rabbit, go in and out of focus at the same time; their inherence in the same form is that union of Conservatism with Toryism, constitutional patriotism with party politics, exemplified by Burke.

They know and they don't know, they have and yet they have not a set of coherent principles. To turn Burkean, Coleridgean, and perhaps Wittgensteinian conservatism into a philosophy of flirtation is no doubt perverse. Conservatives want us to think that they know the practical value of everything and the theoretical price of nothing. But their thinking is stalked by a comic or parodic reversal in which they appear rather as hard-headed utilitarians for whom values are merely theoretical entities. Insofar as Austen's novels engage with Conservative thinking, they acknowledge the danger Conservatism runs of cutting a cynical figure, one knowing the price of everything but the value of nothing because it refuses to systematize its values. Characters embodying this anomie appear in her novels in order to be exposed and condemned. In contrast to their suspect reserve, she wants to express novelistically that ideal constitutionalism unwritten elsewhere, that Conservatism always about to be amalgamated with Toryism, that imagined humanism backing up but, because imaginary, never part of any nineteenth-century Tory manifesto.

In *The Watsons*, Jane Austen teaches the lesson, again too sharply to be included in the same canon as her later writing, that good communication is vital for the coherence of society. An aristocracy incapable of civility, or lacking awareness of how separate class-interests might unite in community, is dangerously lacking in conversibility. Lord Osborne is given an object lesson by Emma Watson in how to behave like a gentleman. Her comic success is to be shamelessly truthful about her impecuniousness in a style which achieves the seemingly impossible, "in words which make his lordship think." He abandons the inconsiderate banter which drove Emma to mention their class difference descriptively rather than deferentially, and he is returned to his social difference from her with a better sense of what it demands. His thinking produces "propriety," the remembrance of "what was due to a woman in Emma's situation," expressed "in the tone of a gentleman" (136–37). This little Burkean vignette assumes the classlessness of Burke's "gentleman," or the general accessibility of Conservative values which, "without confounding ranks . . . produced a noble equality." That "generous loyalty to rank and sex" cannot belong to any particular rank.[26] The recognition of quality makes the person who possesses it superior and those who don't, however lofty, inferior. Without this common ground, acquaintance between the humble and the great produces what the narrator of *The Watsons* calls an embarrassing "inconsistency" (135). Only the cultured knowledge of how properly to talk to each other overcomes this embarrassment and allows different classes literally to inhabit each other's society.

One can put Emma's dilemma the other way round from a feminist rather than a gentlemanly perspective. Their loss of legal personhood in marriage makes women in Austen's novels at once the repositories of property and its idealization. While money can be entailed on a woman, men always have the direction of it in a society where the legal continuation of that society inevitably returns inheritance to male control. All a woman can do to safeguard her property in marriage is to entail it. Women thus have and haven't money, and their flirtations embody this difficult life in which possession can only mean being possessed, with a consequent loss of reputation and power. A woman without property is a burden on others, as the unpleasant Robert Watson tells his penniless sister; yet female disqualification from competence in financial matters means that Emma ought only to have had money secured upon her by her improvident aunt for future use to be directed, of course, by Robert. The transfer of her dead uncle's fortune to her Aunt Turner's new husband, Capt. O'Brien, is nevertheless blamed by Robert on women rather than on a circumstance of law to which they are subject, and so puts them in the impossible position of having responsibility without power. Another way of describing this, though, might be to say that a woman is like a Conservative debarred from being a Tory.

As I said, though, this instruction is presented harshly in *The Watsons.* Its uncomfortable corrections are much more palatable in, for example, the exchanges between Elizabeth Bennett and Mr. Darcy when the latter first declares his inability to repress a love for her at odds with his sense of her "inferiority" (158). There the "incivility" is immediately defused by a surfeit of conversibility which shows Darcy to be right to let his feelings override inconsistency of class and to be wrong in his ungentlemanly expression of them. Not only the erotic charge between the couple, but the force of their social exchange as at last they speak to each other, assure the reader that all will be well. Less spectacularly, Fanny Price's genuine enactment of the role of a daughter at Mansfield Park is recognized by Sir Thomas Bertram on his return and then underestimated by him. Her final union with Edmund is the reward for her proper behavior within that aesthetic space behind social distinction in which characters can discursively or dramatically show their superior or inferior qualifications for whichever rank in society they happen to have. Where culture is not used in that way, then we encounter instead the license for social transgression represented in the novel by *Lovers' Vows* and by the absolute coquetry of Henry and Mary Crawford. A civility out of tune with the social order is unacceptable; on a Conservative definition, it is even not civil, because subversive of established order. In tune with the social order, though, it harnesses fictional energies in the service of its practical renewal. Fanny, conserver of an ideal tradition against its detractors, is allowed to become its actual embodiment.

Fanny's intuition of what is proper, I am claiming, takes place in a space where she had the freedom to think the opposite. There is no reason why the society of people independent of their class positions should necessarily elicit Burke's generous loyalty to hierarchy. One can readily think of reconfigurations of the site of civil society as different as Hegel's matriarchal family, Habermas's literary public sphere and its counterparts, or even of Bohemia and the demimonde of *flâneur* and professional flirt. Can these groupings avoid prefiguring the radical results of the social energies they currently contain? Precisely the fear that the society of individuals might not endorse established society inspired continuing repressive legislation, of which the 1817 Act against Seditious Meetings was the latest during Austen's lifetime. The area where we make ourselves up (whether this be visible as aesthetic experience, flirtation, dandyism, or any other figure of social detachment) is for the Burkean the scene where we encounter the match between our best selves and the time-honored accommodation of them, the match between moral principle and political establishment. Austen's awareness that this outcome is polemical and rhetorical rather than self-evident, and that an absolute abyss has been opened whose results are unknowable in advance, charges her novel with the Tory anxiety of a split with Conservatism, a collapse into sheer political expediency cast off from a legitimacy transcending party. It also shows her metaromantic aliveness to the political stakes in the fictional practice of her time.

Alasdair MacIntyre rightly ascribes importance to Austen "for the way in which she finds it possible to combine what are at first sight disparate theoretical accounts of the virtues"—Homeric, Aristotelian, Christian— and I don't want to reduce his account of her "synthesis" of these to that of an ideological ploy.[27] Her desire for and fear of the experience of a common humanity prior to its particular interpretations by the canons is very different from doctrinaire Conservatism. In her novels, the aesthetic investment in that unstable imaginary life in which we can entertain universal pictures of humanity is very different from retrospective, Tory constructions of what it is to be human out of political precedent—out of how society has traditionally been ordered. Nothing so predictable and self-serving satisfies Jane Austen. The universal can achieve social visibility in politically opposed forms, hence the justice of MacIntyre's praise of her "synthesis" and his startling conclusion linking her to Cobbett and the Jacobins as "the last great representative of the classical tradition of the virtues" (243). He could have wrapped up the same point in a chiasmus: Conservatism has no monopoly on virtue, nor is the good defined by society necessarily productive of Conservatism. All sorts of accommodations are facilitated by the reserve we use in order to maintain our society with people whose political interest is different from our own. The possibility of virtue depends on the society we keep, and, like Jane Austen, we put at risk the stability of our conceptions of society every time we acknowledge the fictional energies and choices with which we make it up. If her novels have a perennial plot or wisdom, that is it.

EIGHT

Romantic Patriotism:
Marvell's Romantics

Wordsworth's most famous eulogies to the Commonwealth writers are his two sonnets of 1802: "Milton! thou shouldst be living at this hour" and "Great Men have been among us." The
former celebrates the radical gentry to which Cromwell belonged, "the
heroic wealth of hall and bower," and the "inward happiness" accompanying their unselfish civic virtue. Milton, whose "soul was like a star and
dwelt apart," is cast here both as an extraordinary luminary of and ordinary participant in these revolutionary times. But the poem's sestet
awkwardly describes Milton's voice as sounding "like the sea; / Pure as
the naked heavens, majestic, free"—a puzzling, synesthetic conflation of
political and natural liberty. It recalls Coleridge's similarly strained equa-
tions in "France: An Ode," a 1798 poem of recantation relocating his sympathies with the French revolutionaries in natural freedoms which could
never be mistaken for a specific political affiliation. The contrast closing
Wordsworth's sestet is also unclear. It says of Milton, "So didst thou travel
on life's common way, / In chearful godliness; and yet thy heart / The
lowliest duties on itself did lay." The words after the "yet" only repeat what
one might have expected of "chearful godliness" along "life's common
way." They betray the rhetorical effort required to stabilize Wordsworth's
historical interpretation. The Commonwealth depicted had perhaps appeared too gentrified to be convincingly revolutionary, and Milton too
elemental or godly to offer an example one could follow—hence that
final, overemphatic domestication of him?

But for the sonnet's argument to work, Milton must stand for the
power to reconceive England precisely because his sublimity offers no
purchase for the discourse of nationalism available in the England of
1802. A well-documented tradition from Byron onward suspects such sublime politics of prettifying Milton's republicanism, of aestheticizing it in

a typically romantic fashion which does not take seriously its radical implications. Against this now fashionable view, one can point out that it neglects to acknowledge that Wordsworth's use of Milton to image a sublime politics derives from a patriot tradition much older than romanticism. This tradition, to which romantics understood Milton and Marvell to belong, was founded on a political engagement—the Commonwealth—which, though real, nevertheless had required the thinking of revolution without a working model, a thinking *beyond*, the very stuff of sublimity. "The homely beauty of the good old cause," as Wordsworth calls it in another sonnet of 1802, will not translate into political practices unconnected with our most native loyalties. But to represent these inner essentials, despite their "homely" tag, has always drawn out the most sublime resources of romantic self-expression.

In "Great Men have been among us," Marvell makes an appearance, flanked by Algernon Sidney, James Harrington, Sir Henry Vane, and "others who called Milton friend." Now the commendations are slightly more specific, though fundamentally still celebrating mental capacity:

> These Moralists could act and comprehend:
> They knew how genuine glory was put on;
> Taught us how rightfully a nation shone
> In splendour: what strength was, that would not bend
> But in magnanimous weakness.

The rest of the sestet shows that the meaning here is to be gained from a contrast with France:

> France, 'tis strange,
> Hath brought forth no such souls as we had then.
> Perpetual emptiness! Unceasing change!
> No single Volume paramount, no code,
> No master spirit, no determined road;
> But equally a want of Books and Men!

Wordsworth's cultural triumphalism seems to sidestep responsible political judgment. He signally fails to historicize both periods under scrutiny and unrealistically expects the same standards to apply to both. Unless, that is, his patriotism is not crude chauvinism but a considered, long-accredited political stance, one significantly deriving from the sublime and therefore unexampled parallel of the Commonwealth men. Support for this interpretation can aptly begin with a later, less well-known Wordsworthian pronouncement.

In the seventeenth issue of Coleridge's journal *The Friend*, published in December 1809, Wordsworth replied to a letter in it written by two young Scottish literary journalists under the pseudonym of *Mathetes*. John Wilson and Alexander Blair had penned a joint plea for Wordsworth to assume an intellectual and moral leadership which could correct the contemporary undervaluing by the young of the achievements of past ages. Education, they argued, was under the control of a "Class" who used it to instill its "hereditary prejudices" in the modern student. The resentful pupil indulged instead in "illusory and exaggerated admiration of the age in which he [lived]." Wilson (who, as "Christopher North," was to become the savage Tory satirist of *Blackwood's Magazine*) and Blair wanted a more effective conservatism attractive in a post-Burkean age. Wordsworth's response to this call, in what is now known as the *Reply to Mathetes*, commends instead a measured historicism. He explains what he means through a fervent evocation of the Puritan tradition and the subsequent struggle to preserve it in the age of Andrew Marvell. We could, he writes,

> throw ourselves back to the age of Elizabeth, and call up to mind the Heroes, the Warriors, the Statesmen, the Poets, the Divines, and the Moral Philosophers, with which the reign of the Virgin Queen was illustrated. Or if we be more strongly attracted by the moral purity and greatness, and that sanctity of civil and religious duty, with which the Tyranny of Charles the first was struggled against, let us cast our eyes, in the hurry of imagination, round that circle of glorious Patriots—but do not let us be persuaded, that each of these, in his course of discipline, was uniformly helped forward by those with whom he was associated, or by those whose care it was to direct him. Then as now existed objects to which the wisest attached undue importance; then as now judgement was misled by factions and parties—time wasted in controversies fruitless, except as far as they quickened the faculties. . . . [1]

Wordsworth argues that the heroism of patriots like Marvell took place in the midst of misjudgment, controversy and delusion. The clear-sightedness of purpose we are tempted to think representative of discrete historical periods is a retrospective construction. He has little of Burke's confidence that the state has grown to perfection as a consequence of sheer longevity. Such confidence in this context looks like a Burkean prejudice to be discarded by the new conservatism Wilson and Blair want him to inaugurate. It is, Wordsworth continues, an "error" to "divide time merely into past and present, and place these in the balance to be weighed against each other, not considering that the present is in our estimation not more than a period of thirty years, or half a century at most, and that the past is a mighty accumulation of many such periods, perhaps the whole of recorded time, or at least the whole of that portion of it in which our own country has been distinguished" (231). In order to understand how Wordsworth's and Marvell's periods might shed light on each other, one ought not simply to compare past and present as if these were discrete separate moments. They were, but we don't understand them as such. The historicism Wordsworth recommends is one which always takes account of the process and continuity by which past and present implicate each other in our interpretations, exposing the ideological character of supposed coincidence or precursiveness. Decisions about what is to count as "distinguished" in British history are the means by which we legitimate successive cultural ascendancies at different times. These interpretations form an "accumulation," not, again as Burke might have wished, an organic growth of one out of the other. Marvell does not anticipate Wordsworth, and straightforward coincidence is not what is desired by Wordsworth in the apostrophe to Milton and his contemporaries—"Milton! Thou shouldst be living at this hour." Rather, we are asked to hear a renewed enjoinder to participate in and add to a distinct part of accumulated tradition which has temporarily been forgotten. We must understand the present as a certain kind of availability of the past, not something to be compared with the past as if detachable from it. Correspondingly, the past must be seen more as the production out of itself of a succession of uncertain presents which reshape it in response to circumstance and ideological opportunity, less as the fixed and prescribed stages of a single teleology. Current education in prejudging the present, resented by Wilson's and Blair's young student, would thus be avoided. Teleology, after all, is itself politically promiscuous and can fuel either the progressive anthropology of the recent Scottish Enlightenment or the royalist conservatism of Burkean set pieces, such as his description (production might be a better word) of Windsor Castle in *Letter to a Noble Lord.*

If Wordsworth is right, then Marvell too must see the past as a series of uncertain presents succeeding each other through the new ideological uses to which they put their predecessors. His "Horatian Ode" might even be argued to have dramatized a particularly difficult instance of the overcoming of a "youth's" education in historical prejudice. Marvell's own primary interest, one would then want to add, though, lies in the question of how to live with the notion of continuity that takes the place of prejudice. How far can disruption go before an apocalyptic or catastrophic language is called for to replace available idioms of historical continuity? We can, as J. G. A. Pocock appears at one point to suggest we do, regard this crisis as simply a question of idiom and the discipline proper to a historian as precisely the archaeology of these idioms. Rather than bewail the impossibility of history, we should catch the inevitable historical expressiveness even of those uses of language which declare a break with the past. Idioms of unproblematic historical continuity do not rest on a more solid bedrock. Nevertheless, as Pocock insists, the problem and challenge of transhistorical values or "universals" cannot be dissolved so easily. The will to create a "republic of letters" in which writers can converse with each other across time is hard to give up. The trouble is, on his own definition of historicism in *The Machiavellian Moment*, that nothing stands still when we couple an attempt to "engage the personality and its integrity in the movement of history [with] an attempt to depict history as generating new norms and values." The separate identity of the past, and corresponding respect for its self-understanding, appears compromised by present modes of transmitting it. Conversely, the awareness that present understanding will be superseded by "new norms and values" can generate a self-understanding calculated *at the time* to be open-ended or strategically uncertain.[2]

Marvell strikes me as concerned to describe the disquieting experience of this historical open-endedness. The romantics, I want to argue, reformulate his historicism in the aesthetic idiom with which they typically imagine metaphysical, ethical, and political possibilities. The stress under which Marvell's own notions of republic and commonwealth labored made the questionableness of a shared patriotism, recognizable only as a *future* common interest, provoke repeated answers over the years in all sorts of ideological, party-political terms. If the romantic response to Marvell's problem is distinctive, it is in the way the romantic construction of the aesthetic raises our consciousness of such ideological opportunity. Like Wordsworth's refusal to let history read like an unequivocal authority, it cultivates a confident individualism in making our choices now, however destined they may seem.

The patriotism for which Marvell is recognized in Wordsworth's republic of letters was of course traditionally attributed to him throughout the eighteenth century. Thomas Moore is knowingly reviving this practiced idiom in his poem, *Corruption: An Epistle*, published in the same year as Wordsworth's *Reply to Mathetes*. Writing "in this hour, when patriot zeal should guide," he shows the ideological versatility of the concept by enlisting it in the service of an Ireland standing as living testimony to the inadequacy of the Revolution of 1688 and testifying to the need for reform throughout Britain generally. "Lives there none, / To act a Marvell's part," he asks; and the negative answer he receives is inevitable, given the current corruption of "public spirit" into a search for "place and power."[3] No doubt this appeal sounds ironic when we remember Marvell's own glossing of Cromwell's Irish campaign. But Moore's tactics would hardly be embarrassed in a poem so vociferously claiming to be above party loyalty. Nevertheless, although he footnotes Burke on Ireland, the recently deceased Charles James Fox attracts his explicit allegiance in this poem and its companion piece, *Intolerance: A Satire* (ll. 137–39).

The Whig inflection given to the tradition of patriotism here is best understood not as an ideology opposing the Tories, which it undoubtedly also was, but as a defusing of the patriotism associated with a more severe radicalism. On hearing of Fox's approaching death, Wordsworth wrote lines in praise of him which style him as a God-sent figure of national unity, and earlier he had sent him a copy of *Lyrical Ballads* with an accompanying fan letter. The Holland House frequented by the young Byron solicitously preserved Fox's memory throughout the Regency among a group of supporters far removed from the patriots of the French Revolution. According to book 9 of the 1805 *Prelude*, Wordsworth had become a patriot before meeting Michel Beaupuy and temporarily espousing the Girondin cause.[4] Subsequently imagination has to "mitigate the force / Of civic prejudice, the bigotry, / So call it, of a youthful patriot's mind" (499–501). In his Jacobinical poem *Religious Musings* of Christmas 1794, the youthful patriot Coleridge calls Benjamin Franklin "PATRIOT SAGE" and his Unitarian hero Joseph Priestley "Patriot, and Saint, and Sage."[5] William Hazlitt's longer-lived Jacobinical sympathies made him write in Leigh Hunt's *Examiner* of June 1815, "*We* have no less respect for the memory of Milton as a patriot than as a Poet."[6] When Blake's Englishness leads him to reconceive "Albion" in his ultimate prophetic book, *Jerusalem*, he carries to a conclusion the patriotic bardic idealizations of James Thomson and Thomas Gray, perhaps thus disguising the extremism of a subversive intent whose idiom had been lost or aestheticized since Dryden's day. In *Britons*, Linda Colley notes that offshoots of the London Corresponding Society called themselves Patriotic Societies and that its members first intended to call the London Corresponding Society itself a Patriotic Club.[7] Highly radical projects could allay fears by echoing a more constitutionalist patriotism in which Marvell was then incorporated, one whose language even Dryden had been able to speak to his honored kinsman—"O true Descendant of a Patriot Line!"[8] I believe Marvell's poetry belies this appropriation, or that it cannot be confined by it; but such euphemistic interpretations of him draw attention to an important staging-post on the way back from the romantics through the historical accumulations which Marvell's reputation gathers.

Zera Fink, in an article of over fifty years ago, details the readings of the English republican tradition lying behind the radicalism of the French Revolutionary period. He argues that Milton, Algernon Sidney, Harrington, Nedham, Moyle, and others are of more importance to the younger Wordsworth than Rousseau. Duncan Wu's recent investigations into Wordsworth's reading demonstrate the poet's familiarity with Marvell's later poems.[9] The patriot tradition into which Marvell seems more evidently inserted for Wordsworth and others after the 1790s has won less consideration. When Dr. Johnson described patriotism as the last refuge of a scoundrel, the patriotism he might well have had in mind was that of Lord Bolingbroke, whom earlier in Boswell's biography he had called "a coward and a scoundrel."[10] Although a Tory, and one implicated in the rebellion of 1715, Bolingbroke in print shied away from the Jacobitism perhaps close to Johnson's heart and advocated instead an opportunistic patriotism transcending party differences.

Johnson, as well as detesting Bolingbroke's deism, probably saw in this public-spiritedness a self-interested attempt to outflank Walpole's hegemony rather than anything more genuine: less an ideal return to true political principle and the divine right of kings and more an effort to stabilize an ideological consensus in a convenient shape. Bolingbroke had been allowed back to England after his Jacobite adventure but not permitted to take a seat in Parliament. My interest here, though, is focused on the more than circumstantial connection between Bolingbroke's patriotism and his ideas of imaginative discourse. His loyalism took two main forms: when disillusioned in 1736 with the opposition Whigs under Pulteney, he wrote *On the Spirit of Patriotism*; slightly later, in 1738, with his supporters regrouped under the dissident Frederick, Prince of Wales, he wrote *The Idea of a Patriot King*, a blueprint for "a sort of standing miracle" surely as idealistic as his earlier Jacobitism.[11] My point, however, is that these two kinds of patriotism are equally implicated in imaginative discourse when they try to gain access to a realm of pure political principle free of the contaminations of current political practice. "Neither Montaigne in writing his essays, nor Des Cartes in building new worlds, nor Burnet in framing an antediluvian earth, no nor Newton in discovering and establishing the true laws of nature on experiment and a sublimer geometry, felt more intellectual joys, than he feels who is a real patriot, who bends all the force of his understanding, and directs all his thoughts and actions, to the good of his country. When such a man forms a political scheme, and adjusts various and seemingly independent parts of it to one great and good design, he is transported by imagination, or absorbed in meditation, as much and as agreeably as they . . ." (203). Bolingbroke then goes on to specify the additional pleasures accruing to the man who can then act on this "speculative philosopher's labour and pleasure." If speculative transports feed the language to which patriotism leads, then when we go still further back in time and look at those poems of Marvell still frequently distinguished from his later political poetry, we can see a comparable patriotic imagination at work. Intellectual retreat and retirement, whether explicitly embodying political themes as in "Upon Appleton House," or indirectly through the mind's redoubling on itself in pastoral or metaphysic, can effectively link to a patriotic purpose. Indeed, in an age of censorship, the indirect speculation may be expected to encode a political alternative to the party line required of the explicitly political statement.

Christopher Hill, writing on Traherne, opposes a tendency to equate the metaphysical bent in seventeenth-century poetry with royalist sympathies. Elsewhere in the same book of collected essays, he concedes that it is "undemonstrable" that the Metaphysicals any more than Jacobean tragedians possessed an "alternative value-system."[12] Metaphysical poetry and the metaphysical attitude of a writer like Marvell can, however (as I think Hill more cryptically seems to imply), be shown to demonstrate an acceptance of historical change to the point of introjecting it as if it were one's own decision, however bewildering or paradoxical such active resignation might appear. Beyond Wordsworth's wise passiveness, this perhaps has more in common with Percy Shelley's self-annihilating figurations of the power of necessity, whether in the conceptual revision of "hope" at the end of *Prometheus Unbound,* or in the sacrifices of personal integrity in poems as varied as "Ode to the West Wind" or "The Triumph of Life." These paradoxes logically dance attendance on an aesthetic attitude creating the space from which one can talk about reality as a whole, physical and political, a poetic position unconstrained by it. On the one hand poetic license seems to guarantee a freedom from necessity; on the other hand it uses the freedom to describe more comprehensively than before the reality of that necessity. The dynamism in necessity, the efficacy of historical change, is the sole guarantee of an alternative to current miseries; but then the first thing to go in the new dispensation would be the poetry of improvements on the former establishment, to be replaced by the improvements themselves.

I don't think this irony is more difficult to handle than the language of Marvell's "Horatian Ode." More obvious in Marvell, though, is the possibility that the metaphysical frame of mind might be a radical political idiom, its overreaching quality conceding the necessarily uncanny appearance possessed by republicanism in a traditionally monarchical society. The poetic force of Marvell's political accommodation of contemporary chiliastic strains of discourse has been described from different perspectives by Christopher Hill and Margarita Stocker. Dryden's *Annus Mirabilis*, as exhaustively interpreted by Michael McKeon, is a royalist act of containment of the same.[13] In the "Horatian Ode," after a lengthy description of the ambiguities and ambivalences of Cromwellian authority, the poem pronounces on the future in such a way as to suggest that its previous *double-entendres* in portraying Cromwell were less intended to be critical than to found a conspicuously new language whose artful agon strives for adequation with a new politics:

> And for the last effect
> Still keep thy sword erect:
> Beside the force it has to fright
> The spirits of the shady Night,
> The same *Arts* that did *gain*
> A *Pow'r* must it *maintain*.[14]

As Nigel Smith has put it: "the ambiguities of the poem are in fact reflections of the tensions which are necessary to the life of republics."[15] Marvell clearly does not underestimate the confidence required to accompany this political leap into the dark. That the poem rests content with these indeterminacies, this new art so different from the consummate performance of Charles on the scaffold, creates reading difficulties for its audience paralleling the gap in political understanding they would also be required to bridge at this time. Similarities with Shelley's irony show the same gap existing and the republic still unestablished. For Shelley, by contrast with Marvell, the paradoxical task is to show that the *existing* legal establishment of Church and State and King doesn't observe the rules and is thus the *Mask of Anarchy*. His upsetting of his readers' expectations of where disorder and unruliness lie has an obvious satirical force. Also, unlike Marvell, Shelley cannot indicate any positive institutional life whose alternative political order he might proselytize. In the absence of a concrete republican alternative in 1819, imagination is obliged to be so self-sufficient in its conjuring of a better society that Shelley can appear to be envisaging not a new citizenry but ideal readers of his own poem, connoisseurs of its visionariness. [16]

Where does this leave patriotism? In a way, it recalls Bolingbroke's un-likely patriot king and how he creates, as Coleridge wanted Wordsworth to do, the taste by which he is to be enjoyed: "A new people will seem to arise with a new king. Innumerable metamorphoses, like those which poets feign, will happen in very deed: and, while men are conscious that they are the same individuals, the difference of their sentiments will al-most persuade them that they are changed into different beings." [17] A consequence of this convergence of patriotism with outright idealism, however, is its susceptibility to charges of aestheticism, just that irrespon-sibility which the genuine political purpose of patriotism was meant to override. In the "Dedication" to *Don Juan*, Byron berated those of his contemporaries who joined in the poetic bowdlerization of art to make "the word *Miltonic* mean *sublime.*" [18] The "intellectual joys" which Boling-broke ascribes to the patriot's political efforts may equate too completely with the enjoyable strenuosities of Marvell's verse or the vertiginous ex-citements of Shelley's visionary resistance. Actual political opposition or radical novelty may be lost or forgotten in a separate appreciation of the linguistic innovations and poetic originality required to do them justice. Miltonic polemic might dwindle into stylistics, as if his Samson, contro-versial hero in defeat, were only an exercise in transforming Biblical epic into Greek tragedy.

This aesthetic reduction or sublimation of politics has been the charge repeatedly leveled at the romantics. But Marvell, I would suggest, sees this danger in his own time in his own way and views it as an inevitable consequence both of political censorship and of aesthetic freedom. The famous lines on poetic heroism in "Tom May's Death" arguably describe a poet who cannot be called to account for his words as much as they delineate poetic superiority to the highly answerable vocations of judges and churchmen over which the poet morally presumes. The language in which the poet sings, seeks, and arraigns brings in tow the paradoxical idiom of the "Horatian Ode," which gives with one hand while taking away with the other: "the World's disjointed Axel . . . wretched good . . . successful crimes." If this idiom has a practical purchase on a real world, it requires us to transvalue our received standards accordingly. Otherwise it remains an impossibly thick description, so rewardingly rich in its ade-quacy as not to take any cognitive or moral decisions at all: metaphysical in a privileged, even royalist sense.

If the charge of aestheticism is actually an attack on a license for political indecisiveness, then it is a charge which readers of Marvell have traditionally had to adjudicate when negotiating opposed allegiances which now look absolute and mutually exclusive. To put it crudely, the very coherence of a Marvell canon has seemed to be threatened if its defining Puritanism has to include elegiac poems to Lovelace, Villiers, and Hastings, poems whose potential royalism is supplemented by equivocations in the poems to Cromwell and an attack on the Parliamentarian Tom May. The easiest way out of this imbroglio is perhaps T. S. Eliot's acceptance of Marvell's experiential variety, a versatility which lets him transcend both affiliations. This disengagement of art from politics, happily for Eliot, inescapably mimes royalism when it consecrates a realm immune to political decision as the proper condition of poetry. It is just such an establishment that royalism proclaims and Puritanism denies. By contrast, the tradition stretching back from the romantics associates him with patriotism. Although most of the romantics who praised Marvell as a patriot hardly ever mention his pastorals, these poems' consistency with his patriotic thought can be supported by the romantic aesthetic. In Marvell's writing retirement and pastoral explore an ideal political structure: not a Platonically fixed ideal but a dynamic oppositional mode which risks contradiction and foregrounds paradox. Patriotic paradoxes present the metaphysical uncertainty of a revolutionary future, one whose authenticity is native to all of us, overriding all current differences and incompatibilities. A patriot imagination, in other words, is so open to transformational historical change that the virtues of the enemy (Charles) become not embarrassments but pointers to a future setting in which they might properly command universal assent.

This sort of view becomes more plausible if we see Marvell's pastoral habit as a way of describing landscape gradually supplanted in the reader's interest by the mental energies, the perspectivism, it takes to produce the sense of place. In *Paradise Lost*, Milton, after all, has Adam's Paradise sent down the river in case we attach more importance to place than the sanctifying attitude we bring to it. [19] Place, for Milton, defines our perspective on God, the extent to which a man can "hold his place" (11:635), a hierarchy complicated of course by the benefits accruing from Eve's fortunate usurpation of Adam's place. The "unfathered vapour" of Wordsworth's imagination profitably overcomes a comparable geographical disappointment in book 6 of *The Prelude* when he misses the climactic moment at which he has crossed the Alps. As poems such as "The Garden" also explicate, the initially cerebral trajectory of Puritanism need no more renege on sensuousness than a Keatsian ode. In the horticultural conceit of the poem, the gardening poet's cultivated transformation of the vegetable world into erotic object or paradise eventually unrealizes itself altogether. The mind retreats into its own ingenuity to create "far other Worlds" rather than perversely sexualize this one. Nevertheless, the computation of the bees busy about the flower-clock of the last stanza shows this willful art finally dovetailing with mortality, the realm of generation disseminated by the bees. The flower-clock tells the time of day, but the pollination carried out by the bee tells the time of life, measured in the generative cycle of experience and not the abstract mathematics of astronomy.

As in "The Mower against Gardens," this return to earth does not refute the poem's imaginative initiatives but accepts the realistic use which imagination may pleasurably exceed but to which it must be put. The bee computes "as well as we," and so it is no come-down next to see how the imaginative powers just demonstrated must refocus and compromise so as to be able to invade reality to transforming effect—not simply, as we have seen, with the effect of trimming their own powers to the times but of rendering bewildering the times they can so radically transform. The poem's realism is as precariously balanced as that last "effect" of Cromwell at the end of the "Horatian Ode." And the same fantastical appropriation of change or metamorphosis as one's own willed decision powers Marvell's famous commendation in *The Rehearsal Transpros'd* of a king so patriotic that he would have abdicated if his people had trusted him to.

On the other hand, to try to identify entirely with what Blake called the world of generation, instead of understanding it as the place which must accommodate the naturally ameliorative and creative energies by which we project the better political life, is to be like the "heavy monarchs" of the "First Anniversarie." It is to embrace the "sluggishness" which Edmund Burke, in his *Reflections on the Revolution in France*, argued was the national character of the conservative English and their property.[20] The opposite of Cromwellian activism, it can also precipitate the dilemma of Marvell's mowers. In the mower poems paradise is lost when figured as a natural function, the harvesting of the grass. The idea of fulfillment within a fixed allotted role works, as for Milton, only in Paradise or in heaven; and to indulge such prelapsarian or divine ideas in the fallen, sublunary world is inappropriate. The Mower's own ideas and passions only enter "Damon the Mower" to disrupt his false idealization of his own role: he cannot be a purely seasonal creature like the disseminating

bee. This realization produces frustration rather than a sharper awareness that he is Aristotle's *zoon politikon*, vocationally bound to imagine
and risk practicing the better society pastorally figured around him. To
do this, to see in pastoral a kind of "country interest," if you like, takes
confidence and a willingness to change perspective—the advantages the
narrator has over the mowers he views in "Upon Appleton House," or the
change urged upon the coy mistress. Marvell, with some irony, presents
himself as "easie Philosopher / Among the Birds and trees" of Appleton
House, and "easy," it is worth remembering, was one of the pejorative
terms of Dr. Johnson's excoriation of Miltonic pastoral. Had he written
a life of Marvell, he might have redoubled his criticism of "Lycidas":
"Where there is leisure for fiction there is little grief." The indulgence
in Miltonic fiction signals, for Johnson, the delusion that the "singular"
can replace the "admirable"; and Milton's singularity links directly with
his republicanism in Johnson's description, the surly assertion of individualism against general nature. Clearly, in Johnson's as well as Milton's
vocabulary, easiness has a ready way with a certain kind of political disruption and defiance of authority.[21]

I have been hinting that an aesthetic self-consciousness characteristic of romantic writing might represent the historical accumulation of
a way of reconceiving political possibility drawing on the patriot tradition at whose head, for the romantics, stood Marvell and his circle. Patriotism in mainstream romantic parlance is usually disguised in other
languages of authenticity, individualistic versions of a loyalty to self—the
"true voice of feeling," the "best self," the "household of man," the "title of Man," "the whole soul of man," "the human form divine," and so
forth. The romantics and many of their interpreters, some approvingly
and some disapprovingly, have seen this outcome as nothing but a sublimation of original political content by aestheticism. But that is, I think,
to miss the point. Pastoral, expressing the mental agility and versatility
of Marvell's describer of place, is like a romantic metaphysic subject to
aesthetic judgment. Aesthetic judgment, as developed by Kant and his
followers, onward, gives us a sense of the limitations of our world in a
language enjoying the license of not being disqualified from figuring
a future it cannot yet get on terms with. In fantasy, in other words, we
can legitimately anticipate the trauma of change or the revolutionary
reordering of experience. In imagination, we can make disorientations
caused by powers outside our control—fate and destiny—our own.[22] Romantic aesthetics can, but need not, assume that political poetry is one
thing—rather prosaic, unvisionary or defined by a satirical assumption of

unproblematic norms—and lyrical self-expression quite another thing altogether.[23] It can, but need not, assume that when the latter *is* political it
has sublimated the character of the former. The political hypothesis embedded in romantic self-exploration might or might not be transformed
into a categorical imperative, depending on one's political persuasion.
But in each case, conservative and radical, a political decision would have
to be taken.

We might then say that what the romantics add, or the spin they give
to the patriot tradition, is a knowledge of how the aesthetic represents
its own political availability. It can also be argued plausibly that patriotism had itself become an even more common political expedient than
Johnson had feared. The romantics took advantage of their situation at
the end of a century in which nationalism and patriotism had become
bywords for the effort to legitimate all kinds of things—so why not the aesthetic enterprise as well? The credibility of writing a history of England,
Wales, and Scotland from 1700 to 1832 and calling it *Britons* depends, as
Linda Colley tells us, on the idea that "being a patriot was . . . ultimately a
means of demanding a much broader access to citizenship."[24] The opportunism with which "the languages of patriotism," as Colley calls them, colored all political complexions of the time inevitably had its aesthetic correlatives, an area beyond her remit but which she commends to future research (336, 8). Romantic patriotism could image an essential humanism
in the Toryism of Scott—"Breathes there the man, with soul so dead, /
Who never to himself hath said, / This is my own, my native land!"—or
in the cosmopolitanism of Dissenting, abolitionist, and other reformist
discourses.[25] But the cross-party appeal of patriotism is bound to favor the
radical side's interest in an expanded citizenship. It therefore emphasizes
the progressive rather than mystifying strain in romantic sublimity.

An obvious dialectic then takes place. Patriotism lets the romantics
see the political content latent in their own aesthetic, a vision we have
seen generating metaromantic discontent with an aesthetic which constitutionally elides that political content instead of registering its impulse
to exceed aesthetics and establish, perhaps, that "subtler language within
language wrought" with which Shelley's revolutionary, Cythna, traces a
larger natural franchise. But romantic philosophical adroitness in conceiving of and formulating their aesthetic helps us read its radical past
despite apparent mystifications. (And no doubt, as Colley's work implies,
this is a timely moment for supplementing critiques of romantic ideology with an appreciation of the rhetorical tactics whereby patriotism
could shed a purely chauvinistic inheritance and be used radically and

salutarily to renovate ideas of social belonging.) In its turn, Romantic aesthetics encourages us to find a language for preserving the political content of Marvell's poetry when it seems most to strain at the limits of conceptual and political consistency. Even if the romantics did not discuss Marvell's earlier, ostensibly less political poems, their aesthetic has provided a rationale for reading into his lyrical forms the patriotic politics of his prose reputation. The romantic use of aesthetics to make patriotism's increased franchise a legitimate political aspiration does not raise the expected question of a transcendental ideal in another form. Rather, as is examined in detail in my final chapter, it moots those more generous kinds of social belonging paralleling those which need to be conceded to multicultural citizenship in a nation-state.

Patriotism for the major English romantics is expressed as a human authenticity which they desire individually but which they also ascribed to the political principles of Marvell's "glorious" circle. This connection explains their frequent nostalgia. Here is Keats writing in 1818 to his brother and sister-in-law who have settled in America. Americans like Franklin and Washington, he tells them, "are great but they are not sublime Man"; and the aestheticizing of Keats's compliment implies the deepening of its political content and distinguishes him (and perhaps the Wordsworth of 1802) from Byron's targets, the effacers of politics from sublime experience. Who are these sublime men who have to be sought in an English past? His answer once more elegizes a patriotic tradition: nowadays "there are none prepared to suffer in obscurity for their Country—the motives of our wo[r]st Men are interest and of our best Vanity—We have no Milton, no Algernon Sidney—Governors in these days lose the title of Man in exchange for that of Diplomat and Minister—We breathe in a sort of Officinal Atmosphere."[26] References like this also begin to explain how, despite their party differences, romantic writers could regard their various internalizations of politics in the quest for authentic self-coincidence as still having a political pedigree. Authenticity, loyalism, patriotism—the words fan out from an original self-assurance to encompass the late-lamented public spirit. J. G. A. Pocock, once more in *The Machiavellian Moment*, retells Machiavelli's story to Francesco Vettori of "how he comes home in the evening, puts on formal clothing, and enters into the presence and conversation of the ancients by reading their books. The conversation," Pocock concludes, "is meant to restore Machiavelli not only to the understanding of politics, but indirectly to actual civic participation" (62). This surprising comparison illustrates the romantic habit I have been trying to describe: the recovery through one's own aesthetic—"formal clothing"—of an intimacy with past writers which can restore their readers to the citizenship of a neglected republic. The "actual" form implied by this virtual solidarity will certainly vary with ideological persuasions. But, as Wordsworth had tried to teach Wilson and Blair, the precision with which we retrospectively specify some political groupings and sympathies and so rule out others traduces the complexities of historical accumulations and transmissions—and, we might add, imagines too scantily the possibilities of political action to which Marvell was so strikingly sensitive.

THEORY

NINE

The Romanticism of
Contemporary Ideology

Tracy, Stendhal, Sade

The afterlife of romantic theory which we inhabit originates in the rough consensus that once existed among British and American romantic scholars that the period was one of intellectual expansion after an age of Enlightenment. However skeptical and emancipatory were its aims, the Enlightenment was pictured as still powered by an inappropriately mechanistic understanding of human creativity. The romantics found or privileged new categories for this unconfinable essence, and their twentieth-century critics largely reproduced them. Disapproving critics of romanticism, such as T. E. Hulme, Irving Babbitt, and T. S. Eliot, still shared the view of romanticism as an intellectually liberationist movement, which was why they disapproved. Their revisionary successors championed romantic range and ambition, even if that imaginative scope was seen by such commentators as Bloom and Hartman to be a fraught, potentially unmanageable freedom from natural determinism.

Subsequent deconstructive and historicist critics, though, looked instead for shades of the prison-house lodged within the very heart of romantic, imaginative license.[1] Rather as Horkheimer and Adorno interpreted the Enlightenment, they have read romanticism as an escape from the constraints of nature into a new prison of its own making. The language of capability, which previously seemed unequivocally to legitimate romantic practice, lost credibility when it was shown to be a discourse impervious to critique, one which just could not fail. "Poetic language can do nothing but originate anew over and over again; it is always constitutive, able to posit regardless of presence but, by the same token, unable to give a foundation to what it posits except as an intent of consciousness."[2] This sharp résumé by Paul de Man repositions romanticism in relation to ideological practice. In other words, poetry of this kind is always incorrigibly buoyant: it is self-writing, self-righting, and self-wrighting. Romantic discourse abounds with poems about the impossibility of producing poetry, poems as different as Wordsworth's *Prelude,* Keats's Hyperion poems, and Byron's *Don Juan.* In each case, failure of the self to achieve its goal is recuperated as autobiography (self-writing). Or an imaginative falling short of effective realization is still imagined, and so still constitutive of the creative category valorized by romantic discourse. This furnishes the ironic (self-righting) logic of the fragment; it also underpins the aura of the symbol as a form that exhibits its own self-fashioning (self-wrighting) as an aesthetic experience replacing the philosophical shortcomings that initially it seemed to record. This literary absolute translates everything into its own terms, which, since they ensure success, elide problems that would have remained visible in a less idealizing discourse.[3]

Romantic poetry described in this way can have no recalcitrant moments; all crises—loss of subject, inability to conclude, idiosyncrasy—merely add to the aesthetic substance of the poem. Sublimation is always sublime rather than escapist, internalization is always symbolic rather than obscurantist, logical opposites are aesthetically reconciled; as soon as the aesthetic transposition takes place, then all its contents become intents and its categories self-originating. Both deconstructive and historicist critics see this self-confirming system as ideological. Ideology has meant a bewildering number of things over the years, but the most recurrent sense has emphasized pretensions to wholeness. And it is the switch from valorizing wholeness absolutely to seeing it as a limiting, exclusive construction that typifies the change in understanding of romanticism I have been highlighting. Characteristic of this ideology is the fact that, in Althusser's words, it "has no history." Once you are inside it, it pretends it is not there, that things were always like this. It tries to preclude the possibility of critique, to make a metalanguage unthinkable. As Alasdair MacIntyre argues, ideology and the end of ideology or end of history are symbiotically related. Both are interested in trying to deprive us of the ability to criticize or see wholes as constructions: "[T]he pragmatism of the attitude involved in the end-of-ideology thesis leaves precisely those whom it seeks to educate vulnerable to almost any ideological appeal by its failure to criticize social wholes. Each party to this dispute provides the other with an opponent made in precisely the required image."[4]

Critics of romantic ideology disagree about the degree of the romantics' awareness of the entrapment in which their imaginative liberationism landed them. Yet some poems, like *The Triumph of Life,* push convincingly against the limits of ideology. *The Triumph of Life* dramatizes ideological constraints as the intolerability of a life lived without the possibility of critique: a life whose naturalness is felt as an imposition. The magnetism of the triumphal car that drags so many in its wake provides the example, par excellence, of a category we cannot step outside—life. Famously, the Yale deconstructionists chose Shelley's poem for the subject of their collaborative *Deconstruction and Criticism*. Their resistance to logocentrism and Shelley's discontent with ideology are immanent to the poem; but the textual reasons for seeing ideology rather than biology as the subject of *The Triumph of Life* particularize that ideology and place it historically in a period discontinuous with the modern and postmodern by specifying it as idealist. The worthies so shockingly in thrall in the *Triumph of Life* stand for "thought's empire over thought." They figure in a review of Western culture that turns its desire for Enlightenment into that self-reflexive, "pure" intellectual virtuosity that was Marx's target in *The German Ideology*. If we see it in this historical perspective, there is a way out of romantic ideology, an alternative to immanent critique: the way chosen by Marx. Although it means giving up "thought's empire over thought," this is still a renunciation that is possible, unlike the romantic dramatization of it as the surrender of life itself. Post-Marxists like Althusser argue that this is an alternative perceived by the *young* Marx, invisible once more after his epistemological break with prescientific Marxism and the restoration of an all-embracing ideology, criticism of which is always symptomatic. Even on this interpretation, the prescientific scenario is still essential to the historical reading of the logic of romantic ideology I attempt here. However, I wish to suggest that the restoration of an inescapable ideology and its consequent restriction of criticism to immanent criticism represent a crucial intersection of modern theory with a definitively romantic dilemma and ought to be understood as such. Metaromanticism, as the next chapter will show, offers a redefinition of immanence, not as the imprisonment of criticism within discourse in general but as the transfer of authority from one discourse to another, a series of "stand-ins" generating corresponding innovations and critical revisions of the original meaning. But first we must look at the question of immanent criticism and its discontents.

Analysis of the ideology of romanticism, then, suggests the romanticism of ideology. A prerequisite for understanding this romanticism of ideology is an appreciation of the eighteenth-century theory of ideology, its transformation within romanticism, and the critique of that inheritance by Marx. This leads us, as it did Marx, into the history of eighteenth-century French thought's adaptation of British empiricism. The term *idéologie* is generally agreed to have been coined by Destutt de Tracy in his *Éléments d'idéologie* (1801–15), that is, right in the middle of the English romantic age and at the end of the French Enlightenment. Tracy's "ideology" followed the philosophes, and etymology, in investigating the logic of ideas: the grammar by which we compose discourse out of strings of ideas validated by sense experience. I will question the coherence of this clear-cut philosophical programme in the second part of this essay. First, though, it is worth noting its democratic, accessible nature. Indeed, Taine alleges that ideology and its proponents achieved such prominence that Napoleon, fearing the dissidence of once sympathetic intellectuals at the *Institut National,* attributed to "ideology, that sinister metaphysics . . . all the misfortune of our beloved France."[5] The change from what ideology means for Napoleon and the ideologue Tracy to what it means for Marx when he writes *The German Ideology* (1845) is a change into the idiom in which our own debates about ideology, however refined their differences, are conducted. From Lukács to Daniel Bell, Althusser to Kenneth Minogue, the proponents and opponents of theories of ideology are arguing about something much closer to Marx's conception than Tracy's. Not that Marx's definition was unequivocal; but I can perhaps leave its definition as vague as this at present in order simply to propose romanticism as a significant rite of passage in the construction of ideology as it features in our arguments today.

In the historical space between Tracy's *Éléments d'idéologie* and Marx's early writings, I want to situate two transformers of the ideological current. Both were primarily novelists: Marie-Henri Beyle, known as Stendhal, and Donatien Alphonse Francois [Marquis de] Sade. In claiming that they make important contributions to the *theory* of ideology, I am building on Jane Gallop's juxtaposition of Sade with Bataille to question more broadly the customary equation of theory with philosophy. As will be seen, their theoretical interventions raised this controversy at the time. Their scandalous meddling argues the important change in the meaning of "ideology" that I want to pinpoint. But a consequence of their philosophical discovery was to open the door to unphilosophical, literary initiatives that question the autonomy and legitimacy of philosophical discourse, a romantic embarrassment that recent theory has been keen to revive.

Stendhal was a great admirer of Tracy, but when he presents his own attempt to analyze an ideology to Tracy, he apparently uses the word in a manner unintelligible to an Enlightenment ideologue. The treatise in question is Stendhal's book *De l'amour.* The other writer who spanned the Enlightenment and what followed, and who pushed the definition of love beyond reasonable understanding to such an extent that his explanation became eponymous is, of course, Sade. Of the two, Stendhal engages more explicitly with the history of ideas. He takes the formal structure of Tracy's reprise of eighteenth-century materialism, exposes its idealist base, and redescribes it as a hermetic belief system. The ingenuity of the author of *De l'amour* is to show that any behavior can be psychologized into love. The central figure for this process of "crystallization," as Stendhal calls it, is the Salzburg bough: "[A]t the salt mines of Salzburg, they throw a leafless wintry bough into one of the abandoned workings. Two or three minutes later they haul it out covered with a shining deposit of crystals. The smallest twig, no bigger than a tom-tit's claw, is studded with a galaxy of scintillating diamonds. The original branch is no longer recognizable. What I have called crystallization is mental process that draws from everything that happens new proofs of the perfection of the loved one."[6]

Similarly, Sade analyzes any aberration into a form of sexual behavior. Sade's modernism, as Angela Carter implies in *The Sadeian Woman*,[7] is to see that once sex is detached from the defining biological function of reproduction, it becomes an ideology: it can explain anything. Stendhal gives us the resourcefulness, whimsy, and pleasure of ideology-making. *De l'amour* may seem to present itself as a critique of the aesthetics of ideology, but it ends up decrying the poverty of a life barren of love's ideology. Sade, conversely, shows the barbarity of his ideology by enjoying it. What makes his critique self-impugning also makes it undeniable. It also makes him the darling of the antihumanists from Bataille onward who do not want their critical alternatives to produce rival forms of legitimation when legitimacy is in fact their target.

Both Stendhal's and Sade's transformations of ideology are shocking—more obviously in the case of Sade, but also in Stendhal's amorous foreclosures of all external explanation or verification. Ideology becomes a partisan phenomenology: one can suffer all manner of self-deceptions, but these too constitute love. Stendhal's conspicuous derivation of the model for explaining love from philosophical method itself then becomes as logically self-lacerating, as much a *trahison des clercs,* as Sadism. But it is under the shadow of the divine marquis that new ideologues claim polemically that the enlightenment they contribute to will escape the presumptuousness of rule, reason, and patriarchy, remaining suitably *sous rature.* "For the *chronique scandaleuse* of Justine and Juliette," claim Adorno and Horkheimer, is "the history of thought as an organ of domination."[8]

The surreally sophisticated appropriation of Sade within French theory by Bataille and Klossowski is redeployed more accessibly by Jane Gallop. In her reading of Sade and his readers, "a Sadeian antihumanism becomes necessarily a feminist disturbance of the distinction masculine/feminine and the correlative principle of the male, ideal sphere." Gallop thus appears to disinfect Sade in critical theory, but she avowedly wants to keep alive the scandalous nature of her association, to "release Sade's stink from the sterilizing tomb of literary history." She figures the effacement of unique authorship ("the male, ideal sphere") as an incrimination of those who replace it. Antihumanism parades rather than muffles the evil-sounding associations of its name, and poststructuralists gather round the corpse of individualism as though participating in a Sadeian scene of instruction. Gallop tells us, "My Sade, (I am at once ashamed and gratified to say) is neither mine nor even 'Sade' [but] a familiar conspiracy of teachers/readers/friends."[9] The implication is that if you don't believe in legitimation you need a highly sophisticated guilt like this to keep your methodology transgressive. Gallop's disingenuous wit is here at one with other postmodern tactics to avoid turning critique into an alternative grand narrative.

In his "Essay on Miracles," the Enlightenment philosopher David Hume had already shown how difficult it is to refute norms without setting up systems parasitical upon the normal: a *lapsus naturae* can only have happened if it is vindicated on the very grounds to which it was supposed to be an exception. The category to be disposed of by the miraculous appears to justify the miraculous. The alternative was for the believer to be "conscious of a continued miracle in his own person, which subverts all the principles of his understanding." If Hume did not dismiss this enthusiasm out of hand, he certainly let it activate his celebrated irony. However, Christian believers, linguistic as well as religious, such as Hamann and Jacobi, were able to equate Hume's skepticism concerning our knowledge of any world external to our impressions and ideas with his refutation of miracles. To continue believing in miracles appeared as commonsensical as to persist in believing in the existence of an external world. Perversely, they used Hume to justify their enthusiastic belief in the miraculous nature of "reality."[10] In other words, despite his ironic disengagements, Hume's so-called empiricism proved flexible enough to accommodate the opposites of skepticism and fideism. Stendhal and Sade exploit the resemblance this Enlightenment epistemology bears to a self-confirming ideology. In their different ways, they romanticize it. Furthermore, the grossly physical abnormal championed by Sade, somewhat different from the perversity of Christian antinomianism, shows how abstract the inherited "way of ideas" had to be for Hume to be able to absorb empiricism within idealism. Stendhal presumes upon the hypothetical comprehensiveness of the idealism, but Sade exposes the ideality of its internalized, disembodied empiricism.

Gallop's still fashionable recourse to Sade, not Stendhal, as a means of illustrating the ideological is therefore a preference for materialism over idealism. Sade is valued for showing the ungovernable body whose materiality exceeds the empiricism rationalized within Humean idealism. The corollary of Stendhal's uncheckable, agglutinative system of ideas is a lawless, unmediated but compulsive physical reality. Things-in-themselves become as potentially alien, mystified, or obstreperous as a body's unbiddable instincts and desires. Consciousness henceforth is shadowed by an unconscious resourceful enough to have produced our actions for reasons other than those we were consciously in possession of while acting. The preference for Sade follows the fate of philosophy after idealism: a series of attempts to abandon idealism and engage with this material power that otherwise would be able to undermine all science and reduce all action to a parody of its real motives.

In *The German Ideology*, idealism is *the* ideology: philosophy's pretense to legislate for reality through logical prescriptions of its conditions of possibility. For Marx, this German-sounding disease is at one with the Enlightenment's absorption of materialism within empiricism. It has two main consequences, corresponding to our Stendhal/Sade axis. Idealist prescriptions ignore materialist contingencies as surely as the madman's study of the weather in *Rasselas* leads to his lunatic belief that he controls it. Marx's vivid attack on the Young Hegelians repeats Dr. Johnson's satire on the enlightenment of his day. "Once upon a time a valiant fellow had the idea that men were drowned in water only because they were possessed with the idea of gravity. If they were to knock this notion out of their heads, say by stating: it to be a superstition, a religious concept, they would be sublimely proof against any dangers from water. His whole life long he fought against the illusion of gravity, of whose harmful results all statistics brought him new and manifold evidence. This honest fellow was the type of the new revolutionary philosophers in Germany."[11]

Marx's first study of ideology investigates "how a theory and history of pure thought could arise among philosophers owing to the divorce between ideas and the individuals and their empirical relations that serve as the basis of these ideas. In the same way, here too one can divorce right from its real basis" (185). Corresponding to the unreality of pure thought, or a self-authenticating system of ideas, must be a symbiotic conception of the material bodily individual as a law unto itself. Hence the frequent sense in reading Sade that the particular horrors are overdetermined in the service of some general *Weltanschauung* as mystified as its idealist counterpart. These grotesque rituals, recipes, protocols, hierarchies, and biographies of cruelty and desire burlesque the idea that there are contexts in which any rituals, recipes, protocols, and so on are necessarily reputable. Anything, Sade wants to demonstrate, can be a turn-on. Both pure thought and utter physical license belong to the same ideological economy and so instantiate what Marx would see as equally false abstractions from the social relations determining how we produce reality. In Sade's description of a modern consensus in *La philosophie du boudoir,* the new materialism subsumes even the most extravagant schemes of mentalism: "[W]hat we call the end of the living animal is no longer a true finis, but a simple transformation, a transformation of matter, what every modern philosopher acknowledges as one of Nature's fundamental laws. . . . death is hence no more than a change of form, an imperceptible passage from one existence to another, and that is what Pythagoras called metempsychosis."[12]

Sade's provocatively uncritical conclusion is that he must have persuaded "any enlightened reader, that for murder ever to be an outrage to Nature is impossible" (332). Social relations are precisely what do not count for anything in this kind of materialism. Marx could have used *La philosophie du boudoir* as his text.

Sade, then, through the obscene tolerance of his dramatization of violence and sexuality, parodies the contemporary resilience of ideology. The critical potential of his writing is compromised, though, first of all by its barbarity, which keeps questionable the postmodern use of perversity as a trope for epistemological sophistication. Sade's ideology, Sadism, is a prison in which people, almost all of them women, are tortured for the sexual pleasure of men and women who have power. Sade's fictions even contain listeners who are meant to take pleasure in the stories of such enjoyments, and so the pornography incriminates its readers in advance. Secondly, the Sadeian parody is limited to a mirror image of the idealism it criticizes. As Roland Barthes points out, Sade's eroticism is "encyclopedic"; but Sade satirizes "the accounting spirit" of the encyclopedic project of the Enlightenment philosophes as amounting to the undiscriminating principle that "pleasure is possible anywhere." Once more, if anything can be a turn-on, then being turned on by something doesn't exactly tell you much about it.[13]

From a postmodern perspective, both these limitations to Sade's critique can appear advantageous. He inspires a form of writing whose transgressive force no longer resides in pretensions to legitimate critique, but in an undeniably offensive *anomie*, powered by a material unconscious capable of undermining all conscious explanation. Defenders of Sade's slighting of moral, political, and economic wisdom hold his transgressions to be characteristic of a new "higher" criticism that locates ideology's defining strength in its power to dictate the terms of our resistance to it. We have seen Scott's *Waverley* try to refuse ideological explanation in order to figure a historical force whose artfully discernible effect is to get us to misdescribe it. Rhetorically, if not sexually, Scott is as sophisticated as Sade. Following Sade, self-impugning writing, such as Bataille's pornography, dovetails with that of unlikely allies (Adorno, Althusser, Foucault) who share a prevailing cynicism about the validity of emancipation and revolt, describing them as movements whose shape and scope are prescribed by a ubiquitous ideology. Rebellion is, therefore, best figured as sexual compulsiveness, non-identity, or disruptions too local to be made sense of in general terms.

These writers counter self-authenticating ideology with self-denying or disreputable critique. This is the provocatively uncritical extreme to which critics working immanently within ideology are reduced. Since the Holocaust, there has been an upsurge of ingenuity for detecting ideologies where none was to be seen before. Science, art, language, politics, race, and gender are not simply traversed or enlisted by ideology but now demonstrably have their own ideologies. In the face of this proliferation, it is hard to be anything other than an immanent critic. All else seems methodological naïveté or hypocritical purity. Adorno and Horkheimer allot a chapter to Sade in *Dialectic of Enlightenment,* arguing that the Sadeian (and sadistic) heroine, Juliette, exhibits "the pleasure of attacking civilization with its own weapons" (94–95). She is the scandalous precursor of the immanent critic; her "merciless doctrines [that] proclaim the identity of domination and reason . . . are more merciful than those of the moralistic lackeys of the bourgeoisie" (111). Romanticism differs from our postmodern situation because, although it provides an explanatory genealogy for the sometimes bizarre pessimism of the immanent critic, there still seems to be a way out: ideological contamination can still be circumscribed. All forms of writing do not fall within its sphere, because romanticism's hermeneutical circle belongs to a particular kind of philosophy, idealism, to which thinkers as varied as Kierkegaard, Schopenhauer, Marx, and Nietzsche are keen to find alternatives. "Criticism," complains Nietzsche in *The Will to Power*, "is never directed at the ideal itself."[14] Nevertheless, criticism's fear of ideological growth is already there in the anxiety typified by *The Triumph of Life*— fear that to step outside ideology is to give up too much. Increasingly, ideology is seen to be enmeshed in valued processes of thinking and imagining. Accordingly, to move outside it threatens further cultural impoverishment.

Romanticism, as I am defining it, moves from a confident exploitation of ideology, Stendhal's "imaginary solution,"[15] to a dissatisfaction at finding in this structure its own completion or ending. This is the pessimism Nietzsche calls "a preliminary form of nihilism,"[16] when nihilism describes the nowhere place left outside romantic ideology's brilliant annexations. On the optimistic side, romanticism legitimates its sense of becoming or pursuit of *Fülle* as the form of universal philosophy; its main devices—imagination, sublimity, irony, symbol, the fragment—exuberantly assimilate apparent exceptions or philosophical shortfalls to a rule of appearance. There are no epistemological defeats that cannot be translated into ironic successes; the collapse of representation becomes its effective supplement when it is reread as the *symbol* of what exceeds representation. Romantic consciousness can now make the boast Marx thought defined ideology, that of "really representing something without representing something real."[17] Appearance is always sufficient.[18]

On the pessimistic side, as Nietzsche saw, romanticism only becomes what it is: what the ideal realizes in "becoming" is itself. Hegel's "dialectical fatalism," like Goethe's, results in "the submission of the philosopher to reality."[19] This reactionary fatalism is very different from the *amor fati*, the affirmative relinquishing of individualism Nietzsche admired in Leopardi, and which entailed a Dionysian participation in life which, to an idealist, would look like life's triumph over us. The crisis literature of late romanticism in Britain—any poems by Shelley, Keats, and Byron, Gothic and historical novels—is at some point given over to criticizing romantic tautology or incorrigibility, searching out another grounding for itself at the risk of hazarding its own mode of imaginative writing. Romantic devices no longer satisfy the appetite for something larger than they can represent; instead, they are more productively read as anticipating the immanent critique we are so conversant with today. Sade's and Stendhal's ability already to imagine a totalizing ideology, one allowing no prosaic escape, shows the danger imaginative license was now posing for critique. The earlier romantic legitimation of the imaginary, its installation at the heart of philosophical explanation, accounts for the difficulties experienced in attempting to forgo so central a form of cultural endorsement. Romantic writing registers the pressure to contrive immanent critiques that would still employ imagination, even if they employ it against itself.

Marx believes ideology is a circle he can break out of because he conceives of ideology as symptomatic of an erroneous development in the history of thought, determined by the division of labor. The premise of his early writings on the subject, that idealism is ideology, comes close to looking like an attack on thought itself, the intellectual "empire" of Shelley's *Triumph of Life*. "Let us revolt against the rule of thought," he announces at the start of *The German Ideology* (159). But Marx believes, of course, that economics is a form of thought. The inversion of the Hegelian dialectic, or the prioritizing of praxis and material circumstance in understanding, is conducive to improved consciousness. It does not imply a handing over of authority to an unconscious power really accounting for consciousness all along. My claim is that to appreciate the cultural pressures Marx had to resist, we have to understand the romanticizing of Enlightenment ideology. Equally, to understand the revolutionary nature of Marx's break with this movement is further to define romanticism. Romanticism, that is, becomes identified with the ploy by which to step outside its ideology is made to appear like a break with thought itself. Romantic writing dramatizes this dilemma. Immanently it criticizes the pass to which it has been brought, and in so doing it expresses dissatisfaction with a criticism that can only be immanent.

The Ideology of Immanent Critique

Let us trace the romanticizing of Enlightenment ideology in more detail. Although Destutt de Tracy is usually commemorated only for his coinage of "ideology," he and Stendhal are preeminently qualified to tell the story of this transformation. Tracy was a liberal aristocrat, a member of the French National Assembly, who wrote a witty reply to Burke in 1790 and was temporarily imprisoned during the Terror. Subsequently, he produced his *Éléments d'idéologie* in four volumes, a work that established him as a successor to the philosophes and constituted an influential, late flowering of the French Enlightenment. In America, Jefferson enthusiastically translated, edited, and published the works Tracy sent him in the hope that, as he put it in a letter of 1818, they would be "be made with us the elementary book[s] of instruction."[20] One piece of writing that Tracy sent him that he did not make available was a chapter on love permissive enough for Tracy to have feared to have it included in the original, Napoleonic edition of *Eléments d'idéologie*. Tracy had met Stendhal, an admirer, around this time, and the novelist became a frequenter of Tracy's salon in the Rue d'Anjou in the 1820s. Despite Stendhal's lasting devotion to Tracy's ideological method, the intellectual differences between the two men became unignorable when Stendhal presented Tracy with a copy of his work on love, *De l'amour*, and the ideologue tried to read it. Mme de Tracy later recalled the incident, suggesting that the decisive disagreement was over the meanings each attached to *idéologie:* "[T]hey soon fell out because of [Stendhal's] book on the theory of love, demonstrated by crystallization, which was the *idéologie* of M. Stendhal. M. de Tracy tried to read this work, understood nothing of it, and declared to its author that it was absurd."[21]

Crystallization, or Stendhal's ideology, exemplifies the romantic departure from Enlightenment methodology. While in Milan, Stendhal had read Tracy's chapter on love in the expanded version he allowed to be published in the Italian translation of the *Éléments d'idéologie*. Before writing his own essay, therefore, he would have seen a typically Enlightenment attempt to define love from first principles, but in an inherently contradictory way. Tracy, one discovers, both analyzes love into its basic elements and yet shows how these elements make sense only in the social context from which philosophical analysis apparently tried to isolate them. Tracy's résumé of his argument draws a comparison from grammar. Just as isolated words have no value outside discourse *(discours)*, so only individuals united in love to create a family form the true social unit. Yet we have no difficulty in conceiving of individuals as a standard against which to check that families are composed of the right stuff. In fact, love must have appeared paradigmatic to Tracy's analysis: not the embarrassing appendage that his consignment of its full exposition to an Italian translation implied, but an analogy easing the way for acceptance of the otherwise awkward hiatus between truth and meaning bedeviling his general theory. For, fundamental to Tracy's ideology are the claims, difficult to reconcile, that "our perceptions . . . are not susceptible of any error, taken each separately, and in itself," and yet that these perceptions have meaning only when their ideas form part of discourse or a system of signs. It is the task of the philosopher to discover the grammar of things, thus perfecting our discursive understanding of them. The difficulty comes when we try to envisage how we would check existing discourse against perceptions. Perceptions must somehow be expected to possess a corrective force prior to having the significance they only acquire when discursively systematized. In other words, the empirical check tends to drop out of consideration because it relies impossibly on meanings existing independently of social context.[22]

The problem recalls Locke's famous barrier of ideas cutting us off from the reality they are supposed to represent (the paradox exploited by Humean skepticism), or his inability to explain the nature of the relation between words and ideas in book 3 of his *Essay*. Overcome one problem and you overcome the other, as fideists like Hamann, Herder, and Jacobi saw. If the relation remains unexplained, then it becomes arbitrary by default, and both Locke's phenomenology and his study of language enter the domain of semiotics; both submit to the rule of appearance rather than reality. Stendhal does not consciously exploit this possibility; he is clearly surprised when Tracy in effect says this is what he has done.

The absurdity of crystallization is its incorrigibility. This embarrassment is shared by Tracy's theory but remains invisible due to his inherited philosophical belief in a correspondence letting him check linguistics against empiricism. Enlightenment ideology from Condillac to Tracy mediates between the two. Thus, Tracy can write, as we have seen him do, about the primacy of perceptions and also claim in his *Éléments d'idéologie* that "all languages have common rules which are derived from the nature of our intellectual faculties."[23] In this context, Cartesian linguistics or the idiom of the grammarians of Port Royal guarantees that appearance still retains its logic even if it loses touch with what it was thought to be the appearance of. We are, as it were, referred in advance to Chomsky rather than to Saussure: to the universals of a deep linguistic structure rather than to the arbitrariness of the sign. We have already seen La Mettrie's brisk way of closing any gap here between mind and matter: the linguistic grids prescribing how we make sense are physically *"marqués ou gravés dans le cerveau."* Assumed by both Chomsky and La Mettrie is a view of language as constituted by an immutable human rationality. Avoided is the post Saussurean surrender of that confidence in an immutable human rationality, as a consequence of realizing that it is constituted by language. It is this second possibility that Stendhal's text anachronistically opens up through its characterization of love as an ideology.

What is happening, then, is that Stendhal's treatise purports to foreclose the arbitrariness of language by producing a scientific definition of love, an ideology of love in Tracy's sense. However, his definition actually restores arbitrariness by characterizing love as a psychological and imaginative overleaping of boundaries: the power to assimilate anything at all to the substance of the original object of study through a process of crystallization. But in seeing how Stendhal fails to become an Enlightenment ideologue of love, we observe how he succeeds in drawing a picture of ideology much closer to a post-Marxist understanding of it as an imaginary relation to the real. And he does this by allowing tendencies in Enlightenment ideology to develop within a new romantic phenomenology that no longer ties them down to external verification.

In such early writings as *The Holy Family, The German Ideology,* and *The Poverty of Philosophy,* Marx still formulates his materialism largely through a critical reading of his philosophical heritage from Descartes to Feuerbach. He sees the empiricist reaction to Descartes's idealism culminating in a combination of the two, stretching from La Mettrie, Holbach, and the philosophes through the work of Tracy's friend Cabanis to the natural science of Marx's own day. Marx's critique of "pure" science, applied retrospectively to this tradition, discredits the materialist half of the "combination," calling it "Cartesian materialism" because in fact all we are being given is a system of ideas or what, in chapter 8, I called "empiricism."[24] Marx then writes his own chapter in this story we have been telling by insisting that such a system must be constructed in conformity with the social relations explaining how people have managed to produce their reality. His explanation exposes how "reality" is tailored to the dominant class's interests and desires. More recently, enlisting Freudian hindsight, post-Marxist thought has concentrated on the ingenuity with which ruling-class power is legitimated or disguised. Althusser's positioning of the ideological in a Lacanian imaginary finally grants it such unlimited resources that it can dispense with ideas altogether, becoming, in a contradiction hard to surpass, both a material and a subjective existence. That damning license is at least partly anticipated by Stendhal's ideology of love: *"[D]ans cette passion terrible,* toujours une chose imaginée est une chose existante."[25]

However, we should keep in mind that if Stendhal's shift in the meaning of ideology characterizes the move from Enlightenment to romanticism, it also depicts romanticism as a misreading, a mistake. There seems no reason to think Stendhal disingenuous in his desire to emulate Tracy and to assume his intellectual heritage. He refers to *De l'amour* in his third and last preface as his "Physiologie de L'Amour." The laws of physics, he claims, are his model, although his treatise is palpably a compendium of everything unsystematic—anecdote, catalog, travelogue, aphorism, reverie, conjecture, autobiography—strikingly in contrast to Tracy's chapter. Stendhal's nostalgia, though, is for the enlightened society of Diderot, fifty years before. He tells us how he finds frightening the change that has rendered Diderot's culture unintelligible and plunged French society into its present ennui, a boredom he satirizes as English, but that will grow monstrous beyond even the capabilities of the English— *"peuple le plus triste de la terre"*—to find again a proverbially French voice in Baudelaire.[26] Stendhal, unlike us, sees no anticipations of a disjunctive modernity in the vivid miscellany (or crystallography, perhaps it should be called) of his own mode of writing. Instead he tries to recover a glittering urbanity and gaiety he associates with the *ancien régime,* virtues, however, that were especially exemplified for him by philosophes like Diderot, who were busy demonstrating that regime's obsolescence. Obviously, it would be unlikely that Tracy would appreciate so contradictory an expression of solidarity. Absurdity was what he saw; but, for us, after Marx, contradiction is fair historical game, the stuff of ideology.

If Stendhal redefines ideology, therefore, he does so inadvertently, in conformity with the contradictions underlying his own stance as a liberal sympathizer, someone expelled more than once from Italy by the Austrian government because of his support for the Carbonari and their revolutionary aspirations. Revolutionaries who take their style from that of radicals shown to best advantage in the regimes they criticize, and liberals who are enabled in their self-criticism by the privileges they wish to do away with—these are familiar knots, *pis-allers* that we can now identify as ideological constraints, but that were repeatedly dramatized during the romantic age. Perhaps this was because there was as yet no metalanguage with which to define and distance their experience, or because the break with a richly contradictory past demanded by a successfully scientific metalanguage implied an unacceptable cultural impoverishment. Stendhal gets as close to articulating this dilemma as any of his contemporaries in his ideology of love; but then his exchange with Tracy over the book shows him to have been mistaken or obscurely contradictory about its achievement. He thinks his picture of love meets the standards of Enlightenment objectivity, but, contaminated by its inexhaustible subject matter, it undermines its own control and distance altogether, miming in its own *mélange* the power of love absurdly to turn anything to its object. The erotic ideology he describes grows into a form that can encompass the position from which he described it. Stendhal himself dramatizes this encirclement when the love of *his* life, Métilde (Mathilde), dies in 1825.

In English, he notes in the margin of his own copy of *De l'amour,* "Death of the author," a surrender of authority sadly accentuated by being in English: none of *la gaïété française* here, the hoped-for complicity with Tracy and his enlightened precursors, but only entrapment within the age's gloomy, English self-image. This is the reality that Stendhal depicts, and, as Marx claimed in *The German Ideology,* "[W]hen reality is depicted, philosophy as an independent branch of knowledge loses its medium of existence."[27] Philosophical detachment from ideology is just what Stendhal's redefinition of ideology precludes. His treatise reveals a philosophical loss, and that is important: its thesis is not complacently self-confirming. But neither can it turn this loss to methodological gain. It can only propose as an alternative to complacency the reenacted awareness of loss and nostalgia for the philosophical position irrecoverably lost.

Sade's exploration of erotic self-confirming systems foregrounds what my discussion of Stendhal's treatise omits: the character allotted to woman by the discourse of male desire. But Sade does so by depersonalizing woman, making her interchangeable with things, refusing her and those who relate to her sexually any subjectivity save the blandness required by pornographic instrumentalism. We can react to this either with straightforward condemnation or else, as antihumanist critics have been led to do, we can find in Sade's perversity a means for raising consciousness of the subjugation women suffer under the contrasting, so-called normality of patriarchy. The French Sadeians, and poststructuralist critics like Jane Gallop, do the latter. Angela Carter tries to value Sadeian excess as a power to demystify gendered stereotype and myth, the achievement of "a moral pornographer."[28] But there is a third response that recovers the historicism implied, I have argued, by romantic texts' dramatized, metaromantic discontent with the immanence of their self-criticism.

Sade's barbarism shows that it is the bought woman or child of pornography who is effaced, silenced, or generally made available to the philosophically anaesthetized reader keen to foreground Carter's "moral pornographer" or the tyranny of contemporary ideology. To vindicate Sade at one point is simply to permit his violence at another. To see him as a deconstructor of representation is also to shelve the victim's pressing problem of how to gain redress through representation. The alternative would be to appreciate more why Marx regarded definition of the subjects of discourse through apparently impersonal economic specifics not as cultural impoverishment but as the only viable recovery of them as persons in the wake of a discredited humanism. Barthes, too, although attracted by Sade's antihumanist precociousness in suggesting "the possibility of a subject-less lexicon," has to concede that "the Sadeian text is reduced by the phenomenological return of the subject, the author, the utterer of Sadism." [29] This historical *birth* of the author risks contradicting Barthes's more famous deconstruction of the author elsewhere. It makes the point that in Sade's time a subjectivity that exploded its self-defining, interpellating ideology from within, immanently, still conveyed the sense that it was defined by external historical circumstances for which it had not yet found the language. Like *Waverley*, it communicates a historiographical crisis. Marx's political economy and Barthes's semiotics provide such a language and such a history. Like the literary children generated by Rousseau's reveries, they extend the existence of his meanings through critical reformulation at a discursive distance from their originals that sublime recuperation could not tolerate. Despite their differences, they are both responding to the historical character of romanticism.

To summarize, then: romanticism, defining itself in the process, mediates the shift in meaning of "ideology" between the Enlightenment and Marx's critique of it in *The German Ideology*, a critique powered by his demonstration of what ideology has become. Romantic dramatizations of the incorrigibility of ideology open up philosophical theories of ideology to all kinds of intervention and illustration. Stendhal and Sade are representative of two poles of this undermining of philosophical autonomy to be completed by Marx. The affront Stendhal's idealist *De l'amour* causes the philosophical ideologue, Tracy, is mirrored by the scandal of Sade's materialism. Both enable us to rethink contemporary theoretical writings, from Adorno onward, which struggle with the legacy of a critique condemned by postromantic ideology to be forever immanent. Finally, I suggest that the young Marx's strong sense that this was a period problem, a romanticism or idealism, both helps explain his subsequent economism and could significantly relativize our postmodern condition.

TEN

The New Romanticism:
Philosophical Stand-ins
in English Romantic Discourse

To read English literature written in the romantic period through emergent and then dominant idealist philosophies has for some time appeared simplistic and reactionary. It's all been done before, hasn't it, from Coleridge onward? Such philosophies appear to favor canonical lyric poetry and so lock into place a familiar canon of English romantic poetry. The philosophers empower poetry to save philosophy from its inability to grasp conceptually its own ideals. Equally, literature which does not serve this expressive, symbolic function lacks philosophical valorization and is consequently disqualified from as serious consideration. In practice, a simplistic aesthetic, unresponsive to the complex variety of romantic period writing, prescribes what is to count as genuine artistic production.

Nowadays, literary critics of romanticism have mostly given up excoriating its philosophical sublimation of real issues and just get on with interpreting the neglected archives. But philosophers, too, habitually revise their own traditions; they have also sought to sidestep this binary opposition and to see that philosophical aspiration and textual practice might always have been much closer than their idealist predecessors officially conceded. The independence of philosophy then seems as much at risk as does the aesthetic it prescribed, now happily no longer constraining scholarship. Something like the metaromantic process of self-dissemination we have been describing in this book is called for to explain the textual delegation of philosophical authority involved. But the absorption of philosophy by textual practice means that literary scholarship must still take on board the philosophical impulse of the period and not, in revenge, issue its own exclusion order. A remedial attempt to record the transactions between a soluble philosophy and an absorbent writing has to respond to interpretative challenges which can arise almost anywhere. First, though, the philosophical revisionism has to be appreciated before the diffuse textual negotiations it makes possible can be observed.

Theories

It must be almost uncontroversial to claim that much mid- to late-twentieth-century philosophy can be characterized by the significance it attributes to language. The "linguistic turn," as it is usually called, takes very different forms in different traditions. Without prejudice to their disagreements, one can say that these different traditions agree that to attribute theoretical authority to discourse is also to reflect upon the status of philosophy. For those who approve the linguistic turn, philosophy no longer independently prescribes the logical conditions under which linguistic behavior is meaningful. It relinquishes this anachronistic imperiousness for a role more in keeping with modernity, one modestly allowing the logic of discourse to predetermine the limits of sensible philosophical speculation. Philosophical clarification must, in Wittgensteinian phrase, leave things as they are. Richard Rorty's philosopher can no longer privilege her insights over the practical knowledge of language-users. At best, ancillaries to Foucault's genealogists, philosophers assist in the job of describing and comparing the ways in which truth is discursively produced at different times. And so on.

This provocation offered to philosophy by discourse becomes especially controversial when we try to account for change or progress. The linguistic turn, as I have just described it, sounds conservative: philosophy's task appears now to be to reconstruct or stand in for the unquestioned rationality of the status quo. Philosophy abandons its purchase on the universal, an ideal against which discursive practice could always be found wanting or to which it always aspired. Idealism of that sort is discredited; but proponents of the linguistic turn sensitive to the charge of conservatism must therefore relocate the idealizing impetus to change in the discourses now designated the only proper sphere of philosophical interpretation. Change in thought must then be something one does: a kind of action not a kind of speculation, possible discursive behavior not an abstract proposal. For Georges Bataille, opposing the "restricted," conservative economy of his day, "No one can say without being comical that he is getting ready to overturn things: he must overturn, and that is all."[1] Jürgen Habermas's own critique of Bataille in *The Philosophical Discourse of Modernity* finally concedes the power of Bataille's poetic practice as an erotic writer to realize in his reader's experience a heterogeneous excess eluding the philosophical "tools of theory."[2] But it is a quotidian, practical realm which Habermas himself envisages absorbing transcendental excess when he resituates the idealizing impulse in unconditioned and normative idioms we unavoidably use in ordinary communication. "Counterfactual presuppositions become social facts."[3] Tensions between our ideals and our actual existence no longer license metaphysics but identify the critical potential in speech itself.

Kant's late guide to Enlightenment divisions of knowledge, *The Contest of the Faculties,* significantly foreshadows this compromise. There he argues for a separation of intellectual and political powers: more specifically, he tries to divide intellectual responsibilities in such a way as to free philosophy from the constraints of government and leave government untouched by philosophical critique. Philosophy, the lower faculty, pronounces upon the truth or falsity of the higher theological, legal, or medical faculties. This might seem to issue a challenge to the various doctrines which a government licenses these faculties to promulgate, but which philosophy finds false. Kant, however, argues that such conflict between philosophy and government is illusory because the pragmatic, utilitarian grounds for wishing unphilosophical institutions to flourish are of a different order from those legitimating philosophical critique. "The Government," as Hans Reiss summarizes Kant, "never protects the higher faculties because their public doctrines, opinions and statements are true."[4]

Nevertheless, Kant (who after the publication of *Religion within the Bounds of Reason Alone* had suffered from the censorship of Frederick William of Prussia) obviously wants there to be possible "a legal conflict of the higher faculties with the lower faculty."[5] The government is to propagandize through the professions, supporting their higher status, while encouraging the public debate of philosophical questions in case a new discovery turns out to be to its profit. It can articulate its policies only through statutes of these state organs or "faculties," which philosophical criticism may show to be "dangerous" or "unsuitable" (55). Kant's government, therefore, maintains a kind of *reserve* in its acceptance of such "writings" or statutes which legitimate the discourses of the faculties pronouncing on legality, physical well-being, and the ultimate questions of religion. Equally, philosophy comes into play, politically, only if its criticisms are adopted for use by the higher faculties for unphilosophical reasons of political expediency. Nevertheless, such changes in policy undeniably follow discoveries resulting from philosophy's search after ideal, universal truth and so, in this case, fit Habermas's reduction of idealizing counterfactuals to social facts. Kant engineers the same straddling of logical and social categories so as both to reactivate philosophy at a discursive level in the modern state and to ascribe a progressive direction to discursive action.

In the tradition founded on revision of his major texts, Kant's later anticipation of Habermas's pragmatism tends to get overlooked. Kant's three earlier *Critiques*, while clearly mapping divisions of experience— scientific, moral, and aesthetic—are also concerned to imply the integrity of that experience. The desired unity is embodied, for Kant, in just that philosophical consciousness which can indeed review experiential variety from a single viewpoint and consequently can criticize infringements of one area of jurisdiction by another. The difficulties for Kant's scheme, difficulties which generate post-Kantian critique of his own *Critiques*, come when he tries to enunciate this unified subject of philosophical consciousness without inserting it into one of the experiential areas it has to lie outside for its disinterested criticism to be possible. How can we know what this transcendental ego is like without reducing it to an empirical object of science? Alternatively, if it is claimed that the philosophical viewpoint experiences itself instead in moral imperative or aesthetic feeling, we are still left with the problem of saying what it is that recognizes itself in these experiences. Every time Kant tries to specify the subjectivity which has made possible his philosophical divisions of experience, he appears obliged to objectify it in terms belonging to one of those divisions it is meant to transcend. At best he can be defended for having deliberately left the thing in mystery or obscurity *(Dunkelheit)*, an aporia tragically constitutive of our essential non-identity with anything, our homelessness in any world we can describe. And for Heidegger, of course, here lies the crucial failure of nerve in idealism, the moment where it cannot acknowledge the larger Being it has disclosed beyond its own powers of ratiocination.[6]

From Kant's immediate follower, Fichte, to Derrida and Habermas, philosophers have been offering alternatives to Kant's problematic account of self-knowledge as a subject knowing an object. Despite their differences, Habermas and Derrida equally participate in the linguistic turn of contemporary philosophy. They both continue to preserve the otherness of self from scientific, moral, or aesthetic prescription by refocusing philosophy on the construction of the self not in reflective self-consciousness but in language. The perpetual self-differing which produced an infinite regress in Kant's philosophy is permissible as the *différance* generating Derrida's grammatology. The otiose transcendentalism of the Kantian self is put to work in the ideal aspirations Habermas characteristically believes we have to attribute to ordinary language in order to make sense of it as communicative action.

Habermas is more useful for my purposes here because latterly he finds his linguistic turn anticipated in the romantic period, most strikingly by Humboldt. Wilhelm von Humboldt, Habermas believes, replaced the eighteenth-century divisions of knowledge, which fragmented rather than mapped a unified subject, with a diversity of linguistic practices. Negotiation between these practices can be rational without this rationality being obliged to appear paradoxically as some unrepresentable, transcendental subject in whom they all inhere. The idea of negotiation indicates sufficiently for Habermas a respect for differences, an individuality preserved on both sides of the table because in each case it is in excess of agreed compromises and so realizes an idealistic, progressive impulse. The sentence from Humboldt on which Habermas seizes to exemplify this postmetaphysical thinking retrieves individuality as an inescapable feature of ordinary communication and so supplements an otherwise entirely structuralist approach. When we communicate, we have different intentions, interests, and so forth, yet we can agree, we can be meaningful to each other. "For this reason," writes Humboldt, "all understanding is always simultaneously non-understanding, and all accord in thoughts and feelings is simultaneously a parting of the ways."[7] Understanding is therefore no longer a struggle between a subject and an object but a significant agreement over differences, potential change, necessary for communication to take place. A working model replaces a theoretical possibility. Kant's contest of faculties rather than his critiques of self-consciousness becomes the paradigm.

The kind of romanticism described by Humboldt's methodological shift in the framing of experience is therefore an *alternative* to the reactionary ideology normally associated with idealism and rightly attacked by a succession of thinkers, from Heine and Marx to contemporary new historicists. The rhetorical strategies we as literary critics or cultural historians habitually try to decipher grow richer in meanings when we keep this in mind. Ideological dispute yields up more secrets of its workings, that is, if we look for this contemporary refiguring of individual difference from an absolute otherness into a discursive reserve necessary for communication between different individuals to be possible. "Reserve," as I commend it throughout this discussion, links surplus, unspoken linguistic competence to respect for the individuality of one's interlocutor—

a discursive ethics, as Habermas might optimistically claim, which is progressive because it continuously increases communicative (and, one might add, literary) resources. Initially this may look like the birth of a fairly simple hermeneutical confidence; in practice, the negotiations are complex and fascinating.

The production of orderly maps of the faculties raised difficulties for late Enlightenment philosophers trying to define the owner of the map. Kant had clearly seen this problem as it applied to past projections. A footnote to *Contest* says of Plato's *Atlantis*, More's *Utopia*, Harrington's *Oceana*, and Allais's *Severambia* that "It is the same with these political creations as with the creation of the world: no-one was present at it, nor could anyone have been present, or else he would have been his own creator" (188 n). But the same objection applies to Kant's *Critiques:* the subject writing them is, by definition, producing the only possible knowledge of herself and so must already be in them, but as if created by another self, equally hers, outside them. Kant sometimes appears to repeat the error, the encyclopedic error it might be proper to call it, he seeks to criticize. The movement beyond this error, though, incurs its own difficulties. We are now rid of that comic embarrassment Bataille attributed to "a vast project" whose "announcement . . . is always its betrayal," or its subsumption by the conditions of definition it purported to circumscribe. But we are left with the description of experience as a miscellany of discourses whose negotiations are often much more oppositional and much less in the service of communication than Humboldt or Habermas appear to allow. Maybe they are right to think that discourses are nevertheless obliged to share ideal aspirations simply in order to be discursive; I don't wish to debate that here. I do wish to suggest that much writing in the romantic period which concerns itself with the dispositions of different discourses often prefers the obliquities of theorizing through discursive practice to systematic philosophical abstraction.

This syndrome is exhibited at different levels. To recognize it helps us get a purchase on otherwise nebulous shifts in writing-practice, such as those which dissolve philosophy in the poetry of Wordsworth and Coleridge, and then that poetic philosophy in the sagacity of Carlyle, Arnold, George Eliot, Ruskin, and further Victorian practitioners of edifying discourse. The poverty of philosophy endows their antitheoretical, prosaic versatility with responsibilities and ambitions originally exemplified by philosophy's metadiscursive range. But pure philosophy can be redeployed in different, local, less well-noticed ways in the romantic period whenever traditions of interpretation or conceptual inheritances are reviewed. Once it is realized that a lack of explicit concern for relations between different kinds of experience—knowledge, labor, gender—may belie a practical engagement with those questions in discourses remote from transcendentalism, then the relocation of what were once explicitly theoretical debates becomes visible, and the continuing pertinence of these debates about a general economics of experience becomes legible.

This is not to say, in defiance of the facts, that the transcendental tradition does not flourish, and that Kantian idealism and its developments are stopped in their tracks. At the beginning of his *Phenomenology*, Hegel seeks to establish the impossibility of describing immediate consciousness without invoking general terms. Among other things, this is a formal reduction of Kant's problem of describing a consciousness existing outside any conceptual scheme. But Hegel's presentation of Kant's crux as a misunderstanding of how language is obliged to work has encouraged, not dissipated, subsequent concern for the individuality his generalizations smoothly efface. Hegel stifles the need for a view of language which, like Humboldt's, will honor particular resistances to hegemonic schemes while acknowledging the necessity of living under their conceptual dispensations. Humboldt, Schelling, and Schleiermacher do concede this point and, as a result, can be rehabilitated by contemporary philosophers as romantic precursors of postmodern singularity. Hegel, though, erases particularity in the interests of tidiness and system, arguing on the side of a traditional map of existence, allowing only for the evolution of new boundaries within its restricted economy. He notoriously neglects the untidiness of particular pressure groups who are provoked by their material conditions to partisan dissent. He ignores them to an extent that invites Marx's verdict in *The German Ideology:* when reality is depicted, philosophy of Hegel's kind has ceased to exist.

English thinkers on the grand scale look more open to the intellectual shift of focus I am describing, perhaps because they are less successfully grand or systematic than Hegel. Coleridge, from within both an idealist and a commonsense tradition, registers the pressure to acknowledge the untidiness of discursive conflict as the arena where philosophical debate about the categories of experience is to be conducted. He usually refers to his Logic as the "Elements of Discourse." The larger project to which it was intended to belong he can describe as an "Anti-Babel," an attempt to discipline obstreperous "logoi" under a single, unifying "Logos." De Quincey's Spinozistic ambition of correcting the human intellect is still more obviously fragmented into energetic polemic of immense discursive variety: the range of "disciplines" which, as Jo McDonagh has recently emphasized, is achieved at the expense of overall intellectual organization. As McDonagh surmises, this phenomenon could concur with Foucault's claim that "at the beginning of the nineteenth century a new arrangement of knowledge was constituted" in which historical and linguistic awareness were at a premium. De Quincey's pathological stylistics, to follow John Barrell's readings here, would then give good grounds for Foucault's belief that the period's defining conviction was that language was an opaque, not a transparent, medium, a new object of knowledge rather than the invisible purveyor of knowledge.[8]

It is hard, certainly, to separate the power of words from notionally different ideological interests which nevertheless could not have been stated in any other way. Foucault's point is recycled in recent claims, from late de Man to Derrida's book on Marx, that there has been an ideological critique inherent in deconstruction all along; but the awareness that language might therefore have its own input into ideological debate need not be the endgame of theory. An escape from, rather than a negotiation of, ideological difference is linguistically impractical. Such emancipation would so defamiliarize language as indeed to leave it as the unusable, meaningless, strange, noumenal material, always to be approached as if for the first time, that is the aesthetic object imagined in Paul de Man's hyperbolic, Kantian suspension of identity. De Man's ideologically disabused view of language actually looks, as Frances Ferguson astutely claims with Rodolphe Gasché's concurrence, "prelinguistic."[9] Imprisonment in a form of words certainly obliges us to use a discourse as the tool of debate; but it also implies a slack which might evoke other, adjacent words not explicitly present in the debate, words whose exclusion is a negotiated compromise, an individual reserve of expression, one silently conceded at the time, there for later changes (progressive, one hopes) in reading to uncover and bring into dialogue.

Discursive Reserve

Examples of this discursive reserve must therefore, by definition, be graspable only in various idealizing practices and not be susceptible of philosophical abstraction and definition. The philosophical reconstructions they facilitate only stand in for and will be superseded by the ideal endpoints aimed at by communicative action.[10] Equally, if philosophy is still to have a function, these ideal termini must be superseded by philosophy's interpretation of how communicative action incorporates them right now.

Habermas's "stand-in" *(Platzhalter)*, I have already suggested, arguably has affiliations with Friedrich Schlegel's description of irony as "perpetual parabasis." Schlegel similarly redefines progress as a lateral, cohering movement rather than one of unremitting, ongoing advancement. He turns the ideal into something produced in communication rather than deferred as the prefiguration of unconditioned knowledge. Habermas's "stand-in" similarly concretizes the ideal of complete philosophical transparency, making a present reality out of something otherwise indefinitely postponed. It interrupts an endless process, or fashions out of a place in the queue for total knowledge a temporary sufficiency. It succeeds by taking account of the pragmatics necessary to keep the specialisms characteristic of modernity in conversation with each other now, an *entretien infini* which is neither the "fruitless discourse" deplored by Carl Schmitt nor that valued for its Orphic disclosures by Maurice Blanchot. This conversational fluency across a historical cross-section of intellectual life—what Schlegel might have called "logical sociability"—lets philosophy be the one to interpret the rationality shared by discursive practices, a rationality traditionally the vanishing-point of philosophical endeavor but ideally prefigured in art. Now, though, this fluency is a presupposition of "everyday communication" whose equivalent function in specialist discourses can be interpreted to us by philosophy. The task remains the one Schiller allocated to aesthetics—to show "how to overcome the isolation of science, morals, and art and their respective cultures."[11] But the solution is pursued sideways, found in contemporary pragmatics based on daily instances of that lived dialectic of respect or otherness within acknowledgement of a common human project.

To begin with a mainline example, cryptography is worth bearing in mind if evaluating the terms of public argument during the romantic period when that argument draws on or represents constituencies that do not share its language. The Revolutionary debate, as represented by Burke and Paine, can seem an exclusive affair: an argument about political theory, a confrontation between Burke's romantic idealism and Paine's Lockean empiricism . Ruled out of court by both their arguments is the wealth of impolite pamphleteering accompanying and provoked by their dispute. If, however, Paine's arguments are read as a cryptic attack on the economy within which formal constitutional debate in Britain traditionally operated, then we should be able to detect at work in his polemic the discursive variety wider than the ostensible terms of his enquiry. Political theory would then be visibly prescribed by the language in which it is conducted, rather than itself be empowered to pass judgment on the admissibility of forms of writing. As Olivia Smith, Kevin Gilmartin, and others have demonstrated, the traditional hierarchy of debate prevailed. Pitt's "terror" largely succeeded in its censorship. But it is still arguable that the dispute rocked conservative apologists because it mobilized current demotics and their different discursive traditions against the weakening notion of a single viewpoint from which the true map of faculties, disciplines, and so on could be charted, or to use Blake's word, "chartered."

Radicalism of Tom Paine's kind holds this kind of cryptic opposition in reserve. Directed against the accommodation of inherited inequity, it is for that reason directed against a mixed economy in politics of any kind. This antagonism opposes him to a government, as he "ludicrously" styles it, "of *this, that and t'other.*" [12] His distaste for compromise obviously targets Burkean conservatism. It also reflects on that older tradition favoring a "balance of powers," one which, growing out of Harrington's *Oceana* (1656) could allow his editor of 1700, John Toland, to describe England as a republic in the frame of a monarchy, and one which Wordsworth surely must assume when he sketches his "perfect *Republic* of Shepherds and Agriculturists" living, nevertheless, "in the midst of a powerful empire like an ideal society" (my emphases) in his *Guide to the Lakes* first published in 1810. [13] As early as his defense of the American Revolution in *Common Sense* (1776), though, Paine suspected such notions of a mixed English constitution, branding their compromises as having "all the distinctions of a house divided against itself," [14] and clearly distrustful of the efficacy of their pragmatic idealism. Already he is discarding the domestic, familial metaphor Burke will use to figure the working relationship obtaining between different ranks of society. Paine regards the synchronic existence of monarchy, aristocracy, and democracy as anachronistic rather than pragmatic or progressive. These different political characters are to be properly explained by his own diachronic narrative. There, each kind of government succeeds the other in a progress from legitimation by superstition, then by power, to a final and convincing corroboration by the rationalization of common social interest in deference only to the rights shared by all men. The halting of progress to institutionalize coexistence of different kinds of government can only be politic in a sense that favors the less rational, whose interest deserves to be superseded.

Paine tells us that "it is in [Burke's] paradoxes that we must look for his arguments" (62). Paradox, here, is an ideological slip, not the calculatedly self-subversive writing for which we saw Burke and Wordsworth berate Rousseau. The demystification, then, of Burke's paradoxical tolerance of constitutional diversity reveals his actual argument to champion a political interest over the rational grounds for its removal, and so, by definition, to support a despotic interest. Paine's plain speaking, by contrast, creates and enfranchises a wider audience of men using their private judgment in the manner so feared by Burke's parliamentarianism. But Paine's meliorist narrative does not simply call for more participation, as his analogy of political republicanism with "the republic of letters" might suggest (166); the asymmetry of democratic and hereditary interest is too pronounced for that. Democratic inclusiveness has to cater for languages, customary practices, and worldviews which blow apart hierarchical understanding mapped from the top down. Paine's writing therefore can retain a cryptic opposition connected to the artisanal background which gives him access to this asymmetrical proletarian culture. It sometimes emerges in the main line of his attack, especially in the way he drives Burke's own hereditary argument to a logical conclusion prior to the authority it wishes to conserve. Burke's pursuit of historical legitimation stops short of that original state in which the rights of man become visible. The language in which Paine chooses to describe Burke's strategy is strongly inflected with a Dissent much more radical than the enlightened words preached in the Old Jewry by Richard Price.[15] Burke's opportunistic attenuation of historical possibility (a fault he himself will ascribe to Bedford in *Letter to a Noble Lord*) provokes Paine to echo seventeenth-century Leveller opposition to political closure or enclosures: "But Mr. Burke has set up a sort of political Adam in whom posterity are bound forever; he must therefore prove that his Adam possessed such a power or right" (57). This same Adam's restrictive politics is also the target of *The Levellers' Standard Advanced: or, The State of Community Opened and Presented to the Sons of Men* (1649). The *Levellers' Standard* attacks an exclusive inheritance or primogeniture and the corresponding property rights which later flesh out Burke's understanding of constitutional liberties as "entailed inheritance": "And since the coming in of the stoppage, or the A-dam, the earth hath been enclosed and given to the elder brother Esau, or man of flesh, and hath been bought and sold from one to another; and Jacob, or the younger brother that is to succeed or come forth next, who is the universal spreading power of righteousness that gives liberty to the whole creation, is made a servant."[16]

Paine echoes the communism of Everard and Winstanley in order to counter Burke's conversion of legislator into testator to justify hereditary succession. For Paine directly to suggest we turn the world upside down would, once again, risk being comical. Blake, or E. P. Thompson's anti-nomian Blake, was prepared to risk ridicule and obscurity and openly tries to turn his Dissenting legacy into a system offering an alternative to cultural staple, resort, or recourse. Despite having occasionally "lost heart," as Morton Paley puts it, evidenced by his modified "Address to the Public" at the start of *Jerusalem* (plate 3), his radicalism appears of a different order from that of primarily Enlightenment polemicists and re-specters of private property like Price and Paine.[17] Nevertheless, Paine's discourse cryptically mobilizes a political vision unconfined by appar-ently inescapable political divisions. In his vision of a shareholders' so-ciety, "Every man is a proprietor in society, and draws on the capital as a matter of right" (79). This is closer to opposing the "divided house" of Burke's constitution with the Levellers' "one house of Israel . . . taking the earth to be a common treasury" than it is to invoking the scholars and philosophers backing Price's claims—Milton, Sidney, Harrington, Hoadley—characters just as likely to appear in Wordsworth's political sonnets of 1802. Eventually the fact that Paine stops short of advocat-ing Leveller ideology aligns his cryptic entertainment of its idiom with the exercise in pragmatic containment practiced by the Putney debates; but even comparison with the generals of the New Model Army obvi-ously exceeds anything Price's ideals could invite. Paine's radicalism hits more significant limits in his gendered scorn of titles—"the counterfeit of woman" (89). He is in turn corrected by the parallel Wollstonecraft draws between titles and the politically degrading construction or "character" of woman as possessing "the arbitrary power of beauty."[18]

"Let it not be concluded that I wish to invert the order of things," we are told in *Vindication of the Rights of Woman* (109); but we know from recent romantic scholarship that feminism can be counterrevolutionary and not the less feminist for that. Men might enforce the "reserve" re-quired of women by popular eighteenth-century conduct books, but they could not prescind its convergence with the radical "reserve" I have been describing. My chapter on Austen tried to show this instability within her Conservatism. Feminist radicalism, more than other types of radical-ism, seems able to work conservatively within given economies of expe-rience, partly because there was so much work to be done simply to get on cultural terms with men before thinking of exceeding those terms of reference. Elizabeth Hamilton, for example, has a character in *Mem-oirs of Modern Philosophers* (1800) unanswerably, one imagines, cite Jesus Christ as the "one philosopher" who "placed the female character in a respectable point of view"; the same Christianity, though, validates "the order of Providence."[19] Thirteen years later, in *A Series Of Popular Essays, Illustrative Of Principles Essentially Connected With The Improvement Of The Understanding, The Imagination, And The Heart,* the conservative acceptance of the map of experience offered by traditional eighteenth-century faculty psychology does not prevent her from criticizing Blackstone's notorious refusal of legal personhood to wives: Hamilton calls it "a gratification of the selfish principle" by which "for ages an heiress was considered in no other light than a promissory note."[20] Hamilton ascribes this abuse to "*a propensity to magnify the idea of self,*" whose perpetrators she then cautiously exculpates by allowing that the fault develops unconsciously, irrespective of conscious desire or affection (271–72). But this care lest her feminist discovery interfere with established psychology nevertheless allows to feminist resistance an autonomy more visible in a post-Freudian age, when unconscious alternatives to conscious explanation can no longer look discreet and unchallenging in the way that Hamilton wants. By not having to be observant of the checks and monitors belonging to established models of experience, Hamilton's analysis of the unconscious begins to set its own agenda. Its unconscious target, male self-magnification, invites her feminism on secret missions, invisible to normal jurisdiction and law-enforcement. Elizabeth Hamilton still thinks she is doing God's work; Christianity's founding philosopher inaugurates feminism; consciousness-raising is all that is called for in her Christian society, in contrast to the conversion of "the barbarian" to which she nevertheless compares modern, European treatment of "the sex." Nevertheless, her gendered division of knowledge constructs the unconscious sphere of feminist critique so as to produce a reserve or difference from public meaning in which a feminist identity can now take shape. Her critical difference now makes a virtue of that "exclusion of 'woman' " which Michele Le Doeuff argues to be "consubstantial with the philosophical" from the eighteenth century onward.[21] According to Le Doeuff, "philosophy is just the formal idea . . . that admissible modes of thought cannot be undefined" (115). But Hamilton cleverly makes the inadmissibility of her "unconscious" evidence stand in for the ideal, still unrealized quality of a Christian perfection: that full, integrated consciousness, toward which her society would claim to be striving.

Failure and Success

What we read into female reserve can be a controversial business. Angela Leighton's revelatory book *Victorian Women Poets: Writing against the Heart*

illuminates how women Victorian poets come to write against their allotted place in the accepted map of experience, partly in reaction to the
unworldly rectitude of sensibility and sincerity practiced by romantic precursors like Felicia Hemans, Laetitia Elizabeth Landon, and, one might
add, by prosaic theorists like Elizabeth Hamilton. Jerome McGann, in his
pathbreaking *The Poetics of Sensibility,* reads back into romantic women's
poetry one of the reactions Leighton attributes to later Victorians—in
her words, "an existential emptying of [sensibility] from within."[22] This
"poetry of loss" (McGann's sobriquet now), by draining writing of reference, leaves high and dry for our better inspection conventions and
communities of feeling instead of the objects they supposedly map. Un-
worldliness ceases to signal sentimental self-indulgence; for the world put
aside creates the space from which we can view critically our construction of it. This optimism is perhaps advisedly tempered by a return to
Leighton's skepticism. Otherwise the critic ends up commending poems,
as Kingsley Amis does Hemans's "The Graves of a Household," for being "superficially superficial," consecrating the shallowness we can't give
up.[23] On this male charity toward female superficiality, Norma Clarke
relevantly remarks, in her analysis of the hostility Hemans met with from
the women of the Wordsworth household: "It was not difficult to regard
sewing as a higher achievement than writing. . . . What was harder was
to notice how these values came from the mouths of those whose shirts
had to be sewn by hand at home."[24] Or there is Leighton's unhappiness
with Marlon Ross's liberalization of literary-critical standards to favor Hemans, turning, she thinks, "historical differences of gender (Hemans is a
woman and therefore dutiful, self-denying and wary of poetic vocations)
into rules of aesthetic value" (20).

These critical responses show different calculations as to the significance of a female reserve lying behind women's deployments of the discourses of knowledge, gender, and labor. Where McGann sees a critical
distance, Leighton tends to diagnose dissociation which only modulated
into criticism later on in the century. To show that the stakes here are
different from male idealizations of women, and the creation of a discursive surplus within erotic literary traditions from Petrarch to Rousseau,
we might briefly mention the startling example of Hazlitt's *Liber Amoris,*[25]
a kind of grotesque parody of *La Vita Nuova,* but one which ultimately
excoriates its own inability to make coherent that slack or give in its own
language created by its abundant discontent with its given forms of knowing. I want to suggest that, by contrast with Hazlitt's stylistic dead-end,
there is a robustness in women romantic poets' reserve which valorizes

the progressive subjectivity about whose power McGann and Leighton have their nuanced disagreement, but concerning whose activism neither seems to be in doubt. .

To understand the depth of the self-critique of the language of *Liber Amoris*, we have to appreciate the policing of the escapes which might have been open to the eroticized object (S) of the narrator's (H) imagination. Had Hazlitt been able to criticize sufficiently the literary tools he lends, with some irony, to his narrator, then the young woman, S, might have been able to elicit alternatives, however cryptic, to the constructions H incessantly puts upon her behavior. He does, it is true, sometimes express strong literary skepticism. Contemporaneous with some of the midlife crisis described in *Liber Amoris* is Hazlitt's article in the *London Magazine* of June 1821, "Pope, Byron and Mr. Bowles," where he declares that it is "the conflict between nature and the first and cheapest resources of art, that constitutes the romantic and the imaginary." The unreadability of S to the infatuated H means that nature drops out of the picture and one is left with the self-confessed "first and cheapest resources of art." The novella is subtitled "the new Pygmalion," thematizing this lack of an original and the tawdriness of the arts substituted for her. However, unable to do anything with such literary reserve, H ends up performing a parodic critique of literariness which turns out to be another fantasy of possessing S. He rents the whole of Southampton Buildings, where he and her family live, in order to offer S the freedom from class and economic circumstance which his idealizing but reactionary literary accommodations of her had professed but of course failed to provide.

The other escape from the literary constructions baffling the relationship between H and S would be downward, dropping out of the polite register. There is a famous kitchen conversation alluded to in *Liber Amoris*, when the servant Betsy gives back to H the books he had lent to S, an allusion incomprehensible without the letter to P. G. Patmore (one of the letters to him and others drawn on by *Liber Amoris*) which details Hazlitt's own eavesdropping. The offending conversation was prompted by the thought of "what a sight there would be" if the trousers of one of Hazlitt's fellow lodgers at Southampton Buildings were to fall down. Hazlitt's frantic conclusion is: "can there be any doubt, when the mother dilates this way on codpieces and the son replies in measured terms, that the girl runs mad for size?" Sarah, Hazlitt's real-life obsession, says something "inaudible, but in connection," but the whole incident remains inaudible within *Liber Amoris*. Again, the lack of an original explanatory context doesn't so much tell the story of Pygmalion as frustratingly perform it. H's confession pretends to a Rousseauian honesty, but primly censors itself in such contrast to the innovative discursive confidence of Rousseau's divulging of childhood likings for being spanked, for masturbation, and for urinating in Mme Clot's cooking pot when she was at church—all within a few pages of beginning his *Confessions.* A realism based on knowing imprisonment within images cannot fail to sound postmodern to our ears. The dilemma of *Liber Amoris*, though, lies precisely in the way that the novella does not redeem through artistic transformation the letters on which it is based, although only in that aesthetic direction, that one-way street, can it envisage transformation happening. Here is no metaromantic, Rousseauian concession to future re-creation in another discourse. Aesthetic through and through, Hazlitt's self-criticism is a profession of discursive bankruptcy.

The same tale can be told of the "little image" of Napoleon which H gives as a present to S and then breaks on the ground in a rage on its return. H gives S the little statue of Napoleon because it reminds them both of hopeless allegiances: in his case the continuation of French Revolutionary hopes in Napoleon, in her case the likeness of a former lover. Her unfaithfulness to H here in this nostalgia is his only, eagerly seized on guarantee that she can be faithful. Since the logic of representation, of being an image of something, cannot be given up, it seems immaterial whether the image in question is in pieces or not. And *Liber Amoris* works for its defenders because its disorder simulates a kind of egalitarianism— "a democratic erotic moment," Michael Neve calls it, in which because you can't get anything right you can't get it wrong either. [26] As Hazlitt tells Patmore in another letter written in the cheap vein of *Liber Amoris*, "For a man who writes such nonsense, I write a good hand." The only redemption possible here is a postmodern one, equivalent to a kind of death, in which Bataille's excess no longer converges with Habermas's discursively constructive reserve but serves instead a "pure expenditure of self."[27] The trouble, again, is squaring this with the book's conventional aestheticizing.

The effective deployment of literary reserve contrasts strikingly with all this tortuousness. Anna Laetitia Barbauld's poem "The Rights of Woman" is now canonical. It is anthologized in collections by Roger Lonsdale, Jerome McGann, Jennifer Breen, and Duncan Wu and in the *Norton Anthology*. The poem presents the constraints on female emancipation in an extraordinarily knowing way. Written circa 1795, it presents an alternative to feminist writing coming out of a Painite framework, like Wollstonecraft's. It mixes cynicism and radicalism, eschewing heterosexual friendship, yet ending in a notion of sexual mutuality. The last line's explosion of the poem's earlier cynicism, apparently with all the force of Blakean innocence, is, however, partly muffled by the recollection, surely solicited as well, that women lose legal personhood in marriage at this time. On the way, Barbauld manages to show that, if men believe their own propaganda about women, they concede to them a power which it was the purpose of their rhetoric to exclude, one generating aggressive successes in a military, masculinist idiom. Barbauld, in short, manages to criticize complacency, conformity, and radical transcendence all at once. Her ambiguities do not concede discursive bankruptcy but orchestrate the senses in which material circumstances will have to change before a new, coherent culture of ideas about gender politics can arise. This is not a poetry of loss of referent, relying on postmodern charity in later interpreters, but a poetry whose multivalencing of the current referent, woman, figures the power to change the referent because narrator and referent are here the same—woman. Discursive versatility and interior distancing already reconfigure their object by being another version of it. The constructions of woman the poem takes as its object are belied by the constructive woman—the new woman—whose creative manipulation of them the reader admires in the poem's subject.

The poem calls for this subject to be given the social, practical, material existence justified by her demonstrated superiority to conventional objectifications of women. However, as Marx saw, idealism is infinitely elastic in its capacity for self-critique because such critique is always internal to the philosophy that mounts it. Barbauld's poem dramatizes a comparable discursive imprisonment, showing metaromantically what *Liber Amoris* cannot show: that it is the very discourses it employs that need to be displaced for the material implications of this new woman to be gathered. To stay with an idealist subject/object paradigm of self-knowledge here would be to describe as a constitutional aporia of self-consciousness a situation which cried out for practical remedies.

This constructive rather than incoherent (Hazlitt's) or aporetic (Kantian) reserve concerning the words she is obliged to use distinctively shapes Barbauld's other poetic productions. She is fascinated by the rhetorical possibilities of reticence, both in political action and in personal expression. Her early pro-Wilkes poem *The Times* (late 1760s) compares the physical but articulate violence lamented by Cicero's *Catiline* (*O tempora! O mores!*) favorably with the unstated corruption of George III's rule through bribery and placemen: "Then, then exclaim 'Oh hapless Times indeed'; / For deeper is the wound that does not bleed."[28] And her much later lines "On the Death of the Princess Charlotte" (1817?) similarly home in on the unspoken misery of Charlotte's Prince Regent father. Unfashionably, the poem argues that his apparently unnatural indifference to his daughter's fate merits not the popular contempt it got but an even greater effort of readerly sympathy. This attractiveness, though, leaves him a vulnerable figure because so removed by his strangely inexpressive grief from the common circle of values and meanings whose legitimate representative he, as royalty, is supposed to be.[29] Barbauld's sympathy is cunningly republican.

Barbauld's most notorious poem, entitled *Eighteen Hundred and Eleven* and published a year later, provoked a review from the *Quarterly* so vicious that it reputedly dissuaded Barbauld from the further publication of poetry.[30] John Wilson Croker is supposed to have succeeded in censoring her where he later failed with Keats; and, as in his criticism of Keats's *Endymion*, he reveals himself to be a reader politically disqualified from responding to the expressive reserve with which writers of his period might deploy traditional poetic tropes and structures. Barbauld's diagnosis of an *annus horribilis* in British history is full of aesthetic double-takes and figurative entrapments whose inescapability provokes the reader to feel more sharply how differently things actually could be under another political dispensation. The cumulative effect of the war with France since 1793 is the departure of prosperity from Britain: "The golden tide of Commerce leaves thy shore," its light "streaming westward," emigrating along with enlightened British intellectual and cultural hegemony, "Science and the Muse" (154).

There are three kinds of skepticism built into this initial gloomy frame of reference. First of all, the British traditions whose passing Barbauld laments are clearly controversial: their composition partly from archives of intellectual dissent (Locke, Paley, Thomas Clarkson, Sir William Jones) compromises other constituents which a Croker would prefer to read as politically conformist. Milton, here, must be a Puritan, James Thomson, a patriot poet writing against the political establishment. Secondly, the *demise* of this mixed loyalist and oppositional heritage turns out to be its *dissemination* in other cultures, lands, and societies—an appropriation and recycling elsewhere which most effectively signals the tradition's lasting value. If readers can just put aside national prejudices for a moment, and with them the partisanship sustaining the war, then the loss of national culture deprecated by the poem can be reinterpreted as an international gain. The poem's final call, after all, will be to replace cultural imperialism with a commonwealth of ideas inspiring the still-

colonized nations of America, the world of Columbus, to gain their freedom. Thirdly, the privileged point of view from which the poem reviews
the sequence of history and the successive ruins of empire is variously figured as that of "a Spirit" or "The Genius": a "capricious," "vagrant Power"
which now appears too arbitrary to offer a convincing gloss on the logic
of cultural and commercial exchange (158–59).

The figure puzzled the poem's first readers, and its progress while
following "the march of Time" scarcely imparts to history a notion of
progression. Croker is witty at its expense in the same way that he is about
Barbauld's pretensions to be a political commentator, a *"dea ex machina."*
His marrying of the figure's implausibility to the political viewpoint he
cannot countenance is a good reason for betting that they are *not* equivalent.[31] But, if explanation is definitely not located in this transcendental overview, then it has to be found in the particularities which such a
high horse loftily soars above. We are returned to the discourses of art,
war, wealth, and commerce which can "destroy the fruits they bring" and
know "no second spring." This inherent obsolescence, however, is tied
to their self-serving, nationalistic modes whose limitations, the poem's
stance implies, can be overcome by a reciprocal, more communal attitude
toward the spread of civilization. Otherwise our identity will perish with a
London Barbauld imagines sunk in future ruin. The alternative is to free
identity from a fixed patriotism and to tie it instead to a cultural center of gravity which will settle wherever civilization renews itself—which
will be multicultural. The pioneers of this future, historically and critically freed from a hegemonic aesthetic, are truly Barbauld's children in a
Rousseauian sense. Chauvinistically regarded, in other words, the individual cycle of mercantile and aesthetic fulfillment is doomed to decay and
frustration: "But fairest flowers expand but to decay; / The worm is in thy
core, thy glories pass away" (160–61). Focused by a militant national interest, the poem does seem to mark, as William Keach rightly points out,
"a decisive break with the meliorist historical perspective" to which "the
progressive Dissenting ideology that motivates all [Barbauld's] work . . .
had previously been attached."[32] By contrast, and more plausibly, we can
read the poem as open to the disseminating values of the *internationale*
typical of the early optimism of the "friends" of the French Revolution,
Richard Price's "citizens of the world" whose enthusiasm Kant located
in a progressive "moral disposition of the human race."[33] *Eighteen Hundred and Eleven* optimistically predicts the recrudescence of what it values
elsewhere, surviving local extinctions.

Reflexively, therefore, the poem has reservations about the received, transcendental viewpoint common to writings as different as Dr. John-son's Juvenalian satire, *London,* or Volney's *Les Ruines,* the viewpoint from which such surveys are traditionally conducted toward pessimistic conclu-sions. History as successive ruination is acceptable to the *Quarterly* when it appears, deceptively, as classical, tragic travelogue in Byron's *Childe Harold,* whose first canto is favorably reviewed in the preceding number of the same volume. Again, Barbauld's elusive reserve in her use of poetic privilege suggests the alteration in political attitude and national outlook needed if that overview is not to be mechanically determined to tell a story of cyclical destruction, inevitable decay and cultural supersession— the same story over and over again. For to describe instead the preserva-tion and resurgence of liberties cherished by the Good Old Cause, the imperialist assumptions of a Croker ("We had hoped . . . that the empire might have been saved without the intervention of a lady-author") and their aesthetic correlatives (". . . in a quarto, upon the theatre where the great European tragedy is now performing") are precisely what must change.

Barbauld's cosmopolitanism is common to moderate sympathizers with the French Revolution such as Price and Kant. Kant's republican ideal, as he emphasized in *The Conflict of the Faculties,* signified the best of all constitutions with which "to banish war, the destroyer of everything good." Barbauld shares Kant's difficulties in persuading his readers that republican pacifism is the conceivable endpoint toward which current national strife might be leading. By way of illustrating his embarrassment, Kant tells one of his rare jokes about an overoptimistic doctor whose re-assurances finally can only persuade his patients that they are dying of improvement.[34] The more influential texts of Kant's critical philosophy, though, emphasize the impossibility of the sensuous appropriation of ideas of reason such as the cosmopolitan republic: a perpetual estrange-ment of the ideal from the real which Lucien Goldmann correctly de-fined as "tragic."[35] Barbauld's skepticism, by contrast, does not so much answer to a logical requirement as constitute a call to the remedial action enjoined by her strictures on war and profiteering. Barbauld's ambivalent poetic presentation of the viewpoint from which the cosmopolitan ideal ought to be seen unfolding invokes the transformation required—and a practicable one if Croker's indignation at her "party pamphlet" is to be credited—if people are to shed the nationalism and accompanying bel-licose behavior impeding that ideal and rendering it implausible. Were people to start believing in it, then the latent meaning of *Eighteen Hun-dred and Eleven* could surface: the poem would now expose and satirize the interests keeping tragic pessimism in place. Progress rather than re-peated tragedy must be the repressed norm against which Barbauld's capricious spirit of genius of history looks an unlikely nemesis, chimerical and fanciful. Barbauld's literary reserve invokes a political unconscious circumscribing the tragic construction of history with which, her poem's intertextuality suggests, she is obliged to deal. As with the subject of "The Rights of Woman," this alternative history demands readers who, under-standing its significant reticence, will stand in for the new society that will let it speak.

In conclusion, I hope we can now understand better why Habermas could think that philosophy, from the romantic period onward, begins to stand in for and interpret those unconditioned idealisms silently em-bedded in discursive practice. So understood, philosophy has nothing to say on its own; nor does it enjoy the privilege of prefiguring the un-reserved communication for which discourse strives. It simply holds a place in our attention for those idealizing elements in which are se-creted discursive desiderata that cannot at present be more fully ar-ticulated. There are clear (if unexpected) similarities in this position to Lyotard's revamping of a Kantian sublime to figure a postmodern reach for the unrepresentable—a philosophical entertainment of what "will have been." Habermas, though, eschews all such aesthetic solutions; perhaps he risks being too systematic in his optimism, where Lyotard is arguably still too romantic in his.

Accordingly, when we consider a selection of the actual transactions between philosophy and writing of the romantic period, we have to rec-ognize both that their sense may emerge from ways in which they criticize aestheticization, and that these criticisms are still powered by the same idealistic, progressive impulse which the aesthetic had tried to monopo-lize and sublimate. Released from aesthetic institutionalization, writing refigures its critical impulse, but varying it with each literary example, each stand-in for a better dispensation. Failure to generalize theoretical and political vision is thus still redeemed by local examples—a particu-larity with which romantic aesthetics supplemented philosophy, yes, but with which postmodern thinkers (as different as Foucault, Lyotard, and Habermas) have continued the work of Barbauld and others to oppose the hierarchical distinctions idealism had otherwise been used to keep in place.

ELEVEN

Sublimity to Indeterminacy:
Dreams of a New World Order

The Postmodern Chiasmus

A chiasmus is oddly reassuring to a modern romanticist, and the unwieldy but chiasmic form of this chapter's title is intended to be apropos. Let me try to unpack it. The romantic trope of sublimity recasts failures of understanding as the successful symbolic expression of something greater than understanding. Postmodernism rereads this success as indicating only the indeterminacy of meaning. Our occasional inability to get on terms merely highlights the condition under which our understanding labors anyway, were we only to examine it more closely: sublimity is more of the same, not the sign for something qualitatively different. Nevertheless, much postmodernist thinking does not regard itself as merely demythologizing romantic pretensions, deconstructing back into understanding the Kantian postulate of a faculty of Reason capable of apprehending metaphysical reality. Postmodernism has its own agenda, one intended to replace former agendas like that of romanticism. Far from being the aftermath of romantic ideology, bound to it in its role of debunker, postmodernism proposes initiatives. Its unseating of the grand, emancipatory narratives of science, history, philosophy, and so on proposes an alternative to the failed Enlightenment which romanticism endeavored to replace in its turn. The postmodern alternative does not rest in Adorno's melancholy disillusionment. The postmodernism of, say, Jean-François Lyotard, advances a new liberalism in which diagnosis of the indeterminacy of meaning will lead to a proper respect for cultural difference, a new world order. A freedom inherent in our inability to define will replace the freedom traditionally aimed at by thought and action.

Postcolonial and feminist criticism have undoubtedly benefited from postmodernist skepticism. But in this aspiration toward a new world order, something qualitatively different from that symbolized in romantic discourse, the romantic ambition, or Idea returns. Postmodernism reconsiders its romantic starting point, and we find Lyotard poring over Kant's writings on judgment and the sublime. Sublimity, then, is deconstructed by postmodernism into indeterminacy; yet, in its escape from the task of mere translator, postmodernism doubles back on the romantic pretension from which it originally differed. A becomes B, and B, however redescribed, becomes A: a chiasmus.[1]

The dialectical structure of the figure of chiasmus suggests transcendence of some kind; its strict containment of that impulse, though, makes sure that the aspiration is securely anchored in the here and now. This is all we know on earth and all we need to know; no temple to Apollo stands at this crossroads, and so forth. The figure is involuted; it gestures outward, but is crucially impaired, drawing attention to its own figurality or the calculated design by which it simulates what it cannot do. Its grounding is in itself, the repetition or traverse of its own structure; the identity it asserts cannot stand as a fact discovered or as a step forward in any grand narrative. Despite first appearances, in other words, it strives for analytical rather than dialectical truth. Relieved of the embarrassment of a full-blown romanticism, with its accompanying religious or mystical overtones, postmodern romanticists can, with proper modesty, skepticism, and self-reflexivity, address the lesser problem of whether or not their chiasmus coheres. They check that in this case the chiasmus follows the pattern, A is B and B is A, with the assumption that if a real difference has crept in they have made a mistake; above all, they have *not* discovered a new grounding for A or B. Or maybe "mistake" is too strong: at best they have committed a catachresis, expressed themselves in another figure of speech, and so continued the rhetorical activity which, for a second, they might have thought they had disrupted by the intrusion of something else.

The name "postmodernism" sounds like where we are at, rather than the indication of a methodology, such as poststructuralism, which we might or might not adopt. However, since so much of our criticism, not only of romanticism, is concerned with showing that where people are at is where they choose to be, perhaps this distinction is illusory. We see what we need to see, even when that is unpleasant. I would like to suggest, here, that from a postmodern perspective, looking at romanticism takes on the chiasmic character I have just been describing. There are two main points to be made. First of all, this is what postmodern readings do to romantic discourse. Dialectical theories which distinguish between appearance and reality or between different orders of being are collapsed into chiasmus. This way of reading is typical both of deconstruction and of historicism. In the former, apparent crossings-over are shown to be crossings-back; A and B mean differentially, in relation to each other and not because they refer to different things; B does not denote something on the other side of a threshold from A. In the latter, historicist readings, the romantic sublimation of practical, political issues is detected by the cool glass of a criticism on whose surface the supposedly unfathered vapor condenses or solidifies. Again, an apparent transformation into something else turns out to contain its own reversal into the same. The second main point is that postmodernists repeat this groundlessness in their own discourse. That, on most descriptions, is just what postmodernism is about: the failure to ground any story of what is happening is the failure to legitimate any explanation in terms other than those already belonging to it. It can hardly be a coincidence that the postmodernist reads this absence of foundations into romantic literature and philosophy.

In this scenario, romanticism cannot anticipate postmodernism: since the postmodernist cannot see it any other way, it must always have been like this. But, equally, romantic refinements of the theoretical set postmodernism must think it shares show a theoretical initiative of their own. For example, postmodern criticism seems to reiterate Hegel's phenomenological critique of Kant. Hegel's *Phenomenology of Mind* does away with the distinction between Kant's two worlds, the world of things as they appear to us and the world of things in themselves in which appearances are grounded. Hegel argues that the second, noumenal world is nothing more than the mirror image of the first. In this inversion, we encounter the familiar turn-around in which transgression is demystified, and the voyage out becomes the voyage home; the noumenal world only retraces the outline of the phenomenal world in a different direction. We get the "others" we deserve, opposites tailored to our images of the normal, the ordinary, and the sane. For the postmodernist, the price of this epistemological xenophobia is that we never learn anything new. Like Satan in *Paradise Lost,* our journeys are never original, only perverse, and the country into which we travel has already been mapped by a moral orthodoxy we can refract or invert in various ways, but never escape. Nevertheless, as I have already recalled, Lyotard looks to Kant's aesthetics rather than Hegel's phenomenology for his model of philosophical judiciousness. Hegel's philosophy appears much more like a grand narrative in this context, whatever its success in ungrounding Kant's thought. In returning to Kant's aesthetics, Lyotard finds a championing of the recalcitrance of particularity to abstraction, the resistance of specificity to universal. Kant's aesthetic judgments remain indeterminate, judgments made prior to the imposition of concepts enabling us to generalize about the experience in question. Indeterminacy, Lyotard seems to be implying, produces differences in the definitions of things which ought to be tolerated in the way that we accept differences in how people might paint things, or tell stories about them. The act of artistic expression may well be an attempt to win our assent, to get us to see something in the artist's way, but it is not an attempt to universalize, produce a rule, or define the world through representation. We want other people to accept our judgments of taste and would feel these judgments needed reconsideration if they did not succeed in winning agreement. But the sureness of touch demonstrated in sound aesthetic judgment is, for Kant, a cultural norm rather than a logical axiom. The *sensus communis* Kant argues is displayed in aesthetic agreement is indeed the sense of a community, a polis, which is why Hannah Arendt regarded Kant's aesthetic writings as the core of his political thought. Where Lyotard's politics differs from Kant's and Arendt's is in its emphasis on the individual *sensus* over the *communis* that validates or accredits it. Provided it still makes sense to talk of a judgment whose rationale is *still to be argued for,* Lyotard has all that he wants. Having got rid of Kant's grounding of knowledge in a noumenal world of Reason, Lyotard also gets rid of his grounding of aesthetic judgment in cultural consensus. For him, such consensus is a kind of cultural indifference, callous as capital, shadowing the tyrannical grand narratives he is at such pains to refute. Lyotard spells out the political consequences, as he sees them, of this privileging of the aesthetic particular over the cultural unanimity which, for Kant, guarantees that the particular is aesthetic rather than plain peculiar or eccentric.

> Within the tradition of modernity, the movement toward emancipation is a movement whereby a third party, who is initially outside the *we* of the emancipating avant-garde, eventually becomes part of the community of real (first person) or potential (second person) speakers. Eventually, there will only be a *we* made up of you and me. Within this tradition, the position of the first person is in fact marked as being that of the mastery of speech and meaning; let the people have a political voice, the worker a social voice, the poor an economic voice, let the particular seize hold of the universal, let the last be first! Forgive me if I over-simplify. It follows that, being torn apart between

the present minority situation in which third parties count for a great deal and in which you and I count for little, and the future unanimity in which the third parties will, by definition, be banished, the *we* of the question I am asking reproduces the very tension humanity must experience because of its vocation for emancipation, the tension between the singularity, contingency and opacity of its present, and the universality, self-determination and transparency of the future it is promised.[2]

Lyotard's overriding sense of cultural relativism leads him to prioritize "singularity, contingency and opacity" over "universality" or a welcoming consensus. However emancipatory its plans for the "self-determination" of minorities, the consensus will, he thinks, efface the cultural difference, the particularity which defines each minority and it alone.

But doesn't this break with Kantian aesthetics also break open the chiasmus which I was arguing explained the relation between romanticism and postmodernism? The new world order implied by Lyotard's pluralism dispenses with exactly what makes it possible for Kant to call aesthetic experience a judgment, and so to have a philosophy of it. Isn't the new world order of postmodernism not a return to Kantian aesthetics, but its deconstruction? Well, I think Lyotard has not broken completely from Kant; his model, after all, is Kant's judgments of the sublime rather than of the beautiful, and it is in his account of sublimity that Kant accords most to the cultural construction of aesthetic experience. Sublimity, for Kant, is certainly a pretty *recherché* experience, to be clearly distinguished from the gawpings of the uneducated. Kant subsequently needs his account of "genius" to show how it might ever be possible for so unique an experience to filter down to the rest of the community. Yet the fact that it does become assimilated distinguishes genius from irrational raving or fanaticism. In *The Postmodern Condition* Lyotard focuses on the tense-logic of the sublime: in sublime experience, our judgment of what is happening is always one of what "will have been," future-perfect, never one which provides a rule for the present. The particularity of the experience does seem to predominate, and all rationalizations of it look belated. Only afterward can we tell that the genius was not raving; that his source was an Idea of Reason which he could not, by definition, represent directly; that the eccentric particularity of his discourse was after all symbolic. There is, in other words, a Kantian cue for Lyotard's ideal of a kind of judgment, and so a philosophical position, which emancipates particularity from any general rule.

However, what this continuing link with Kant's theory of a sublimity shows is also something typical of romantic discourse. The romantic dislike of abstraction and distrust of rules fosters a cult of individual genius which constantly threatens to explode the romantic aesthetic from within. But the scope allowed to ordinary, unexceptional particularity by Kant's theory of the sublime was also exploited at the time. Romanticists nowadays, alert to the prescriptions of romantic ideology, are constantly looking for different kinds of writing in the period, writings which exceed ideological prescription, or, in falling short of what romanticism requires, remain significantly recalcitrant. The cutting edge of this internal difference from romantic ideology is an explicitly antisymbolic writing. Many recognizably new developments in romantic criticism at the moment, I would suggest, come from attempts to find a critical vocabulary for those writings of the period which fail to satisfy the dominant aesthetic. The critic wishing to defend or champion these writings must decide whether they work on *different* aesthetic lines. Within the canon, Jerome McGann's Byron or John Barrell's Clare have provided role models; outside, the most persistent pressure for a revised aesthetic comes especially from the writing of women.

The Uses of William

But I am arguing that postmodernism helps us see how some nonstandard romantic writings might also be widening a fault in the *prevailing* aesthetic at its most presumptuous and exalted: that is, in the Kantian theory of sublimity. The scandal of this writing, then, would lie in its immanence within the dominant aesthetic, not its alterity. It circumscribes the pretensions of symbolic writing with a relish for particularity which simply pushes the implications of sublimity that bit further. John Clare, and the difficulty of writing about him, is perhaps the best canonical example; but we have also seen Keats's sensuousness bid to foreclose on aesthetic idealizations which postpone such immediate satisfaction. Women's poetry and journals in the period furnish extracanonical satisfactions. Both popularity and unpopularity were reasons for subsequent critical exclusions, perhaps showing that consensus culture had as heavy and selective a hand as Lyotard suspected. In due course I should like to focus on Dorothy Wordsworth's *Journals* as examples of antisymbolic particularity, but first I will summarize where I think my comparison of postmodernism and romanticism has reached.

On the one hand, postmodernists like Lyotard are attracted to romantic aesthetic theory because it provides the model of a groundless judgment. It allows a review of experience in which objects are savored in their particularity, and agreement about their character is solicited by an openly collaborative, cultural activity. An accurate judgment, in this context, is achieved through a consensual activity about which one can be more or less cynical. Lyotard is extremely cynical, and I shall have more to say about postmodern cynicism and its reprise of romantic cynicism in the last part of this chapter. However, I have so far been stressing the positives claimed by Lyotard's approach, principally how the freedom he detects in indeterminacy allows for an exemplary respect for the particular. Here, he again takes off from a Kantian model of sublimity, but implies that the time-lapse between the sublime experience and the critical recognition or judgment of its sublimity allows the particular experience a distinct preeminence and authority of its own. Quotidian particularity, on this theory, is privileged prior to judgment and is no longer necessarily part of a larger narrative, as it is in *The Prelude* or in William's figurings of his sister in "Tintern Abbey," articulated and valued only by the maturity into which it grows.

Dorothy Wordsworth was one of the principal romantic dealers in quotidian reality. Her critics and biographers have always had to cope with the symbiosis of her writing and her relationship with her brother, William Wordsworth. There have been two main lines of interpretation. Her journals either occupy a helpfully ancillary position to her brother's poetry: in Mary Moorman's edition of the *Alfoxden* and *Grasmere Journals,* it is a nice point as to which is the primary, which the secondary text, the journals or the poems of William Wordsworth listed at the end. The other main critical view is that the "self-baffling" De Quincey detected in Dorothy Wordsworth's life is repeated in her writings. Her readers witness an embryonic poet failing to rise to the highest aesthetic challenges. Dorothy's frequent literary downgrading of her own work shows that she shared a romantic ideology in which journal entries become highlighted where they are demonstrably the occasional stuff out of which lasting poetic transformations can be made. Recent criticism, though, has read her journals as unconsciously opposing this kind of ideology. Far from "baffling" her literary self, Dorothy's prose threatens the aesthetic hegemony of romantic poetry and proposes an alternative model for understanding the individual's place in nature and the community.[3]

Feminist critics, such as Margaret Homans, Susan Levin, and Susan Wolfson have taken the lead here, emphasizing in different ways and to varying degrees the extent to which Dorothy's failure to sustain the romantic sublime in fact succeeds in defining sexual difference. Once that success is acknowledged, a new stylistics comes into play, and different critical criteria must be invoked to judge Dorothy's rendering of her quotidian reality. Her writing shrugs off the verdicts of those who praise or downgrade it by comparing it with William's poetry or poetry in general. Instead, it challenges readers to become aware of the options with which literary particularity confronts them: to realize the possibilities for judgment raised by the individual character or scene when presented in a mode which initially appears to prevaricate over which judgment is solicited—aesthetic, social, political, economic, and so on. Or, perhaps more accurately, we should say that we experience as prevarication representation whose lack of fit with a prevailing, historically expected literariness makes its readers hang judgment temporarily. As I have claimed already, this experience leaves the reader with two options: to find a nonhegemonic aesthetic which *does* fit or to understand the recalcitrant writing as combatively engaged with the prevailing taste which seems to exclude it. The fact that the idea of the aesthetic gained unprecedented prominence during the romantic period dovetails with Dorothy's relation to one of its main English constructors. Dorothy's attempt to establish her own discourse—however unwilling, unconscious, or inadvertent—allegorizes her life as spinster sister with the married couple, William and Mary, whose interests she then served with such devotion and apparent self-effacement as to attract the pity of De Quincey and the eventual dismissal of Coleridge. Had she written novels, Dorothy might have ridden the crest of a wave of success in women's writing which already had its allotted place in the contemporary economy of taste. Her early journals, though, and the critical problems they raise, are just those arising from their match with her domestic subordination and from William's use of them as source-material for his conventionally superior, sublime poetic project.

In other words, one can first of all look around for another rationale for Dorothy's writings, a rationale that might remove them entirely from the artistic hierarchy in which they occupy so low a position. John Barrell, Michael Rosenthal, and others have written persuasively about the presence of a Virgilian, Georgic ethic in some late eighteenth- and early nineteenth-century painting and literature. Kurt Heinzelman has successfully fed these perceptions into the reading of Dorothy. The aesthetic potential of her writer's interest in a domestic economy which, despite its lack of obvious pattern or symmetry, retrieves artistic value from labor itself, becomes highlighted. It infiltrates her descriptions of Lakeland characters, foregrounding their work and interests in an unusually collaborative way, striking because those she meets are not prized as the symbolic motivators of a separate literary activity but as coworkers in a way of life which Dorothy's literature indifferently records. The possibility that writer and worker are doing the same or analogous or mutually illuminating things is not at issue, as it always is for William. Rather, romantic criticism must be repositioned so as to appreciate that it is this kind of writing, the *Grasmere Journals,* say, which is answerable to various modes of production, from the industrious to the beggarly, the residential to the transient, in Cumbria at this time. Labor has its art, as much as do reading, musing, or learned lucubration; labor is exhibited in the kind of writing required to describe it adequately and in the critical exercise required to read it with propriety.[4]

My free expression here of a kind of Georgic materialism clearly reverses the idealist aesthetic usually associated with romanticism. But, allied with the first, is the second stage of reading I have been arguing for, which sees that Dorothy's kind of writing is possible within the idiom of the sublime when that idiom is given the inflection postmodernism foregrounds: one in which materialist particularity is at odds with its idealist, judgmental endpoint. In a tellingly reflexive incident of March 1802 in the *Grasmere Journals,* Dorothy reads to William an earlier episode, "that account of the little boy belonging to the tall woman," which she had written about two years previously. William is composing a poem anyway about the incident, but this rereading of his supposed source material stops him in his tracks. Dorothy writes of the effects of her reading, "and an unlucky thing it was, for he could not escape from these very words, and so he *could not write the poem.* "[5] Clearly there is an integrity or propriety to Dorothy's literalism that resists poetic translation.

William is halted temporarily, but after a night's sleep he *can* write the poem. His judgment is suspended, for a while, but then, after having slept on it (badly), he can reorganize the details of Dorothy's account in such a way as to demonstrate that, finally, his aesthetic judgment of it stuck. But the hiatus is symptomatic: Dorothy's writing no longer need be understood merely as a source for William's poem. It speaks in its own character through its power to delay judgment; in that pause we become aware of other possible judgments, judgments different from the aesthetic one producing William's poem. Dorothy's writing thus contrives a twin critique of the romantic aesthetic. Its symbolism is bypassed by her miscellaneous record of a life which permits natural objects and people their own ordinary, unsymbolic existence without thereby forfeiting connection with them. Secondly, this relish for the particular forces a way through the passage of sublimity into a space which solicits comparable approval, recognition, and agreement. But the judgment formed is one whose imagined community need not be poetic.

Let us look at an example in more detail. The *Grasmere Journal* is periodically symbolic; it plots the story of an unmarried woman anxious that her brother's impending marriage will not affect her life and relationship with him adversely. In the shadow of these fears, landscape, incident, and person can unsurprisingly wear a psychological or emotional character. Nevertheless, by far the main substance of the *Grasmere Journal* is its circumscription of these symbolic distillations, demystifying their portentousness and lodging the significance of what is described in a laboring social and domestic context. Here is almost all the entry for 14 February 1802:

> After dinner a little before sunset I walked out about 20 yards above Glowworm Rock. I met a Carman, a Highlander I suppose, with 4 Carts, the first 3 belonging to himself, the last evidently to a man and his family who had joined company with him, and who I guessed to be Potters. The Carman was cheering his horses, and talking to a little Lass about 10 years of age who seemed to make him her companion. She ran to the wall, and took up a large stone to support the wheel of one of his carts, and ran on before with it in her arms to be ready for him. She was a beautiful creature, and there was something uncommonly impressive in the lightness and joyousness of her manner. Her business seemed to be all pleasure—pleasure in her own motions, and the man looked at her as if he too was pleased, and spoke to her in the same tone in which he spoke to his horses. There was a wildness in her whole figure, not the wildness of a Mountain lass but a *Road* lass, a traveller from her birth, who had wanted neither food nor clothes. Her Mother followed the last cart with a lovely child, perhaps about a year old, at her back, and a good-looking girl, about 15 years old, walked beside her. All the children were like the mother.—She had a very fresh complexion, but she was blown with fagging up the hill, with the steepness of the hill and the bairn that she carried. Her husband was helping the horse to drag the cart up by pushing it with his shoulder. I got tea when I reached home, and read German till about 9 o'clock. Then Molly went away and I wrote to Coleridge. Went to bed about 12 o'clock. Slept in Wm.'s bed and I slept badly, for my thoughts were full of William. (*Journals*, 90)

The anxious ending reminds us that Dorothy is writing in the year of William's marriage. Dorothy sleeps badly thinking of her brother, as we saw him doing thinking, if not of Dorothy's person, then of her untranslatable words. They might well have posed him the same problem here. The description of the Scottish Carman, little lass, mother, children, and husband looks a picture but inventories hard work. "There was a wildness in her whole figure"—the light and joyous manner of the "little lass" echoes the register of William's poetic celebration of Dorothy. John Barrell has alerted us to "The Uses of Dorothy," principally the use in "Tintern Abbey" of the figure of Dorothy to engineer various kinds of poetic legitimation for William.[6] But here we have the "uses of William" put to work in her writing. Dorothy is not attributing any preeminence to this incident, nor, by implication, to the mind alive to its symbolic potential. But it is as if we read her passage through the pattern of William's "obscure sense of possible sublimity" to arrive somewhere else by the same road.

Can I make clear that in this reading of Dorothy I am not, I hope, shamelessly dabbling in opportunistic anachronism. I am not saying that Dorothy Wordsworth is a proto-postmodernist. Rather, I am saying that postmodernist interpretations of the romantic sublime allow it to include a sheer particularity usually thought to be inimical to its symbolic discourse. I do not think one can find this possibility considered by earlier critics of the sublime, even those as exploratory of its structures as Thomas Weiskel and Neil Hertz. Were Dorothy Wordsworth, wonderful to relate, to be a postmodernist, then she would also be a cynic. It would not be enough for her to see sublimity and particularity, the exalted and the quotidian, as connected means of constructing culture or consensus. It would not even be enough for her to suspect the truth of her observations because they were *constructed;* she would have to suspect them especially when they were *consensual.* She would have to possess a cynicism concerning consensus, one which led her to doubt that any consensus could, at bottom, be anything other than the temporary imposition of a particular group's views, disguised under the title of the common interest. Yet even this cynical stance recrosses a romantic path.

The Political Cynic

A "hypermystical, hypermodern, hypercynic"—who is being described? Jean Baudrillard? No, but, as might be expected in this book, Friedrich Schlegel, caught in the words of a Novalis worried about the reception that Schlegel's novel, *Lucinde,* was going to attract, a novel subtitled "Cynical Fantasies or Satanisms." But Schlegel's cynicism is, of course, part of his romantic irony, a detachment from what he professes, powered by a sense of inner reserve far in excess of any outward show it might make. In the service of irony, Schlegel's wit produces a heroic cynicism. Its refusal to accept material values and definitions allies it with a Christianity which Schlegel calls "universal cynicism" (*AF,* no. 16).[7] In another of the *Athenaeum Fragments,* Schlegel and Schleiermacher coauthor an aphorism in which the dazzle of cynicism belies its bad faith: "A *cynic* should really have no possessions whatever: for a man's possessions, in a certain sense, actually possess him. The solution to this problem is to own possessions as if one didn't own them. But it's even more artistic and cynical not to own possessions as if one owned them" (*AF,* no. 35). As is typical in a display of Schlegelian *Witz,* this *aperçue* either outsmarts its own content and through a chiasmus collapses discovery into tautology, or else it does present a radical departure. Either, that is, the cynic here is the last word in balletic intellectual display or dandyism, or else what the aphorism advances is a notion of public ownership, and with it a notion of pubic belonging, one which outdoes any of the satisfactions supposed to be unique to or inseparable from private property. This protosocialism moots the idea of possession as an at-homeness with or self-conferring orientation toward things which remains nevertheless independent of the ascription of these things to the individual as exclusively theirs. Cynicism maintains rather than undermines this politics. If no one owns things but everyone expresses their identity in relation to them, then the public construction of identity and public ownership of things essential to our self-esteem are shown to go together. Not a collective identity, but a highly individualized identity, inflected by as provocative a self-display as any aristocrat might desire, is what this socialism guarantees. Each particular reorientation of what we have in common creates new possibilities, new roles, for us all.

I will try to take further the political implication of Schlegel's pluralism in the last chapter. To anticipate a little, we can have a first look at that moment when Schlegel's cynic does explicitly politicize the Kantian aesthetic of particularity, turning its resistance to rules into a democratic programme: "Poetry is republican speech: a speech which is its own law and end unto itself, and in which all the parts are free citizens and have the right to vote" (*AF,* no. 65). The pronounced spin given to Kantian aesthetics here by Schlegel can be measured by contrasting statements of romantic organicism by his brother and a host of other romantics. In *Biographia Literaria,* Coleridge famously compares Shakespeare's choice of words to bricks integral to a building; in this Burkean analogy, aesthetic particulars are reciprocally means and ends, as Kant prescribes. But Schlegel's adaptation suggests that Kant might have left it open for the autonomy of his aesthetic citizens to generate a centrifugal rather than a centripetal force, thus symbolizing an as yet unrealized order rather than cementing the propriety and fitness of the present one. Schlegel's irony rather prefigures his admirer Walter Benjamin's aesthetics of history, learned from Paul Klee's "Angelus Novus," which imagines strategies for blasting historical particulars out of the progressive narratives in which they have been imbedded. Benjamin, famously, is intent on the task of politicizing aesthetics by reconceiving progress; but it is questionable whether or not he ever envisages a republic in which these particulars, liberated, as Lyotard wants them to be, from grand interpretations, would speak with individual voices. The messianic moment in which he conceives the shedding of explanatory contexts, this tiger's leap in the dark, initially looks obscure and apocryphal in comparison to Schlegel's confident skepticism. But perhaps Walter Benjamin's early study of Schlegel's aesthetics has left its mark? For Schlegel, "skeptical method would more or less resemble a rebellious government" (*AF*, no. 97). Again, this logical finesse seems to transvalue its own terms. Either government becomes impossible if composed of Schlegel's skeptical socialism; or else a communitarian form of political participation is envisaged. This innovation would do away with authoritarian ideas of what is proper to political (hierarchical) representation, and it would do so on analogy with the manner in which the aesthetic offers a way of grasping things itself constitutive of an addition to the wealth of common sense. In both cases, the commonwealth is remapped and negotiated anew with each judgment. There is an unignorable historical difference between Benjamin and Schlegel, though. Benjamin is driven to messianic philosophical exigencies by the attempt to conceive of a proletarian revolution unprescribed by past bourgeois revolutions or by deficient contemporary revolutionary examples. Schlegel responds to the French Revolution with a skeptical poetics which refuses to see it as a failure but recuperates it as part of the explanatory dynamic of his age. Taking on the conventions of his day and locating freedom in the resulting indeterminacy is, for him, immediately suggestive of political action in the likeness of the recent French Revolution—one of the main "tendencies of the age," impossible to escape. Unlike Lyotard, and perhaps Benjamin, Schlegel's revolution does have a model.

Yet Schlegel happily develops irony to the cynical extremes that worried Novalis, "Only cynics make love in the market place" (*AF*, no. 119), he claims, critiquing bourgeois marriage settlements but also meaning that for the true ironist public and private can never coincide. No scandalous exposure of self is therefore involved. But his dismissal of authentic expression of the private perhaps leaves nowhere to make love except in the marketplace. Schlegel seems to think that the private can be expressed only in debased images because the *consensual* is always devalued by its provisional, constructed nature. But, in this case, how long can the private experience's notional independence of the public survive? Does not it gradually drop out of consideration like the beetle in the box with which Wittgenstein used to allegorize the redundancy of private sense-data to any theory of meaning? Don't we have to admit that we are obliged to live our life in public images, in which case a *contrasting* inner richness becomes merely an act of faith. Or, since we *never* have authentic expressions of the private alternative to the marketplace, perhaps all we can do is live a life of false consciousness, but a life of knowing false consciousness, unhappy but not taken in by the straits to which we are reduced? Schlegel is sure such disillusionment evinces "superiority," analogous to that of the Goethean artist hovering over his creations or the Fichtean philosopher brimming with his own egotistic reserves. But why should not such alienation rather produce an irony that looks more like the last recourse of the inner city slum-dweller or the victim of a poverty trap? Sometimes Schlegel sounds like a philosophical slummer. Unless, that is, each act of cynical disaffiliation in fact registers a vote within a new poetic republic in which all of us can share through similar acts of citizenship.

What Novalis feared, carried to its logical, postmodern conclusion, threatens Benjamin too. Benjamin's exploded histories, no longer a part of any linear progressive, logical sequence, have to sink or swim in competition with each other for our attention. Market forces may again become the final arbiter. Benjamin's apparent democratization of historical facts frees them from the hierarchies of privilege or repression through which traditional historical narratives supposedly conferred on them significance. But a postmodernist could argue that he succeeds only in leaving history vulnerable to a cynical eclecticism. This would be to simplify Benjamin, and simplification is one of the main targets of Peter Sloterdijk when he investigates postmodern cynicism at great length in his *Critique of Cynical Reason*. If, when carried to extremes, the groundlessness of romantic aesthetics leaves us with nothing except a knowing reflection of our unauthentic state, then Schlegelian superiority does indeed degenerate into the "enlightened false consciousness" which Sloterdijk excoriates in his book. Symptomatically, Sloterdijk's starting point is Kantian.

In his preface, he describes the "occasion" for writing a critique of cynical reason:

> This year (1981) is the 200th anniversary of the publication of Immanuel Kant's *Critique of Pure Reason*—a date in world history. Seldom has there been a jubilee as dull as this one. It is a sober celebration; the scholars keep to themselves. Six hundred Kant experts gathered in Mainz—that does not produce a carnival atmosphere. . . . Is it not a sad festival where the invited guests secretly hope that the person being celebrated is prevented from appearing because those who constantly invoke him would have to be ashamed on his arrival . . . ? Who could bring himself to give Kant a summary of history since 1795, the year in which the philosopher published his essay *On Perpetual Peace*? Who would have the nerve to inform him about the state of the Enlightenment—the emancipation of humanity from "self-imposed dependency"? Who would be so frivolous to explain to him Marx's "Theses on Feuerbach"? I imagine that Kant's splendid humour would help us out of our stunned state.[8]

Humor is important to the alternative which Sloterdijk's book goes on to propose. A "cheeky" tradition of what he calls "low theory" or different versions of carnival, from Diogenes to the film *M.A.S.H.*, is called in to reinvigorate the cynicism of the *conferenciers*. Although he does not mention Friedrich Schlegel, it as if Sloterdijk tries to restore the optimism and rebellion to Schlegelian irony in order to close up its fatal trajectory toward a cynical postmodernism deprived of any agenda. Reading Kant becomes funny, like Musil's description of the young Törless's attempt: "When he stopped in exhaustion after about half an hour, he had only reached the second page, and sweat stood out on his brow."[9]

And the rest of Sloterdijk's complex book evokes a multitude of such apparently naive or ingenuously physical responses to the philosophical texts which have produced our contemporary mental set, doing so in order to rehabilitate the language of ideology critique. The targeted mental set is "Cynicism . . . *enlightened false consciousness*. It is that modernized, unhappy consciousness, on which enlightenment has laboured both successfully and in vain. It has learned its lessons in enlightenment, but it has not, and probably was not able to, put them into practice. Well-off and miserable at the same time, this consciousness no longer feels affected by any critique of ideology: its falseness is already reflexively buffered" (5). Sloterdijk's critique of this cynical reason is his "attempt to enter the old building of ideology critique through a new entrance" (3). He thinks that the tradition of ideology critique which he inherits is disabled by the ubiquity of ideology. Ideology, after all, has been *the* intellectual growth industry of recent times. In his recent book *Spinoza and the Origins of Modern Critical Theory,* Christopher Norris emphasizes the ancestry of Spinoza in recent all-embracing definitions of ideology. He is especially convincing in his description of Althusser's debt to various of Spinoza's ideas, and sensitive to the degree to which Spinoza is read through a romantic interpretation. [10] The most notorious characteristic of the romantic adaptation was pantheism. Commentary on the romantic pantheistic tradition, such as Thomas McFarland's, has stressed the doctrinal problems which pantheism posed for Christian poets who, like Coleridge, were especially alive to the symbolic possibility pantheism opened up to the poet of nature. But the monism resulting from pantheism, in which, since you cannot find God "outside" you must find him everywhere, has all sorts of other implications. Fundamentally, it makes all critique immanent. It leads to that equality of particulars, which temporarily silenced William Wordsworth, and a potential democracy of subject matter which so troubled Coleridge about Wordsworth's own "Immortality Ode." In other words, it sets up the opposition we have seen at work between a cynical refusal to believe in appearance, and a rebellious celebration of the destructive effect this has on received hierarchies of meaning A footnote in Sloterdijk suggests that he thinks this ideological consciousness leads to a kind of Jacobinical sublime. He misquotes the famous words of the Abbe Sieyès—"What is the Third Estate? Nothing. What does it want to be? Everything" [it should actually read "something"]—and finds in this "all-or-nothing logic" a cynical lack of objectivity in need of critique. [11]

Sloterdijk tries to find a legitimate role for cynicism which takes account of the postmodern condition but does not connive at it. As I tried to show was the case with romantic sublimity, and its privileging of particularity, romantic cynicism also contains an inner, destabilizing dynamic which undoes its pretensions. A quotidian individuality, a varied relish for "minute particulars" often celebrated by romantic writing, goes against the idea of sublimity, but it can be seen through postmodern eyes to be a consequence of the most thoroughgoing rationale provided for sublimity, that expounded by Kant's *Critique of Judgement.* In the case of romantic cynicism, Schlegelian ebullience also exposes a perspective different from the one in which it ostensibly places its reader. The ego's skepticism of the adequacy of public institutions to represent it either produces a Wordsworthian sublimity in need, I suggest, of Dorothy's correctives— cynical in a feminist sense theorized as Schlegel's poetic republic—or else what takes over is a cynical flouting of convention which acknowledges that it has no new language to substitute for a public sphere assumed, by definition, to be debasing. The particularity promoted by Lyotard and Sloterdijk as exceptions to the rule of ideology do seem as far cry from Dorothy Wordsworth's records, but all rework the same structure of sublimity in similar ways. Perhaps I can be cheekily sure that my initial chiasmus is more plausible now: the postmodern championing of particulars undetermined by any rule exceeds its romantic heritage but only as it reworks romanticism to serve different historical uses. I should, in justice, though, repeat Friedrich Schlegel's warning in the *Athenaeum Fragments* about the uses of Kant: "The Kantian philosophy resembles that forged letter—which Maria puts in Malvolio's way in Shakespeare's *Twelfth Night*. With the only difference that in Germany there are countless philosophical Malvolios who tie their garters crosswise, wear yellow stockings, and are forever smiling madly" (*CF*, no. 21). The forged letter and the pretension to authority of a myriad Malvolios, though, possibly indicate only Schlegel's necessarily cynical view of that politically constructive cynicism he wrested from the *Critique of Judgement*. Like the irony of irony, this self-impugning authority, the self-irony which Carl Schmitt insisted Schlegel did not possess, advances into the footlights with each cynical disavowal.

Finally, what does this tell us about metaromanticism? Dorothy Wordsworth undoes the structure of the sublime by writing in such a way as to present a particularity the precise nature of whose exemplariness is still undetermined. She writes so as to engage our attention with the ordinary sight, but with a propriety that exposes the presumptuousness in assuming that her success must be aesthetic, William's presumption. It takes a Schlegel, though, to raise to the pitch of cynicism the consciousness that even the aesthetic railroads judgment along preconcerted lines rather than allows the individual freely to set new standards of communal understanding. Dorothy Wordsworth's artistic labor could be classed in a number of ways. The feminist resistance to a male aesthetic that her literary work might embody unconsciously suggests a politics. Schlegel's cynicism comparably but more knowingly reposes on a sense of the individual's power to assert a new sense of propriety. What is proper to oneself is no longer to be understood as private property but as a superiority to such private identifications, a disowning of them which immediately throws them open to public ownership or a kind of self-conferring communal sense of things belonging which has nothing to do with possessing them. Cynicism generates a kind of republican speech in which every citizen can renew the law, not annul it, with each vote cast; each exercise of individuality can offer an end for all to enjoy. But Schlegel calls this republican speech poetry, and so the chiasmic structure of thought more often associated with postmodernism reasserts itself. Cynicism displaces (sublime) aesthetics but in so doing moots a Jacobin politics, a republican speech best described as poetry. The metaromanticism at work here, the critical edge of romantic discourse's reflection upon itself, might seem at first self-serving. But here the journey has not, as in Schiller's aesthetics, been through aesthetics to get to a politics worthy of the name but, conversely, through politics to recover a seriousness for poetic generosity. As Benjamin famously desired, aesthetics has been politicized rather than politics aestheticized.

TWELVE

Romantic Republicanism and Multicultural Progress

Negotiating the Universal

"The ethical is the universal, and as the universal it applies to everyone, which from another angle means that it applies at all times."[1] Thus writes Johannes de Silentio, Kierkegaard's narrator in *Fear and Trembling*. Exceptions to the law, in other words, mean the suspension of the ethical. The ethical is suspended when the law does not apply universally. This may happen in the religious experiences whose irreducibility to other explanations, especially moral explanations, Kierkegaard wishes to assert. But, extrapolating from the specific case of religion, we can say that the ethical is suspended when it is historically relativized so as not to apply at all times. It appears that the ethical becomes compromised when it is interpreted historically.

The philosophical tradition stretching from Kant to Hegel establishes the doctrine that interpretation, hermeneutics, and aesthetic particularity are separate from ethical thinking. It is a very influential tradition. Kierkegaard quarreled with its demarcations in order to defend the paradox of a particular, absolute call to action experienced in religious vocation. His paradigmatic example of religious vocation in *Fear and Trembling*, the binding of Isaac by Abraham on Mount Moriah, the *akidah*, could hardly be prescribed generally as a morally desirable course of action for every father; equally undeniable was the sense of obligation under which Abraham acted. Nor could this compulsion be rationalized as a particular, intermediate stage in the Hegelian unfolding of an ultimate universal. For it is precisely in the exaltation of the individual's conviction *over* the ethical obligations applying to the rest of us that religious vocation takes shape. Hermeneutically speaking, Abraham's action could only be saved from the charge of attempted murder by a reading of it which went against the equation of ethical behavior with universal-izability per se. But where a religious calling is not at issue, and reason is not displaced by faith, to go against this traditional commensurability of the ethical and the universal can appear nonsensical. To permit individual exemptions from duty can seem straightforwardly to oppose notions of fair play, impartiality, and justice habitually presented as part of the meaning of what it is to behave ethically.

I want to look at alternatives to such universalizing views of ethics, especially as they are bound up with interpretative activities. Most forms of moral and legal thinking have built into them—through ideas of equity, mitigation, judicial discretion, and so on—provision for creating exceptions to strict application of the law. It has, though, been a characteristic of thinking from Adorno to Deleuze to try to turn the exceptions into the rule, contradictorily mooting the idea of a rule which changes with each application, the idea of a rule which is always only an approximation of an ideal, of something better, more comprehensive. If not dispensable, then rules are, on this reading, at least radically historicizable.

These attempts to recognize the provision ethics makes for recognizing and judging exceptions are often tied to exemplary historical moments. They use historical periods to articulate themselves. They interpret themselves historically, relatively. They are case-studies. The classic study of the "case" in relation to romantic historicism is now James Chandler's *England in 1819.* Modeled on the aesthetic respect for particularity, romantic historicism both treats the individual on its own merits and, in that manner of proceeding, shows itself to be exceptional too. Where our emphases differ is perhaps evident from Chandler's "recognition that, whereas poststructuralist historicism most immediately derives from Continental intellectual traditions, the romantic historicism in question, insofar as it can be nationalized, is associated primarily with Britain." My work tries to uncover the historicizing power those more highly theorized "Continental intellectual traditions" possess still to support the British case Chandler makes for romantic historicism. That we are nevertheless contributing to a common project appears from my much more limited study's exact agreement with Chandler's premise that "we most invoke the terms of a historicism that is emergent within romanticism when we make the historicist critique."[2]

I want to review the well-documented differences between Habermas and Lyotard but to focus primarily on their common interest in late eighteenth-century and romantic philosophy. In particular, I want to argue that if we read further into romantic reactions to Kant we arrive

at ways of thinking which shed light on attempts to think through multiculturalism now, perhaps in a fashion which sidesteps an otherwise
inevitable-looking opposition between Habermas and Lyotard. Habermas first exerted a serious influence on cultural studies in Britain and
America through his *Habilitationschrift* which he published in revised
form as *The Structural Transformation of the Public Sphere.*[3] How does this
study look now if read in the context of the questions just raised? Habermas isolated a critical area of public discussion existing at a distance
from the jurisdiction of state apparatuses—a potentially utopian forum,
one proposing the impermanence of current social universals. Publicity
(Öffentlichkeit) is seen as possessing a radical force irrespective of what is
actually publicized. Habermas is interested in *public* opinion rather than
what those opinions are. He reworks, commentators such as Geoff Eley
have argued,[4] Gramscian notions of civil society as a contested consensus,
although modeled ultimately on the negotiations that take place in the
intimate sphere of the family or an analogously autonomous market prior
to institutional or cultural expression (sec. 6). Habermas's historicized
version records transformations from the coffee-houses of the late seventeenth to the late eighteenth century of a public sphere developed out of
earlier resistance to princely absolutism through "critical public debate
among private people" (53). The public sphere was created by "private
people making use of their reason" (51), an activity already qualifying
the universal qualities of reason: reason does not legislate a priori but
by gaining publicity for private interests not identical with state interests.
Put simply, we encounter "the idea of a public opinion born of the power
of the better argument" (54).

Habermas offers two main generative models for this critical difference of private and public. One is the bourgeois family which, in a sense
"more than just ideology," offers experience of "ideas of freedom, love
and cultivation" (48), ideas of living "without coercion" in a "community of love" (46). Although Habermas admits from the start that he has
picked a particular example, the desire by his readers that his theory apply generally produced strong critiques. These pointed out that there
could be more than one public sphere, even a counterpublic sphere.
Feminist critiques emphasizing the role of patriarchy turn Habermas's
model inside out. In Seyla Benhabib's words, "Any theory of the public,
public sphere, and publicity presupposes a distinction between the public
and the private. . . . What the women's movement and feminist theorists
of the last two decades have shown, however, is that traditional modes of
drawing this distinction have been part of a discourse of domination that

legitimizes women's oppression and exploitation in the private realm."[5] In other words, we need to be able to describe a counterpublic sphere in which these grievances or interests can get aired, a public sphere in relation to which Habermas's public sphere looks like a patriarchal universal and to which the feminist countersphere provides exceptions. Habermas's description is still used, but grounded at another, feminist level. Nancy Fraser seems to accept this, not dispensing with Habermas's model but rethinking it to publicize postbourgeois interests. Here, feminism is allowed to set the example.[6]

Habermas's second, related model for the public sphere is the republic of letters. "The process in which the state-governed public sphere was appropriated by private people making use of their reason and was established as a sphere of criticism of public authority was one of functionally converting the public sphere in the world of letters already equipped with institutions of the public and with forums for discussion" (51). Again, Habermas is openly historicizing his own theory. The invitation to rethink it, to reapply it, is one which *he* makes. Disappointment that it is not a general theory seems to miss the book's argument that it can only be *progressively* formulated by further "structural transformations." These changes make the public sphere better honor its own commitment to represent the private individual. Habermas's literary model, after all, is epistolary writing typical of mid-eighteenth-century novels. He believes this technique to be founded on a private subjectivity which, through the forum of letter writing, "attained clarity about itself" (51). Also, increasingly, letters were written for publication. Hence literature of this kind at this time provides a model of private people gaining in awareness of autonomy and finding a market for this new publicity. Indeed, the liberalized market can be seen as the product of such a sensibility which brings its individuality into a public sphere confident that its private properties will be recognized as exchangeable without need of state mediation.

In his more recent writings, Habermas is still preoccupied with the historicizing or individualizing of universals in a progressive cause.[7] Unlike Hegel, he does not plot a path toward complete communication and a knowing retreading of it to understand it still better. The ideal speech situation remains ideal because it describes functions discourse cannot do without—hypotheticals, counterfactuals, and other strategic reserves—functions necessary for historical intercourse to be practicable between different individuals, cultures, and interests. We only grasp the ultimate goal in the form of a "stand-in" *(Platzhalter)*.[8] This refigured aesthetic function keeps the seat warm for what we can't as yet conceptualize but which we can experience in each compromise and negotiation which furthers communication. Dissolution of the problems negotiated by the idealisms embedded in speech would deny us this experience; it would also self-defeatingly remove the cultural differences that such discursive latitude is there to respect. Recognition of cultural differences, in other words, depends on the current idealizations with which we forgo complete communication. Habermas's use of the aesthetic, idealizing function facilitates sociopolitical practice now; it does not, as in Schiller, temporize on possible sociopolitical outcomes or benefits. On this reading, Habermas can be made to sound closer than expected to a project akin to Jean-François Lyotard's. They are joined through their typically postmodern interest in how individual interests might be introduced without loss into a public sphere; or, to put it the other way round, how one might conceive of a public sphere tolerant and alive to the highly individualized and historicized forms in which rational pursuits appear.

Lyotard's pluralism, however, favors cultural difference at the expense of an overall theory of meaning or ethics. The extravagant liberalism of what Lyotard confidently calls "that severe reexamination which postmodernity imposes on the thought of the Enlightenment"[9] imagines societies as numerous as differences in meaning but, inevitably, at the cost of any coherent notion of society itself, promoting a version of the occasionalism lambasted by Carl Schmitt. Consistent with his adaptation of the Kantian model of aesthetic judgment, Lyotard takes "society as a suprasensible nature, as something that is not there, that is not given."[10] For the romantics, he claims, this amounted to "the appearance of the people as potential public." Unlike Kant, he does not think that the finding of such community in the act of judgment is culturally continuous with past communities formed in the same way. The romantic audience has become alarmingly indeterminate.[11] Lyotard wishes his intervention to leave behind the structure of Kant's philosophy. "It is not true that one can do an aesthetic politics"; Lyotard's use of aesthetic judgment to focus the "intensities" of individual circumstance and event pursues "justice" at the expense of received (Enlightenment) ideas of either aesthetics or politics: "with justice, we have to do, of necessity, with the regulation of something else."[12] This new kind of regulation, itself always a "case," is redefined again and again *by* each instance coming under its purview. "Is a politics, regulated by such an idea of multiplicity possible?," asks Lyotard, and answers, "And here I must say that I don't know."[13]

A respect for cultural difference so fastidious that it refuses all critique perhaps fails the test of fairness in other respects. Refusal to apply to others standards we apply to ourselves often turns out in practice to look like condescension. Alasdair MacIntyre has pointed out that "the incommensurability between two schemes of belief in no way precludes their logical incompatibility": the fact that they are incommensurable in Lyotard's sense need not stop the one from being able to criticize the other. [14] MacIntyre's point also exposes the static, nonprogressive quality Lyotard attributes to individual language-games. His philosophically self-annihilating abandonment of the grand emancipatory narratives of the Enlightenment is one thing, and can indeed be staged as a magnanimous, liberal gesture. His consequent refusal of the idea of progress to language games as individual belief-systems is another thing altogether, and one that seems potentially diminishing.

But if Lyotard allows language games the possibility of improvement, he surely must allow that this improvement can come about comparatively, through the rational acceptance that one culture can furnish the means for another to criticize itself just because its difference makes the latter culture aware that it could benefit from and be enriched by resources not at present within its own tradition. Neither culture masters the other in this exchange; the kind of knowledge produced is not that of a subject making the other its object. To insist contrary to this latitude that a culture's self-criticism be autochthonous is precisely to deprive it of the chance to learn from you the difference you have learned from it. MacIntyre's argument is that a culture which denies itself this possibility can attach no content to its idea of truth and falsity which is not "idealized." [15] One could also stress that a view of another culture which thus collapsed together incommensurability and logical incompatibility would deprive that culture of access to a rationality by which it might improve, progress, and change in all sorts of ways, ways different from the linear progress prescribed by the grand narratives attacked by Lyotard and, before him, by Walter Benjamin. A culture may make wrong or self-destructive decisions, but to deny it the chance to weigh the effects of incommensurability with other cultures and respond accordingly is to deny it a basic recourse of rationality. it is the perfect mirror-image of colonialism, almost as destructive, certainly as patronizing. Perfect translation is not required for one culture to assimilate aspects of another culture for its own enrichment. Otherwise, incommensurability of this radical kind would also disqualify us from knowing when we *had* interfered with another culture's norms in our treatment of it. But the rationality making possible these negotiations, stand-offish or welcoming, appears ruled out by Lyotard's definition of heterogeneity. Habermas's notions of discursive reserve, by contrast, make mutual progress toward greater communication and cultural respect dependent on the same discursive mechanisms.

Sometimes Lyotard refers to his desideratum of philosophy without critique, or judgment without law, as "pagan." Paganism leaves prescriptions hanging, observes the different protocols of several language games at once, and is generally adept in "dispensing justice without models."[16] Lyotard's paganism is condensed into the Aristotelian virtue of prudence. The Aristotelian judge responds to the fact that "each situation is singular," and what fascinates Lyotard about the Kant of the third *Critique* is the presence of this Aristotelian, pragmatic recognition of the uniqueness of each event on which we are asked to judge, a recognition pressing though the juridical, universalist ethical and logical structure binding the Kant of the other two *Critiques*.[17] The "pagan" Kant ceases to be an autonomous lawgiver and becomes someone who realizes that his own prescriptions are themselves prescribed by the language games in which he finds himself. Like Sophocles's Oedipus, he must become aware that he belongs to a narrative already; to this extent he is fated, and, consistently with such awareness, he must acknowledge the heteronomy of those judgments in which he imagined himself entirely autonomous or self-legislating. Instead of applying universal principles of justice, the good judge now proves an adept at recognizing the boundaries differentiating other language games from his own.

One need not accept Lyotard's definition of "paganism," for a while a major category in his philosophical self-characterization, nor his view of Aristotle, to find "paganism" nevertheless rehearsing an old conflict in philosophy. Lyotard's postmodernism reworks the dispute, noticed by a number of modern philosophers, between two ethical traditions: Aristotle's account of the virtues, and Kant's account of moral judgment. Our starting point, therefore, in asking whether we can have a historicist ethics of interpretation now appears to feed into a long-standing dispute within ethics itself. Lyotard fastens upon the Kantian sublime as especially expressive of this tension. The first two *Critiques* and the *Groundwork of the Metaphysic of Morals* confidently advance a view of rationality as above all universalizable. Reason powers the transcendental deduction of binding scientific laws and obligatory ethical maxims. Lyotard exaggerates the contrary sense gained from the third *Critique* that we might escape from this jurisdiction, that every judgment might be different, rhetorically conjuring up its own legitimating community.[18] The difference in meaning between each judgment is at the same time a cultural difference. I would argue that there is truth in this to the extent that it shows Kant's philosophy registering the imprint of an Aristotelian tradition, one which holds that in ethics what we find worthy and admirable is not necessarily universalizable. One's ability to exercise virtues must to some extent depend on individual circumstances—social, political, economic, and personal. Philosophers within the analytic tradition as different as Bernard Williams, Alasdair MacIntyre, and John Casey have pointed out that many ethical judgments cannot be proved rational with reference to a universal law to which all human beings, high and low, are subject. In Williams's memorable phrase, our chances of being judged to have behaved morally frequently depend on "moral luck," accidents of circumstance and situation belonging to people's material conditions of existence. Of course it would seem intolerable to push ethics toward a materialist or historicist *reductio* in which only the fortunate aristocrat or even Aristotle's great-souled man can lead a fully moral life. Lyotard's free-for-all would be better than this. Nevertheless, as Casey puts it, "we are of necessity of two minds in our thought about ethics."[19] Equally intolerable would be the idea that you can impoverish and diminish people's lives with impunity because they possess some primal, self-determining rationality, shared with their oppressors—a guarantee that, whatever is done to it, the moral creature remains unscathed. As the Lady in Milton's *Comus* says to her aristocratic oppressor, "You cannot touch the freedom of my mind"; but the audience is relieved, to put it mildly, that it does not have to witness her reduction to that final saving essence.

We do think that our ethical judgments are explicable and consistent, and that good politics is the putting of them into social practice. But if the rationality of this attempt cannot be dovetailed with the universals grounding logic and science, then the fissure spectacularly widened by Lyotard definitely exists. On the other hand, since Kant, this historicism has in some form or another—Hegelianism, perspectivism, existentialism, and so on—been taken as the starting point not the endpoint of philosophy. Determining the shape negotiations between rationalities should take has been the prime endeavor in a tradition extending to Habermas. I have cited MacIntyre's description of a genuine logic of cultural difference allowing for the rational decisions explaining cultural change or improvement: a lateral series of comparative reckonings within existing possibilities rather than a projection into an ideal future. Also worth emphasizing is the fact that if judgment, justice, and the rest exist within a juridical language game, this form of life can possess several courts, not just one. For a dispute or claim to be ruled out of court does not discredit the law entirely if exceptions to it can still be handled properly in another legal chamber, one occasionally convened to rule equitably on just such cases.

At all events, we can say that postmodernism of Lyotard's kind defines itself by an attack on law. [20] In the process he recovers a romantic relativism which the Enlightenment had tried to bypass. This relativism resurfaces in Kant's critique of judgment, bearing traces of an Aristotelian tradition of moral realism alive in our day most notably in problems of legislating and theorizing across different cultures. Such questions, though, were alive in the romantic period. The solutions offered were not postmodern, but they were in their own way as daring and radical. The romantics take to poetic extremes the opportunity to imagine a community of particular interests and then to offer that integration as a model of political inclusiveness. A public sphere capable of grasping the diversity of content managed by poetry becomes the "dry run" (*Platzhalter* again) for a multicultural republic. How is this contemporary-sounding conclusion reached?

Schlegel's Republicanism

Germany appears to be the place where British culture left its theorizing conscience, aesthetic and political, during the romantic period. It has long been maintained that German theory rationalizes much English romantic practice, if you want to do that sort of thing. The political implications of German poetic theory are less often discussed, except as they match the passage from radicalism to reaction characterizing major British romantic figures. Hamann, Herder, and Kant had absorbed what they needed from the early eighteenth-century British philosophy of Shaftesbury, Hutcheson, Hume and his commonsense opponents, and others. Their redeveloped ideas of an expressive humanism lent to language, creativity, and feeling a *logical* necessity previously described as psychological or animal contingency. They argued for a necessary correlation between the world and the essential composition of the human being experiencing it. They disagreed strongly over the nature of those human essentials but agreed about their constitutive role in knowledge. Kant refined on the idea of universal reason; Herder argued for a much more diversified humanity, one varying with history, nation, culture, race, and language. The young Friedrich Schlegel paradoxically united both these universalist and individualist strains of thought. And he did so in a poetic, republican idiom.

Kant had argued that since we are inside our constitution and, by definition, can't get outside it, it falls to fiction, poetry, and the aesthetic to imagine what things might look like in the round, as it were. Shouldn't the same hold true of political constitutions? Shouldn't it be the case that the political accommodation of our world-creating nature is best grasped through a kind of poetic generosity? Isn't this task the one which properly exercises the poetic faculty? If, with Herder, one adds that our worlds change with historical period, language, and the other variables I mentioned, then the challenge to a political poetics increases proportionately. The post-Kantians temporarily seized on this possibility—the necessarily poetic imagining of political diversity and the political vocation of the poetic faculty. Through poetry they tried to think uniformity as difference, and, initially at least, they cast this paradox as a kind of republicanism.

Let us look again at Schlegel's most confident remark on the subject: "Poetry is republican speech: a speech which is its own law and end unto itself, and in which all the parts are free citizens and have the right to vote."[21] This aphorism is, above all, smart—smart in the manner of the Jena romantics, a manner Schlegel took with him to Berlin in 1797 and which informed his period of closest collaboration on such aphorisms with Schleiermacher. It cynically revises Kant's idea of an aesthetic whole whose organic parts are reciprocally means and ends, and flaunts instead the possibility of a constitutional free-for-all. Nietzsche would have called such license "decadent." He repeats the terms of Schlegel's literary democracy in a stern denunciation. "What is the sign of every *literary decadence*? That life no longer dwells in the whole. The word becomes sovereign and leaps out of the sentence, the sentence reaches out and obscures the meaning of the page, the page gains life at the expense of the whole—the whole is no longer a whole. But this is the simile of every style of *decadence*: every time, the anarchy of atoms, disintegration of the will, 'freedom of the individual,' to use moral terms—expanded into a political theory, '*equal* rights for all.' "[22] It leads, he says, to equal rights for all, and all that nonsense. Unfortunately, Nietzsche's culprit here is Wagner, hardly a convincing champion of "equal rights for all." These little embarrassments occur in the history of ideas. Nietzsche's wittiness lies in the discomfiture Wagner, now dead, would have felt had he seen that his art led in this egalitarian direction. Wagner brought this humiliation upon himself through his failure to confer organic form on his works. He patently strives to do so. The *Leitmotif*, however, cannot perform the unifying task. Democracy beckons, however hard Wagner labors against its individual style. "One feels," Nietzsche concedes with some exquisiteness, "a kind of compassion for so much distress." Wagner, he pitilessly adds, "had the virtue of all decadents: pity." Pity, Blake had said, divides the human soul, and it is into such divisions that Nietzsche, unlike Schlegel and Schleiermacher, thinks the aesthetic must *not* disintegrate or fragment. He compares Wagner to "the old Kant," surely the Kant of the last, third *Critique*, the critique of judgment, aesthetic and teleological. Wagner "posits a principle where he lacks a capacity," while Kant "wherever he lacked a principle . . . posited a special human capacity."[23] However it was the aesthetic and teleological faculties which Friedrich Schlegel, anticipating Nietzsche, removed from the Kantian role of exonerating philosophy from its failure to locate its reality-principle (noumena) in the world we all know and live in (phenomena). As much as Nietzsche did, Schlegel opposed the nihilistic view of a Kantian world deserted by ideals. But his romanticism led him to do so with a different kind of aestheticism, one which relocates these ideals in an ironic creativity, a performance, a perpetual discontent with holistic definitions; progressive in its continual disillusionment with authority, and demystifying in its eschewal of otherworldliness except as this progressive, skeptical impetus. Hence the startling assertion of *Athenaeum Fragment* 262: "Every good human being is progressively becoming God. To become God, to be human, to cultivate oneself are all expressions that mean the same thing."[24] Schlegel's republican poetry is central to this bringing down to earth of ideals.

Schleiermacher did not follow Friedrich Schlegel back to Jena in late 1799. His own lectures on religion to its cultured despisers were published that year, mapping out a more orthodox theological vocation. Nevertheless, in those discourses Schleiermacher certainly transgresses the limits Kant had mapped out in his prescription of a religion properly bound "within the limits of reason alone." And the romanticism with which Schlegel and Schleiermacher went on to promulgate worldviews joyfully exceeding the austere boundaries prescribed by Kant's critical philosophy was also evident behind the witty and often somewhat scabrous aphorisms they had already produced together, with occasional help from Friedrich's brother and his wife, the extraordinarily talented Caroline, from Friedrich's partner, Dorothea Veit, and from Novalis. Kant would have felt justified in predicting for these accesses of the infinite a mystificatory and unenlightened conclusion. As Ernst Behler, the *Kritische Ausgabe*'s editor of Schlegel's writings on history and politics points out, Schlegel's idea of freedom becomes later on not republican but monarchist. He favors a constitution founded on privilege, not parliament, and adopts political principles no longer secular but sacramental. If not purely reactionary, these changes represent what Behler calls a "genuine German special form of European conservatism," a suitably contradictory idea of empire *(Kaisertum)* culminating in "germanic, free, hierarchical, legal, Christian, universal monarchy."[25] Yet prior to Berlin and Schleiermacher, Schlegel had outdone Kant's republican zeal in a study of the older man's essay "On Perpetual Peace" which must have connected in his mind with a desire he had just expressed in a letter to his brother to write something popular on republicanism.[26]

Schlegel's early study of republicanism appeared in Johann Friedrich Reichardt's journal *Deutschland,* a publication competing with Schiller's *Horae.* Schlegel's exposition of republicanism contrasted sharply with *Horae*'s political quietism resulting from Schiller's horror at the French Terror of 1793–94. In fact, the political disagreement with Schiller extends beyond the conventional political sphere to include disputes about feminism, to which Schlegel, encouraged particularly by his sister-in-law, Caroline, eventually contributed.[27] Carl Schmitt predictably misunderstands Schlegel's feminist collaboration as intellectual dilution or frivolity typical of someone "who gave lectures under the protection of ladies with literary pretensions."[28] Schmitt's suspicion of coterie or salon culture, but not his sexism, is perhaps apt here. But it is also undeniable that Schlegel's notion of who might be the audience for his republican thoughts, and the different interests they might constitute, already anticipates a much more variegated and mixed body than that assumed by Kant or Schiller. One shouldn't exaggerate the emancipation of female members of the Jena group, whose undoubted contributions to major works never bore their signature, and champions of whose originality have to make dialogical virtues out of their signed correspondence. Their contributions were fragmentary, but then the whole effort of Jena philosophy was to persuade us of each fragment's unique possession, inviolable as a hedgehog, of universal significance—that ideal experienced in negotiating the reserved or fragmentary expression of others. Undeniable is the Jena group's incorporating of such oppositional but collaborative experience in the "symphilosophy" and "sympoesy" professed under the male authors' names.[29]

Schlegel's "Essay on the Concept of Republicanism" at first appears, if anything, more abstract than Kant in its insistence that republicanism embodies a freedom which can only be endlessly approached through a process of perpetually progressive approximation. He stirs up the Rousseauian sources of Kant's constitutionalism and asks how it is possible for such a spontaneous identification of particular and general wills to exist outside the world of pure thought. Only through a *Salto mortale* can the gap between the actual interests of an individual citizen and the state be crossed and a republic can cease to be hypothetical and come into existence. The fatal leap can only be avoided through putting more trust than Kant is prepared to do in fiction. Schlegel thinks that we have, knowingly, to accept the fiction that the a priori legitimacy of the general will, underwriting the ideal republic, can have as its surrogate a particular empirical will or example. A purer solution is not of this world. The legal fiction that an imperfect constitution can "stand in" for a perfect republic becomes a practical necessity.

The compromise Schlegel recommends amounts to accepting that in the real world the will of the majority must substitute for the general will. Equally, the will of the majority is only legitimate *if it is* standing in for the general will. Kant thought democracy despotic. But if democracy is a fiction to make available an empirical approximation of the general will, it would be mistaken to regard the institutionalization of what we all have in common, or what I can without contradiction will everyone else to do, as an imposition. It all comes down to what one makes of the fiction; or, better, it all depends on how profound your sense of fiction is. It was, after all, through a sense of fiction or aesthetic judgment that Kant himself hoped, in his third *Critique*, to justify a concrete sense in our practical lives of things as they might exist independently of our knowledge of them. Schlegel's much greater tolerance of philosophical fiction has first radical and then reactionary consequences.

The key to this is an ironic attitude, developed more famously in Schlegel's epistemology. The fragment is the form of universal philosophy. It obliges us to accept its claims to significance ironically or provisionally. It publicly confesses the approximate character which all claims to knowledge ought to concede. All pretensions to tell the truth are necessarily fragmentary, and the more one mixes up these different pieces, the more one increases the number of perspectives one has on reality. In science, these different perspectives tend to compete and contradict each other. Poetry is exemplary in its toleration of a mixture of genres or radically opposed views of life—comic, tragic, epic, lyrical, and so on. The poetic view of the fragment is not synecdochal: the fragment is not the inadequate part of the whole, but (following Benjamin's reading of

Schlegel again) *is* the truth as experienced in extended practical negotiation with other versions of it, other fragments, all possessing their own standards of coherence and representation.

Schlegel's own fragments try to gain philosophical accreditation for this poetical flexibility. In politics he similarly rejects any a priori principle by which to clarify *political* representation.[30] His political skepticism, in other words, matches his epistemological skepticism. My interest is in the way things get mixed up as a result. He goes beyond the opposition of aristocratic and democratic republicanism to imagine their mixtures *(Mischungen)* on models that must have seemed to him literary *(Mischgedichte)*. Again, with hindsight, this imaginative generosity may seem to head toward a reactionary conclusion, a willingness to accept increasingly symbolic and religiose surrogates for that ideal republic. But in its inception, it is radical.

Schlegel has no time for Kant's careful sequestration of the aesthetic in a realm of its own. His fictions take their chance in the real world. They stand as the persuasive representatives of what can only be fully instantiated in an ideal world but whose practical function in this world is independent of that instantiation. If they succeed in attracting sufficient subscribers, they create an approximation of a political essence, a common human ground. Ironically, most ironically, we can show our grasp of that transcendental common factor only through our willingness to compromise or our ability to fictionalize about its representatives here and now. The truest republic is the best story. Fichte had described the vocation of humankind as an "endless aspiration."[31] The young Schlegel interprets this aspiration politically, politicizing Kant's aesthetics in the process. The *sensus communis,* which Kant believed was created through persuasion by particular example, becomes Schlegel's republic. It represents the endless task of representing *as community* the different ways in which we express what we have in common.[32] The passage through politics shows us what aesthetics is capable of. Perhaps you can now anticipate my multicultural conclusion?

It is worth dwelling on the romanticism of this a little. At first Schlegel's skeptical tolerance might appear to make him a pluralist. The poetic housing of incompatible political ends perhaps accepts that there are equally compelling values belonging to different political systems. His difference from pluralism, though, lies in the poetic or fictional activity necessary to create such tolerance. Liberals such as Isaiah Berlin believe that we choose between different goods but should acknowledge the relativism of our choices. An ironist like Schlegel is more interested in the exercise of imagination by which we can represent these different goods as goods belonging to the same human being. Or, another way of putting it, he is interested in the different kinds of human being we could have been, the mixture that one potentially is. Initially he defines the expressive transitions we can make from one set of values to another as "progressive." The undermining of one establishment by moving on to the precepts of another points to an ideal resolution we are always seeking but never achieve. The seeking makes us better people, and its negotiations stand in for—give us practical experience of—the ideal as we go along. Thus we defer to difference, treating otherness as something to reckon with, something satisfying an idealizing function within discursive practice rather than aesthetically euphemizing discursive limitations, following Benjamin's rather than Nancy and Lacoue-Labarthe's reading of Schlegel.

Schlegel, reputedly at his sister-in-law Caroline's instigation, had reviewed one of the great texts of ameliorative Enlightenment, Condorcet's *Essay on the Progress of the Human Mind*, around the same time as his writing of his essay on the concept of republicanism. Schiller's inaugural lecture at the university of Jena in 1789 had been on "What Is and to What End Does One Study Universal History." Schlegel's concentration on Condorcet, victim and ideologue of the French Revolution, no doubt distanced him further from Schiller. But it is within the same tradition that he affirms the worth "as Idea" of infinite perfectibility. History requires the art of a *historischen Kunstler* rather than a *Chronikenschreiber*, a historical artist rather than a chronicler, an expansion giving methodological point to the "literary pretensions" of Caroline sneered at by Schmitt. Only in a *Kunstwerk* could the historian avoid either the violence incurred by making history conform to the idea, or the chaos invited by leaving events uninformed by the idea. Isaiah Berlin suspects Condorcet, "one of the best men that ever lived," of harboring the Enlightenment prejudice that at a certain stage of human development the incompatibility between different values will dissolve.[33] Schlegel never claims that. But he does say that if it were, wonderfully, to happen, that all differences could be identically represented, then the polity in which this would happen would be an ideal republic. And, crucially, he adds that the creation of the fictions to which this ideal is necessarily reduced in the here and now is a republican poetic activity. This takes us back to the original Schlegelian aphorism from which we set out.

In conclusion, what is one to make of all this? Perhaps Schlegel's theory is only a dispensable romantic exaggeration of the political significance of literature, one soon to be magisterially historicized by Hegel in his *Aesthetics*. On the other hand it might represent the bringing to reflection, the theorizing, of a recurrent need to be utopian in a poetic or a literary way and, to use a passing defense of utopian thinking by Quentin Skinner, aesthetically to "critique our practice as insufficiently attentive to our principles."[34] I would like to think that the examples and arguments I have brought together support this second verdict. Thus defended, romanticism is a particular instance of literary reflexivity— metaromanticism—whose self-critical practice of engaging in new forms of poetic or aesthetic organization stand in for or temporarily do the work of a desirable political order of representation.

Such manifestos are sometimes forgetful of their function as surrogates, as the working mothers of, rather than alternatives to, forms of political order. Contemporary postmodern theory has often been accused of thus forgetting itself. Rather like Mr. Sleary's circus in *Hard Times*, it leaves one puzzled as to whether it is the solution or the problem. Presumably few of us want what Martha Nussbaum calls "a postmodernism concluding that, in the absence of transcendent standards, we should understand value judgments as attempts to maximize expected utility." Utilitarianism, after all, has been a traditional object of aesthetic disdain, although the connections between utilitarian thought and technological advance have often made aesthetic opponents look reactionary. Writers as different as Jane Austen and the Shelleys, Marvell and the Wordsworths demand critical theories which show this need not be necessarily so. To understand them one is obliged to recall their exemplariness; one has to become a member of the new, modern conventions they call to order. To be a good reader is to work out the implications of belonging to that readership, to use fiction not just to interpret the world but to change it.

My quotation from Nussbaum is to be found in an article called "Human Capabilities, Female Human Beings." Her essay is an extended gloss on Catherine MacKinnon's remark to the effect that to be a woman is still not a way of being human—not a way in which one is allowed to be representatively human, is how Nussbaum understands it. Nussbaum both strongly agrees with MacKinnon's skepticism, yet also claims her own understanding of human capabilities to be "frankly universalist and essentialist."[35] How can she believe in a human essence and also believe that in their specificity women are unfairly excluded from being its bearers? These paradoxical commitments to particular and general causes led her to write her next book, called *Poetic Justice*. There she argues in inadvertently Schlegelian mode that we get at the law, what universally applies, via a theory of how aesthetic sensibility negotiates the differences between particular cases, reconstructing sympathetically background information justifying different treatment. She moves toward, in other words, a more defensible version of the postmodern idea that what is uniform, what eternally returns, is difference, and that the individuality of the particular example always embodies more considerations than we can legislate for in advance. Human beings themselves escape our generalizations. Everyone finally merits a fictional estimation.[36]

Nussbaum's argument here sounds like those I have been tracing. Literature's purpose once more is to figure human universals, laws, which can't be metaphysically established or prescribed. In the language of Aristotle's *Poetics* (rather than Lyotard) literary probability allows us to discuss historical impossibilities. Its idealizations are practically facilitating not pleasurably substitutive. But a contradiction looms, for imagine a law which from the start was a law of equity, one which established its universality through repeatedly tailoring itself to individual cases. Its critics would call it casuistical. Even equitable use of the law, especially equitable use of the law, will always be ideological. Yet it was precisely in order to counter the hegemonic force of the law itself that poetic justice entered the arena.

It is difficult to decide between these two views. All I can say is that their disagreement presses on us today. Currently, the idea of universal interests or a common culture is attacked from both sides. For some, it imposes a majority view on a society composed of minorities. For others, the commonness of a common culture smuggles multiculturalism in by the back door and renders the idea of culture incoherent. The former can be fiercely sectarian, the latter completely paranoid. Unspeakable and unthinkable to both is a republic founded on the ability of each to imagine the position of the other. But perhaps in this case the best do indeed lack all conviction. The ability to compromise opens the transcendental door. I return to Alasdair MacIntyre's condemnation of out and out relativism because it denies any culture, hegemonic or minoritarian, the chance to improve itself by comparison with others. For MacIntyre, as for the young Schlegel, a progressive background explains our imaginative participation in new groupings we can't *actually* belong to. But the ideal republic, to which we then *do* belong, stands in for the best future we have.

Schlegelian republicanism reviewed in a multicultural context suggests why we might want to communicate and why, indeed, the act of communication might be an imperative. Critics of Habermas have often argued that his theory of communicative action is in need of a teleology. For Robert Pippin, he needs a *Phenomenology of Spirit*; or, to paraphrase Bill Readings, we need a reason for answering a telephone other than the fact that it is ringing and communication is possible. Charles Larmore asks, in effect, the same question of the political application of Habermas's ideas, and I will finish by reiterating the motive I believe to be provided by the metaromantic support this book has been laboring to provide for Habermas.[37]

Larmore rightly points out a difficulty in construing as a valid *political* aspiration the communication between different discourses, achieved by philosophically interpreting them to each other. First of all, a novel view of philosophical and political activity is being introduced, one attenuated in comparison with traditional groundings of the subject. But this is consistent with Habermas's deliberate abandonment of a magisterial role for philosophy and his celebration of communicative logic as the only respectable form left for a transcendental ideal. Secondly, though, Habermas is adopting what Larmore calls a "constitutional patriotism." On Habermas's theory, all "fundamental political aspiration would have to be cosmopolitan."[38] Habermas's description thus ignores the way in which modern political identity has been bound up with the idea of the nation-state and the contrast it needs to have in order to define itself in opposition to the citizens of other nation-states. The freedoms that the civic republican tradition has always defended require that opposition or separation from equivalents as their *raison d'être*. Without division into nation-states, political associations would be communitarian, unhelpfully unsure of the territories and boundaries which political activity has always been about policing and demarcating legitimately.

This objection appears well-founded. Nevertheless, it is also fair to say that the concept of the nation-state is precisely what is being compromised by multicultural politics at the present time. In other words, *within* a nation-state nowadays citizens have to be capable of being cosmopolitan because their ethnic backgrounds and origins completely lack the homogeneity of the exemplars of any civic republican tradition. The new republic, too, must not only itself foster a constitutional patriotism but must be able to survive the lasting allegiances of its citizens to the transnational communities they belong to. Current postcolonial theory is typically exercised by the problem of providing effective formulations for these equally defining affiliations—imagined communities, hybridity, the black Atlantic, tricontinentalism.[39] Walter Benjamin's Schlegelian *Mischgedicht* is both urbane about its own generically conflicted integrity and sanguine about its critical afterlife, ready to perpetuate its original existence beyond the jurisdiction of its founding intention. In this it arguably exemplifies not communitarian vagueness but a timely increase in republican generosity, in keeping with Habermas's communicative ideal and its romantic sources. The "reasonable disagreement" Larmore thinks Habermas's practical ideal rules out might, when translated back to its metaromantic source, look more like a framework for thriving on contradiction. Certainly, the new nation-state, simply to hold together, needs such republican latitudinarianism that can find in successful negotiation now the transcendental common ground it could once afford to defer to some ideal realm. That is reason enough.

NOTES

Introduction

1. My wording comes from Tilottama Rajan's and Julia Wright's introduction to the book of the first proceedings of the North American Society for the Study of Romanticism, *Romanticism, History, and the Possibilities of Genre: Re-forming Literature 1789–1837*, ed. T. Rajan and J. Wright (Cambridge: Cambridge University Press, 1998), 16. See too Jerome Christensen's stirring defense in *Romanticism at the End of History* (Baltimore: Johns Hopkins University Press, 2000): "Now that the long haul has been aborted, and Marx's beautiful theory has withered, the Romantic Movement marks time as the reviving possibility of change that is not merely normal, the hope for justice that is not merely the confirmation of property rights" (41).

2. David Simpson, *Romanticism, Nationalism, and the Revolt against Theory* (Chicago: University of Chicago Press, 1993), 159. Simpson is addressing "The Wordsworth Question," but even the radical efforts of Blake, Shelley, and Keats "run aground on a form of inwardness whose variations are beyond prescription and sometimes even description" (170). It is a Rousseauian impulse to translation that I try to read into such moments.

3. See Rosemary Ashton, *The German Idea: Four English Writers and the Reception of German Thought, 1800–1860* (Cambridge: Cambridge University Press, 1980).

4. Along with Abrams ought to be mentioned the distinctive approaches of Anne K. Mellor's *English Romantic Irony* (Cambridge: Harvard University Press, 1985), Mark Kipperman's *Beyond Enchantment: German Idealism and English Romantic Poetry* (Philadelphia: University of Pennsylvania Press, 1986), and any work by Tilottama Rajan. Terry Eagleton's *The Ideology of the Aesthetic* (Oxford: Basil Blackwell, 1990) admirably takes on the task of making available for critical debate now the defining passage of aesthetic theory through German thought; and Isobel Armstrong's *The Radical Aesthetic* (Oxford: Blackwell, 2000) opens up new dimensions for this debate now and in the future. I engage below with Frances Ferguson's admirably rigorous *Solitude and the Sublime: Romanticism and the Aesthetics of Individualism* (New York: Routledge, 1992).

5. *Immanuel Kant in England—1798–1838* (Princeton: Princeton University Press, 1931).

6. *Coleridge and the Pantheist Tradition* (Oxford: Clarendon Press, 1966).

7. See Walter Benjamin, "Theses on the Philosophy of History," in *Illuminations*, trans. Harry Zorn (London: Fontana, 1974), and Julian Roberts's helpful discussion

of anti-Kantian messianism in his introduction to *German Philosophy: An Introduction* (Cambridge: Polity Press, 1988), esp. 6–8.

8. Kantians justify intentionality (shorthand for the embedded orientation of our perceptions within a world) with reference to nature's apparent ("as if") abstraction from all sorts of other possibilities to make our experience possible. But this is simultaneously to say that only in seeing through intentionality, as it were, do we get a sense of that plenitude. But since we cannot step outside intentionality, we are reduced to repeating what we know in order to evoke what we don't know. This is the "unboundedness of the conceptual," recognized by Hegel and recently reiterated by John McDowell—*Mind and World* (Cambridge: Harvard University Press, 1994), lecture 2, esp. 44–45. Equally, the disinterestedness of the Kantian aesthetic, its solitude (Ferguson's useful nomenclature again), frees sublimity and beauty from intentions and purposes, but only to let us savor the finality of our own faculties. Intentionlessness and intentionality are again interchangeable. Hence, we see one way of understanding the provocation to produce a more dynamic dialectic felt not only by Schlegel, Schelling, and Hegel, but also registered in Keats's exploration of poetic redundancy (see chap. 4 below).

9. See Howard Caygill, *The Art of Judgement* (Oxford: Blackwell, 1989); Paul Collins Hayner, *Reason and Existence: Schelling's Philosophy of History* (Leiden: E. J. Brill, 1967); F. Schlegel, *Ideen*, no. 28, in *Philosophical Fragments*, trans. Peter Firchow (Minneapolis: University of Minnesota Press, 1991), 96. See Robert B. Pippin's authoritative summary of the way the "perceived failure of Hegel's attempt at a complete, self-justifying account by reason itself split apart" to form all sorts of philosophical reactions which lie at "the heart of all the familiar claims of the late Schelling, Kierkegaard, Schopenhauer, Adorno, and most recently Habermas . . ." (*Modernism as a Philosophical Problem* [Oxford: Basil Blackwell, 1991], 166).

10. J. G. Fichte, *Science of Knowledge (Wissenschaftslehre)*, trans. Peter Heath and John Lachs (New York: Appleton Century Crofts, 1970). See esp. 223: " If, say, the not-self were posited without quantity, as infinite and unlimited, the self would not be posited at all. . . . Hence it requires to be posited in a determinate quantity, and the reality of the self will be restricted by the amount of reality posited in the not-self.—The expressions *to posit a not-self* and *to restrict the self* are completely equivalent, as was shown in the theoretical Science of Knowledge." The classic study of the transformation of Fichtean "reflection" into Schlegelian "connectedness" is Walter Benjamin's "The Concept of Criticism in German Romanticism," in *Selected Writings—1913–26*, ed. Marcus Bullock and Michael W. Jennings (Cambridge, Mass.: Belknap Press, 1996), 1:116–21. See also Rodolphe Gasché's discussion of foundational performativity from Fichte's idealism to de Man's rhetoric in *The Wild Card of Reading: On Paul de Man* (Cambridge: Harvard University Press, 1998), chap. 1.

11. Dieter Henrich's classic account of Fichte's exposure of circularity in the reflective model of self-consciousness is equally alive to "elements of the reflective theory . . . insinuating themselves into Fichte's counterproposal." See "Fichte's Original Insight," trans. David R. Lacherman, in *Contemporary German Philosophy* (University Park: Pennsylvania State University Press, 1982), 1:26 and passim. Frederick Neuhouser's carefully historicized attempt to defend Fichte from the critical side of Henrich's advocacy nevertheless concedes that it is "misleading to say, as Fichte does, that intellectual intuition is 'directed at' the activity of consciousness," but this separation of knower and known keeps resurfacing to undermine Fichte's attempt to make aware-

ness "internal" to the act of consciousness ("Self-Positing as Nonrepresentational Self-Awareness," in *Fichte's Theory of Subjectivity* [Cambridge: Cambridge University Press, 1990], 83–84 and passim.

12. I am drawing here on Andrew Bowie, *Aesthetics and Subjectivity: From Kant to Nietzsche* (Manchester: Manchester University Press, 1993); and also his *From Romanticism to Critical Theory: The Philosophy of German Literary Theory* (London: Routledge, 1997). In the latter, especially helpful is the chapter "Understanding Walter Benjamin," 193–238. Bowie himself draws on Manfred Frank, *Einführung in die früromantische Ästhetik* (Frankfurt: Suhrkamp, 1989), as does Charles Larmore in his excellent exposition of romantic alternatives to reflective understanding in *The Morals of Modernity* (Cambridge: Cambridge University Press, 1991), 198–203.

13. See the claim of Isobel Armstrong's "Benjamin Reader," in "And Beauty? A Dialogue?" chap. 6 of *The Radical Aesthetic:* "What Adorno calls 'the unstillable longing in the face of beauty,' the something, the 'what was promised' in the artwork, can only be got at by making it *appear* in prose criticism, manifesting itself rather than being discursively analysed. It can only appear through understanding the dense contradictions which bring it into being" (179).

14. Schlegel, *Ideen*, no. 108, in *Philosophical Fragments*, 104.

15. F. W. J. Schelling, *The Philosophy of Art*, ed. and trans. Douglas W. Stott, (Minneapolis: University of Minnesota Press, 1989), 28. See also the discussion of the relation of art to philosophy in the "Corollaries" at the end of the 1800 *System of Transcendental Idealism*, trans. Peter Heath (Charlottesville: University of Virginia Press, 1978, 1993), 229–36. "The work of art merely reflects to me what is otherwise not reflected by anything, namely that absolutely identical which has already divided itself even in the self" (230). Schelling's *Ideas for a Philosophy of Nature* (trans. Errol E. Harris and Peter Heath [1797, rev. 1803; Cambridge: Cambridge University Press, 1988]) had asserted that "the first idea of philosophy already rests on the tacit presupposition of a possible indifference between absolute knowing and the absolute itself. . . . An absolute knowing is not one in which subjective and objective are united as opposites, but one in which the entire subjective is the entire objective and *vice versa*" (44–46).

16. *Kritische Friedrich-Schlegel Ausgabe*, ed. Ernst Behler with Jean-Jacques Austett and Hans Eichner, vol. 18 (Munich: Verlag Ferdinand Schöningh Thomas—Verlag—Zurich, 1966), frag. 927, p. 106.

17. Compare A. Benjamin, *The Plural Event: Descartes, Hegel, Heidegger* (London: Routledge, 1993), 196 n. 13. Here, the messianic quality of Walter Benjamin's later ideas of redemption seems to disrupt an ontology affiliated to the power to produce interpretations, and hence, retrospectively, to question the ontology of an original heterogeneity—the plural event—momentarily celebrated in Walter Benjamin's dissertation on Schlegel.

18. Theodor Adorno, *The Culture Industry*, ed. Jay Bernstein (London: Routledge, 1991).

19. Ferguson, *Solitude and the Sublime*, 3.

20. Ibid., 75, 7. Ferguson's main purpose is to distinguish Kant from the Burkean "aesthetic empiricism" (2) into which his difference from Burke has been deconstructed or historicized by the critical tradition in which she works. The clarity of her grasp of this also makes it easier to see why Kant's romantic successors might have struggled against the "fate" he assigned art. For a comprehensive critique of that

attenuation, see Jay Bernstein, *The Fate of Art: Aesthetic Alienation from Kant to Derrida and Adorno* (Cambridge: Polity Press, 1992).

21. From "The Rhetoric of Temporality" onward, de Man, too, subscribes to the Kantian attenuation. He reads Schlegelian irony as a repetition of the non-identitarian structure of Kantian aesthetics in which, unlike Peter Szondi (*On Textual Understanding and Other Essays*, trans. Harvey Mendelsohn [Minneapolis: University of Minnesota Press, 1986], 68) or Lucien Goldmann, he sees no "tragedy" but the possibility of a continuing critique of the "aesthetic ideology" he thinks peddled by Schiller and others. Jochen Schulte-Sasse partly follows de Man in his many-sided introduction to *Theory as Practice: A Critical Anthology of Early German Romantic Writings* (Minneapolis: University of Minnesota Press, 1997): "In their critique of the possibility of a coincidence of subject and object, the romantics came quite close to defining what was to become de Man's target, aesthetic ideology . . . the delusion of coincidence . . . nationalism" (39). As "nationalism" suggests, though, Schulte-Sasse also sees at work in romantic irony a characteristic attempt to present a coherent alternative to totality, a subtending "indifference," escaping specificity or differentiation, absolutely accommodating the multicultural interests exceeding the notion of a nation-state investigated in my last chapter (27–28).

22. See my "The Republican Prompt: Continuities in English Radical Culture," in *Radicalism in British Literary Culture,* ed. Timothy Morton and N. Smith (Cambridge: Cambridge University Press: 2002), 201–16.

23. Friedrich Engels, *Ludwig Feuerbach and the Outcome of Classical German Philosophy* (London: Martin Lawrence, 1888), 69–70.

24. Heinrich Heine, *Historische-Kritische Gesamtausgabe der Werke,* ed. Manfred Windfuhr (Hamburg: Hoffmann & Campe, 1979), Band 8, 1:115, 79. Margaret A. Rose has a good summary of Marx's relations with Feuerbach and Schelling, its intellectual and academic politics, in *Marx's Lost Aesthetic: Karl Marx and the Visual Arts* (Cambridge: Cambridge University Press, 1984), 31–33.

25. Engels, *Ludwig Feuerbach,* 69.

26. Georg Lukács, *The Destruction of Reason,* trans. Peter Palmer (1962; London: Merlin Press, 1980), 153, 147. I have altered the translation of *Problemstellung.* See G. Lukács, *Die Zerstörung der Vernunft* in *Werke,* vol. 9 (Darmstadt: Hermann Luchterhand Verlag, 1960), 131.

27. For an informed and comprehensive survey of the kinds of regeneration enjoyed by materialist philosophy after the collapse of idealism, see Herbert Schnädelbach's *Philosophy in Germany, 1831–1933,* trans. Eric Matthews (Cambridge: Cambridge University Press, 1984), esp. chap. 5, "Life," 139–61, and, in chap. 3, "Science," section 3, iv—"The Rehabilitation of Philosophy," 103–8.

28. Engels, *Ludwig Feuerbach,* 29.

29. P. Lacoue-Labarthe and J.-L. Nancy, *The Literary Absolute: The Theory of Literature in German Romanticism,* trans. Phillip Barnard and Cheryl Lester (Albany: SUNY Press, 1988). For example, Schlegelian criticism is naturally the dangerous supplement of Derrida's grammatology (110–11, 147 n. 14) and recalls "the Stoic theory of the sign" (113) dear to Deleuze.

30. Schlegel, "Critical Fragments," no. 117, in *Philosophical Fragments,* 14–15.

31. "The Concept of Criticism," 1:173–75. Benjamin thinks Schlegel grasped this less "purely" than did Novalis, through "multiplicity of forms" rather than "the purely prosaic."

32. *The Theory of Communicative Action,* vol. 1, *Reason and the Rationalization of Society,* trans. Thomas McCarthy (Cambridge: Polity Press, 1991), 382–84, 453 n. 52. See *Theorie des Kommunikativen Handelns,* Band 1: *Handlungsrationalität und gesellschaftlische Rationalisierung* (Frankfurt am Main: Suhrkamp Verlag, 1981), 512 n. 111, where the word Habermas uses for the "placeholder" role Adorno gives art is *Statthalter,* with more of a sense of "governor," the legislative capacity which Habermas wants philosophy to give up.

33. *Theory of Communicative Action,* vol. 1, 385–86; "Philosophy as Stand-in and Interpreter," in *Moral Consciousness and Communicative Action* (Moralbewusstsein und kommunicatives Handeln), trans. C. Lenhardt and S. W. Nicholsen (Cambridge: Polity Press, 1990), 15.

34. Paul de Man, "The Rhetoric of Temporality," in *Blindness and Insight* (London: Methuen, 1983), 187–228. See also "Intentional Structure of the Romantic Image," in *The Rhetoric of Romanticism* (New York: Columbia University Press, 1984), 1–19. The epochal readings by Hartman and Bloom I am thinking of are, of course, Hartman's *Wordsworth's Poetry—1787–1814* (New Haven: Yale University Press, 1964) and Bloom's *Shelley's Mythmaking* (New Haven: Yale University Press, 1959).

35. It helps here to think of a Lacanian rereading of Freud in which the unconscious ceases to be an irretrievable past whose reality we cannot face up to directly and is disclosed in just the present modes of action by which we fail to close on it scientifically. To say that the unconscious is therefore never possessed as an object of knowledge is precisely the point; the unconscious is the constitutional lack which we are exorbitant, disturbed, immaturely Oedipal, mad, and so on to resent. The unconscious, too, has the structure of a language and gets said one way or another.

36. The *OED* defines parabasis principally as " . . . a going aside, digression. . . . In ancient Greek comedy, a part sung by the chorus, addressed to the audience in the poet's name, and unconnected with the action of the drama." For de Man's understanding of parabasis through "a slight extension of Friedrich Schlegel's formulation," see also *Allegories of Reading: Figural Language in Rousseau, Rilke and Proust* (New Haven: Yale University Press, 1979), 300–301.

37. Paul de Man, *Aesthetic Ideology,* ed. Andrzej Warminski (Minneapolis: University of Minnesota Press, 1996), 90. De Man concedes that *The Critique of Judgement* "depends on a linguistic structure (language as a performative as well as a cognitive system) that is not itself accessible to the powers of transcendental philosophy" (79). For the chiasmic structure to his argument, whose postmodern idiom I look at more closely in chap. 11, see his conclusion to "Kant's materialism" (my emphasis): "To parody Kant's stylistic procedure of dictionary definition, the radical *formalism* that animates aesthetic judgment in the dynamics of the sublime is what is called *materialism.* Theoreticians of literature who fear they may have deserted or betrayed *the world* by being too formalistic are worrying about the wrong thing: in the spirit of Kant's third *Critique,* they were not nearly *formalistic* enough" (128).

38. Walter Benjamin, *Der Begriff der Kunstkritik in der deutschen Romantik,* ed. H. Schweppenhäuser (Frankfurt am Main: Suhrkamp Taschenbuch Verlag, 1973), 22–23. *Selected Writings* translates *erfüllte* as "full," but the material instantiation of infinitude which Benjamin's word also suggests is anticipated by his own footnote earlier on Schlegel's romantic point of view where he endorses Charlotte Pingoud's verdict that "Fulfilment at every point of existence, realised ideal on every level of life: this is the categorical imperative out of which Schlegel's new religion emerges" (*Selected*

Writings—1913–26, 186 n. 3). See also Benjamin's distinction between *Fortschritt* and *Progredibilität.* The latter, a "*qualitative* infinity, is an endless process of fulfilment, not a bare process of becoming" *(ein unendlicher Erfüllungs-, kein blosser Werdeprozess) (Der Begriff,* 86). In Ferguson's brilliant reading, Kant's mathematical sublime eschews quality for quantity because of the impersonality of numerical description desirable for its disinterestedness ("supremely egalitarian") and its honoring of nature's other-ness, aware that "nature can only speak in such an uncolloquial idiom" (*Solitude and the Sublime,* 31, 85). This non-identitarian rationale is again what prohibits Kant an idea of Benjamin's *Progredibilität.*

39. *Der Begriff,* 62–63.

40. See Ken Hirschkop, *Mikhail Bakhtin: An Aesthetic for Democracy* (Oxford: Oxford University Press, 1999): "By insisting on it as a cultural category Bakhtin endows democracy with a depth and reach into the lifeworld which any Kantian—Habermas included—would be wary of" (37). Hirschkop's book details for the first time Bakhtin's neo-Kantian training and his post-neo-Kantian reaction, which perhaps makes him a future for Schlegel.

Chapter One

1. Herbert Marcuse, *The Aesthetic Dimension: Toward a Critique of Marxist Aesthetics* (London: Macmillan, 1979), 27–28. For Marcuse on Schiller's "de-sublimation of rea-son" and "self-sublimation of sensuousness," see *Eros and Civilisation* (London: Sphere Books, 1969), 148–58.

2. See Habermas's essay, "Walter Benjamin: Consciousness-Raising or Rescuing Critique," in *Philosophical-Political Profiles,* trans. Frederick G. Lawrence (London: Heinemann, 1983), 133–36. In "Habermas and Modernism" (in *Habermas and Modernity,* ed. R. Bernstein [Cambridge: Polity Press, 1985]), Martin Jay provides the best introduction to Habermas's suspicion of aesthetic autonomy from Schiller to Adorno, and sympathy for Benjamin's project interpreted as leading to communicative interaction between aesthetic and other discourses. To assign philosophy the specific task of understanding this process both reconceives its role and demystifies its traditional authority. See Peter Dews's account of Habermas's arrival at this conclusion in "Habermas and the Desublimation of Reason," introduction to *Habermas: A Critical Reader* (Oxford: Basil Blackwell, 1999), 1–25. In *Romanticism, Aesthetics, and Nationalism* (Cambridge: Cambridge University Press, 1999), David Aram Kaiser takes a more conciliatory line than I do toward Schiller's "aesthetic statism," as he calls it. But our accounts are in many ways complementary, and he ends up with a chapter opposing Adorno and Habermas as a consequence of Schiller's aesthetic understanding of symbol being "no longer a viable option for contemporary theory" (41). He chooses not to develop the contemporary alternative to Schiller, Schlegel, and Schlegel's affinities with Benjamin.

3. Friedrich Schiller, *On the Aesthetic Education of Man, in a Series of Letters,* English and German facing, ed. and trans. Elizabeth M. Wilkinson and L. A. Willoughby (Oxford: Clarendon Press, 1967), 147–49, 167. All references to *On the Aesthetic Education of Man* are to this edition. In the case of other works, German references are to the five-volume *Sämtliche Werke,* ed. J. Perfahl, vol. 4, *Historische Schriften;* vol. 5, *Philosophische Schriften/Vermischte Schriften* (Munich: Winkler Verlag, 1968).

4. For an unambiguously reductionist account of *On the Aesthetic Education of Man,*

in which Schiller's theory is attuned entirely to his own commercial interests, see Martha Woodmansee, *The Author, Art, and the Market* (New York: Columbia University Press, 1994), chap. 3. Woodmansee does not go on to look at the contemporary manipulation of the prestige achieved for poetry by the Kantian tradition, the critical reflection of a metaromanticism well aware of the political finesses on which that prestige or cultural capital is based. But that consideration restores a poetic and philosophical substance to romantic writing not exhausted by its conformity to "the market." Woodmansee is critical of Terry Eagleton for conceding a "progressive" purpose to *On the Aesthetic Education of Man* that "the market" can demystify, but in fact it was the task of reconceiving "progress" that Schiller's radical opponents undertook, and for that they needed the critical leverage of metaromanticism.

5. Søren Kierkegaard, *Either / Or,* trans. David F. Swenson and Lillian Marvin Swenson, 2 vols. (Princeton: Princeton University Press, 1959), 1:439.

6. See below, chs. 11 and 12.

7. Tom Paine's skepticism of the radicalism of mixed constitutions is discussed below in chap. 12. For Machiavellianism, see J. G. E. Pocock's classic, *The Machiavellian Moment: Florentine Political Thought and the Atlantic Republican Tradition* (Princeton: Princeton University Press, 1975), and the large literature it provoked. I argue for Marvell's relevance in more detail below, chap. 9.

8. *On the Aesthetic Education of Man,* 5.

9. T. Adorno, *Minima Moralia: Reflections from Damaged Life,* trans. E. F. N. Jephcott (London: Verso, 1974), 247.

10. Friedrich Nietzsche, *The Birth of Tragedy,* trans. W. Kaufmann (New York: Vintage Books, 1967), 37; *Sämtliche Werke,* ed. G. Colli and M. Montinari (Berlin: Verlag de Gruyter, 1999), 1:29.

11. As Josef Chytry puts it briskly in his extensive study of "the aesthetic state," "Schiller's theory of history violates its own premises." And Chytry rightly sees the "primacy of self-consciousness of spirit" interrupting Schiller's historical location of the aesthetic ideal as proto-Hegelian (*The Aesthetic State: A Quest in Modern German Thought* [Berkeley: University of California Press, 1989], 92–93).

12. Franco Moretti, *Signs Taken for Wonders,* rev. ed., trans. Susan Fischer, David Forgacs, and David Miller (London: Verso, 1988), 245.

13. Naive and Sentimental Poetry *and* On the Sublime, *Two Essays,* trans. Julius A. Elias (New York: Frederick Ungar, 1966). All references to these works are to this edition.

14. Theodor Adorno, *Aesthetic Theory,* ed. Gretel Adorno and R. Tiedemann, trans. C. Lenhardt (London: Routledge & Kegan Paul, 1984), 282.

15. Schiller, *Sämtliche Werke,* 5:267.

16. Schiller, *On the Aesthetic Education of Man,* 9.

17. David Bromwich, *Disowned by Memory: Wordsworth's Poetry of the 1790s* (Chicago: University of Chicago Press, 1998), 149. Bromwich is discussing the two-part *Prelude* of 1799 (2:26–31), but his remarks apply to the later versions which retain the lines.

18. Contrast Theresa M. Kelley's study of Wordsworth's "aesthetics of containment" in *Wordsworth's Revisionary Aesthetics* (Cambridge: Cambridge University Press, 1988).

19. Paul de Man, "Autobiography as De-facement," *MLN* 94 (1979): 919–30.

20. F. Schiller, *The History of the Thirty Years' War in Germany, Translated from the*

Original German of Frederic Schiller, Aulic Counsellor, and Professor of Philosophy at Jena, by Captain Blaquiere, of the Royal Irish Artillery (London, 1799), xxv.

21. *History of the Rise and Progress of the Belgian Republic, until the Revolution under Philip II,* trans. Thomas Horne (London, 1807), iii–iv.

22. G. W. F. Hegel, *Aesthetics: Lectures on Fine Art,* 2 vols., trans. T. M. Knox (Oxford: Clarendon Press, 1975), 1:527.

23. This traditional criticism of Hegel begins with Schelling's *Lectures on Modern Philosophy,* continues through Marx's *The German Ideology,* and still demands ingenious defenses by Hegelians now such as Robert B. Pippin in *Idealism as Modernism: Hegelian Variations* (Cambridge: Cambridge University Press, 1997): "Hegel claims to be able to show that [human beings] must enact the only historical drama that historical and rational beings could enact," but apparently does not mean that human beings "must be rational because we know a priori that history is rational" (259, 422).

Chapter Two

1. I cite both the English and French editions of Rousseau's works. Quotations in English are from the following translations, some slightly altered by me: *Discourse on the Origin of Inequality,* trans. Donald A. Cress (Indianapolis: Hackett, 1992); *The Social Contract,* in *The Social Contract and Discourses,* trans. G. D. N. Cole, rev. J. H. Brumfitt and John C. Hall, updated by P. D. Jimack (London: J. M. Dent, 1993); *Émile, or On Education,* trans. Allan Bloom (Harmondsworth: Penguin, 1991); *The Confessions of Jean-Jacques Rousseau,* trans. J. M. Cohen (Harmondsworth: Penguin, 1954); *Rousseau, Judge of Jean-Jacques, Dialogues,* ed. and trans. Roger D. Masters, Christopher Kelly, and Judith R. Bush, vol. 1 of *The Collected Writings of Rousseau* (Hanover, N.H.: University Press of New England, 1990); *The Reveries of the Solitary Walker,* trans. Charles E. Butterworth (Indianapolis: Hackett, 1992). References to the French are to the *Pléiade* edition (ed. Bernard Gagnebin and Marcel Raymond [Paris: Gallimard, 1959–69]) and are given directly after the citations from the translations.

2. Lester G. Crocker, *Jean-Jacques Rousseau: The Quest, 1712–1758* (New York: Macmillan, 1974), 179.

3. F. R. Leavis, "The Wild, Untutored, Phoenix" (1939), in *The Common Pursuit* (London: Peregrine, 1962), 239.

4. See Edmund Duffy on the use of *Confessions* to discredit Rousseau's political ideas in England: *Rousseau in England: The Context for Shelley's Critique of the Enlightenment* (Berkeley: University of California Press, 1979).

5. Thomas McFarland, *Romanticism and the Heritage of Rousseau* (Oxford: Clarendon Press, 1995), 53–55.

6. Stanley Cavell, *The Claim of Reason: Wittgenstein, Skepticism, Morality, Tragedy* (New York: Oxford University Press, 1979), 464.

7. See Ernst Cassirer, *Rousseau, Kant, Goethe,* trans. James Gutmann et al. (Princeton: Princeton University Press, 1970); and *The Question of Jean-Jacques Rousseau,* trans. Peter Gay (Bloomington: Indiana University Press, 1963).

8. Keith Ansell-Pearson, in *Nietzsche contra Rousseau: A Study of Nietzsche's Political Thought* (Cambridge: Cambridge University Press, 1991), claims that the interpretation of Rousseau's thought as nothing more than "concealed resentment" (229) is a Kantian one, ahistorical and idealizing (36–37, 221–22). He follows Judith Schklar in finding in Rousseau a more Nietzschean will to make *amour propre* become *amour de soi.*

9. But for affinities between Wordsworthian and Rousseauian rhetorics of free-dom, see Celeste Langan, *Romantic Vagrancy: Wordsworth and the Simulation of Freedom* (Cambridge: Cambridge University Press, 1995).

10. *Corréspondance complète de Jean Jacques Rousseau,* ed. R. A. Leigh (Geneva: Institut et Musée Voltaire, 1965–1991), 2:142–43.

11. Jacques Derrida, *Of Grammatology,* trans. Gayatri Spivak (Baltimore: Johns Hopkins University Press, 1974), 297–98.

12. Edmund Burke, *A Letter From Mr. Burke To A Member Of The National Assembly In Answer To Some Objections To His Book On French Affairs,* in *Reflections on the Revolution in France,* ed. A. J. Grieve (London: J. M. Dent, 1967), 263.

13. See Hunt Williams's clear formulation in *Rousseau and Romantic Autobiography* (Oxford: Oxford University Press, 1983): "Yet the very act of becoming an autobiographer, of telling the story of his life and claiming to understand it, leads Rousseau to want his personal image to be real, to be himself. This closes down the distance that was necessary to make the claim of understanding in the first place" (219).

14. Cavell, *The Claim of Reason,* 464.

15. Pierre Bourdieu's work is obviously relevant here. For a discussion of the "run" on high art set off by calling the bluff of its protestations of value, see chap. 5 below.

16. Marian Hobson, "Kant, Rousseau et la musique," in *Reappraisals of Rousseau: Studies in Honour of R. A. Leigh,* ed. Simon Harvey, Marian Hobson, David Kelley, and Samuel B. Taylor (Manchester: Manchester University Press, 1980), 303.

17. Samuel Taylor, "Rousseau's Romanticism," in *Reappraisals of Rousseau,* ed. Harvey, Hobson, Kelley, and Taylor (Manchester: Manchester University Press, 1980), 16.

18. Jean-Louis Lecercle's bicentennial "reappraisal" in "Rousseau critique littéraire: 'le coeur' et 'la plume'" summarizes closest, to my mind, Rousseau's historicism, describing that fraught but unavoidable passage through present distortions into a new sophistication, a new writing neither aesthetically resigned to the absence of wholeness, applauding a tragedy, nor theoretically naive about the difficulties in recovering an experience congruent with nature: "For him, the pen must be placed at the service of the heart if it isn't to be a contemptible instrument, and the literature of his time has gone off the rails because the men of letters write for other reasons than to express useful truths. If literature has corrupted society, society has returned the compliment. We must relearn the secrets of the ancients, think justly, translate simply authentic sentiments, find the true language of the heart. But it isn't nature which gives these to us. It is in the most refined society, the most corrupt that we learn to master language; and it is at the cost of an immense labour that we succeed in making nature speak without betraying her, nature being here none other than our authentic feelings. In the sense that he refused to pass judgement on the literary object, Jean-Jacques wasn't a literary critic. However, he forged a critical doctrine, expressed in a language insufficiently precise to our eyes, but sufficing to guide him in his patient progress towards perfection . . ." (ibid., 231).

19. I say "postmodern" to distinguish the rhetorical plausibility of "longing for total revolution" from the "contradiction" generating the interpretation of it as paradox at the time. See Bernard Yack, *The Longing for Total Revolution: Philosophic Sources of Social Discontent* (Princeton: Princeton University Press, 1986), 31.

20. *Reflections on the Revolution in France,* ed. C. C. O'Brien (Harmondsworth: Penguin, 1968), 92–93.

21. Gregory Dart, *Rousseau, Robespierre, and English Romanticism* (Cambridge: Cam-

bridge University Press, 1998), 58, 74. On Hazlitt's difficulties, see chap. 10 below, and contrast discussions by Dart (chap. 7 in *Rousseau, Robespierre, and English Romanticism*), John Whale (*Imagination Under Pressure, 1789–1832: Aesthetics, Politics, and Utility* [Cambridge: Cambridge University Press, 2000]), and Kevin Gilmartin (*Print Politics, the Press, and Radical Opposition in Early Nineteenth-Century England* [Cambridge: Cambridge University Press, 1996]). For a good defense of Hazlitt's consistency, see Uttara Natarajan, *Hazlitt and the Reach of Sense: Criticism, Morals, and the Metaphysics of Power* (Oxford: Clarendon Press, 1998).

22. Langan, *Romantic Vagrancy*, 33.

23. Ibid., 15.

24. Ibid., 221. Langan cites Steven Goldsmith, who, applying Derrida's "On an Apocalyptic Tone . . . ," "calls attention to a 'transformation of matters of power into matters of language' that occurs in Romantic poetry and the theoretical discourses that would interrogate the implicit privileging of the literary" (Steve Goldsmith, *Unbuilding Jerusalem: Apocalypse and Romantic Representation* [Ithaca, N.Y.: Cornell University Press, 1993]), 75). Both are to some extent anticipated by Marjorie Sabin's distinction of the "sentiment of being" in book 2 of *The Prelude* from *"le sentiment de l'existence"* of the fifth *Rêverie*, venerated phrases in which "the secret of Romanticism in general has been thought to lie." She does so by referring Wordsworth's rhetoric to the aesthetics of sublimity, or "a vague exaltation of tone," and Rousseau's language to "a theoretical vocabulary of extraordinary continuity and coherence in his career." Rousseau's more systematic expression supports his continuing critique of the institutional history of humankind, including, of course, aesthetics (*English Romanticism and the French Tradition* [Cambridge: Harvard University Press, 1976], 104, 107, 113).

Chapter Three

1. *The Watchman,* ed. Lewis Patton, in *The Collected Coleridge* (Princeton: Princeton University Press; London: Routledge & Kegan Paul, 1969–), 2:4.

2. Nigel Leask, *Coleridge and the Politics of Imagination* (London: Macmillan, 1988), 18. Leask persuasively demonstrates how Coleridge's Unitarian interests mediate between his "One Life" theories and the politics of the "Commonwealth Men." He charts the fate of this civic ideal in Coleridge's thought and its decline into "spiritual *consolation*" as Coleridge saves it from "dispersal" only at the cost of "political efficacy" (33–34).

3. *Lectures 1795 on Poetry and Religion,* ed. Lewis Patton and Peter Mann, *The Collected Coleridge,* 1:11, 43.

4. On "opinion" as either "safety valve" or "part of the political action" in pre-Reform English society, see Marilyn Butler, introduction to *Burke, Paine, Godwin, and the Revolution Controversy* (Cambridge: Cambridge University Press, 1984), 6–7.

5. *Collected Coleridge,* 1:126, 2:4.

6. William Hazlitt, "The Spirit of the Age," in *The Complete Works of William Hazlitt,* ed. P. P. Howe (London: Dent, 1930–33), 11:17.

7. Page references in the text to *St. Leon: A Tale of the Sixteenth Century* are to the *Standard Novels,* no. 5 (London: Henry Colburn & Richard Bentley, 1831). References to *Things as They Are; or, The Adventures of Caleb Williams* are to the edition edited by David McCracken (London: Oxford University Press, 1970).

8. Marilyn Butler, "Godwin, Burke, and *Caleb Williams,*" *Essays in Criticism* 32, no. 3 (July 1982): 240.

9. Mark Philp, *Godwin's Political Justice* (London: Duckworth, 1986), 142–48. See Jon Klancher's use of Philp in relation to the question of genre in T. Rajan and J. Wright, eds., *Romanticism, History, and the Possibilities of Genre* (Cambridge: Cambridge University Press, 1998). Pamela Clemit's *The Godwinian Novel: The Rational Fictions of Godwin, Brockden Brown, Mary Shelley* (Oxford: Clarendon Press, 1993) makes an original, groundbreaking case for Godwin's establishment of a new kind of philosophical novel.

10. William Godwin, *Thoughts On Man, His Nature, Productions. And Discoveries. Interspersed With Some Particulars Respecting The Author* (London: Effingham Wilson, 1831), 42–43, 101–5; John Thelwall, *The Tribune,* 3 vols. (London: 1795–96), 2:vii: "nothing is more remarkable than that it should at once recommend the most extensive plan of freedom and innovation ever discussed by any writer in the English language, and reprobate every measure from which even the most moderate reform can be rationally expected" (quoted in Roe, *Wordsworth and Coleridge: The Radical Years* [Oxford: Oxford University Press, 1988], 167).

11. Roy Porter, "The Enlightenment in England," in Roy Porter and Mikulas Teich, *The Enlightenment in National Context* (Cambridge: Cambridge University Press, 1981), 4–5. See also Lewis Patton's introduction to *The Watchman:* "Coleridge had lived for several years in a milieu in which journalism had seemed a natural and inevitable means of expressing one's views, marketing one's verse, and making one's living" (*Collected Coleridge,* 2:xxvii).

12. See Andrew McCann, "William Godwin and the Pathological Public Sphere: Theorizing Communicative Action in the 1790s" (*Prose Studies* 18, no. 3 [December 1995]: 199–223), for support for seeing Habermas's works as "broadly continuous" with Godwin's. Jürgen Habermas, *Strukturwandel der Offentlichkeit: Untersuchungen zu einer Kategorie der burgerlichen Gesellschaft* (Herman Luchterhand Verlag, 1965), 31–55; Roy Porter, "Enlightenment in England," 12; see also Porter's *English Society in the Eighteenth Century* (Harmondsworth: Penguin, 1982), 322.

13. William Godwin, *An Enquiry Concerning Political Justice and Its Influence on General Virtue and Happiness,* 2 vols. (London: G. G. & J. Robinson, 1793), 1:212–13.

14. Philp, *Godwin's Political Justice,* 173.

15. I am drawing here on Jon P. Klancher's excellent account of the dialectic of class and audience in *The Making of English Reading Audiences, 1790–1832* (Madison: University of Wisconsin Press, 1987). On Coleridge's displaced radicalism, see my *Coleridge's Poetics* (Oxford: Basil Blackwell, 1983).

16. See Don Locke, *A Fantasy of Reason: The Life and Thought of William Godwin* (London: Routledge & Kegan Paul, 1980), 60; Philp, *Godwin's Political Justice,* 229; and Godwin, *Enquiry Concerning Political Justice* (1793), 20.

17. Philp, *Godwin's Political Justice,* 199–200; "Recollections of William Godwin," quoted from Abinger MSS, in Peter H. Marshall, *William Godwin* (New Haven: Yale University Press, 1984), 381.

18. William Godwin, *Cloudesley,* 3 vols. (London: Henry Colburn & Richard Bentley, 1830), 1:xi.

19. "Of History and Romance," quoted from Abinger MSS, in D. McCracken, "Godwin's Literary Theory: The Alliance between Fiction and Political Philosophy," *Philological Quarterly* 49 (1970): 124.

20. Kelvin Everest, "William Godwin's *Caleb Williams:* Truth and 'Things as They Are,'" in *1789: Reading, Writing, Revolution* (Colchester: Essex Sociology of Literature Conference, 1982), 135; Leslie Stephen, "William Godwin's Novels," in *Studies of a Biographer,* 2d ser. (New York: 1902), 3:140.

21. *Lectures 1795 on Poetry and Religion,* 60.

22. See D. G. Dumas, "Things as They Were: The Original Ending of *Caleb Williams,*" *Studies in English Literature* 6 (1966): 583; William Godwin, *Uncollected Writings (178–1822)* introductions by J. W. Marcken and B. R. Pollin (Gainesville, Fla.: Scholars Facsimiles and Reprints, 1968), 8–9, 17–18; Marshall, op. cit., 142–43.

23. Godwin, *Enquiry Concerning Political Justice and Its Influence on Modern Morals and Happiness,* 3d edition of 1798, ed. Isaac. Kramnick (Harmondsworth: Penguin, 1985), 279–80.

24. Gary Kelly catalogs this eclecticism, but condemns it as a weakness rather than as part of the plot in "History and Fiction: Bethlem Gabor in Godwin's *St. Leon,*"*English Language Notes* 14, no. 2 (December 1976): 117–20.

25. Hazlitt, *Complete Works,* 11:24.

26. *Enquiry Concerning Political Justice* (3d ed. of 1798), 274.

27. Robert Kaufman, "The Sublime as Super-Genre of the Modern, or *Hamlet* in Revolution: Caleb Williams and His Problems," *Studies in Romanticism* 36 (winter 1997): 541–74. In Kaufman's exhilarating reading, it is the novel which offers Godwin the means of framing this new, sublime narrative which can accommodate both a radical ideal—"a *presentation* of the only form in which his previous commitment to uncoerced judgement could be instantiated"—and also a "non-identical alienated relation to a postfeudal and ostensibly unknowable world" (550, 552). Kaufman's point—though, *contra* Leslie Stephen's questioning of the literary propriety of *Caleb Williams*'s hybridity—is the Kantian one of praising Godwin's preservation of undecidability, so as perpetually to keep "unpredictable" the "experience of genuine judgement" (570). William Godwin, *Lives Of The Necromancers: Or, An Account Of The Most Eminent Persons In Successive Ages, Who Have Claimed For Themselves, Or To Whom Has Been Imputed By Others, The Exercise Of Magical Power* (London: Frederick J. Mason, 1834), vii.

28. *Collected Letters of Samuel Taylor Coleridge,* ed. E. L. Griggs, 6 vols. (Oxford: Clarendon Press, 1956–71), 1:570.

29. Ronald Paulson, *Representations of Revolution (1789–1820)* (New Haven: Yale University Press, 1983), 239.

30. T. Rajan, *The Supplement of Reading: Figures of Understanding in Romantic Theory and Practice* (Ithaca, N.Y.: Cornell University Press, 1990), 184–85; and, "Framing the Corpus: Godwin's "Editing" of Wollstonecraft in 1798," *Studies in Romanticism,* 39 (winter 2000): 530.

31. *The Enquirer. Reflections On Education, Manners, and Literature* (Dublin, 1797), 80.

32. *The Friend,* ed. Barbara Rooke, in *The Collected Coleridge,* vol. 4, book 2, p. 52.

33. I develop this argument at more length in "Coleridge," in *The Romantic Period—Penguin History of English Literature,* vol. 5, ed. David Pirie (Harmondsworth: Penguin, 1994), 185–221.

34. Godwin, *Enquiry Concerning Political Justice* (3d ed. of 1798), 301.

35. [Edward Dubois], *St. Godwin: A Tale Of The Sixteenth, Seventeenth, And Eighteenth Century,* By Count Reginald De St. Leon (London, 1800), 233.

Chapter Four

1. *The Letters of John Keats: 1814–21,* ed. Hyder E. Rollins, 2 vols. (Cambridge: Harvard University Press, 1958), 2:323. All quotations from Keats's letters come from this edition. References to Keats's poems are to *The Poems of John Keats,* ed. Miriam Allott (London: Longman, Norton, 1970).

2. Susan Wolfson, introduction to "Keats and Politics: A Forum," *Studies in Romanticism* 25, no. 2 (summer 1986): 171.

3. N. Roe, ed., *Keats and History* (Cambridge: Cambridge University Press, 1995); and N. Roe, *Keats and the Culture of Dissent* (Oxford: Oxford University Press, 1997). Roe's introduction to *Keats and the Culture of Dissent* gives an excellent résumé of developments in political criticism of Keats since the *Studies in Romanticism* issue of 1986.

4. Marjorie Levinson, *Keats's Life of Allegory: The Origins of a Style* (Oxford: Basil Blackwell, 1988), 291, 23, 5–6, 141.

5. I am here following Hannah Arendt's interpretation of Kant's third *Critique* as containing "perhaps the greatest and most original aspect of Kant's political philosophy. . . . Culture and politics, then, belong together because it is not knowledge or truth which is at stake, but rather judgement and decision, the judicious exchange of opinion about the sphere of public life and the common world" (*Between Past and Future* [New York: Viking Press, 1961], 219–24). Pierre Bourdieu, in *Distinction: A Social Critique of the Judgement of Taste* (trans. R. Nice [London: Routledge & Kegan Paul, 1984]), sees a relation between Kant's separation of taste from the bodily and his separation of art from kitsch or "schmaltz." Bourdieu thinks the separation can be maintained only by a sublimation of the lower, "popular" term by the "higher," bourgeois one. The consequence when this sublimation, in working, wears thin is the subject of my chapter, rather than the straight confrontation with bourgeois aesthetics engineered by Bourdieu's sociology of taste. Bourdieu criticizes Derrida's critique, in *La Vérité en peinture,* of Kant's third *Critique:* "Because he never withdraws from the philosophical game, whose conventions he respects, even in the ritual transgressions at which only traditionalists could be shocked, he can only philosophically tell the truth about the philosophical text and its philosophical reading, which (apart from the silence of orthodoxy) is the best way of not telling it . . ." (493). In Bourdieu's convergence of opposites here, Derrida could preserve his oppositional stance only by critically energizing "the silence of orthodoxy," much as he does "*sous rature*" in *De la grammatologie.* It is a similar response to Bourdieu that I have tried to elicit for Keats. Derrida, of course, would hardly regard his own work as exhausting a paradigm in preparation for cultural materialism. For an epistemological defense of Kant, see Ferguson, *Solitude and the Sublime* (New York: Routledge, 1992); and Robert Kaufman, "Legislators of the Post-Everything World: Shelley's Defence of Adorno," *ELH* 63 (fall 1996): esp. 732 n. 36. For an accessible and provocative handling of these subjects, see Terry Eagleton's *The Ideology of the Aesthetic* (Oxford: Basil Blackwell, 1990).

6. See *Hegel's Aesthetics: Lectures on Fine Art by G. W. F. Hegel,* trans. T. M. Knox, 2 vols. (Oxford: Oxford University Press, 1975), 1:524–29. I think Richard Rand uncovers the same historical entrapment in Keats when he links the ambitious improprieties of Keatsian "translation" of all kinds—metamorphosis, conveyancing, displacement, dissemination—to his immanent attack on a "neoclassical" aesthetic and our own "classical" modes of reading it. See "O'er brimm'd," *Oxford Literary Review* 5 (1982), nos. 1 and 2: 42–43, 53–55; and "Ozone: An Essay on Keats," in *Post-structuralist Read-*

ings of English Poetry, ed. Christopher Norris and Richard Machin (Cambridge: Cambridge University Press, 1986), 294–307.

7. Jerome McGann, *The Beauty of Inflections* (Oxford: Clarendon Press, 1985), 44–45.

8. Friedrich Schiller, *On the Aesthetic Education of Man, in a Series of Letters,* ed. and trans. Elizabeth M. Wilkinson and L. A. Willoughby (Oxford: Clarendon Press, 1967). See Peter Bürger's critique of the tradition of viewing art as inefficacious from Schiller to Adorno in *Theory of the Avant-Garde,* trans. Michael Shaw (Minneapolis: University of Minnesota Press, 1984).

9. John Bayley, "Keats and Reality," *Proceedings of the British Academy* (1962): 118, 98.

10. Kean's popularity and commercial success is emphasized in biographies of him as much as the distinction with which, in B. W. Proctor's near-contemporary *Life,* he impressed *"character* on almost everything which he attempted." Proctor refers to both under the Keatsian rubric of "Return of the Golden Age." He also describes how Kean typically "determined to make the hero the most conspicuous object in the play," and helps show how Kean's egoism, so apparently different from Keatsian "disinterestedness," could nonetheless provide the example for Keats's literary utilitarianism. Bertram Joseph, in *The Tragic Actor* (London: Routledge & Kegan Paul, 1959), could be describing Keatsian practice when he catalogs Hazlitt's and contemporary critics' accounts of Kean's seizing on "the parts" of a character, sometimes to the neglect of "the broad and massy effect," but often in order to translate character "with great freedom and ingenuity into a language of his own." Too great a sacrifice of the integrity of line and plot to climactic "points" resulted in "a clap-trap" or precocious fulfillment retrievable only in a performance of what Crabb Robinson called "pure feeling" (quoted by Joseph, 265–66, 275). Byron's remark is in Leigh Hunt's *Lord Byron and Some of His Contemporaries* (London: 1828), 266. For Scott's defense, see *Keats: The Critical Heritage,* ed. G. M. Matthews (London: Routledge & Kegan Paul, 1971), 116. Other reviewers focus on *Endymion*'s "beauties" and describe its "poetical concentrations" as "flowers of poetry" or "pure poetry" (Francis Jeffrey, in *Keats: The Critical Heritage,* 203–4); "if it be not, technically speaking, a poem," concludes Patmore, it "is poetry itself" (in *Keats: The Critical Heritage,* 135). The burlesque of Hunt's and Keats's style by "Beppo" in the *Literary Journal* (20 March 1819, 92)—"Pleasant Walks: A Cockney Pastoral, In the manner of Leigh Hunt, Esq."—transforms the second line of Hunt's sonnet "To John Keats" ("Whose sense discerns the loveliness of things") into " 'Tis well I see the beautiful of things," making this distillation its refrain, and extracting most of its humor from the miscellaneous quality of "Cockney" catalogs. See Lewis M. Schwartz, *Keats Reviewed by His Contemporaries: A Collection of Notices for the Years 1816–21* (Metuchen, N.J.: Scarecrow Press, 1973), 151–55. See Jeffrey N. Cox, *Poetry and Politics in the Cockney School: Keats, Shelley, Hunt, and their Circle* (Cambridge: Cambridge University Press, 1998) for a lucid and compendious discussion of the area.

11. Matthews, ed., *Critical Heritage,* 326.

12. Ibid., 111; the reviewer in *The Champion,* probably Richard Woodhouse, recognizes and describes the unmethodical habit: "Let [the reviewers] . . . refer to principles: let them show us the philosophic construction of poetry, and point out its errors by instance and application. . . . If, however, they follow their old course, and having tackled the introduction of the first book, to the fag end of the last, swear the whole is an unintelligible jumble . . ." (*Critical Heritage,* 87–88).

13. On these tactics of parody, and *Blackwood's* paranoia about the alternative, see Kim Wheatley, "The *Blackwood's* Attacks on Leigh Hunt," *Nineteenth-Century Fiction* 47 (June 1992), 1–31.

14. For the extent of German influences on Lockhart, see G. Macbeth, *John Gibson Lockhart—a Critical Study* (Urbana: University of Illinois Press, 1935), 62–83. Francis R. Hart gives a helpful account of the Coleridgean tendency of Lockhart's writings in *Lockhart as Romantic Biographer* (Edinburgh: Edinburgh University Press, 1971): "Peter . . . comes equipped with a Coleridgean 'idea' of Scotland" (56). Lockhart could later write a crudely anti-Semitic review of Heine's *De l'allemagne* in the *Quarterly* on the basis of a warped understanding of nationalistic elements in Herder's and the Schlegels' writings ("Heine on Germany," *Quarterly* 55 [December 1835]: 1–34); but his ambition in 1825 of "throwing materials of History into the ever attractive form of Biography" (Hart, *Lockhart as Romantic Biographer*, 25) shows the Carlylean part he played in the general diffusion of idealism in Britain. Sir William Hamilton's "On the Philosophy of the Unconditioned" (*Edinburgh Review* 50, no. 99 [1829]: 194–221) engages directly with Kant and Schelling. See also René Wellek, *Immanuel Kant in England* (Princeton: Princeton University Press, 1931). Wellek's magisterial dismissal of English attempts to understand Kant has perhaps led subsequent commentators to underestimate the extent to which German idealism worked itself into English romantic sensibility, despite Wellek's equal emphasis on the variety of ways in which Kant was assimilated, however inaccurately. For Wellek, Sir William Hamilton "genuinely assimilated some of Kant's thought and appropriated some of his ideas for his own purposes" (51).

15. John Gibson Lockhart, *Peter's Letters to His Kinsfolk*, 3 vols. (Edinburgh: William Blackwood, 1819), 2:144–45, 1:176–77.

16. See Ronald Paulson's discussion of its Burkean sources in *Literary Landscape: Turner and Constable* (New Haven: Yale University Press, 1982), 147–48; and Theresa M. Kelley's excellent analyses of its dominant Wordsworthian forms in *Wordsworth's Revisionary Aesthetics* (Cambridge: Cambridge University Press, 1988).

17. Matthews, ed., *Critical Heritage*, 326.

18. Ibid., 112; See William Keach's useful discussion of Keats's couplets, "Cockney Couplets: Keats and the Politics of Style," in "Keats and Politics: A Forum," *Studies in Romanticism* 25, no. 2 (summer 1986): 182–96.

19. John Jones, *John Keats's Dream of Truth* (London: Chatto & Windus, 1969).

20. Theodor Adorno, *Aesthetic Theory*, trans. C. Lenhardt, ed. Gretel Adorno and Ralph Tiedemann (London: Routledge & Kegan Paul, 1984), 113.

21. *Letters of John Keats*, 1:218.

22. C. Ricks, *Keats and Embarrassment* (Oxford: Clarendon Press, 1974), 13 ff; M. Aske, *Keats and Hellenism* (Cambridge: Cambridge University Press, 1986).

23. See Clement Greenberg's discussion in "Avant-Garde and Kitsch" (1939), in *Art and Culture* (London: Thames & Hudson, 1973), 14; for Keats's use of "caviare," see McGann, *The Beauty of Inflections*, 32–39.

24. I am trying here to expand on Adorno's remarks in *Aesthetic Theory:* "Implicit in the concept of art is the phenomenon of kitsch" (175); "It lies dormant in art itself" (339); "A critique of kitsch, if it is radical and unrelenting, passes beyond kitsch and encompasses art *per se*" (435); and also 53, 70–71. See too Stephen Bungay's brief but illuminating discussion in *Beauty and Truth: A Study of Hegel's Aesthetics* (Oxford: Clarendon Press, 1984), 95.

25. *Letters of John Keats,* 1:266–67.

26. See, for example, David Ricardo's summary of the problem in the chapter "Value and Riches, Their Distinctive Properties," in *The Principles of Political Economy and Taxation* (1817; London: Dent; 1973): "Many of the errors in political economy have arisen from errors on this subject, from considering an increase of riches, and an increase of value, as meaning the same thing, and from unfounded notions as to what constituted a standard measure of value" (183). Equally relevant to Keats would be Thorstein Veblen's critique of the "pecuniary canons of taste" of the *nouveaux riches* for whom "terms in familiar use to designate categories or elements of beauty are applied to cover this [otherwise] unnamed element of pecuniary merit" (*The Theory of the Leisure Class—an Economic Study of Institutions* [1899; London: Unwin Books, 1970], 108). Keatsian "diligent indolence" similarly parallels the capitalism and aesthetics of a class for whom, in Veblen's description, "leisure is the conventional means of pecuniary repute" (49).

27. John Locke, "Some Considerations of the Consequences of the Lowering of Interest and the Raising of the Value of Money . . ." (1691), in *Several Papers Relating to Money, Interest, and Trade, &c.* (London: 1696), 32.

28. *The Halliford Edition of the Works of Thomas Love Peacock,* ed. H. F. B. Brett-Smith and C. E. Jones, 10 vols. (London: Constable, 1924–34), 5:2:95–147.

29. Sir James Steuart, *An Inquiry into the Principles of Political Oeconomy,* ed. A. S. Skinner, 2 vols. (1767; Edinburgh: Oliver & Boyd, 1966), 1:479.

30. John Law, *Money and Trade Considered: With a Proposal for Supplying the Nation with Money* (Edinburgh: 1705), 11.

31. G. Berkeley, *Querist* (1735–37), part 1, 32.

32. D. Hume, *Essays Moral, Political, and Literary,* ed. T. H. Green and T. H. Grose, 2 vols. (London: Longmans, Green, 1875), 1:321, 311; for Hume as a moderate inflationist, see his approval of increasing the money supply if it "keeps alive a spirit of industry in the nation, and increases the stock of labour, in which consists all real power and riches" (1:315).

33. See Michael G. Gootzeit, *David Ricardo* (New York: Columbia University Press, 1975), 2, 22.

34. Ricardo, *Economic Essays,* ed. E. C. K. Gonner (London: Frank Cass, 1923), 40; see also W. L. Taylor, *Francis Hutcheson and David Hume as Predecessors of Adam Smith* (Durham, N.C.: Duke University Press, 1965).

35. See Douglas Vickers, *Studies in the Theory of Money 1690–1776* (London: Peter Owen, 1960), 133; Gareth Stedman Jones, in *Languages of Class: Studies in English Working-Class History, 1832–1982* (Cambridge: Cambridge University Press, 1983), 137–40, discusses the relevance of Shelley's bullionism to the Chartists.

36. Ricardo, *Economic Essays,* 45.

37. For Keats's use of "speculative" and "speculation," see *Letters of John Keats,* 1:175, 184–85, 223–24, 243, 277, 387; 2:80–81, 115. His aesthetic "speculation" echoes the vocabulary which Burke, in *Reflections on the Revolution in France* (1790; London: Dent, 1967), famously attributed to an ungrounded dissenting imagination opposed to "our nature . . . [and] the great conservatories and magazines of our rights and privileges" (32–33); but Keats is able culturally to accredit it because it lies, paradoxically, at the heart of that establishment's economic self-perpetuation. Burke had consistently inveighed against "paper circulation, not founded on any real money ," and constantly punned on the theoretical and financial senses of "speculation" in his

attack on a revolutionary France "founded . . . upon gaming," in which moral and political "speculation [are] as extensive as life" (187–89). His diatribes against the "fictitious wealth" of paper money are compromised both by his own use of all the resources of fiction to make his case, as Paine and others pointed out, and by the unspoken complicity between economic systems in France and England, which were increasingly founded on sheer confidence. Keats's aesthetic, then, figures the departure from Burkean principle which made practicable Burkean constitutionalism.

38. David Simpson, *Wordsworth and the Figurings of the Real* (London: Macmillan, 1982), 159.

39. Kurt Heinzelman, *The Economics of the Imagination* (Amherst: University of Massachusetts Press, 1980), 133.

40. [John Wilson Croker], *The Life, Adventures, & Serious Remonstrances of a Scottish Guinea Note, Containing a Defence of the Scottish System of Banking, and a Reply to the Late Letters of E. Bradwardine Waverly* (Edinburgh, 1826).

41. Karl Niebyl, *Studies in Classical Theories of Money* (New York: Columbia University Press, 1946), 164; Levinson, *Keats's Life of Allegory*, 288–89 and chap. 6. passim.

42. Marc Shell, *Money, Language, and Thought: Literary and Philosophical Economies from the Medieval to the Modern Era* (Berkeley: University of California Press, 1982), 14. Levinson, reading the character Lamia as "the money form," invokes support from the way in which G. Simmel's "understanding of the renunciation inherent in the money form leads him to associate money with art" and argues that "Simmel's definition of art is also a definition of the art we associate with the Romantic period" (*Keats's Life of Allegory*, 295–96).

43. *Letters of John Keats*, 2:167.

44. See Marilyn Butler's chapter in *Romantics, Rebels, and Reactionaries* (Oxford: Oxford University Press, 1981); Nicholas Roe, *Keats and the Culture of Dissent;* Jeffrey Cox, *Poetry and Politics in the Cockney School;* Ian Jack, *Keats and the Mirror of Art* (Oxford: Oxford University Press, 1967). On the radical potential within Della Cruscan poetry, see J. J. McGann, *The Poetics of Sensibility* (Oxford: Oxford University Press, 1996).

Chapter Five

1. The implied author's progressive construction of himself throughout the Waverley novels as a kind of editor, not only of their sources but also of their extraordinary range of dialect and literary register, leaves him a detached spectator like Goethe in Schlegel's review of *Wilhelm Meister.* This literary cosmopolitanism, a dry run for multiculturalism, also lets him become the Scottish synthesizer of a modern national literature described in Robert Crawford's *Devolving English Literature* (Oxford: Clarendon Press, 1992), 129, 133.

2. Sir Walter Scott, *Waverley,* ed. Claire Lamont (Oxford: Oxford University Press, 1986), 5. I have used this edition throughout.

3. Sir Walter Scott, *The Life Of Napoleon Buonaparte, Emperor Of The French. With A Preliminary View Of The French Revolution. By The Author Of "Waverley," &c.,* 9 vols. (Edinburgh: Ballantyne & Co., 1827), 1:63.

4. Georg Lukács, *The Historical Novel,* trans. Hannah Mitchell and Stanley Mitchell (London: Peregrine Books, 1962), 61–63.

5. Katie Trumpener, *Bardic Nationalism: The Romantic Novel and the British Empire* (Princeton: Princeton University Press, 1997), 130.

6. See Ian Duncan's subtle treatment of Scott and romance in "The Romance of Subjection: Scott's *Waverley*," chap. 2 of *Modern Romance and Transformation of the Novel: The Gothic, Scott, Dickens* (Cambridge: Cambridge University Press, 1992).

7. David Kaufmann, *The Business of Common Life* (Baltimore: Johns Hopkins University Press, 1995), 113–14; Ian Duncan, "Romance of Subjection," 62. Reopening "the case of Scott," James Chandler points out that "Scott foregrounds . . . just those questions about historiographical performativity that have recently claimed attention under a variety of slogans and rubrics. . . . Not all subjects have their origins in Scott, needless to say, but the originality of the Waverley novels consists largely in his inventive handling of them" (*England in 1819: The Politics of Literary Culture and the Case of Romantic Historicism* [Chicago: University of Chicago Press, 1998], 307–8).

8. James Hogg, *Memoirs of the Author's Life* (1807) and *Familiar Anecdotes of Sir Walter Scott* (1834), ed. D. S. Mack (Edinburgh: Scottish Academy Press, 1972), 129, 132.

9. *The Journal of Sir Walter Scott,* ed. W. E. K. Anderson (Oxford: Clarendon Press, 1972), 644.

10. See especially, Paul de Man, "Form and Intent in the American New Criticism" and "The Rhetoric of Temporality," both reprinted in *Blindness and Insight,* 2d ed. (London: Methuen, 1983), 20–36, 187–229; and "The Intentional Structure of the Romantic Image, " originally published in French in 1960, revised English version reprinted in *The Rhetoric of Romanticism* (New York: Columbia University Press, 1984). There is a good, accessible exposition of de Man on intentionality in the first chapter of Tilottama Rajan's *Dark Interpreter* (Ithaca, N.Y.: Cornell University Press, 1980).

11. William Hazlitt, "The Spirit of the Age," in *The Complete Works of William Hazlitt* (London: Dent, 1930–33), 11:65. Among recent examinations of "romance," see Rajan, *Dark Interpreter;* and Marjorie Levinson, *Keats's Life of Allegory* (Oxford: Basil Blackwell, 1988).

12. David Hume, *A Treatise on Human Nature* (1739), ed. L. C. Selby-Bigge (1888; Oxford: Oxford University Press, 1968), 264–65.

13. William Wordsworth, *The Prelude: 1799, 1805, 1850,* ed. J. Wordsworth, M. H. Abrams, and S. Gill (New York: Norton, 1979) (1799) 2:473–96; (1805) 2:435–66. I take my view of Hazlitt here to complement David Bromwich's fine account of why "Hazlitt, alone of Burke's rivals, saw that an anti-rhetorical prejudice would be no help in defeating him" (*Hazlitt: The Mind of a Critic* [Oxford: Oxford University Press, 1983], 292–96).

14. See Gary J. Handwerk, *Irony and Ethics in Narrative: From Schlegel to Lacan* (New Haven: Yale University Press, 1985), 15.

15. Revisionism is usually described as starting with Alfred Cobban's inaugural lecture as Professor of French History at London University, "The Myth of the French Revolution" (1955), expanded as *The Social Interpretation of the French Revolution* (Cambridge: Cambridge University Press, 1964). Cobban's work is still abrasive enough to remain the presiding idea of more recent studies, like William Doyle's *Oxford Book of the French Revolution* (Oxford: Clarendon Press, 1989); and Simon Schama's *Citizens* (London: Viking, 1989). Henri Lefebvre, Albert Soboul, and Claude Mazauric were the main targets for the brilliant French revisionist François Furet. Marxist reformulations rather than defenses of the idea of the "bourgeois" Revolution are propounded in G. Comminel's *Rethinking the French Revolution, Marxism and the Revisionist Challenge* (London: Verso, 1987). There are useful general summaries and introductions to this vast area of historiography going back, after all, to Tocqueville and Michelet, in the

first chapter of Doyle's *Origins of the French Revolution* (Oxford: Clarendon Press, 1980); and in T. W. Blanning's *The French Revolution: Aristocrats versus Bourgeois* (London: Macmillan, 1987).

16. Doyle, *Origins,* 210, 213; see also Schama, *Citizens,* 62, 116.

17. François Furet, *Interpreting the French Revolution,* trans. Elbourg Forster (Cambridge: Cambridge University Press, 1981), 46; see Blanning, *French Revolution,* 41–42. In his review of Carlyle's *The French Revolution,* John Stuart Mill attributes Carlyle's success to "showing" rather than "reasoning." Mill worries, though, that Carlyle's spectacular epic power will replace entirely inductive reasoning from general principles (*London and Westminster Review* 27, no. 10 [July 1837]: 27, 48). In his recent book on the subject of eighteenth-century spectacle, *Realizations: Narrative, Pictorial, and Theatrical Arts in Nineteenth-Century England* (Princeton, N.J : Princeton University Press, 1983), Martin Meisel likens Carlyle to Scott and argues that "Carlyle's protagonist is the people as such," therefore, we might add, Rousseau's unrepresentable general will and so a moving force which Carlyle must strive to let us experience immediately. From Meisel's discussion it emerges that what Carlyle *can* represent is just this dilemma for representation: so a reality experienced in his undistanced way becomes one which we readers experience as if we were thrust into a play. Carlyle's realism, if we try to understand it through conventional oppositions of life and art, or spectacle and action, becomes self-defeating. "It is perhaps," concludes Meisel, "only the reflective irony that keeps the style sane" (212–13).

18. In "Telling It Like a Story: The French Revolution as Narrative" (*Studies in Romanticism* 28, no. 3 [fall 1989]: 345–46, 350–52), Marilyn Butler has pointed out that Burke's "plot" *is* to foreclose other possible narratives of the Revolution and that our postmodern use of narrative to unseat philosophical seriousness therefore connives at this pessimism, denying us academic critics and historians a voice as powerful as Burke's. In this chapter I try to keep visible the Tory condemnation of the Revolution as an event undermining all kinds of historiography.

19. In John O. Hayden, ed., *Scott: The Critical Heritage* (London: Routledge & Kegan Paul, 1970), 78.

20. Darline Gay Levy, Harriet Branson Applethwaite, and Mary Durham Johnson, eds. *Women in Revolutionary Paris, 1789–1795: Selected Documents, Translated with Notes and Commentary* (Urbana: University of Illinois Press, 1979).

21. Ina Ferris, *The Achievement of Literary Authority: Gender, History, and the Waverley Novels* (Ithaca, N.Y.: Cornell University Press, 1991), 60.

22. *The Letters of Sir Walter Scott,* ed. H. J. C. Grierson (London: Constable & Co., 1935), 11:455.

23. *Journal,* 656; see also Edgar Johnson, *Sir Walter Scott—The Great Unknown* (London: Hamish Hamilton, 1970), 2:117–18.

24. *Letters of Sir Walter Scott,* 8:376.

25. Quoted by John Prebble in *The King's Jaunt: George IV in Scotland, August 1822* (London: Fontana, 1989), 206. Prebble's polemical account effectively juxtaposes actual contemporary radical disturbances and the Highland Clearances with the make-believe Jacobitism of George's visit. See also Basil C. Skinner, "Scott as Pageant-Master—The Royal Visit of 1822," in *Scott: Bicentenary Essays,* ed. Alan Bell (Edinburgh: Scottish Academic Press, 1973), 231–32; for a more general and witty account of the fraudulent "tartanizing," as J. G. Lockhart called it, of Scotland, see Hugh Trevor-Roper, "The Invention of Tradition: The Highland Tradition of Scotland," in *The*

Invention of Tradition, ed. E. Hobsbawm and T. Ranger (Cambridge: Cambridge University Press, 1983), 15–43.

26. Jonathan Clark, *English Society 1688–1832* (Cambridge: Cambridge University Press, 1985), 143; *Revolution and Rebellion* (Cambridge: Cambridge University Press, 1986), 111–16; James Boswell, *The Life of Samuel Johnson,* rev. ed., ed. D. Fleeman (Oxford: Oxford University Press, 1970), 305. Scott's most explicit description of the "public confusion" caused by the alliance of Covenanting and Jacobite interests around the time of the Union of the Parliaments is in chapter 1 of *The Black Dwarf.* Hogg's version of this troubled period is given in his novel *Confessions of a Justified Sinner* (1824).

27. Scott, *Journal,* 28, 245, 678.

28. This might explain the otherwise puzzlingly religious orientation of the impression Scott gave to Hogg that "he was always keeping a sharp look out on the progress of enthusiasm in religion as a dangerous neighbour [to revolution]" (*Familiar Anecdotes,* 129).

29. E. P. Thompson, *The Making of the English Working-Class* (Harmondsworth: Penguin, 1968), 134.

30. *Letters of Sir Walter Scott,* 1:30; Johnson, 1:102.

31. *Letters of Sir Walter Scott,* 6:234–35, 209).

32. Ibid., 1:35; Marianne Elliott's exhaustive study, *Partners in Revolution: The United Irishmen and France* (New Haven: Yale University Press, 1982), suggests that genuine complicity between the London Corresponding Society (LCS) and the United Irishmen's revolutionary republicans took place much later in 1797–98 as a result of the LCS's decline (173–76, 185–88).

33. *Letters of Sir Walter Scott,* 1:34–35.

34. E. P. Thompson, *Making of the English Working-Class,* 136.

35. See John Gibson Lockhart, *Memoirs of the Life of Sir Walter Scott* (Edinburgh: Constable, 1837–38, 1902), 1:60–61; Thompson, *Making of the English Working-Class,* 140.

36. Furet, *Interpreting the French Revolution,* 48, 54.

37. François Furet, *Marx et La Révolution Française* (Paris: Flammarion, 1986), 98 ff. The use by modern French philosophers, most famously by Bachelard, Althusser, and Foucault, of the idea of epistemological "breaks" to explain philosophical and historical difference can be understood as incidentally attacking the uniqueness claimed by their inherited Revolutionary model of the "break" in a way that, say, Thomas Kuhn's theory of successive scientific paradigms could not. For Althusser on the "reactionary tradition" in French philosophy since the Revolution which he takes his own work (after Jean Hyppolite) to oppose, see *Montesquieu, Rousseau, Marx—Politics and History,* trans. B. Brewster (London: Verso, 1982), 163 ff. J.-F. Lyotard once offered advice, intriguing in this context, to Richard Rorty on the necessity of understanding French thought under "the sign of the crime," the execution of Louis XVI, which necessarily raises questions of legitimacy. Lyotard calls this French discourse "tragic," a description which, I think, catches at his sense of trying to escape an original determination threatening to shape every intellectual departure precisely in proportion to its radicalism or break with the past ("Discussion entre Jean-Francois Lyotard et Richard Rorty," *Critique* [May 1985]: 583–84).

38. I think Kathryn Sutherland implies this interpretation in her excellent introduction to *Redgauntlet* (Oxford: Oxford University Press, 1985), xvii. Hugh Redgauntlet and Charles's other Jacobite supporters fear that he is presumed upon by his

mistress, whom they happily demonize. They thus apparently displace, but in fact reemphasize, their leader's womanish inefficacy. Judith Wilt cleverly retraces this pattern of Jacobite recrimination to the unexpiated original sin with which began the myth of Scottish kings' legitimacy—Robert Bruce's sacrilegious murder of his rival for the crown, the Red Comyn. The feminization of Jacobite rebellions and Pretenders, depriving them of legal entitlement or personage, also damns them with too true a lineage. "The crime being expiated in the feminizing of the last Scottish King is not the degrading of power by association with women but the outlaw grasping of power by the red hand of man" (Judith Wilt, *Secret Leaves: The Novels of Sir Walter Scott* [Chicago: University of Chicago Press, 1985], 129).

39. Compare Jon Klancher's adventurous argument in "Romantic Criticism and the Meanings of the French Revolution," *Studies in Romanticism* 28, no. 3 (fall 1989): 463–91. Klancher gains a perspective from which he can see romantic criticism's vested interest in having " 'English Romanticism' . . . reproduce its own circuitous history of making 'the meanings of the French Revolution' " (491).

Chapter Six

1. *Shelley's Prose, or The Trumpet of a Prophecy,* ed. David Lee Clark (Albuquerque: University of New Mexico Press, 1954), 174. Shelley's French argument against thought as an independent substance is clearest in his "Essay on a Future State," 175–78.

2. *The Holy Family,* in *Karl Marx: Selected Writings,* ed. David McLellan (Oxford: Oxford University Press, 1977), 150.

3. See Ann Thomson, introduction to her translation of *Machine Man and Other Writings* (Cambridge: Cambridge University Press, 1996); and Justin Leiber, introduction to *Man a Machine and Man a Plant,* trans. Richard A. Watson and Maya Rybalka (Indianapolis: Hackett, 1994). See also, Ann Thomson, *Materialism and Society in the Mid-Eighteenth Century: La Mettrie's Discours Preliminaire* (Geneva: Librairie Droz, 1981), part 3. References to La Mettrie will be to the *Oeuvres Philosophiques,* 2 vols., ed. Michel Serres (Paris: Fayard, 1987); followed by references to Thomson's *Machine Man and Other Writings.*

4. Thomson, introduction to *Machine Man,* 3.

5. Thomson, introduction to *Machine Man.* For Rousseau's reputation, see Edmund Duffy, *Rousseau in England: The Context for Shelley's Critique of the Enlightenment* (Berkeley: University of California Press, 1979).

6. For a discussion of the materialism of this view of "difference" see Jay Bernstein's discussion of comparable philosophical turns from idealism in Schelling and Derrida in *Textual Practice* 1, no. 1 (spring 1987): 99–101.

7. Epicurus, "Collections of Maxims," in *Hellenistic Philosophy, Introductory Readings,* trans. Brad Inwood and L. P. Gerson (Indianapolis: Hackett, 1988), 31.

8. All references to Shelley's poems are by line reference to the texts given in *Shelley's Poetry and Prose,* ed. Donald H. Reiman and Sharon B. Powers (New York: Norton, 1977).

9. Timothy Morton, *Shelley and The Revolution in Taste* (Cambridge: Cambridge University Press, 1994).

10. Lucretius, *On the Nature of the Universe,* trans. R. E. Latham, rev. by John Godwin (Harmondsworth: Penguin, 1994), book 5, ll. 55–64. See D. P. Fowler, "Lucretius and

Politics," in Miriam Griffin and Jonathan Barnes, *Philosophia Togata: Essays on Philosophy and Roman Society* (Oxford: Clarendon Press, 1989): "The behaviour of the atoms is not governed by an external law laid down by a divine ruler but is controlled by pacts they have freely entered into. In this respect atomic society is strongly republican" (147).

11. Edward Duffy's major study *Rousseau in England: The Context for Shelley's Critique of the Enlightenment* (Berkeley: University of California Press, 1979) reads Rousseau's self-division as one of genre. He mediates through reverie the different receptions accorded his theoretical and his confessional writings, dialectically working to discredit each other, the autobiography showing the dire consequences of the radical political ideas and the political theory leading readers to expect the worst of the biography. Duffy writes that Shelley "sat down to write a poem that would be a reclamation of Rousseau's work from the corrosive influence of his life and hence a model for the way the benign impulse of the French Revolution ought to be similarly distinguished from its pragmatic failures" (151). I am trying to argue that Shelley's poem opposes seeing Rousseau's life as something to be reclaimed from Enlightenment interests. I believe a materialist, Lucretian reading tries to dissolve "the choice between stances allowed by transference"—which the poem poses for J. E. Hogle (in *Shelley's Process: Radical Transference and the Development of His Major Works* [New York: Oxford University Press, 1988], 340)—by identifying knowledge with its own material production. Better to get away from critical categories of Freudian etiology altogether and opt for a Deleuzean/Guattarian confidence that "There is no difference between what a book talks about and how it is made. . . . the only question is which other machine the literary machine can be plugged into, must be plugged into, in order to work" (Gilles Deleuze and Felix Guattari, *A Thousand Plateaus,* trans. Brian Massumi [London: Athlone Press, 1992], 4). Timothy Morton's *Shelley and the Revolution in Taste* shows the possibilities here. See especially, "Introduction: Prescriptions," 7, passim.

12. All references are to *Matilda,* ed. Pamela Clemit, in *The Novels and Selected Works of Mary Shelley,* vol. 2 (London: William Pickering, 1996).

13. See "The Right to Death," in *The Gaze of Orpheus,* trans. Lydia Davis (Barrytown, N.Y.: Station Hill Press, 1981).

14. *Literary Gazette,* no. 949 (1835): 194. Quoted by Morton Paley in "The Last Man: Apocalypse without Millennium," in *The Other Mary Shelley: Beyond "Frankenstein,"* ed. Audrey Fisch, Anne K. Mellor, and Esther H. Schor (New York: Oxford University Press, 1993), 107–23.

15. Barbara Jane O'Sullivan, "Beatrice in Valperga: A New Cassandra," in *The Other Mary Shelley,* 151. All references to *Valperga* are to the edition edited by Nora Crook as vol. 3 of *The Novels and Selected Works of Mary Shelley.*

16. Lucretius, *De Rerum Natura,* with English translation by W. H. D. Rouse (London: William Heinemann; and Cambridge: Harvard University Press, 1947), 251 n.

17. See Simon Schaffer's placing of Kant's notion of Genius in scientific historical context in "Genius in Romantic Natural Philosophy," in *Romanticism and the Sciences,* ed. Andrew Cunningham and Nicholas Jardine (Cambridge: Cambridge University Press, 1990), 82–101.

18. *Shelley's Prose,* 295.

19. See D. P. Fowler, "Lucretius and Politics," in Griffin and Barnes, *Philosophia Togata,* 120–50, for a good review of the state of scholarship on the subject of Lucretius's

politics. Very helpful also is James H. Nichols, Jr., *Epicurean Moral Philosophy: The De rerum natura of Lucretius* (Ithaca, N.Y.: Cornell University Press, 1976).

Chapter Seven

1. Robert Blake, *The Conservative Party from Peel to Thatcher* (London: Fontana, 1985), 6.

2. Henry St. John, Lord Bolingbroke, *Letters on the Spirit of Patriotism and on the Idea of a Patriot King* (Oxford: Clarendon Press, 1917); Benjamin Disraeli, *Vindication of the English Constitution in a Letter to a Noble and Learned Lord by Disraeli the Younger* (London: Sanders & Otley, 1835), 185–86.

3. Roger Scruton, *The Meaning of Conservatism* (Harmondsworth: Penguin, 1980), 15. Scruton's praise of Hegel comes from the introduction to his *Conservative Texts: An Anthology* (London: Macmillan, 1991), 9.

4. Ian Gilmour, *Inside Right: A Study of Conservatism* (London: Hutchinson, 1977), 60.

5. Edmund Burke, *Reflections on the Revolution in France*, ed. J. G. A. Pocock (Indianapolis: Hackett, 1987), 66 (my emphasis).

6. Norman Gash, *Lord Liverpool: The Life and Political Career of Robert Banks Jenkinson, Second Earl of Liverpool, 1770–1828* (London: Weidenfeld & Nicolson, 1984), 5.

7. Disraeli, *Vindication*, 185–86, 192.

8. William Waldegrave, *The Binding of Leviathan: Conservatism and the Future* (London: Hamish Hamilton, 1978), 56

9. *Emma*, 351. References to Jane Austen's novels are to the following editions: *Love and Friendship and Other Early Works* (London: Women's Press, 1978); and *Lady Susan / The Watsons / Sanditon*, ed. Margaret Drabble (Harmondsworth: Penguin, 1974). All other references are to the new Penguin editions: *Persuasion*, ed. Gillian Beer (1998); *Northanger Abbey*, ed. Marilyn Butler (1995); *Sense and Sensibility*, ed. Ros Ballaster (1995); *Pride and Prejudice*, ed. Vivien Jones (1996); *Mansfield Park*, ed. Kathryn Sutherland (1996); *Emma*, ed. Fiona Stafford (1996).

10. Roger Gard, *Jane Austen's Novels: The Art of Clarity* (New Haven: Yale University Press, 1992), 43.

11. Toril Moi, *Simone de Beauvoir: The Making of an Intellectual Woman* (Oxford: Basil Blackwell, 1994), 4, 125–48. For the idea of the "proper" and "professional" lady of Austen's era, see Mary Poovey's classic, *The Proper Lady and the Woman Writer: Ideology and Style in the Works of Mary Wollstonecraft, Mary Shelley, and Jane Austen* (Chicago: University of Chicago Press, 1984); and Catherine Gallagher, *Nobody's Story: The Vanishing Acts of Women Writers in the Marketplace* (Berkeley: University of California Press, 1994).

12. Scruton, *Meaning of Conservatism*, 36.

13. Jacques Derrida, "Structure, Sign and Play," in *Writing and Difference*, trans. Alan Bass (Chicago: University of Chicago Press), 283. See the discussion by Vincent Descombes in *Modern French Philosophy* (Cambridge: Cambridge University Press, 1980), chap. 4.

14. Gilmour, *Inside Right*, 192.

15. *Jane Austen's Letters*, ed. Deirdre Le Faye, 3d ed. (Oxford: Oxford University Press, 1995).

16. Adam Phillips, *On Flirtation* (London: Faber, 1994), xii.

17. See Roger Sales, *Jane Austen and Representations of Regency England* (London: Routledge, 1994).

18. Disraeli, *Vindication*, 173.

19. Linda Colley, *Britons: Forging the Nation, 1707–1837* (London: Pimlico, 1992).

20. Quoted in Bruce Coleman, *Conservatism and the Conservative Party in Nineteenth-Century Britain* (London: Edward Arnold, 1988), 42 n.

21. Georg Simmel, *On Women, Sexuality and Love*, trans. Gary Oakes (New Haven: Yale University Press, 1984).

22. Scruton, *Meaning of Conservatism*, 11.

23. Scruton, *Conservative Texts*, 3.

24. Ludwig Wittgenstein, *Philosophical Investigations*, trans. G. E. M. Anscombe (Oxford: Basil Blackwell, 1963), par. 201.

25. Simmel, *On Women, Sexuality and Love*, 134.

26. Burke, *Reflections on the Revolution in France*, 66.

27. Alasdair MacIntyre, *After Virtue: A Study in Moral Theory*, 2d ed. (London: Duckworth, 1985), 185. Austen's political inventiveness is much more economically and tellingly summarized than here at the end of Vivien Jones's introduction to *Pride and Prejudice:* "Austen's post-revolutionary achievement in *Pride and Prejudice* is to put Wollstonecraft's revolutionary femininity at the service of the Burkean 'family party' by writing what is still one of the most perfect, most pleasurable and most subtle—and therefore, perhaps, most dangerously persuasive—of romantic love stories" (xxvii).

Chapter Eight

1. *The Friend*, no. 17 (14 December 1809), ed. Barbara E. Rooke, *The Collected Coleridge*, vol. 4: book 2, p. 230.

2. J. G. A. Pocock, *The Machiavellian Moment: Florentine Political Thought and the Atlantic Republican Tradition* (Princeton: Princeton University Press, 1973), 63–64, 551.

3. Thomas Moore, *Poetical Works*, ed. A. D. Godley (London: Oxford University Press, 1910), 133–37.

4. *The Prelude 1799, 1805, 1850*, ed. Jonathan Wordsworth, M. H. Abrams, and Stephen Gill (New York: Norton, 1979), 1805, 9:121–25. Typical of Beaupuy is that "Man he loved / As man" (313–14), a mode of address he shares with the presumably similarly "patriot" poet of the "Preface" to *Lyrical Ballads?*

5. Samuel Taylor Coleridge, *Poems*, ed. John Beer, new ed. (London: Everyman, 1993), 86, 90.

6. William Hazlitt, *A View of the English Stage* (1818), in *The Complete Works of William Hazlitt* (London: Dent, 1930–33), 5:233.

7. Linda Colley, *Britons: Forging the Nation, 1707–1837* (London: Pimlico, 1992), 336.

8. *The Poems of John Dryden*, ed. James Kinsley (Oxford: Clarendon Press, 1958), 4:153–54.

9. Zera Fink, "Wordsworth and the English Republican Tradition," *Journal of English and Germanic Philology* 47 (1948): 107–26; Duncan Wu, *Wordsworth's Reading, 1770–1799* (Cambridge: Cambridge University Press, 1993), 96–97.

10. James Boswell, *Life of Johnson*, ed. R. W. Chapman, new ed. corrected by J. D. Fleeman (London: Oxford University Press, 1998), 615, 189.

11. Bolingbroke, *Political Writings,* ed. David Armitrage (Cambridge: Cambridge University Press, 1997), 251.

12. J. C. E. Hill, *Collected Essays,* vol. 1, *Writing and Revolution in 17th-Century England* (Brighton: Harvester Press, 1985), 226, 25.

13. Hill, *Writing and Revolution;* M. Stocker, *Politics and Poetry in Restoration England* (Cambridge: Harvard University Press, 1975).

14. All references to Marvell are to the Margoliouth (3d) edition of *The Poems and Letters* (Oxford: Oxford University Press, 1927); and the Smith edition of *The Rehearsal Transpros'd* (Oxford: Oxford University Press, 1971).

15. Nigel Smith, *Literature and Revolution in England, 1640–1660* (New Haven: Yale University Press, 1994), 278.

16. "And that slaughter to the Nation / Shall steam up like inspiration, / Eloquent, oracular; / A volcano heard afar" ("The Mask of Anarchy," in *Shelley's Poetry and Prose,* ed. Donald H. Reiman and Sharon B. Powers [New York: Norton, 1977], p. 310, ll. 360–65).

17. Bolingbroke, *Idea of a Patriot King,* in *Letters on the Spirit of Patriotism and on the Idea of a Patriot King,* 85, 251.

18. Lord Byron, *The Complete Poetical Works,* ed. Jerome J. McGann (Oxford: Clarendon Press, 1986), 5:6.

19. John Milton, *Paradise Lost,* ed. Alastair Fowler (London: Longman, 1971), 11:829–38.

20. Edmund Burke, *Reflections on the Revolution in France,* ed. J. G. A. Pocock (Indianapolis: Hackett, 1987), 44, 75.

21. "Milton," in *Lives of the English Poets,* ed. G. B. Hill (Oxford: Clarendon Press, 1905), 1:163.

22. David Norbrook uncovers a contemporary tradition of reading sublimity into Cromwellian politics which brings a new political self and its destruction into rhetorical relationship in "Marvell's Horatian Ode," in *Literature and the English Civil War,* ed. Thomas Healy and Jonathan Sawday (Cambridge: Cambridge University Press: 1990), 147–70—"[the revolution's] greatest defender and its destroyer might be one and the same man" (164).

23. See, for example, Frederick Burwick's argument in "What the Mower Does to the Meadow: Action and Reflection in Wordsworth and Marvell" (in *Milton, the Metaphysicals, and Romanticism,* ed. Lisa Low and Anthony John Harding [Cambridge: Cambridge University Press, 1994]), that Wordsworth's "main difficulty may well stem from his very act of prescinding the poetry of political consciousness and treating it as if it were an essentially different kind of poetry. For Marvell, as I will try to show in a brief examination of the Mower Poems, there is no such difference" (172). Prescinded here, though, appears to be Wordsworth's use of history, in particular his transformations of the patriot tradition.

24. Colley, *Britons,* 5.

25. Sir Walter Scott, "The Lay of the Last Minstrel," in *The Poetical Works of Sir Walter Scott, with the Author's Introductions and Notes,* ed. J. Logie Robertson (London: Oxford University Press, 1940), 39. Richard Price's epochal sermon preached at the Old Jewry in 1789 supporting the French Revolution, was, of course, "A Discourse on the Love of Our Country." Christine Gerrard's *The Patriot Opposition to Walpole: Politics, Poetry, and National Myth, 1725–1742* (Oxford: Clarendon Press, 1994) is an excellent attempt to disentangle the main meanings of patriotism in the preceding eighteenth

century, as is also Brean Hammond's *Pope and Bolingbroke: A Study of Friendship and Influence* (Columbia: University of Missouri Press, 1984), esp. chap. 8, "The Common Language."

26. *The Letters of John Keats, 1814–1821,* ed. Hyder E. Rollins (Cambridge: Cambridge University Press, 1958), 1:396–97.

Chapter Nine

1. I discuss in detail the intellectual history of this indictment in the introduction, above. Its best-known revivalists are Jerome McGann's new historicism and Paul de Man's deconstruction. See, principally, McGann, *The Romantic Ideology* (Chicago: University of Chicago Press, 1983); *The Beauty of Inflections* (Oxford: Clarendon Press, 1988); and *Social Values and Poetic Acts* (Cambridge: Harvard University Press, 1988). Paul de Man, *The Rhetoric of Romanticism (New* York Columbia University Press, 1984); "Sign and Symbol in Hegel's Aesthetics," *Critical Inquiry* 8, no. 3 (spring 1982): 509–13; "Hegel on the Sublime," in *Displacement: Derrida and After,* ed. M. Krupnick (Bloomington: Indiana University Press, 1983), 139–52; and "Phenomenality and Materiality in Kant," in *Hermeneutics: Questions and Prospects,* ed. G. Shapiro and Alan Sica (Amherst: University of Massachusetts Press, 1984), 121–44. On ideology in general, see Howard Williams, *Concepts of Ideology* (Brighton, England: Wheatsheaf, 1988), and, especially useful here since it supplements his major work on romantic ideology *(The Ideology of the Aesthetic),* Terry Eagleton's *Ideology: An Introduction* (London: Verso,1991). The placing of an imagination creative of ideology at the center of understanding, or of figurality at the heart of discourse, recalls Coleridge but finds support today. See John B. Thompson, *Studies in Ideology* (Cambridge: Polity Press,1984). Striking studies of the elided articulation of political issues within romantic ideology, alive to European studies from Gramsci to Althusser, are to be found in the work of Marjorie Levinson, Alan Liu, David Simpson, and others.

2. Paul de Man, "Intentional Structure of the Romantic Image," in *The Rhetoric of Romanticism,* 6.

3. On the romantic construction of a "literary absolute," see P. Lacoue-Labarthe and J.-L. Nancy, *The Literary Absolute: The Theory of Literature in German Romanticism,* trans. Phillip Barnard and Cheryl Lester (Albany: SUNY Press, 1988).

4. L. Althusser, "Ideology and Ideological State Apparatuses," in *Essays on Ideology* (London: Verso, 1984), 33; Alasdair MacIntyre, *Against the Self-Images of the Age: Essays on Sociology and Philosophy* (London: Duckworth, 1971), 11.

5. H. Taine, *Origines de la France contemporaine: la régime moderne,* 5th ed. (Paris: 1898), 2:219–20; also quoted in Jorge Larrain, *The Concept of Ideology* (London: Hutchinson, 1979), 215. Kenneth Minogue, in *Alien Powers: The Pure Theory of Ideology* (London: Weidenfeld & Nicolson, 1985), warns against histories of ideology that "in some measure [confound] the history of an idea with the history of a word. The real source of the excitement generated by the idea of ideology lies elsewhere, and this is the reason why Marx tends to be so dismissive of eighteenth-century socialists who are, in other respects, so closely related to both his projects and his enthusiasm" (39). I would argue that to appreciate the reasons for dismissal you have to understand the history of both idea and word.

6. [Marie-Henri Beyle] Stendhal, *Love,* trans. G. Sale and S. Sale (Harmondsworth: Penguin, 1975), 45.

7. Angela Carter, *The Sadeian Woman: An Exercise in Cultural History* (London: Virago, 1979).

8. T. Adorno and M. Horkheimer, *Dialectic of Enlightenment*, trans. John Cumming (London: Verso, 1979), 117.

9. Jane Gallop, *Intersections: A Reading of Sade with Bataille, Blanchot, and Klossowski* (Lincoln: University of Nebraska Press, 1981), 3–4, 115–16.

10. David Hume, "On Miracles," in *Essays Moral, Political, and Literary*, ed. T. H. Green and T. H. Grose (London: Longmans, Green, 1875); Friedrich Jacobi, *David Hume über den Glauben, oder Idealismus und Realismus* (1787), a text which, like Jacobi's letters two years earlier to Moses Mendelssohn *Über die Lehre des Spinoza*, are usually read in the context of the *Pantheismusstreit*, rather than to shed light on Hume's ambivalences. Isaiah Berlin is good on the Humean paradoxes involved in *Against the Current: Essays in the History of Ideas* (Oxford: Oxford University Press, 1981), 181. Alasdair MacIntyre adds to the Humean picture when he points out the ironies of a similar, native allegiance between the Scottish Evangelicals and Secessionists, who preceded Hume, and philosophical skepticism in *Whose Justice? Which Rationality?* (London: Duckworth, 1988), 243 ff.

11. K. Marx, "The German Ideology," in *Selected Writings*, ed. D. McLellan (Oxford: Oxford University Press, 1977), 160.

12. Donatien Alphonse François [Marquis de] Sade, *Justine, Philosophy in the Bedroom, and Other Writings*. ed. and trans. Richard Seaver and Austryn Wainhouse (London: Arrow Books, 1991), 331.

13. Roland Barthes, *Sade, Fourier, Loyola*, trans. R. Miller (London: Jonathan Cape, 1977), 31; Barthes, "The Metaphor of the Eye," trans. J. A. Underwood, in G. Bataille, *Story of the Eye* (Harmondsworth: Penguin, 1982), 126. Marcel Henaff gives a lucid account of the Sadeian economy of loss and its peculiar kind of romantic recuperation: "Si le cri de la victime consacre une impossibilité du parler, le cri du libertin gaspille somptuairement les reserves du langage. En passant dans le cri la jouissance devient asymbolique [i. e., not of the Lacanian symbolic order, so symbolic of the extradiscursive in a romantic sense] mais ce blanc de signification, cette rupture de l'ordre sont le luxe de la dépense delirante que s'offre la maitrise discursive" (*Sade, l'invention du corps libertin* [Vendome: Presses Universitaires de France, 1978], 218).

14. F. Nietzsche, *The Will to Power*, trans. W. Kaufmann and R. J. Hollingdale (New York: Random House, 1968), par. 253.

15. Stendhal, *De l'amour* (Paris: Garnier-Flammarion, 1965), 43. The Penguin translation unaccountably renders the French as plural.

16. Nietzsche, *Will to Power*, par. 9.

17. Marx, "German Ideology," 168.

18. Nietzsche, *Will to Power*, par. 6.

19. Ibid., pars. 95, 253, 422.

20. See *Translation Of A Letter From Monsieur De Tracy, Member Of The French National Assembly, To Mr. Burke, In Answer To His Remarks On The French Revolution* (London, 1790). Thomas Jefferson's letter is prefaced to *A Treatise Of Political Economy To Which Is Prefixed A Supplement To A Preceding Work On The Understanding; or, Elements Of Ideology By The Count Destutt De Tracy, Translation Edited By Thomas Jefferson* [1817], Reprints of Economic Classics (New York: Augustus M. Kelley, 1970).

21. Destutt de Tracy, *De l'amour* (Paris: Société d'editions "Les Belles Lettres," 1926), xliv.

22. Ibid., 59–60; de Tracy, *A Treatise Of Political Economy,* 5. Jacques Derrida, in *The Archaeology of the Frivolous: Reading Condillac* (trans. John Leavey [Lincoln: University of Nebraska Press, 1987]), argues that, in the case of Condillac, Enlightenment philosophy's dichotomy is held together by a biologism "which develops sensationalism into semiotism" (46). Otherwise the frivolity of which Derrida thinks Condillac provides the archaeology "consists in being satisfied with tokens. It originates with the . . . empty, void, friable, useless signifier" (118). See also Brian William Head, *Ideology and Social Science: Destutt de Tracy and French Liberalism* (Dordrecht: Martinus Nijhoff, 1985), 27, 40, 54, for discussion of Tracy's empiricist corrective to Cartesian linguistics

23. Destutt de Tracy, *Eléments d'idéologie,* 2 vols. (Paris: Librairie Philosophique, J. Vrin, 1970), 1:xxiii–iv. For a placing of Tracy's praise of the Port Royal grammarians within a history of philosophers who combine (Condillac) or supplement Arnauld's and Lancelot's work with empiricism, see Antoine Arnauld and Claude Lancelot, *The Port Royal Grammar,* trans. J. Rieux and B. E. Rollin (The Hague: Mouton, 1975), 25–27.

24. Marx, *Selected Writings,* 149–55, 179.

25. Stendhal, *De l'amour,* 119.

26. Ibid., 325–26.

27. Marx, *The German Ideology,* 165.

28. Carter, *The Sadeian Woman,* 19.

29. Barthes, *Sade, Fourier, Loyola,* 134.

Chapter Ten

1. Georges Bataille, *The Accursed Share: An Essay on General Economy,* 2 vols., trans. Robert Hurley (New York: Zone Books, 1988), 1:9.

2. Jürgen Habermas, *The Philosophical Discourse of Modernity,* trans. Frederick Lawrence (Cambridge: Polity Press, 1987), 286–87.

3. Jürgen Habermas, *Postmetaphysical Thinking: Philosophical Essays,* trans. William Mark Hohengarten (Cambridge: MIT Press, 1992), 47.

4. *Kant's Political Writings,* ed. Hans Reiss, trans. H. B. Nisbet (Cambridge: Cambridge University Press, 1977), 176.

5. I. Kant, *The Conflict of the Faculties (Der Streit der Fakultaten),* trans. Mary J. Gregor (Lincoln: University of Nebraska Press, 1992), 53.

6. See in Germany, for example, Manfred Frank's *Der Unendliche Mangel an Sein: Schelling's Hegelkritik und die Anfange der marxischen Dialektik* (Frankfurt am Main: Suhrkamp, 1975). For English developments of Frank's thought see Andrew Bowie, *Aesthetics and Subjectivity* (Manchester: Manchester University Press, 1992); and *Schelling and Modern European Philosophy: An Introduction* (London: Routledge, 1993); as well as Peter Dews's "Deconstruction and German Idealism: A Response to Rodolphe Gasché's 'The Tain of the Mirror,' " in *The Limits of Disenchantment: Essays on Contemporary European Philosophy* (London: Verso, 1995), 115–51.

7. Jürgen Habermas, *Postmetaphysical Thinking,* 48.

8. Michel Foucault, *The Order of Things,* trans. Alan Sheridan (London: Tavistock, 1970), 262, 300. See Jo McDonagh, *De Quincey's Disciplines* (Oxford: Clarendon Press, 1994).

9. See de Man's materialist transvaluations of Kant's terminology in "Phenomenality and Materiality in Kant," "Kant's Materialism," and "Kant and Schiller," in *Aes-*

thetic Ideology. 70–91, 119–28, 129–63. Frances Ferguson, *Solitude and the Sublime*, 154; Rodolphe Gasché, *The Wild Card of Reading: On Paul de Man* (Cambridge: Harvard University Press, 1998), 272 n. 10. Ferguson has wonderfully lucid summaries of the de Man agon, suggesting its motivation: the material language has to be forever new, noumenal as I describe it, or prelinguistic as she says, in order to preclude all the ways other materialisms are not necessarily meaningless *because* they are material (163–64).

10. See Jürgen Habermas, "Philosophy as Stand-in and Interpreter," in *Moral Consciousness and Communicative Action*, trans. Christian Lenhardt and Shierry Weber Nicholsen (Cambridge: Polity Press, 1990), 15–16.

11. Ibid., 19.

12. Thomas Paine, *Political Writings*, ed. Bruce Kuklick (Cambridge: Cambridge University Press, 1989), 137.

13. James Harrington, *The Oceana and Other Works of James Harrington, with an Account of His Life by John Toland* (1700); see J. G. A. Pocock's edition of *Harrington's Political Works* (Cambridge: Cambridge University Press, 1977), 141–43. William Wordsworth, *Guide to the Lakes*, ed. Ernest de Selincourt (Oxford: Oxford University Press, 1977), 67–68; see Nigel Leask's discussion of Commonwealth influences on Wordsworth and Coleridge in *The Politics of Imagination in Coleridge's Critical Thought* (London: Macmillan, 1988), part 1.

14. Paine, *Political Writings*, 7.

15. As mentioned earlier, in 1789 Richard Price preached an epochal sermon at the Old Jewry supporting the French Revolution. The sermon was entitled, "A Discourse on the Love of Our Country."

16. Gerard Winstanley, "The True Levellers Standard Advanced," in *The Law of Freedom and Other Writings*, ed. Christopher Hill (Harmondsworth: Penguin, 1973), 79.

17. Morton D. Paley, *The Continuing City: William Blake's Jerusalem* (Oxford: Clarendon Press, 1983), 6–7.

18. Mary Wollstonecraft, *Vindication of the Rights of Woman*, ed. Miriam Kramnick (Harmondsworth: Penguin, 1982), 103.

19. [Elizabeth Hamilton], *Memoirs of Modern Philosophers, in Three Volumes* (London: G. G. & J. Robertson, 1800), 1:198.

20. Elizabeth Hamilton, *A Series Of Popular Essays, Illustrative Of Principles Essentially Connected With The Improvement Of The Understanding, The Imagination, And The Heart* (Edinburgh: Manners & Miller, 1813).

21. Michele Le Doeuff, *The Philosophical Imaginary*, trans. Colin Gordon (London: Athlone, 1989), 111.

22. Angela Leighton, *Victorian Women Poets: Writing against the Heart* (New York: Harvester Wheatsheaf, 1992), 299; J. J. McGann, *The Poetics of Sensibility* (Oxford: Clarendon Press, 1996).

23. Quoted with approval by Peter W. Trinder, in *Mrs. Hemans* (Cardiff: University of Wales Press, 1984), 2.

24. Norma Clarke, *Ambitious Heights: Writing, Friendship, Love—The Jewsbury Sisters, Felicia Hemans, and Jane Welsh Carlyle* (London: Routledge, 1990), 65.

25. William Hazlitt, *Liber Amoris, or The New Pygmalion* (London: Hogarth Press, 1985).

26. Michael Neve, introduction to *Liber Amoris*, xii.

27. *The Letters of William Hazlitt*, ed. Sikes, Bonner, and Lahey (New York: New York

University Press, 1978), 269. See the interesting attempt at a postmodern reading by Kurt M. Koenigsburger in "Liberty, Libel, and *Liber Amoris:* Hazlitt on Sovereignty and Death," *Studies in Romanticism* 38 (summer 1999): "The death by libel to which Hazlitt subjects himself cannot be redeemed by being understood as a means of maintaining psychic integrity or as a representative part of the English confessional tradition. Only the 'law of the law' can be gestured towards, the illogic of Hazlitt's actions serving to expose, over a century in advance of Bataille . . ." (309).

28. *The Poems of Anna Laetitia Barbauld,* ed. William McCarthy and Elizabeth Kraft (Athens: University of Georgia Press, 1994), 27.

29. Ibid., 174–76.

30. Ibid., 152–61.

31. *Quarterly Review* 7 (1812): 309–13.

32. William Keach, "A Regency Prophecy and the End of Anna Barbauld's Career," *Studies in Romanticism* 33, no. 4 (winter 1994): 577. James Chandler provides an excellent discussion of the complexities of the stadial view of history Barbauld would have inherited from the Scottish Enlightenment in *England in 1819.* Particularly helpful here is his highlighting of her posthumously published letters "On the Uses of History," which reinforces her relativism (*"When* is a relative term") and her insistence on a global perspective with which to understand "One consoling idea . . . [our] tendency towards amelioration" (*A Legacy For Young Ladies, Consisting Of Miscellaneous Pieces In Prose And Verse By The Late Mrs. Barbauld* [London: 1826], 148, 134).

33. Kant, *Conflict of the Faculties,* 153.

34. Kant, ibid., 169.

35. L. Goldmann, *Immanuel Kant,* trans. Robert Black (London: New Left Books, 1971).

Chapter Eleven

1. For a good discussion of chiasmus in Kantian aesthetics, see Elizabeth M. Wilkinson and L. A. Willoughby, introduction to *On the Aesthetic Education of Man, in a Series of Letters,* by Friedrich Schiller, ed. and trans. E. M. Wilkinson and L. A. Willoughby (Oxford: Clarendon Press, 1967).

2. "Universal History and Cultural Differences," trans. David Macey, in *The Lyotard Reader,* ed. Andrew Benjamin (Oxford: Blackwell, 1989), 315–16; translation slightly modified. For Lyotard's fuller, earlier discussion of the tense-logic of the sublime, see "Answering the Question: What Is Postmodernism?" (1982), trans. Regis Durand, in *The Postmodern Condition: A Report on Knowledge,* trans. Geoff Bennington and Brian Massumi (Manchester: Manchester University Press, 1984), 71–82. David Ingram helpfully distinguishes "The Postmodern Kantianism of Arendt and Lyotard," in *Judging Lyotard,* ed. Andrew Benjamin (London: Routledge, 1992), 119–45. A balanced overview of different politicizations of Kantian aesthetics is given in Martin Jay's " 'The Aesthetic Ideology' as Ideology: Or What Does It Mean to Aestheticize Politics?" in *Force Fields: Between Intellectual History and Cultural Critique* (New York: Routledge, 1993), 71–84.

3. I discuss traditions of reading Dorothy Wordsworth at greater length in the introduction to *Dorothy Wordsworth: Selections from the Journals,* ed. Paul Hamilton (London: William Pickering, 1992), ix–xxii.

4. See the discussion of "Georgic" in Michael Rosenthal, *Constable, the Painter and*

his Landscape (New Haven: Yale University Press, 1983); John Barrell, *Poetry, Language, Politics* (Manchester: Manchester University Press, 1988) and *The Birth of Pandora* (London: Macmillan, 1992); Kurt Heinzelman, "The Cult of Domesticity: Dorothy and William at Grasmere," in *Romanticism and Feminism,* ed. Anne K. Mellor (Bloomington: Indiana University Press, 1988).

5. Dorothy Wordsworth, *Journals,* 99.

6. John Barrell, "The Uses of Dorothy: 'The Language of the Sense' in 'Tintern Abbey,' " in *Poetry, Language, and Politics* (Manchester: Manchester University Press, 1988), 137–68.

7. All references to Friedrich Schlegel's *Athenaeum Fragments* and *Critical Fragments* are from *Lucinde and the Fragments,* trans. Peter Firchow (Minneapolis: University of Minnesota Press, 1971); further references are cited in the text as *AF* or *CF* followed by the number of the fragment.

8. Peter Sloterdijk, *Critique of Cynical Reason,* trans. M. Eldred (London: Verso, 1988), xxx.

9. Ibid., xxxi.

10. C. Norris, *Spinoza and the Origins of Modern Critical Theory* (Oxford: Blackwell, 1991), 21–23.

11. Sloterdijk, *Critique of Cynical Reason,* 21 n. The third estate *is* everything according to Sieyes, and so the "all-or-nothing-logic" is still there.

Chapter Twelve

1. Søren Kierkegaard, *Fear and Trembling,* ed. and trans. Howard V. Hong and Edna H. Hong (Princeton: Princeton University Press, 1983), 53.

2. James Chandler, *England in 1819: The Politics of Literary Culture and the Case of Romantic Historicism* (Chicago: University of Chicago Press, 1998), 35–36.

3. Jürgen Habermas, *The Structural Transformation of the Public Sphere: An Inquiry into a Category of Bourgeois Society,* trans. Thomas Burger (Cambridge: Polity Press, 1989).

4. Geoff Eley, "Nations, Publics, and Political Cultures," in *Habermas and the Public Sphere,* ed. Craig Calhoun (Cambridge: MIT Press, 1992), 289–340.

5. Seyla Benhabib, "Models of Public Space: Hannah Arendt, the Liberal Tradition, and Jürgen Habermas," in *Habermas and the Public Sphere,* ed. Craig Calhoun (Cambridge, Mass: MIT Press, 1992), 93.

6. Nancy Fraser, "Rethinking the Public Sphere: A Contribution to the Critique of Actually Existing Democracy," in *Habermas and the Public Sphere,* ed. Calhoun, 109–43.

7. His most recent collection of essays published in English (1998) enjoys the title, so apt for my purposes here, of *Including the Other.*

8. See Jürgen Habermas, *Moral Consciousness and Communicative Action,* trans. C. Lenhardt and S. W. Nicholsen (Cambridge: Polity Press, 1990), 1–21; see also chap. 10 above.

9. Jean-François Lyotard, *The Postmodern Condition: A Report on Knowledge,* trans. Geoff Bennington and Brian Massumi (Manchester: Manchester University Press, 1984), 73.

10. J.-F. Lyotard and J. L. Thébaud, *Just Gaming,* trans. W. Godzich (Minneapolis: University of Minnesota Press, 1985), 82.

11. Ibid., 11. For a good discussion of the anxiety of reception this could have caused, see Andrew Bennett, *Romantic Poets and the Culture of Posterity* (Cambridge:

Cambridge University Press, 1999); and Timothy Clark, *The Theory of Inspiration: Composition as a Crisis of Subjectivity in Romantic and Post-Romantic Writing* (Manchester: Manchester University Press, 1997).

12. *Just Gaming,* 90.

13. Ibid., 94.

14. Alasdair MacIntyre, *Whose Justice? Which Rationality?* (London: Duckworth, 1988), 380.

15. Ibid., 387–88.

16. *Just Gaming,* 16, 39, 59, 62, 26.

17. Ibid., 27.

18. There are obvious similarities here to Stanley Fish's position on interpretative and legal hermeneutics; see *Is There a Text in This Class?* (Cambridge: Harvard University Press, 1980).

19. John Casey, *Pagan Virtues* (Oxford: Clarendon Press, 1990), vii. Casey uses Aristotle's *megalopsychos* as an example of "moral luck" on p. 201.

20. The key text here is Gillian Rose's *Dialectic of Nihilism* (Oxford: Blackwell, 1984), to which I am much indebted.

21. *Philosophical Fragments,* trans. Peter Firchow (Minneapolis: University of Minnesota Press, 1991), 8.

22. F. Nietzsche, *The Case of Wagner,* trans. and commentary Walter Kaufmann (New York: Random House, 1967), 170.

23. Ibid., 171–72.

24. *Philosophical Fragments,* 55.

25. "Studien zur Geschichte und Politik, "in *Kritische Friedrich-Schlegel Ausgabe,* ed. Ernst Behler, vol. 7 (Munich: Verlag Ferdinand Schöningh Thomas—Verlag—Zurich, 1966), xvii–xviii.

26. Ibid., xx. In what follows, I have drawn not only on Ernst Behler's excellent "Einleitung" to this volume, but also on his account of the Schlegels at this period in *German Romantic Literary Theory* (Cambridge: Cambridge University Press, 1993), 72–131. Most valuable also is Frederick Beiser's introduction to *The Early Political Writings of the German Romantics,* trans. and ed. F. Beiser (Cambridge: Cambridge University Press, 1996). My chapter can be read as putting a multicultural spin on Beiser's description of the romantic ideal of the "organic state," which, "rather than consisting of only a central government and a mass of isolated individuals, like the machine states of Prussia and France . . . will also comprise many autonomous groups," xxvi. See also Beiser's *Enlightenment, Revolution, and Romanticism* (Cambridge: Harvard University Press, 1992), esp. 245–64.

27. *Kritische Friedrich-Schlegel Ausgabe,* 7:xxv. See Jon Klancher's helpful discussion of the literary politics contextualizing Schlegel's republican utterances in "Criticism and the Crisis in the Republic of Letters," *Cambridge History of Literary Criticism,* vol. 5, *Romanticism,* ed. Marshall Brown (Cambridge: Cambridge University Press, 2000), 306–12.

28. *Political Romanticism,* trans. Guy Oakes (Cambridge: MIT Press, 1986), 36–37.

29. For a good account of dialogism in Caroline's letters, see Sara Friedrichsmeyer's "Caroline Schlegel-Schelling: 'A good woman, and No Heroine,'" in *In the Shadow of Olympus: German Women Writers around 1800,* ed. by Katherine R. Goodman and Edith Waldstein (Albany: SUNY Press, 1992), 115–37. Katherine R. Goodman, *Amazons and Apprentices: Women and the German Parnassus* (New York: Camden House,

1999), finds an apprenticeship for Caroline in the earlier Gottshed circle whose inclusiveness the Jena circle reproduced but, unlike, say, Rachel Levin/Varnhagen's salon in Berlin, actually made part of their philosophy. For a clear-sighted presentation of the philosophical gains and limitations connected to the sexual politics of the Jena circle, see Lisa C. Roetzel, "Feminizing Philosophy," in Jochen Schulte-Sasse, *Theory as Practice: A Critical Anthology of Early German Romantic Writings* (Minneapolis: University of Minnesota Press, 1997), 361–81. On "symphilosophy" and "sympoesy," see esp. F. Schlegel, *Lucinde and the Fragments*, trans. Peter Firchow (Minneapolis: University of Minnesota Press, 1971), *Critical Fragments*, no. 112, p. 14; *Athenaeum Fragments*, no. 112, p. 31; *Blütenstaub*, no. 20, p. 17 (no. 2). Gasché's foreword to Firchow is good on the fragment as "an *essential* incompletion, an incompletion that itself is a mode of fulfilment," xxx.

30. *Kritische Friedrich-Schlegel Ausgabe*, 7:19.

31. See Behler, *German Romantic Literary Theory*, 18.

32. In "Community," chap. 2 of *The Romantic Legacy* (New York: Columbia University Press, 1996), Charles Larmore sets out clearly the varieties of affinity between community and the state as formulated in German romanticism, from the mature Hegel's collapse of societal possibility into the state to the freeing from it entirely of a fully imagined citizenry as conceived by the young Hegel, Schelling, and Hölderlin in *Das sogennante "Älteste Sytemprogramm" des deutschen Idealismus* and Friedrich Schlegel's dialectical compromise. However, he leaves Schlegel's imagined politics unrelated to his literary theory, and, as a result, subject to "his regrettable fixation on simply national community" (61).

33. Isaiah Berlin, "Two Concepts of Liberty," in *Four Essays on Liberty* (Oxford: Oxford University Press, 1969), 167.

34. Quentin Skinner, *Liberty before Liberalism* (Cambridge: Cambridge University Press, 1997), 78–79.

35. Martha Nussbaum, "Human Capabilities, Female Human Beings," in *Women, Culture, and Development: A Study of Human Capabilities*, ed. M. Nusbaum and J. Glover (Oxford: Clarendon Press, 1995), 63.

36. Martha C. Nussbaum, *Poetic Justice: The Literary Imagination and Public Life* (Boston: Beacon Press, 1995).

37. Robert B. Pippin, *Idealism as Modernism: Hegelian Variations* (Cambridge: Cambridge University Press, 1997), 178–79. Charles Larmore, *The Morals of Modernity* (Cambridge: Cambridge University Press, 1996), see chap. 10, "The Foundations of Modern Democracy: Reflections on Jürgen Habermas," passim.

38. Larmore, *Morals of Modernity*, 212.

39. See Benedict Anderson, *Imagined Communities: Reflections on the Origins and Spread of Nationalism* (London: Verso, 1983); Homi K. Bhabha, *The Location of Culture* (London: Routledge, 1994); Paul Gilroy, *The Black Atlantic: Modernity and Double Consciousness* (London: Verso, 1993); Robert J. C. Young, *Postcolonialism: An Historical Introduction* (Oxford: Basil Blackwell, 2001).

INDEX

Abrams, M. H., 6, 31
Addington, Henry, Viscount Sidmouth, 158
Adorno, Theodor W., 11, 18, 35, 42, 52, 102, 103, 231, 250, 271n. 18, 275n. 9, 295n. 8; *Aesthetic Theory,* 35, 275n. 14, 283nn. 20, 24; *Dialectic of Enlightenment,* 193, 197–98, 201
Alighieri, Dante. *See* Dante
Allais, Denis Vairasse d', 215
allegory: of art, 109; and Coleridge, 84; and Godwin, 83; of reading, 109; and Scott, 117
Althusser, Louis, 194–95, 201, 206, 246, 288n. 37, 294nn. 1, 4
American Revolution, 219
Amis, Kingsley, 223
Anderson, Benedict, 301n. 39
Ansell-Pearson, Keith, 276n. 8
Applethwaite, Harriet Branson, 127, 287n. 20
Arendt, Hannah, 234, 282n. 5
Armstrong, Isobel, 269n. 4, 271n. 13
art: and Benjamin, 10; critical and prosaic ontology of, 10–11, 17–18, 21, 66, 210, 271n. 3; run on, 5, 104–5; and Schelling, 10; and F. Schlegel, 11; and subject/object knowledge, 9–10, 15–16
Ashton, Rosemary, 269n. 3
Aristotle, 50, 154, 187, 255, 256; *Poetics,* 264

Arnauld, Antoine, 296n. 23
Arnold, Matthew, 81, 215; and Keats, 94
Aske, Martin, 283n. 22
Austen, Cassandra, 166
Austen, Charles, 166
Austen, Jane, 12–13, 156–74, 221, 264, 291n. 9; and conversibility, 171–73; *Emma,* 160, 164, 168, 172; on feminism and politics, 172; *Lady Susan,* 156, 161; *Love and Friendship,* 162; *Mansfield Park,* 169, 173; *Persuasion,* 159; *Pride and Prejudice,* 164; reserve, 164, 173–74; *Sanditon,* 159, 164; *The Watsons,* 159, 171–72

Babbitt, Irving, 1, 45–47, 193; *The New Laokoon,* 46–47; *Rousseau and Romanticism,* 46
Bachelard, Gaston, 288n. 37
Bagehot, Walter, *The English Constitution,* 170
Bailey, Benjamin, 94
Bakhtin, Mikhail, 21, 274n. 40
Bank of England, 105, 106, 107
Barbauld, Anna Laetitia, 84, 225–26, 298nn. 28, 29, 30; *Eighteen Hundred and Eleven,* 227–28, 229–30; "On the Death of the Princess Charlotte," 227; "On the Uses of History," 298n. 32; "The Rights of Woman," 225–26, 230; *The Times,* 226
Barrell, John, 217, 236, 238, 241, 299nn. 4, 6